BETTER UNDERSTANDING LEARNING DISABILITIES

BETTER UNDERSTANDING LEARNING DISABILITIES

New Views from Research and
Their Implications for
Education and Public Policies

edited by

G. Reid Lyon, Ph.D.
Psychologist
Human Learning and Behavior Branch

David B. Gray, Ph.D.
Acting Deputy Director
National Center for Medical Rehabilitation Research

James F. Kavanagh, Ph.D.
Deputy Director
Center for Research for Mothers and Children

and

Norman A. Krasnegor, Ph.D.
Chief
Human Learning and Behavior Branch

National Institute of Child Health and Human Development
National Institutes of Health
Bethesda, Maryland

·P·A·U·L·H·
BROOKES
PUBLISHING Co

Baltimore · London · Toronto · Sydney

Paul H. Brookes Publishing Co.
P.O. Box 10624
Baltimore, Maryland 21285-0624

Typeset by The Composing Room of Michigan, Inc.,
Grand Rapids, Michigan.
Manufactured in the United States of America by
The Maple Press Co., York, Pennsylvania.

Library of Congress Cataloging-in-Publication Data
Better understanding learning disabilities : new views from
   research and their implications for education and public
   policies / edited by G. Reid Lyon . . . [et al.].
      p.   cm.
   Includes bibliographical references and index.
   ISBN 1-55766-116-2
   1. Learning disabilities—United States—
Congresses.   2. Learning disabled children—
Education—United States—Congresses.   I. Lyon, G.
Reid, 1949–   .
LC4705.B48   1993
371.9′0973–dc20   92-27605
                                                CIP

(British Library Cataloguing-in-Publication data are
available from the British Library.)

CONTENTS

CONTRIBUTORS

The Editors

G. Reid Lyon, Ph.D., Psychologist, Human Learning and Behavior Branch, National Institute of Child Health and Human Development, National Institutes of Health, 6100 Executive Boulevard, Room 4B05D, Bethesda, MD 20892. Dr. Lyon is responsible for the development and management of research programs in learning disabilities, language development and disorders, and disorders of attention in children. Dr. Lyon's background is in developmental neuropsychology and special education, and he has served as a classroom teacher, special education teacher, research neuropsychologist, school psychologist, and university professor prior to coming to the NIH. His current research interests include biobehavioral mechanisms related to language and learning and intervention practices with children with learning and language disorders.

David B. Gray, Ph.D., Acting Deputy Director, National Center for Medical Rehabilitation Research, National Institute of Child Health and Human Development, National Institutes of Health, 6100 Executive Plaza South, Room 450W, Bethesda, MD 20892. Dr. Gray has worked as a scientist in the fields of behavioral genetics and psychology and has served as a health science administrator in the areas of human learning and behavior. Improving communicative skills of people with disabilities through better research and best practices remains an area of great interest to Dr. Gray.

James F. Kavanagh, Ph.D., Deputy Director, Center for Research for Mothers and Children, National Institute of Child Health and Human Development, National Institutes of Health, 6100 Executive Boulevard, Room 4B05G, Bethesda, MD 20892. Dr. Kavanagh's research interests are in speech science, human communication, and the relationship between language development and reading and written language disorders in children.

Norman A. Krasnegor, Ph.D., Chief, Human Learning and Behavior Branch, National Institute of Child Health and Human Development, National Institutes of Health, 6100 Executive Boulevard, Room 4B05, Bethesda, MD 20892. Dr. Krasnegor is a physiological and experimental psychologist whose current research interests lie in developmental behavioral biology, learning, and cognitive development.

The Chapter Authors

Duane Alexander, M.D., Director, National Institute of Child Health and Human Development, National Institutes of Health, 9000 Rockville Pike, Building 31, Room 2A04, Bethesda, MD 20892. As a pediatrician, researcher, and administrator, Dr. Alexander's career has focused on the development of research and clinical programs to help ensure that children are born healthy and wanted, and have the opportunity to fulfill their potential unhampered by disease and disorders of learning and behavior.

Roger K. Blashfield, Ph.D., Professor, Department of Psychiatry, Box 100256, University of Florida, Gainesville, FL 32610-0256. Dr. Blashfield's research has focused on psychiatric classification and personality disorders.

John L. Doris, Ph.D., Director, Family Life Development Center, College of Human Ecology, G20 MVR Hall, Cornell University, Ithaca, NY 14850. Dr. Doris's research and scholarly endeavors have been in the area of child clinical psychology with special focus on child maltreatment, mental retardation, and learning disabilities.

Jack M. Fletcher, Ph.D., Psychologist and Professor, Department of Pediatrics, MSB 3.136, The University of Texas Medical School at Houston, 6431 Fannin, Houston, TX 77030. Dr. Fletcher's research has focused on the classification of reading disabilities and on the development of children with different types of brain injuries.

David J. Francis, Ph.D., Associate Professor, Department of Psychology, The University of Houston, Houston, TX 77030. Dr. Francis's research focuses on the measurement of change in behavior over time and structural equation modeling.

Stephen Hooper, Ph.D., Assistant Professor, Department of Psychiatry, Center for Development and Learning, CB 7255, BSRC, University of North Carolina, Chapel Hill, NC 27599-7255. Dr. Hooper is also a clinical scientist at the Clinical Center for the Study of Development and Learning and a Clinical Assistant Professor in the School of Education at the University of North Carolina. His research has focused on the classification of learning disabilities, disorders of written language, and measurement of neuropsychological outcomes in a variety of pediatric and psychiatric disorders.

Kenneth A. Kavale, Ph.D., Professor, Department of Special Education, University of Iowa, N235 Lindquist Center, Iowa City, IA 52247. Dr. Kavale currently serves as Editor-in-Chief, *Learning Disabilities Research and Practice*. His primary research interest focuses on the scientific and theoretical development of learning disabilities.

Barbara K. Keogh, Ph.D., Emeritus Professor of Educational Psychology, Graduate School of Education, University of California, Los Angeles, 405 Hilgard, Los Angeles, CA 90024. Dr. Keogh has been a member of the National Advisory Committee on the Handicapped and was the recipient of the 1992 Research Award of the Council for Exceptional Children. Her research activities include study of developmental problems in young children, temperament, and learning disabilities.

Melvin D. Levine, M.D., Director, Clinical Center for the Study of Development and Learning, CB 7255, BSRC , University of North Carolina, Chapel Hill, NC 27599-7255. Dr. Levine is also Professor of Pediatrics, School of Medicine, University of North Carolina. His research, clinical activity, and teaching are focused on developmental phenomenology in children with learning disorders.

Donald L. MacMillan, Ed.D., Professor, School of Education, University of California–Riverside, Riverside, CA 92521. Dr. MacMillan's research has focused on the educational plight of students with mild disabilities, including dropouts. In addition, he has conducted longitudinal studies of self- and school attitudes in these students. Dr. MacMillan is the recipient of the Edgar Doll Award from the American Psychological Association (Division 33) and the 1990 Education Award from the American Association on Mental Retardation.

Edwin W. Martin, Ph.D., President and Chief Executive Officer, National Center for Disability Services, 201 I.U. Willets Road, Albertson, NY 11507-1599. Dr. Martin served as Director of the U.S. Bureau of Education of the Handicapped under four presidents and as the nation's first Assistant Secretary of Education and Rehabilitative Services. He is also Professor of Education (Adjunct), Teachers College, Columbia University, and has served as Lecturer in Education, Harvard Graduate School of Education.

Louisa C. Moats, Ed.D., Director, Upper Valley Associates in Psychology, and Assistant Professor of Clinical Psychiatry (Adjunct), Dartmouth College, Box 253, East Thetford, VT 05403. Dr. Moats is also on the Faculty of St. Michael's College where she prepares special educators and classroom teachers for careers in schools and clinics. Dr. Moats's background is in linguistics, special education, and psychology, and her current research interests include development and disorders of reading and spelling behavior and the development of intervention programs for such disorders.

James Montgomery, Ph.D., Clinical Speech/Language Pathologist, Clinical Center for the Study of Development and Learning, University of North Carolina School of Medicine, Chapel Hill, NC 27599. Dr. Montgomery's research focuses on the psycholinguistic processes (i.e., perceptual and memory) underlying language comprehension in children with and without language impairments.

Robin Morris, Ph.D., Associate Professor, Department of Psychology, Georgia State University, University Plaza, Atlanta, GA 30303. Dr. Morris's research has focused on the classification of learning and attention disorders, developmental neuropsychology, and the effects of various interventions on children with acquired brain injuries.

Martha Reed, M.Ed., Educational Diagnostic Specialist, Clinical Center for the Study of Development and Learning, CB 7288, BSRC, University of North Carolina, Chapel Hill, NC 27599-7255. Ms. Reed's work and research have focused on educational assessment techniques that explore the developmental interaction of academic demands, learning variability and dysfunction, and the effectiveness of interventions with differing learning-performance profiles.

Byron P. Rourke, Ph.D., Professor, Departments of Psychology and Neuropsychology, University of Windsor, Windsor, Ontario N9B 3P4, Canada. Dr. Rourke's research interests are in the development of neuropsychological models of learning disabilities and the classification of learning disorders.

Adrian Sandler, M.B., B. Chir., M.D., The Clinical Center for the Study of Development and Learning, CB 7255, BSRC, University of North Carolina, Chapel Hill, NC 27599-7255. Dr. Sandler is a behavioral- developmental pediatrician whose research interests include the neurodevelopmental underpinnings of writing disorders and the assessment of learning difficulties in adolescence.

Bennett A. Shaywitz, M.D., Professor and Chief of Pediatric Neurology, Yale University School of Medicine, Department of Pediatrics, 333 Cedar Street, New Haven, CT 06510. Dr. Shaywitz's primary and long-standing research has focused on the neurobiological influences in learning and attention disorders. His most recent area of investigation involves the nosology and classification of learning and attention disorders. Most recently, Dr. Shaywitz has been named Co-Director of the Yale Center for the Study of Learning and Attention Disorders, one of three federally funded Centers for the Study of Learning and Attention Disorders. He has served on advisory boards of the National Institute of Child Health and Human Development, National Institute of Neurological and Communicative Disorders and Stroke, and the National Academy of Sciences, and the Editorial Board of *Pediatric Neurology*. He currently serves on the Professional Advisory Board of the National Center for Children with Learning Disabilities and of the Reye Syndrome Foundation.

Sally E. Shaywitz, M.D., Director, Learning Disorders Unit, and Professor, Yale University School of Medicine, Department of Pediatrics, 333 Cedar Street, New Haven, CT 06510. Dr. Shaywitz is particularly interested in utilizing epidemiological and biological strategies to more clearly elucidate the nature of learning and attention disorders. She has addressed issues relating to gender, measurement, and conceptual models for, and the emergence of, learning and attention disorders over time. A co-author of the "Report to Congress on Learning" and Co-Director of the Yale Center for the Study of Learning and Attention Disorders, Dr. Shaywitz currently serves on the Professional Advisory Board of the National Center for Learning Disabilities, on the Editorial Board of the *Journal of Learning Disabilities*, and as Editorial Consultant to the National Institute of Child Health and Human Development and the Department of Education.

Deborah L. Speece, Ph.D., Associate Professor, Department of Special Education, 1308 Benjamin Building, University of Maryland, College Park, MD 20742. Dr. Speece's research focuses on issues related to the classification of children at risk and ecological aspects of school failure.

Keith E. Stanovich, Ph.D., Professor, Departments of Instruction and Special Education and Department of Curriculum, The Ontario Institute for Studies in Education, Department of Special Education, Toronto, Ontario M5S 1V6, Canada. Dr. Stanovich's research interests are in the theoretical, conceptual, and educational aspects of reading disabilities.

H. Lee Swanson, Ph.D., Professor, Department of Educational Psychology, School of Education, University of California–Riverside, Riverside, CA 92521. Dr. Swanson's research has focused on the information processing differences between children with and without learning disabilities. Primary areas of focus have been memory, problem solving, and intellectual processes.

Carl Swartz, Ph.D., Center for the Study of Development and Learning, C B 7255, BSRC, University of North Carolina, Chapel Hill, NC 27599-7255. Dr. Swartz's research focuses on the effects of intervention to prompt self-regulated learning. He also teaches self-efficiency for teaching students with disabilities.

Joseph K. Torgesen, Ph.D., Professor, Psychology Department R-54, Florida State University, Tallahassee, FL 32306. Dr. Torgesen is interested in the cognitive development of children with learning disabilities. His research has focused specifically on the development of strategic processors in memory and on the construction of phonological processing deficits to certain kinds of memory problems. Most recently, he has been involved in a longitudinal study of phonological processes and reading.

Thomas Watson, Ph.D., was the Director of Research at the Clinical Center for the Study of Development and Learning, a University Affiliated Program at the University of North Carolina, Chapel Hill. He was responsible for research design, statistical analyses, and the maintenance of data bases within the Center for Development and Learning. Dr. Watson died in April 1992.

Naomi Zigmond, Ph.D., Professor of Special Education, School of Education, 5N25 Forbes Quad, University of Pittsburgh, Pittsburgh, PA 15260. Dr. Zigmond's research has focused on the development and validation of service delivery models and curricular approaches for students with learning disabilities at both elementary and secondary school levels.

FOREWORD

By the time this book is published, 30 years will have passed since the first major organizational meeting that launched the use of the term "learning disabilities." Prior to the 1960s, children with such problems had been recognized but, depending on their primary symptoms, they were given labels such as "brain damaged," "neurologically impaired," "aphasic," and "dyslexic." The primary intention behind the new category was to highlight the needs of children who were not being served in special education or who were inappropriately placed in groups of children with other disabilities. In addition, professionals hoped to avoid fragmentation of services and stigmatizing labels. However, the global term "learning disability" resulted in problems with classification and operationalization of the definition. The group was homogeneous because all of the children had difficulty learning even though they had at least average mental ability, sensory acuity, and motivation. However, the group was heterogeneous because the symptoms varied, as did the levels of severity. In addition, some children had multiple problems. Consequently the broad term "learning disabilities" sometimes resulted in problems related to diagnosis, program development, and research. Nevertheless, scholars and practitioners have grappled with these issues and are attempting to reach solutions. The problems are not unique to learning disabilities; similar concerns have been expressed with regard to other disabling conditions. However, the resolutions are somewhat easier in fields such as hearing and visual impairment, where classifications are made primarily according to levels of severity (albeit type of loss must be considered). In learning disabilities, we are concerned with both the type of disorder and the level of severity.

The National Institute of Child Health and Human Development should be commended for sponsoring the "Wingspread" conference that resulted in the thought-provoking, timely, and scholarly chapters in this volume. They reflect concerns but also provide constructive suggestions. The chapters on classification are enlightening because they discuss classification theories from various disciplines. These perspectives allow us to see the potential value of each system for the study of atypical learners. The polythetic approach appears particularly promising because of the complexity of learning disabilities. The current practice of using a severe discrepancy between potential and achievement for identification is questionable because the patterns of problems are not always detected. Furthermore, if the diagnosis is based only on severe discrepancies, children with mild to moderate disorders may not be identified. In addition, as Stanovich states, there are many issues surrounding the construct and measurement of potential.

Keogh and others have long emphasized that the purposes of classification vary. In this volume, she says the three purposes are advocacy, services, and scientific study. Others say the purposes may be for nomenclature, information retrieval, description, prediction, or concept formation. Thus, one classification system may be needed for eligibility for services while another may be required for subject selection in research.

Whatever the purpose, Morris emphasizes the need for theory-driven work. Both clinical and empirical researchers should specify their theoretical model and how it is operationalized. He also says classification systems should be developed that can be used by clinicians and researchers from different theoretical perspectives. However, he reminds us that any classification model biases a clinician's observations of a child and a researcher's interpretation of empirical results. Such is the case with definitions in general. They may either expand or restrict one's vision.

According to Morris, the integration and translation of concepts and models between clinicians and empirical researchers may be useful in the development of more valid classification models that will benefit both groups. Such systems should be standardized and reliable. They should predict developmental courses or treatment requirements for different types of children and should yield etiological information that can be used for developing prevention strategies. However, because philosophies of education and values vary, prediction is somewhat dependent on the content, quantity, and quality of instruction.

The chapters in this volume also highlight the need to consider comorbidity of problems. Both clinical observations and empirical research suggest that disabilities often co-occur. For example, learning disabilities may occur with attention deficits or subtle motor problems. Hence, classification systems should be broad and flexible enough to describe the scope of the conditions. In many respects, this process is similar to a giant class inclusion task.

As we attempt to improve the classification process, we must be aware of the technical problems with many tests. Few have adequate ceilings and floors across a wide age range and ability level. Many tests have both conceptual and practical problems and were standardized only on individuals without disabilities. They may not measure what they purport to measure among persons with disabilities because various processing deficits may interfere with performance. In addition, we lack many good measures, particularly in the area of listening comprehension, written language, and reasoning. These weaknesses should not deter us, but should provide the impetus for developing new procedures.

Swanson's chapter illustrates the need for incorporating concepts from cognitive psychology in future assessment, research, and intervention. These constructs are particularly relevant for studying higher order thinking and those aspects of learning for which we have few assessment tools. Nomenclature also needs to be refined. Broad terms such as "perception" or "memory" should be used cautiously. Rarely does a child have difficulty with memory in general. Therefore, the theories or approaches to classification should address content as well as process.

Several authors in this volume emphasize the need for studying learning disabilities from a developmental perspective. Both the learner and the environmental demands change over time. Consequently, the diagnostic profile may change. Often the assessment is like a snapshot when, in reality, we need a moving picture over time and across context in order to understand the problems.

The need to study ecological variables is well documented. Children should not be studied without an analysis of the context because environmental factors clearly affect development and learning. Information regarding the type and level of stimulation at home, the types of instruction in school, the setting, the peer group, and other factors is needed for studies of risk factors and outcomes.

Speece highlights the importance of effective instruction; however, few studies include comprehensive descriptions of either the population or intervention. Therefore, it is difficult to interpret results of studies and to determine why certain children improved or failed to respond. Many theorists, particularly in fields such as written language, emphasize the need for studying both product and process. Hence, investigators should attempt to describe the activity of the learner as well as the activities of adults and peers in the environment. Predictions about achievement will be enhanced if we look at more than test results. Zigmond reviews several issues to be considered when conducting studies in schools. We need to know what is expected of students and the specific procedures teachers are using.

Various approaches to subclassifications have been used over the years; however, they often focused only on domain-specific problems (e.g., language or reading) rather than the broader range of learning disabilities. In addition, subtypes that emerge depend on the types of data that are collected and the theoretical models used. For example, neuropsychological theories might yield different subtypes than psycholinguistic models of reading. Labels for subtypes should be selected and defined carefully to avoid ambiguity. For instance, a "language subtype" would need to be clarified to determine whether the population had receptive, expressive, or mixed problems and whether there were co-occurring thinking problems. In general, the attributes of the individuals should be defined so that one can determine who is included or excluded. Levine and colleagues remind us that, although classification is desirable, subtyping should not result in artificial clusters that are too global or that have little resemblance to clinical reality.

Despite the differences in theoretical perspectives and approaches, a certain amount of cognitive dissonance can be enlightening. A single theory may be neither necessary nor desirable. Multiple perspectives often highlight unique factors in learning. The field has been strengthened as professionals from many disciplines have conducted research with children with learning disabilities. The methodologies from neuropsychology, cognitive psychology, psycholinguistics, anthropology, and other fields represented in this book provide new insights into the problems. However, as stated above, the theories that are used should be broad enough to encompass the range of problems that might be found within the population. Learning disabilities are not synonymous with reading disabilities. Indeed, many children with learning disabilities have no reading problems. Similarly, not all have academic disorders.

Despite the problems raised throughout the literature and this volume, professionals in the field are actively engaged in trying to improve the "state of the art." The quality of research is improving, and many studies are more replicable because of the demands for better subject descriptors and research designs. If the ideas and concepts in this volume are applied, the scientific base and understanding of learning disabilities will be enhanced.

Doris J. Johnson, Ph.D.
Head, Program in Learning Disabilities
Department of Communication Science and Disorders
Northwestern University
Evanston, IL

PREFACE

Over the past decade, the field of learning disabilities has grown to represent over one third of the students receiving special education nationally. At the same time, learning disability remains one of the least understood of the various disabling conditions that affect school-age children. Although much of the confusion about learning disabilities can be attributed to its relatively recent recognition as a disabling condition, much of our current thinking about this heterogeneous array of disorders has been based on fragmentary evidence, typically derived from technically inadequate measurement instruments, and interpreted within the context of theoretical and conceptual frameworks that have not been clinically or scientifically validated. Moreover, there is scant evidence that current classification and diagnostic models used to identify children with learning disabilities provide clinicians and researchers with useful information to enhance communication or improve predictions, the two primary reasons for using any classification system in science. This state of affairs is unacceptable given the deleterious impact learning disabilities have on the educational and social well-being of developing children.

If we are to ultimately understand learning disabilities from a scientific and clinical perspective, the field must undertake a systematic effort to establish a precise definition for the disorder and a theoretically based classification system that is open to empirical scrutiny. Such a classification system must not only provide a valid framework for clinical scientists to identify different types of learning disabilities, but must be robust enough to recognize the distinctions and interrelationships (comorbidities) between learning disabilities and other childhood learning disorders, including attention-deficit disorder, general academic underachievement, mental retardation, and emotional disturbance. This is not an easy goal to achieve, as can be noted by even a cursory perusal of literature relevant to the history and current status of learning disabilities. The field has been, and continues to be, beset by pervasive and, at times, contentious disagreements about definitions, diagnostic criteria, assessment practices, teaching/intervention procedures, and educational policy. Nevertheless, difficulties and failures in the past must not deter new efforts to develop conceptualizations that provide a critical description and characterization of learning disabilities. Indeed, as noted in the Interagency Committee on Learning Disabilities Report to Congress (1987), the development of a reliable and valid definition and classification system for learning disabilities is the most pressing scientific goal currently facing the field.

In response to this challenge, the National Institute of Child Health and Human Development (NICHD) convened, in the fall of 1990, a working symposium at the "Wingspread" Conference Center in Racine, Wisconsin. The senior scholars who were invited to this conference were charged with two major goals: 1) to identify the major reasons for the field's persistent difficulty in establishing a reliable and valid definition and classification system, and 2) to identify the conditions that must be in place if the field of learning disabilities is to establish a firm definitional, theoretical, conceptual, and methodological base from which to prosper as a valid clinical science.

In attempting to accomplish these goals, the Symposium participants noted that a precise definition of learning disabilities rests on our ability to identify the fundamental characteristics of a classification system as well as the theories and the social, political, and educational factors that can shape the system in the most powerful and appropriate manner. The participants also noted that, in the field of learning disabilities, a number of basic questions that must be answered before a robust classification and definition can be developed have typically not been asked, much less addressed. Such questions include the following: What constitutes precision in definition and classification? What methodological conditions and principles must be considered when one attempts to identify similarities and differences among children who fail to learn in school? What methodologies currently exist to achieve this purpose? How is theory linked to classification efforts? Which theories are the best candidates for informing classification efforts and why? Are different theories, models, and classification solutions necessary for establishing eligibility, for making a diagnosis, for remediation, and for social, public, and education policy?

This book and the research symposium on which it is based reflect our initial attempts to answer these very complex questions. In doing so, it is our goal to provide professionals and students interested in learning disabilities with a state-of-the-art review of critical issues in classification and definition of learning disabilities; the development of theory in learning disabilities; the development of cognitive, developmental, and educational models of learning disabilities; and social and public policy in learning disabilities. The contents of the book are centered on the premise that scientific and clinical advances in the field must be based on an informed understanding of the critical conditions that must be in place if we are eventually to define and classify learning disabilities in a reliable and valid manner, develop theories that are open to empirical scrutiny, and provide efficacious interventions for students with learning disabilities within school and social contexts.

The book is organized in four sections. The chapters in Section I are concerned with addressing critical issues in the classification of learning disabilities. The writing in this section is focused on delineating the fundamental methodological conditions essential for nosological frameworks that can aid in the recognition of distinctions and interrelationships between learning disabilities and other childhood disorders. In addition, the content in this section provides a comparison and contrast of classification methodologies for clinicians and researchers, providing a much needed discussion in the field. The chapters in Section II address the development of definitions and theories of learning disabilities and the relationship between the two. Moreover, an emphasis is placed on identifying similarities between the fields of learning disabilities and mental retardation in their respective quests to establish operational criteria for assessment and identification. It should be noted that both the "Wingspread" Conference and the preparation of chapters in this book were concluded prior to the completion of the revised American Association on Mental Retardation (AAMR) definition of mental retardation. As such, the comparative analyses carried out for definitions of learning disabilities and mental retardation by several of the authors reflect findings and conclusions primarily relevant to the 1983 AAMR definition of mental retardation. Nevertheless, even if a new definition of mental retardation is ultimately accepted, the comparisons and contrasts between the development of definitions in the two fields with respect to advocacy, social/political factors, and external validation remain highly instructive. It is also our contention that, if learning disabilities are ultimately going to reflect a valid diagnostic category, we must "stand on the shoulders" of other disciplines within child health and education that have had to grapple with similar definitional issues. In Section III, the authors have provided an analysis of four perspectives for understanding learning disabilities. Specifically, learning disabilities are conceptualized through the eyes of cognitive, developmental, educational, and reading researchers. These four different conceptualizations provide a range of opportunities for developing a better understanding of learning disabilities and how best to teach students with such disabilities. Finally, the chapters in Section IV address how prevailing social and public policy trends and priorities influence research and practice in learning disabilities. In this regard, it is our contention that scientists and practitioners engaged in work with individuals with learning disabilities must appreciate the relevance of "extrascientific" forces that influence and modify how findings from research are interpreted and used. If such forces are ignored, limited practical and educational value will be derived from even the strongest of scientific efforts.

This book is intended for a wide range of audiences that includes active researchers, clinicians, teachers, methodologists, and administrators. If the contents of this book help to promote a critical understanding of the factors necessary for a definition and classification system for learning disabilities, then we have achieved our goal.

G. Reid Lyon, Ph.D.

REFERENCE

Interagency Committee on Learning Disabilities. (1987). *A report to Congress*. Washington, DC: U.S. Government Printing Office.

This book is dedicated to Matthew,
whose strength brought him through the storm,
and to Heather, who never had the chance.

ACKNOWLEDGMENTS

W e owe a number of debts of gratitude to individuals who have contributed to the birth, evolution, and fruition of the work presented in this book. Without the faith, support, and very hard work of Melissa Behm, Victoria Thulman, Megan Westerfeld, Sarah Cheney, and Susan Vaupel, all of Paul H. Brookes Publishing Co., the concepts, methodologies, and visions brought forth at the NICHD "Wingspread" Conference would have been available only to a few. These members of the Brookes staff are outstanding in their abilities and a genuine delight to work with. We are particularly pleased to acknowledge them. We are also grateful to Dr. Doris Johnson and Dr. Louisa Moats, who read and commented on each of the chapters.

The interest and support of Richard Kinch of the Johnson Foundation in Racine, Wisconsin, provided the scientists writing in this book the opportunity to meet and solve problems in a warm, stimulating, and historic environment. We are indebted to him and the Foundation. Finally, it is with utmost gratitude that we acknowledge the leadership and prescience of Dr. Duane Alexander, Director of the National Institute of Child Health and Human Development. His persistent encouragement and steadfast resolve to develop a robust theoretical, conceptual, and methodological foundation for the study of learning disabilities has led to a number of major discoveries during the past decade, with several more on the near horizon. Undoubtedly, the children will benefit.

1

An Examination of Research in Learning Disabilities
Past Practices and Future Directions

G. Reid Lyon and Louisa C. Moats

The field of learning disabilities has grown since learning disabilities were recognized as a federally designated disabling condition in 1968 to represent almost one half of the students receiving special education services nationally. At the same time, learning disabilities remain one of the least understood yet most debated disabling conditions that affect children in the United States. Indeed, even a cursory perusal of the literature relevant to the history and current status of learning disabilities reveals that the field has been, and continues to be, beset by pervasive and, at times, contentious disagreements about definition, diagnostic criteria, assessment practices, teaching procedures, and educational policy (Lyon, 1987; Lyon & Moats, 1988; Moats & Lyon, in press).

Clearly there are many reasons for the field's persistent struggles, and we attempt to identify some of the most important in this introductory chapter. However, it seems obvious that the field of learning disabilities is at a critical juncture where an examination of the basic constructs, concepts, and operating principles that undergird current thinking about learning disabilities is in order. More importantly, in assessing where the field has been and where it currently stands, leaders in the field must now write forcefully about where the field needs to go. No longer can science take a back seat, and more accurately the rumble seat, to the social and political forces that have shaped the field to date. The blueprint for productive change and new directions for understanding the complexities

1

inherent in the concept of learning disability lies in our ability to conduct systematic research. By systematic research we are referring to investigative efforts that have at their core a firm grounding in classification methodology, including the construction of theory-driven hypotheses, the selection and development of tasks and measures to test the hypotheses, a determination of the reliability and replicability of findings, and an external validation of the findings. By systematic, we are also referring to research that is conducted within a developmental, longitudinal framework. Within this context, the same children are repeatedly observed and studied, without the need for any a priori assumptions about which of them are children with learning disabilities, particularly if children are studied as they enter school and then are followed with consistent probes for several years.

It is a goal of this book to identify research directions and methodologies that have a probability of establishing a clinical scientific framework for learning disabilities. It is important, however, that such directions and methodologies be discussed within the educational, social, and political contexts that have always accompanied, and in some cases informed, the field of learning disabilities. The authors of the chapters in this book present what can be considered state-of-the-art thinking about: 1) linkages between theory and the development of a valid and useful definition and classification system for learning disabilities and other disorders, 2) linkages between theory and the assessment and teaching of children with learning disabilities, and 3) the role social and educational policies play in setting priorities for research and practice. In this first chapter, we attempt to provide a brief context for the need to entertain new research directions and methodologies in learning disabilities with an eye toward identifying scientific and social factors that have influenced the field's development, or lack thereof. In doing so, we hope to provide a clear message that the field must recognize the theoretical, conceptual, definitional, and social/political quandaries that persistently limit our progress. We also want to stress the need to address these quandaries effectively so we can move forward as a valid clinical science. In conclusion, we provide a brief overview of each author's contribution to this volume and how the contribution addresses the critical issues that face us.

UNDERSTANDING THE PRESENT
BY EXAMINING PAST PRACTICES

There are numerous sources that provide detailed histories of the development of the concept of learning disabilities, and Doris (chap. 6, this volume) provides one of the most recent overviews to date.

(Readers may also be interested in reviews by Coles, 1987; Fletcher & Morris, 1986; Kavale & Forness, 1985; Kavanagh & Truss, 1988; and Vaughn & Bos, 1987.) When perusing the history of the field, many readers have difficulty understanding that the field, as we know it today, emerged not from initial scientific discoveries about difficulties learning to read or write, but because many children who ostensibly should have been able to learn in school could not (Moats & Lyon, in press; see also Zigmond, chap. 12, this volume). More specifically, 25 years ago, children who displayed unusual learning characteristics in the context of seemingly average or above-average general intellectual ability were disenfranchised from any formal special education services because their cognitive and educational features did not correspond to any of the recognized categories of disability. This disenfranchisement has since successfully driven a social, political, and educational movement designed to protect children from being underserved by our educational system (Moats & Lyon, in press). The strength and success of this advocacy movement has played a far greater role in establishing a concern and visibility for children with learning disabilities than any scientific study has, past or present.

Yet can a movement born from fierce and well-intentioned advocacy continue to prosper if its growth has preceded, rather than followed, scientific development? We do not think so. Although the initial political and social forces that led to the recognition of learning disabilities as disabling conditions were necessary at the time of the field's birth (Zigmond, chap. 12, this volume), they will not continue unchallenged until we have established credible scientific and clinical validation of learning disabilities. To be sure, the field risks promoting its own destruction unless it responds systematically and objectively to pressures to overstate our knowledge for social, political, and educational purposes. As mentioned earlier, the field appears to be at a critical point in its history where, if we are to ever understand the tremendously heterogeneous array of disorders manifested by children identified as having learning disabilities, we must first establish precise definitions for research purposes (Keogh, chap. 14, this volume) and a theoretically based classification system that is open to empirical scrutiny (Fletcher, Francis, Rourke, Shaywitz, & Shaywitz, chap. 3, this volume; Morris, chap. 5, this volume; Torgesen, chap. 8, this volume). Such a classification system must not only provide a valid framework for clinical scientists to identify different types of learning disabilities, but must be robust enough to recognize the distinctions and interrelationships (comorbidities) between learning disabilities and other childhood disorders, including general academic underachievement, attention-deficit disorder, mental retardation, and emotional disturbance

(Fletcher et al., chap. 3, this volume; Morris, chap. 5, this volume; MacMillan, chap. 7, this volume).

To review, the field of learning disabilities has emerged from a genuine social and educational need and, for the time being, is robust and viable in law, policy, and practice. Historically, parents and other advocates for children with learning disabilities have successfully negotiated a category subsuming educational problems as a means to educational protection (Zigmond, chap. 12, this volume; Keogh, chap. 14, this volume; Martin, chap. 15, this volume). Only in passing have parents, advocates, and the research community also defined an arena for scientific inquiry in which persistent and complex questions have been entertained with less than satisfactory results (Moats & Lyon, in press). Who has entered that arena, and why has research not led to a better definition and scientific understanding of learning disabilities and their educational, linguistic, genetic, physiological, and neuropsychological correlates? There are many influences that historically have contributed to difficulties in validating the learning disabilities construct, and a few of the more important ones are reviewed here.

Influences on Validation of the Learning Disabilities Field

Youth of the Field The current limitations of the learning disabilities field as a clinical science may be related to its young chronological age. Learning disabilities, as a federally designated disability, has been in existence only since 1968 (U.S. Office of Education, 1968). Therefore, there simply may not have been enough time to collect and consolidate all of the necessary information that could lead to a better understanding of the nature of learning disabilities and to identify teaching methodologies that have a high probability of success (Lyon, 1987; see also Doris, chap. 6, this volume; Martin, chap. 15, this volume).

Theoretical and Conceptual Heterogeneity Probably more significant than the field's limited history in impeding scientific progress are the many different theoretical and conceptual views that reflect the multidisciplinary nature of the field (Lyon & Moats, 1988; see also Zigmond, chap. 12, this volume). As Torgesen (chap. 8, this volume) eloquently points out, learning disabilities have been considered the proper and legitimate concern of many disciplines and professions, including education, psychology, speech and language pathology, neurology, psychiatry, ophthalmology, optometry, and occupational therapy, to name a few. Each of these disciplines has traditionally focused on different aspects of the problems of the child with learning disabilities, so that there frequently are extremely divergent ideas and contentious disagreements about the importance of etiology, diagnostic methods, the significance of different characteristics, instructional content, teaching methodologies, and professional roles and responsibilities (see Torgesen, chap. 8, this volume). Obviously, such theoretical, conceptual, and territorial variation leads to the examination of idiosyncratic research issues and the conduct of research on entirely different types of samples, although all children have been labeled "learning disabled." This state of affairs leaves little room for replication and generalization of findings, the cornerstones of scientific inquiry (Blashfield, chap. 2, this volume; Kavale, chap. 9, this volume).

Limitations in the Criteria for Diagnosis Historically, the concept of "unexpected underachievement," as operationalized by a discrepancy between IQ and achievement, has served as the driving clinical force in the diagnosis of learning disabilities (Stanovich, chap. 13, this volume; Zigmond, chap. 12, this volume). However, although this has been a widely accepted criterion for the identification of learning disabilities, there is considerable variation in how the discrepancy is derived and quantified (Siegel, 1989; see also Stanovich, chap. 13, this volume), and concern about whether it constitutes a valid diagnostic marker (Fletcher et al., chap. 3, this volume; Morris, chap. 5, this volume; Stanovich, chap. 13, this volume; Swanson, chap. 10, this volume). Federal regulations and extant clinical criteria (e.g., the *Diagnostic and Statistical Manual of Mental Disorders,* 3rd ed., rev. [American Psychiatric Association, 1987]) do not specify particular formulas or numerical values to objectively assess discrepancy. The effect of such variation on both clinical and research practices is substantial. From a clinical standpoint, consider that a child can be identified as having learning disabilities in one state but not in its neighbor because of differences in the discrepancy criterion used. From a research perspective, different approaches to discrepancy measurement clearly lead to different sample characteristics and different prevalence estimates, again undermining the ability to replicate and generalize findings. Until recently, there literally has been no well-designed research conducted that could compare children identified according to different discrepancy criteria on external validation measures. The reader is referred to Fletcher et al. (chap. 3, this volume), Francis, Shaywitz, Steubing, Shaywitz, and Fletcher (in press), and Stanovich (chap. 13, this volume) for reviews of such research.

Other Limitations in Measurement Practices In addition to the difficulties associated with the discrepancy issue, many diagnostic decisions and research studies are guided by technically inadequate tests and measures. Recent reviews (Lyon, in press) suggest that fewer than one third of the psychometric tools used in the diagnosis of learning disabilities meet criteria for adequate norms, reliability, and validity. In addition, the valid measurement of behavioral change over time, clearly of critical importance in the study of learning and learning disabilities, is virtually impossible at present because few instruments have the necessary scaling properties to satisfy conditions for longitudinal measurement (Francis et al., in press). Even more alarming is that few standards for measurement of behavior and academic skills in learning disabilities research have been discussed and identified.

In response to this shortcoming, the National Institute of Child Health and Human Development (NICHD) recently convened a working conference to identify reliable and valid measurement strategies, approaches, and instruments that could be applied to the assessment of cognitive development, attention, executive functions, listening skills, expressive language skills, phonological and orthographic skills, and aptitude–achievement discrepancies (Lyon, in press). To meet the NICHD conference goal, leading scientists and clinicians who are highly experienced in each of these domains were asked to address the following questions:

1. Within the domain in which you specialize, what are the most important constructs that should be identified for measurement? (In identifying these fundamental constructs, each expert was required to provide specific suggestions for *core* areas that should be measured in all studies of the domain, across all laboratories, and all projects.)
2. Given the critical constructs within each domain, what *conditions* must be in place (e.g., coverage, reliability, validity, levels of precision, number of measurement points, types and levels of scaling procedures, assessment approaches) to measure the domain in the most robust manner?
3. Given these identified conditions, what measures, strategies, and approaches currently exist that meet the criteria specified and should be employed within a *core* battery, and can be employed across studies, laboratories, projects, and clinics?
4. Given the probability that a discrepancy exists between the conditions identified and those that currently exist, what steps must be taken to develop the necessary measurement technology to ensure proper assessment and diagnostic practices?
5. What measures, strategies, methods, and approaches are most appropriate and powerful for the measurement of behavior change over time, particularly in response to intervention?

The writings and recommendations prepared by the participants of the NICHD Measurement Conference are being made available in 1993 in book form (Lyon, in press). Interestingly, during the process of addressing each of these questions in detail, the participants found that these aspects of measurement have not been aggressively researched previously, despite the fact that valid research and clinical practices in learning disabilities are dependent on solid measurement foundations. Given the vagaries inherent in traditional measurement practices used with children with learning disabilities, it is not surprising that our research efforts over the past quarter century have been somewhat disappointing (Keogh, chap. 14, this volume).

Parochial Classification Efforts   Until recently (Francis et al., in press; see also Blashfield, chap. 2, this volume; Fletcher et al., chap. 3, this volume), classification research conducted with children with learning disabilities has not included comparisons with children who manifest other disorders. As Morris (chap. 5, this volume) points out, this isolation of disorders has created substantial debate within the field and has led directly to the use of exclusionary criteria to select samples for study, despite the fact that such criteria have never been validated effectively. Moreover, the separation of children into possibly artificial categories negates our ability to understand how multiple and comorbid difficulties influence learning and response to instruction (Moats & Lyon, in press). As mentioned earlier, until classification efforts can provide a valid framework for clinical scientists to identify different types of learning disabilities as well as the distinctions and interrelationships between learning disabilities and other childhood learning disorders, communication and the making of predictions about the children we are studying will be impossible to achieve.

Limitations in Sampling Practices   Unfortunately, a significant amount of what is known or thought about learning disabilities has been based on data collected from "school-identified" and "clinic-referred" samples (Lyon 1987; see also Keogh, chap. 14, this volume). As has been pointed out repeatedly (Fletcher & Morris, 1986; see also Keogh, chap. 14, this volume), such sampling practices undermine the reliability and validity of any information obtained because of the lack of consistency in the way in which school and clinic professionals identify learning disabilities. As has been stated several times before, such variability in sample characteristics prohibits replication and generalization of findings, a significant impediment to the development of any clinical science.

How does one address this very critical concern? In 1991, the NICHD invited the editors of the major journals that publish research relevant to learning disabilities to a meeting to discuss subject selection criteria. At this meeting, a consensus was achieved that any study conducted with children with learning disabilities should define the sample in a rigorous manner so that *complete* replication could be accomplished at another site. Furthermore, it was suggested that authors should provide clearly documented and operational definitions for their subject sample criteria in an a priori manner. Moreover, the selection of "school-identified" or "clinic-referred" children with learning disabilities should be clearly discouraged unless the diagnostic characteristics in such cases match the author's a priori established selection criteria. Finally, all children selected for study should be defined with reference to age; gender; grade level; length of time in special education placement; type of current special education placement; previous special education placement(s), including indices of intensity and duration; ethnicity; socioeconomic status; primary learning disability; comorbid disabilities; severity of disabilities; familial and/or genetic findings; intellectual status; cognitive-linguistic status; neurophysiological/neuropsychological status; levels of academic achievement in reading, written language, and mathematics; and presence or absence of attention-deficit disorder (see Morris, Lyon, Alexander, Gray, & Kavanagh, in press).

To date, few, if any, journal editors have required this level of specificity in sample selection and description. This is understandable given the necessary time that it will take to collect the information required and factor the data into the relevant statistical analyses. However, many editors may believe that the proposed level of specificity is too great a task to accomplish and may not require adherence to the suggested criteria. The real question that remains is, if we do not provide the suggested level of specificity in selecting and defining samples, how can adequate understanding of the sample and complete replication take place? We do not believe that it can, and the NICHD, for instance, will require this peak level of sample description in responses to requests for grant applications for research with children with learning disabilities.

Limited Developmental, Longitudinal Research Efforts With few exceptions (Fletcher & Morris, 1986; McKinney, 1989; Shaywitz, Escobar, Shaywitz, Fletcher, & Makuch, 1992; Shaywitz, Shaywitz, Fletcher, & Escobar, 1990), the majority of research on learning disabilities has consisted primarily of "single-shot" investigations that compare children achieving normally with children with learning disabilities on one or more dependent variables of interest, at one point in time. In the main, this research has been conducted without a clear understanding of what constituted the independent variable; that is, which children should be identified as having learning disabilities and which should not. Such research seemingly also was conducted without a clear understanding that children with learning disabilities may not differ in some abilities from learners achieving normally at one point in time, but could clearly show differences at other ages or in eventual outcome.

It is understandable that investigators interested in learning disabilities have typically eschewed the use of longitudinal designs, given the difficulty and costs of conducting such research. However, we must begin to realize that the developmental nature of learning requires an analysis of change over time, and how such change interacts with different interventions, subject characteristics, teacher characteristics, and classroom climates. Such an analysis is difficult to carry out with cross-sectional designs, and impossible with investigations carried out at one point in time.

SUMMARY AND OVERVIEW OF THE BOOK

In summary, much of our research thinking about learning disabilities is based on information obtained from ambiguously defined samples of children with school-identified learning disabilities who have been measured by technically inadequate tests at a single point in time. Moreover, the research problem is confounded further by our tendency to interpret these test data within the context of theoretical and conceptual frameworks that have not been scientifically or clinically validated or informed by robust classification methodology. The result is that the field of learning disabilities lacks a logically consistent, easily operationalized, and empirically valid definition and classification system. Therefore, it is extremely difficult to make solid predictions about the behavior and learning outcomes of youngsters with learning disabilities and equally difficult for clinicians and teachers to communicate about the specific needs of these children and what to do about those needs. We need to address these concerns in an informed and systematic fashion, and we are hopeful that the chapters in this book provide a healthy first step in this direction. Each author has been charged with the task of: 1) identifying the major reasons for the field's persistent difficulty in establishing a reliable and valid definition and classification system, and 2) identifying the conditions that must be in place if the field of learning disabilities is to establish a firm definitional, theoretical, conceptual, and methodological base from which to prosper as a valid clinical science.

The chapters in this book have been organized into four sections. The first section is composed of Chapters 2 through 5, and addresses critical issues in the application of classification methodology to learning disabilities. In Chapter 2, Roger Blashfield provides a clear overview of classification science and its relevance to learning disabilities. His explanations of the different classification models that are available should provide excellent guidance for researchers addressing questions related to development of taxonomies. In Chapter 3, Jack Fletcher, David Francis, Byron Rourke, and Sally and Bennett Shaywitz bring their collective experience together and produce a much needed review of the factors that have hindered research progress in learning disabilities. They also have provided a series of specific guidelines for the development of a valid classification system for learning disabilities that shows interrelationships with and distinctions among other childhood disorders, including mental retardation and childhood psychopathology.

Deborah Speece broadens the discussion of classification of learning disabilities in Chapter 4 by demonstrating that any classification effort must be informed by an examination of the ecological context within which the children develop. Her call for an analysis of instructional environments as well as an analysis of the child provides researchers with a number of guidelines for enhancing the ecological validity of their work. Finally, in Chapter 5, Robin Morris delineates those conditions that must be in place for both clinicians and researchers to make valid diagnostic decisions. By showing that the process of establishing internal and external validity is equally important to clinical and scientific problem solving, Dr. Morris provides a much needed blueprint for how practitioners and researchers can communicate effectively and how clinical findings can inform research initiatives, and vice versa.

In Section II, four chapters are devoted to a discussion of definition and theory in learning disabilities. John Doris's work in Chapter 6 details the historical influences that have contributed to past and current definitions of learning disabilities. Dr. Doris points out that we cannot understand present definitions and plan for better ones in the future unless we have a clear grasp of where we have been. In Chapter 7, Donald MacMillan brings his rich and varied experience to the task of providing an in-depth comparison and contrast of definitions and classification efforts in mental retardation and learning disabilities. Dr. MacMillan demonstrates that there are a number of similarities in how both fields have developed, particularly with respect to the role of advocacy, social/political factors, and difficulties validating particular definitions. Dr. MacMillan also shows very clearly that researchers and clinicians in the field of learning disabilities can learn much from the definition and classification efforts carried out in the field of mental retardation.

In Chapter 8, Joe Torgesen provides a much needed and articulate explanation of what a theory must contain if it is to be useful in guiding research and the development of a valid definition and classification system. Ken Kavale extends the discussion of the role of theory in Chapter 9 by delineating the critical scientific factors that must be considered if we are ever to establish a "metatheory" of learning disabilities. Dr. Kavale demonstrates the complexity of such an endeavor via discussion of a series of theoretical models.

In Section III, four authors address perspectives for conceptualizing learning disabilities as a research and clinical domain. For example, in Chapter 10, Lee Swanson demonstrates the power of addressing theoretical, conceptual, and clinical issues relevant to learning disabilities through the perspective of cognitive psychology. In this work, Dr. Swanson shows how a particular theoretical framework can stimulate important questions, guide the development of hypotheses and tasks to measure the hypotheses, and provide a context for interpreting data in a manner useful to both research and practice. Likewise, in Chapter 11, Mel Levine, Steve Hooper, James Montgomery, Martha Reed, Adrian Sandler, Carl Swartz, and Thomas Watson show how the study of learning disabilities, guided by a developmental perspective, can be used to investigate the multidimensional mechanisms underlying normal and atypical learning. Impressively, Dr. Levine and his colleagues demonstrate how such an interactive developmental paradigm can be used as a clinical heuristic by teachers in classrooms so that they can more effectively describe learner characteristics and develop and implement intervention strategies to address those characteristics.

In Chapter 12, Naomi Zigmond provides a compelling look at the effect of past and current research and educational practices on how learning disabilities are conceptualized in the public school domain. Dr. Zigmond points out the real problems that can occur in the development of a clinical science when one confuses the definition and diagnosis of learning disabilities for administrative purposes with those for research purposes. By means of his efforts in discussing research through a reading researcher's eyes, Keith Stanovich, in Chapter 13, orients us to the key conceptual issues that continue to plague current efforts to conceptualize learning disabilities and argues for the use of domain-specific models and definitions to replace the use of a generic definition of learning disability. In making his points, Dr. Stanovich provides a concise review of the research issues in the area of reading disability and offers a number of excellent suggestions for establishing conceptual coherence in this specific domain.

Trends in research in learning disabilities have been, and will surely continue to be, influenced and modified by prevailing social and public policy priorities. In Section IV, two chapters focus on those issues and events both within and outside the field that guide and reinforce educational trends. Specifically, in Chapter 14, Barbara Keogh provides the reader with a well-articulated mosaic of how "extrascientific" forces play a role in how we ultimately come to define and classify learning disabilities. Dr. Keogh's clear point is that, given the social and political context, different conceptualizations and definitions of learning disabilities may be necessary for different purposes. Similarly, in Chapter 15, Edwin Martin brings his wealth of experience in the public policy domain to a discussion of a number of myths about learning disabilities that must be countered if the field is eventually to move forward. Dr. Martin also calls for an outcome orientation in the field, with an eye toward documenting the effects of well-defined educational practices and procedures.

Finally, in Chapter 16, Drs. Duane Alexander, David Gray, and G. Reid Lyon outline the future for research in learning disabilities as conceptualized from an NICHD perspective. Specific directions for future initiatives are provided.

In closing, we are hopeful that the following chapters serve to promote a return to attempting to understand the critical factors that must be in place if we are ultimately to define and treat children with learning disabilities and other children who display individual differences in learning. Without such understanding, progress will continue to be limited.

REFERENCES

American Psychiatric Association. (1987). *Diagnostic and statistical manual of mental disorders* (3rd ed., rev.). Washington, DC: American Psychiatric Press, Inc.

Coles, G.S. (1987). *The learning mystique: A critical look at learning disabilities.* New York: Pantheon Press.

Fletcher, J.M., & Morris, R. (1986). Classification of disabled learners: Beyond exclusionary definitions. In S. Ceci (Ed.), *Handbook of cognitive, social, and neuropsychological aspects of learning disabilities* (Vol. I, pp. 55–80). Hillsdale, NJ: Lawrence Erlbaum Associates.

Francis, D.J., Shaywitz, S.E., Steubing, K.K., Shaywitz, B.A., & Fletcher, J.M. (in press). The measurement of change: Assessing behavior over time and within a developmental context. In G.R. Lyon (Ed.), *Frames of reference for the assessment of learning disabilities: New views on measurement issues.* Baltimore: Paul H. Brookes Publishing Co.

Kavale, K., & Forness, S.R. (1985). *The science of learning disabilities.* San Diego, CA: College-Hill Press.

Kavanagh, J.F., & Truss, T.J. (1988). *Learning disabilities: Proceedings of the national conference.* Parkton, MD: York Press.

Lyon, G.R. (1987). Learning disabilities research: False starts and broken promises. In S. Vaughn & C. Bos (Eds.), *Research in learning disabili-*

ties: Issues and future directions (pp. 69–85). San Diego, CA: College-Hill Press.

Lyon, G.R. (Ed.). (in press). Frames of reference for the assessment of learning disabilities: New views on measurement issues. Baltimore: Paul H. Brookes Publishing Co.

Lyon, G.R., & Moats, L.C. (1988). Critical issues in the instruction of the learning disabled. Journal of Consulting and Clinical Psychology, 56, 830–835.

McKinney, J.D. (1989). Longitudinal research in the behavioral characteristics of children with learning disabilities. Journal of Learning Disabilities, 22, 141–150.

Moats, L.C., & Lyon, G.R. (in press). Learning disabilities in the United States: Advocacy, science, and the future of the field. Journal of Learning Disabilities.

Morris, R., Lyon, G.R., Alexander, D., Gray, D.B., & Kavanagh, L.J. (in press). Proposed guidelines and criteria for the description of samples of learning disabled persons. Journal of Clinical and Experimental Neuropsychology.

Shaywitz, S.E., Escobar, M.D., Shaywitz, B.A., Fletcher, J.M., & Makuch, R. (1992). Evidence that dyslexia may represent the lower tail of a normal distribution of reading ability. New England Journal of Medicine, 326, 145–150.

Shaywitz, S.E., Shaywitz, B.A., Fletcher, J.M., & Escobar, M.D. (1990). Prevalence of reading disability in boys and girls: Results of the Connecticut longitudinal study. Journal of the American Medical Association, 264, 998–1002.

Siegel, L.S. (1989). IQ is irrelevant to the definition of learning disabilities. Journal of Learning Disabilities, 22, 469–478.

U.S. Office of Education. (1968). First annual report of the National Advisory Committee on Handicapped Children. Washington, DC: U.S. Department of Health, Education, and Welfare.

Vaughn, S., & Bos, C. (1987). Research in learning disabilities: Issues and future research directions. Austin, TX: PRO-ED.

I

CLASSIFICATION OF LEARNING DISABILITIES

Classification plays a pivotal role in producing operationally meaningful accounts of human learning and behavior. In a general sense, classification is closely linked to human cognition and conceptual ability. Specifically, mankind has evolved through the ability to distinguish, order, and describe similarities and differences among people, objects, and events. Classification serves a significant scientific function by structuring domains of study for more precise description and analysis. Within the social and behavioral sciences, classification methodology is instrumental in testing hypotheses relevant to dimensions and categories of childhood learning and behavioral disorders. In essence, by creating classifications, the scientist establishes the foundation for theory development, communication, and prediction.

For a number of reasons cited and elaborated in the chapters within this section, the field of learning disabilities could benefit from the appropriate application of classification efforts. For example, it is apparent that the category of learning disabilities represents an extraordinarily diverse population of learners with disabilities who will form a continuous distribution across the majority of tasks administered to assess their characteristics. Unless well-designed studies are conducted to classify this diverse group of individuals into relatively homogeneous subgroups and to distinguish them from persons with other hypothesized disabilities, research findings will continue to be contaminated by factors associated with unaccounted for heterogeneity. In addition, the classification of children with learning and other disabilities could provide insight into the assessment of useful clinical dimensions and categories and their treatment. Moreover, identification of specific patterns of performance across cognitive, linguistic, and social/behavioral measures within the context of longitudinal designs could enhance knowledge of meaningful developmental continuities and their relationship to school learning.

The chapters in this first section are devoted to examining, in depth, these reasons for the development of taxonomies and the application of classification methodology to the identification and description of learning disabilities. Blashfield provides us with an informative overview of different classification models and a rationale for selecting one model over another. With Blashfield's chapter as background, Fletcher and his colleagues explicate how different classification models can be used as processes *and* methods to develop refutable hypotheses about learning disabilities and their relationship to other disabilities, and then test the hypotheses using robust sampling and measurement techniques. Speece follows with a reasoned argument that the classification of students with learning disabilities must take into account environmental variables as well as child characteristics. In making this argument, Speece provides an ecological perspective that examines the youngster as well as the instructional milieu. Finally, Morris's chapter provides the much needed bridge between classification efforts in research and clinical practice. Morris also ably demonstrates why and how the principles applied in classification research are equally important and applicable in clinical practice.

2

MODELS OF CLASSIFICATION AS RELATED TO A TAXONOMY OF LEARNING DISABILITIES

Roger K. Blashfield

Imagine a small child almost 2 years of age trying to learn what a bird is (Rosch & Lloyd, 1978). A mother who is trying to teach the child will *not* attempt this task by sitting the child down and saying, "Becky, a bird is an animal that flies. It lives in nests. It eats bugs. And it is rather small." Instead, the mother is more likely to teach the child by pointing at a robin outside the window and saying the word "bird" to the child. When Becky sees a cat and says, "Bird," the mother corrects her by saying, "That is a cat," and then points to a sparrow on a tree and says, "That is a bird."

Gradually, as the child experiences repeated instances of things that fit the concept of bird, the child will begin to abstract the characteristics that separate birds from other things. For example, Becky may note that birds have wings. From this observation, she decides that anything that has a wing is a bird. This principle works rather well until one day, when being bothered by an annoying fly, Becky takes a swat at it and says, "Naughty bird." Her mother laughs and tells Becky that the insect bothering her is a "fly," not a "bird."

Confused, Becky decides that her rule that things with wings are called "bird" does not seem to hold true. So she thinks about the things that are birds, and she develops a more complicated rule. Birds not only have wings, but they lay eggs and they have feathers. Flies do not have feathers, so they are not birds. Eagles are big, but they do have wings and feathers and lay eggs, so they are birds. Becky's new rule does much better.

That is, her rule does better until one day, when she is older, Becky goes with her parents to the zoo. While walking around, Becky listens to her parents discussing the unusual animals she sees. One of them is a penguin. Her parents say that the penguin is a type of bird. Becky is very confused. How could a penguin be a bird? A penguin does not have feathers, nor does it have wings. Moreover, it cannot fly. How can a penguin be a bird? Her parents explain to Becky that penguins really do have feathers, but oil mats the feathers so that they can swim; the "flippers" of the penguin have the characteristic bone structure of birds; and it is true that penguins cannot fly, but neither can chickens or ostriches.

Becky puzzles about this. She decides that she must adopt a new rule for defining "bird." So she enumerates a list of seven features of birds, including: 1) the ability to fly, 2) having wings, 3) eating bugs or fish, 4) living in nests, 5) laying eggs, 6) having feathers, and 7) having a beak. Any animal that has at least four of these seven features, she decides, is a bird. Having arrived at a definition of birdness similar to the diagnostic criteria of the *Diagnostic and Statistical Manual of Mental Disorders (3rd ed., rev.)* (*DSM–III–R*), this allegorical story will end.

MODELS OF CLASSIFICATION

The intention of the preceding story was *not* to accurately portray how children learn concepts. The story was intended to be an allegory to introduce five approaches to classification. These five approaches are labeled:

1. Prototype model
2. Dichotomous perspective
3. Monothetic model
4. Polythetic model
5. Dimensional model

The five models are discussed using psychiatric classification as the content area to exemplify how these models function. However, these models are not limited in application to psychiatric classification. The prototype model, for instance, was originally developed in cognitive psychology to understand how children learn nouns. The monothetic and polythetic models have been largely developed in the literature on biological classification. The dimensional model has an extensive history in the studies of human abilities and of personality styles.

Classification is a fundamental process for all sciences. The intent of this chapter is to suggest models used in other areas of classification that might profitably be applied to the classification of learning disabilities.

Prototypes

Briefly stated, the prototype model suggests that classificatory concepts are learned not by memorizing lists of features associated with a concept, but instead by learning "exemplars" that represent the concept (Cantor, Smith, French, & Mezzich, 1980; Smith & Medin, 1981). By comparing new instances to an exemplar, a decision can be made as to whether the new instance belongs to the concept or not.

In the story of Becky, the prototype view suggested that Becky learned what a bird is by associating the word "bird" with an instance of robin. Thus, when confronted with other stimuli in her environment, presumably Becky compared the new stimulus to what she remembered of the robin, decided if the new stimulus was relatively similar to the robin, and assigned the term "bird" or not depending on her judgment of the similarity. Notice that, according to the prototype model, not all instances of birds are equally good exemplars. Robins and sparrows are good exemplars because they manifest all or most of the characteristic features of birds. In contrast, chickens and ostriches are not good exemplars, although both clearly are birds.

In the clinical setting, the prototype model, which employs explanations of case histories, often is used to teach diagnostic concepts. The case histories are representations of concepts that students who are unfamiliar with the language of psychopathology (or learning disabilities) can readily grasp. For instance, recent research using the prototype model (Livesley, 1985a, 1985b) has focused on the classification of personality disorders. A popular, perhaps faddish, diagnosis concerning personality disorders is the concept of borderline personality disorder. To individuals who are unfamiliar with this diagnosis, the easiest way of teaching what this diagnosis means is to have them watch the movie *Fatal Attraction*. Glenn Close's character in the movie is a prototype of the borderline personality. The use of case histories also is common in the psychotherapy literature. In this literature, the formation of a standard clinical language is still an evolving process. Given this lack of a uniform language, case histories help communication because the cases provide concrete representations of therapeutic issues that all therapists can understand.

The use of case histories and prototypes to develop scientific and clinical languages is important. There are five purposes to a classification: 1) nomenclature, 2) information retrieval, 3) description, 4) prediction, and 5) concept formation (Blashfield & Draguns,

1976). The first of these, nomenclature, is the most fundamental. Every science must develop a language and, eventually, develop testable theories to explain the phenomena of the science. A classification provides the nouns for the language of the science.

The prototype view is important to the classification of psychopathology, and of learning disabilities, because it focuses on the nomenclature function of a classification. Using methods developed in cognitive psychology to study concepts from a prototype model, research methods can be used to take a census of how clinicians handle diagnostic concepts as well as to analyze how well accepted a classification is as a nomenclature.

Dichotomies

Using structural terms, the prototype view of classification can be said to emphasize exemplar, extensional definitions of concepts. An extensional definition of a concept is a definition in which the members of the concept are enumerated (Hull, 1988). For instance, one could define the concept of "baseball teams" by listing all teams in the American and National leagues. An exemplar definition is a particular type of extensional definition in which the most salient, usually an ideal, representation of the concept is listed. For instance, a baseball team could be defined by referring to the 1957 New York Yankees.

The problem with exemplary definitions is that these definitions do not describe the boundaries of a concept. How does one know whether a new instance is a member of the concept or not? For example, suppose that an immigrant to this country is trying to learn what a baseball team is. An American friend tells him that the 1957 New York Yankees is the best example of a baseball team. Another friend says that the best example of a football team is the 1973 Pittsburgh Steelers. Later, on television, he hears a sports commentator discussing the Detroit Pistons. The immigrant wonders whether the Pistons are a football or baseball team. Using the prototype model, he might decide, since Detroit is closer to Pittsburgh than to New York, that the Pistons probably are a baseball team. And, of course, he would be incorrect.

To define the boundaries of a concept, *intensional definitions* are needed. Intensional definitions define a concept by listing the features that are required for membership in the concept. The most primitive type of intensional definition for a concept is a dichotomy. This is the type of definition that was popular in Aristotle's classification of animals (Hull, 1988). For instance, Aristotle distinguished between animals with hooves and animals without. He also separated fish into those with scales (e.g., trout, bass) and those without (e.g., sharks, sea lions, whales—i.e., animals living in the sea that we would not describe as fish). In the *DSM–III* classification of psychopathology of children, a parallel classification of the form "A and not A" is the subdivision of attention-deficit disorder (ADD) into ADD with hyperactivity and ADD without hyperactivity.

There are several problems with dichotomous classifications. First, the use of dichotomies could lead to a large number of classifications. Suppose that children were classified into those with and without reading problems, those with and without arithmetic problems, those with and without emotional problems, and those with and without language problems. Just using those four dichotomies would lead to 2^4, or 16, categories. If there were eight dichotomies, there would be 256 different categories. Thus, the total number of categories in a dichotomous classification grows exponentially as a function of the number of dichotomies.

The second problem concerns selecting variables to dichotomize. Because not every variable of interest can be used in a dichotomous categorization, which dichotomies are the most important? Aristotle thought that this was a very important question and argued that not all dichotomies led to "natural" classifications. In other words, some variables, when dichotomized, are more likely to lead natural or correlated splits in other variables. For instance, modern zoologists believe that Aristotle's dichotomy of animals with hooves versus those without was reasonable because this dichotomy was associated with many other morphological features of animals.

Finally, the third problem of a dichotomous classification is that the "A" category is usually the category of interest while the other— the "not-A" category—is likely to be a grab bag, heterogeneous category. For instance, when ADD without hyperactivity was first proposed as a diagnosis, it was a "wastebasket" category. Attention-deficit disorder with hyperactivity was the category of interest.

Although dichotomous classifications largely have fallen into disfavor, both in psychopathology and in other sciences, dichotomous classifications do have their advantages. First, they are easy to learn. Humans can dichotomize almost any observable variable easily. Second, dichotomous classifications work particularly well for the second purpose of a classification—information retrieval. There is a cliché in biological classification that "the name of a plant is the key to its literature" (Sneath & Sokal, 1973). The concepts from a classification serve as title headings to organize the literature of a science. Dichotomous classifications are a particularly easy method of organizing information because they are efficient and understandable.

Monothetic

The third view of classification also is associated with a particular type of intensional definition: the monothetic. A monothetic definition of a concept is a definition in which the necessary and sufficient features for membership in the concept are listed. For instance, a square can be defined as: 1) a closed figure 2) composed of four straight lines 3) of equal length 4) that are at right angles to each other. *All* of these features must occur for a geometric figure to be called a square. Objects with curved sides are not squares, nor are three-sided figures, nor are trapezoids that do not have right angles between the sides.

The monothetic approach to classification is associated with a popular etiological view of classification, the disease model of psychopathology. Very broadly speaking, the disease model is a reductionist model that attempts to explain abnormal behaviors in terms of physiological processes (genetics, faulty biochemical mechanisms, slow viruses, etc.). Most diseases are defined using monothetic definitions. For example, diabetes is defined as faulty glucose metabolism associated with malfunctions in the pancreas. Paresis is defined as tertiary syphilis of the central nervous system. Some day, schizophrenia may be defined as something like faulty dopamine metabolism in a particular limbic pathway of the brain.

This leads to another important point about the monothetic view of classification. This view supports an *essentialist* approach to classification. That is, most advocates of monothetic definitions believe that there are certain underlying, "essential" features that explain a category. From this perspective, the job of classifiers is "to carve nature at its joints," to use a colorful phrase that Meehl (1973) has popularized. The essentialist view of classification is opposed to the *functionalist* view of classification. This view suggests that categories of a classification are convenient fictions that are imposed on a scientific area for a particular purpose, and that there are as many classifications as there are purposes (Lakoff, 1987).

Most modern commentators concerned with the classification of psychopathology and learning disabilities have attacked monothetic classifications because this type of definitional form requires complete homogeneity on the defining characteristics. Yet, complete homogeneity is almost impossible to achieve for concepts referring to natural categories (see Shaywitz, Escobar, Shaywitz, Fletcher, & Makuch, 1992). As noted in the discussion of Becky's attempt to define birds, being able to fly is often seen as a feature associated with birds, yet not all birds fly. Nor do all birds give birth by laying eggs. In other words, monothetic definitions are problematic for the third purpose of a classification system—description (Blashfield &

Draguns, 1976). Because of the apparently restrictive condition of complete homogeneity on the defining characteristics, monothetic classifications have been dropped in favor of polythetic classifications in the *DSM* systems (see Fletcher, Francis, Rourke, Shaywitz, & Shaywitz, chap. 3, this volume, for an in-depth application of this thinking to the classification of learning disabilities).

Polythetic

The fourth view of psychiatric classification, and the one that has become dominant in the last 15 years, is the polythetic approach. According to the polythetic view, all of the characteristics used to define a category need not be present in order to make a positive classification; rather, some subset of the characteristics is sufficient. More concretely, polythetic intensional definitions usually are in the form of a list of characteristics (e.g., the eight *DSM–III–R* diagnostic criteria for borderline personality disorder). Also, there is a specification that a subset of the characteristics is needed to make a classification. In a polythetic classification in which any five of eight features are used to make a diagnosis, no one single characteristic is necessary. Subsets of the defining characteristics are sufficient for the diagnosis.

Polythetic definitions have become the standard in psychiatric classification because these definitions do not make the strong requirement that every patient with a diagnosis must manifest all defining symptoms of the disorder. Not every borderline patient must have a history of multiple suicide attempts. Not every child with ADD must have abnormal findings on a neurological examination.

Notice that the polythetic approach to classification, when compared to the monothetic view, relaxes the homogeneity required within concepts. According to the monothetic view, all members of a diagnostic concept must manifest all defining features. Thus, there was complete homogeneity on the defining features for the concept. Moreover, the expectation was that the concept would be associated with relative homogeneity on other descriptive characteristics. However, for the polythetic approach, complete homogeneity is not required, even on the defining characteristics. Instead, relative homogeneity is expected on the defining characteristics and, additionally, there also should be relatively good homogeneity on the other, associated characteristics.

In effect, what the polythetic view of classification suggests is that diagnostic concepts should be associated with "clusters" of patients whose symptom patterns are similar (Jain & Dubes, 1988). To understand this, imagine data from a group of patients plotted in a two-dimensional space. If there is a relatively dense grouping of patients in this space that is separate from other patients, this group then forms what has been called a "cluster" of patients. The polythetic view of classification assumes that descriptive clusters of patients exist. These clusters represent patients whose symptom patterns are relatively similar and homogeneous. The defining features for these clusters are the variables that organize the dimensions of the space and serve to discriminate a cluster from the remainder of patients. This view serves as the basis for empirical classification studies of children with learning disabilities.

Dimensions

Notice that, in the previous example, the data on patients were conceptualized in terms of a two-dimensional space. Associated with finding clusters is the issue of how to define the dimensions of the multivariate space. This brings up what can be called the dimensional view of classification (Blashfield, 1984; Millon & Klerman, 1986).

According to the dimensional view, the major task for descriptive psychopathology is to identify the latent variables that are needed to account for symptoms. In many ways, the dimensional view is a measurement model because it assumes that the symptoms can be organized in terms of higher order factors that represent the systematic variance in observable measurements. Also, superiority often is claimed for the dimensional model because this model does not make the additional assumption that clusters must exist in the measurement space (Kendell, 1975). In effect, the dimensional model is descriptively more parsimonious than the polythetic model because it does not require the additional assumption of homogeneous grouping of patients that the polythetic model does.

However, the dimensional model has its shortcomings as a view of classification. In particular, the dimensional model has difficulty being a nomenclature. A dimensional view does not provide the nouns (i.e., categories containing sets of patients) that are necessary for forming a language of psychopathology. This aspect of a dimensional model can be viewed as positive, however. Because the dimensional model refers not to sets of patients but to collections of variables, it is less stigmatizing. However, the failure to provide names that refer to groups of patients is the reason that most clinicians usually avoid dimensional models. Patients are the "things" that clinicians deal with, and clinicians need terms to describe groupings of these "things."

A related problem with the dimensional model is that it has not proven very useful for organizing the scientific information in the field. The basic underlying dimensions of psychopathology could be used as chapter headings in a textbook of psychopathology. For instance, when organizing a textbook about adult mental disorders, one could have chapters about hallucinations, delusions, affective symptoms, somatic symptoms, interpersonal issues, and so forth. Such books have been written (Kraupl-Taylor, 1979). Psychopathology textbooks that are organized by groups of symptoms have not had much success because both students and clinicians want to understand patients and they are likely to be frustrated if they cannot find information that is organized around types of patients.

FINAL COMMENTS

The brief story that begins this chapter suggests that classification is simple, and in one sense it is. Classification represents an early, elemental stage in the development of most sciences. However, classification, like any superficially simple topic, has an underlying complexity. There are five purposes for classification: nomenclature, information retrieval, description, prediction, and concept formation. Only the first three of these purposes have been discussed in this chapter, largely because of limitations in the current state of knowledge about psychopathology and learning disabilities. In other sciences, debates over alternative classifications involve references to information about the predictive utilities of the classifications and to the relationships of these classifications to alternative theories in the sciences (Hull, 1988).

The scientific study of learning disabilities is a topic of growing interest. Moreover, the study of learning disabilities represents an area of significant concern to a number of disciplines, including education, psychology, psychiatry, and neurology. Researchers from these different disciplines will tend to apply the models that they have learned from their respective backgrounds. Because of this, forming a coherent, useful classification that will be both acceptable and generative for the study of learning disabilities is a major challenge. This is particularly true if researchers from those disciplines do not grasp the differences between, and the strengths and weaknesses of, the major classification models presented here. As Keogh (chap. 14, this volume) points out, different classification models and definitions of learning disabilities may be applied at different times and for different purposes. This can only be accomplished correctly and for useful purposes if these fundamental classification models and principles are understood.

REFERENCES

American Psychiatric Association. (1987). *Diagnostic and statistical manual of mental disorders* (3rd ed. rev.). Washington, DC: American Psychiatric Press, Inc.

Blashfield, R.K. (1984). *The classification of psychopathology.* New York: Plenum.

Blashfield, R.K., & Draguns, J.G. (1976). Towards a taxonomy of psychopathology: The purposes of psychiatric classification. *British Journal of Psychiatry, 129,* 574–583.

Cantor, N., Smith, E.E., French, R., & Mezzich, J. (1980). Psychiatric diagnosis as prototype categorization. *Journal of Abnormal Psychology, 89,* 181–193.

Hull, D.L. (1988). *Science as a process.* Chicago: University of Chicago Press.

Jain, A.K., & Dubes, R.C. (1988). *Algorithms for clustering data.* Englewood Cliffs, NJ: Prentice-Hall.

Kendell, R.E. (1975). *The role of diagnosis in psychiatry.* Oxford, England: Blackwell Scientific Publications.

Kraupl-Taylor, F. (1979). *Psychopathology: Its causes and symptoms.* Baltimore: Johns Hopkins University Press.

Lakoff, G. (1987). *Women, fire and dangerous things: What categories reveal about the mind.* Chicago: University of Chicago Press.

Livesley, W.J. (1985a). Classification of personality disorders: I. The choice of category concept. *Canadian Journal of Psychiatry, 30,* 353–358.

Livesley, W.J. (1985b). Classification of personality disorders: II. The problem of diagnostic criteria. *Canadian Journal of Psychiatry, 30,* 359–362.

Meehl, P.E. (1973). *Psychodiagnosis: Selected papers.* Minneapolis: University of Minnesota Press.

Millon, T., & Klerman, G.L. (Eds.). (1986). *Contemporary directions in psychopathology.* New York: Guilford Press.

Rosch, E., & Lloyd, B.B. (Eds.). (1978). *Cognition and categorization.* Hillsdale, NJ: Lawrence Erlbaum Associates.

Shaywitz, S.E., Escobar, M.D., Shaywitz, B.A., Fletcher, J.M., & Makuch, R. (1992). Distribution and temporal stability of dyslexia in an epidemiological sample of 414 children followed longitudinally. *New England Journal of Medicine, 326,* 145–150.

Smith, E.E., & Medin, D.L. (1981). *Categories and concepts.* Cambridge, MA: Harvard University Press.

Sneath, P.H.A., & Sokal, R.R. (1973). *Numerical taxonomy.* San Francisco: W.H. Freeman.

3

CLASSIFICATION OF LEARNING DISABILITIES
Relationships with Other Childhood Disorders

Jack M. Fletcher, David J. Francis,
Byron P. Rourke, Sally E. Shaywitz,
and Bennett A. Shaywitz

The classification, definition, and identification of children with learning disabilities represent a complex set of empirical and sociopolitical issues that are presently diffᵢcult to unravel. Despite many years of effort, satisfactory classifications (and corresponding definitions) that permit the identification of the child with learning disabilities in a manner uniformly acceptable to scientists, practitioners, and policymakers are not available. Unfortunately, similar problems plague other childhood disorders, which for simplicity's sake we will depict as mental retardation and childhood psychopathology. The central thesis of this chapter is that many of the problems involved in developing satisfactory classifications of learning disabilities, mental retardation, and childhood psychopathology reflect the tendency for nosologic efforts in these areas to develop independently of each other. This is particularly true for classifications that simply attempt to describe and catalog subgroups and subtypes within these disorders. Unfortunately, substantial overlap occurs at the level of these major groups and subtypes. The failure to develop classifications that account for this comorbidity may be a

This research was supported in part by National Institute of Child Health and Human Development Grants P01 HD21888 and P50 HD25802.

significant factor in the absence of uniformly acceptable classifications in learning disabilities, childhood psychopathology, and mental retardation.

From a classification perspective, the nature of this comorbidity is easily described. For example, children with mental retardation can also have attention-deficit hyperactivity disorder (ADHD) and conduct disorders, children with ADHD can manifest conduct disorder and learning disabilities, and many children with learning disabilities also have conduct disorder and ADHD. Finally, what about those children with composite IQ scores between 70 and 85? Should they be classified as having mental retardation, which was the case before 1961? Should they be classified as having learning disabilities? The latter classification has never really been viable because of the emphasis on definitions of learning disabilities based on measurement of ability potential as an IQ score (Francis, Espy, Rourke, & Fletcher, 1991). How many children in the 70–85 IQ range fall where they do because of behaviors (e.g., inattention, oppositionality, depression) that influence their ability to take IQ tests? Perhaps they represent a separate classification of "slow learners," a potentially pejorative label. Presently, these children are generally ineligible for educational services in many settings, partly because of the use of test scores with measurement error of about 5–10 points per instrument (Sattler, 1988).

These examples demonstrate some of the issues involved in the classification of learning disabilities, mental retardation, and childhood psychopathology. Classification and definitional issues are inherently intertwined in the three areas. The resolution of these issues depends in part on the purpose of the classification. To the extent that the purposes are descriptive and oriented toward definition and identification, classification efforts should probably occur simultaneously across the three areas. It is our view that progress in the descriptive classification of learning disabilities will not occur unless relationships with mental retardation and childhood psychopathology are addressed. With coordinated attempts at classification, policy can be similarly coordinated, resulting in a more streamlined attempt to serve children. The net result would likely be fewer children identified as needing service and more funds for treatment because of lower expenditures devoted to establishing eligibility.

CLASSIFICATION AS A PROCESS AND AS A METHOD

We have written extensively on the nature of classification research, with specific applications to childhood disorders (Fletcher, 1985; Fletcher, Francis, & Morris, 1988; Fletcher & Morris, 1986; Fletcher,

Morris, & Francis, 1991; Fletcher & Satz, 1985; Morris, 1988; Morris & Fletcher, 1988; Morris, Blashfield, & Satz, 1981; Rourke, 1985, 1989, 1991b). These articles outlined various theoretical models and empirical approaches to classification with specific application to learning disabilities.

In approaching this type of research, classification as a *process* must be separated from classification as a set of *methods*. When the process of classification is considered, it can take a number of forms. These forms can be primarily *rational,* representing a clinician's attempt to observe the phenomenon of interest, describe subgroups, and even delineate criteria for defining subgroups. The approach could also be primarily *statistical,* as in the application of cluster analyses to a set of behavior questionnaires completed by parents. At this point, classification is simply the process of forming small groups from larger groups.

Regardless of whether the approach is more rational or statistical, the *process* of creating subgroups will lead to viable classifications only if the typology is developed in a manner that permits empirical scrutiny. It is at the point where subgroups are delineated that classification as a *method* becomes important.

Methodologically, a viable classification must be replicable and valid. In other words, the subgroups must be based on reliable attributes, provide homogeneous members, cover an adequate portion of the population of interest, and be sufficiently operationalized to permit replicability at other sites by other investigators (Morris & Fletcher, 1988). For validity, the classification should predict treatment response or be differentiated on criteria that have some independence from the criteria used to develop the classification (Fletcher, 1985; Rourke, 1991a). Classification as a method will be facilitated when classification as a process is based on some theory leading to the classification. This theory should specify modal types and provide specific classification attributes and relationships with external criteria (Morris & Fletcher, 1988; Rourke, 1989; Skinner, 1981; Torgesen, chap. 8, this volume). Again classification as a process or as a method can be rational or statistical, and can involve multiple approaches depending largely on the ultimate purpose of the classification. These steps are nicely outlined in Skinner's (1981) framework for classification research.

IMPLICIT NATURE OF CLASSIFICATION

It is important to recognize that classification is a broad endeavor that underlies any attempt to communicate or predict a set of phenomena (Blashfield & Draguns, 1976). Many investigators in each of the three major areas discussed in this chapter have argued that classification is either unnecessary or not possible, usually because of difficulties determining relationships of treatment response and subgroups, or the heterogeneity of the disorders. However, even the most rudimentary attempt to discuss a single child yields an implicit classification, which leads to identification of the case as "important."

One of the major problems with behavioral research is the failure to make such implicit criteria explicit, which is why research in the areas of learning disabilities, mental retardation, and childhood psychopathology is plagued with sampling issues and problems. Indeed, there has been a tendency to focus on dependent variables, such as phonological awareness or inattention, without adequate consideration of the independent variables used to define the group (i.e., classification).

In the area of learning disabilities, this problem has been compounded by attempts to "subtype" without adequate attention to determining which children should be subtyped. The controversy over "socioemotional learning disabilities," which now appears in some standard definitions of learning disability with few systematic attempts to study the validity of this hypothetical type (see Rourke, 1989), epitomizes this problem. The fact that the *Diagnostic and Statistical Manual of Mental Disorders* (in its third revised [*DSM–III–R*] and fourth editions) and the *International Classifications of Diseases* (ninth and tenth revisions) include definitions of learning disabilities based on discrepancies in IQ and achievement, despite any significant evidence for the exclusive validity of these definitions, illustrates these problems.

At this point, the current status of classification and definition in learning disabilities may represent what Golden, Galob, and Watt (1983) described as "bootstraping effects," wherein classifications that should be hypotheses have become self-perpetuating myths akin to "the emperor with no clothes" and "the six blind men and the elephant." The notion of dyslexia is a prime example of this phenomenon (Rutter, 1974) because it reflects the absence of specifically operationalized and validated criteria for identifying children with the disorder.

Classifications must be treated as refutable hypotheses requiring empirical investigation from a falsifiable framework (Goodall, 1966; Skinner, 1981). There has been a persistent tendency in behavioral research to treat the derivation of groups as the end point of the research. This represents the process of classification, but little of the methods necessary to establish reliability and validity. Classifications evolve when process is embedded within method and the results of method-based studies alter the theories underlying the classification, leading to new investigations. Neither theory nor classification develops rapidly when it is treated as an independent process. Classification is a dynamic, evolving process.

There are many other issues concerning classification that are addressed in other chapters of this book. These issues concern 1) models of classification (chaps. 2, 3, 5, 11, and 14); 2) the hypothetical nature of classifications (chap. 4; also Morris & Fletcher, 1988); and 3) sampling and measurement problems (chaps. 2, 4, 5, and 14). As we turn to a review of classification issues in mental retardation, childhood psychopathology, and learning disabilities, the reader is encouraged to review these chapters.

CLASSIFICATION IN MENTAL RETARDATION

Many of the issues pertaining to the classification of mental retardation are discussed elsewhere in this book (see MacMillan, chap. 7, this volume). In general, mental retardation is an intervention-oriented area that attempts to be noncategorical. A major emphasis is on the development of individualized treatment plans for children. These plans are often based on principles from social learning theory and the experimental analysis of behavior (Crnic & Reid, 1989). However, some classifications can be observed. Historically, the differentiation of mental retardation into exogenous and endogenous types by Strauss and Lehtinen (1947) had a profound influence on conceptualizations of learning disabilities because the concept of minimal brain damage was directly derived from this work (see Doris, chap. 6, this volume, for a detailed discussion of historical trends). Applied to children with learning disabilities and ADHD, this concept underwent several evolutions into minimal brain dysfunction, which was embedded into policy in 1962 (see Satz & Fletcher, 1980). This policy-based definition served as the foundation for the U.S. Office of Education definition of specific learning disability in 1966, representing the minimal brain dysfunction definition without etiology. The historical thread of these classification hypotheses can be traced back as far as Still (1902). Even today, many theories of mental retardation distinguish between "organic" and "familial" types, with considerable controversy over definitions of these two subgroups (Zigler, 1969).

There are several classifications of mental retardation based on both etiology and treatment (Forness & MacMillan, 1989). As MacMillan (1988; see also chap. 7, this volume) pointed out, much of the controversy in classification of mental retardation has concerned definitions of mild, educable, or borderline mental retardation. This controversy concerns whether to include children with IQs from 70 to 85. Before 1961, the American Association on Mental Deficiency (now the Association on Mental Retardation) classification included a group with "borderline" mental retardation with IQs from 70 to 85. Currently, this group of children is difficult to serve because they are not accounted for in mental retardation classifications and are generally excluded from learning disabilities classifications (Mac-Millan, Hendrick, & Watkins, 1988).

Most classifications of mental retardation are rational and rarely subjected to empirical investigation. More recently, empirical approaches were used by Silverstein, Lozano, and White (1989), who applied cluster-analytic techniques to a sample of 161 individuals with mental retardation living in institutions. Three subtypes emerged based on cluster analysis of five factor scores from an adaptive behavior scale, supporting the presence of individual differences within the sample of interest. There was, however, no validation of these types; thus, the study represented the process of classification without the method.

Similarities and Differences in the
Classification of Learning Disabilities and Mental Retardation

When the relationship of classification efforts in mental retardation and learning disabilities is considered, it is important to return to the historical roots of definitions of learning disabilities. Basically, by defining learning disabilities as not including children with low IQs, an implicit definition of mental retardation was developed that basically classified children with mental retardation as those children not meeting learning disabilities definitions—a true exclusionary definition! When it was realized that including children with IQ scores between 70 and 90 in mental retardation definitions may be discriminatory (MacMillan et al., 1988), definitions of mental retardation were revised without any attempt to reevaluate learning disabilities definitions. This practice illustrates the need to coordinate both classification and policy attempts for all children with developmental disabilities. Major classification problems for learning disabilities and mental retardation are: 1) whether IQ scores are either necessary or sufficient components of the definition of the disorder; and 2) if IQ scores are necessary and/or sufficient, what cutoff should be used. Until these two problems are addressed and at least understood in terms of the effects on sampling, studies such as that of Silverstein et al. (1989), similar to earlier attempts at subtyping in learning disabilities, are not likely to be definitive. Again, the problem is how to define the major group (mental retardation), which must be addressed in order to subclassify individuals within this major group.

A major similarity between mental retardation and learning disabilities is that their definitions at this juncture are inherently psychometric. More specifically, definitions based on etiology, responsiveness to treatment, or biological correlates presently are not possible. Even if they were possible, it is likely that such definitions would be too nonspecific to be useful. Indeed, research into etiology and treatment has been hampered by an absence of acceptable, well-validated psychometric definitions. Another similarity is that, unlike childhood psychopathology, categorical definitions, with inclusion based on interviews or symptom checklists, are not viable for either learning disabilities or mental retardation. In the *DSM–III–R*, the only purely dimensional diagnoses are mental retardation and learning disabilities, with most other *DSM–III–R* subgroups potentially having either a *categorical* or a *dimensional* definition (see Blashfield, chap. 2, this volume, for a discussion of these models of classification). Major problems with dimensional definitions include: 1) difficulties in defining the relevant dimensions of classification, and 2) difficulties defining the cutoffs for these dimensions. For mental retardation, the first problem is not critical because most approaches use scores on IQ tests and adaptive behavior scales as the most relevant dimensions. In contrast, there is considerable controversy in learning disabilities (and childhood psychopathology) concerning the most relevant dimensions. The second problem, that of defining cutoff points, is difficult for all three areas of classification.

In contrast to childhood psychopathology, definitions of both learning disabilities and mental retardation tend to be *monothetic*. In other words, these definitions specify a set of unique attributes that are both necessary and sufficient for group membership. There is little consideration of *polythetic* or *prototype* models of classification (see Blashfield, chap. 2, this volume). Because most groups in nature are formed on the basis of *shared* features as opposed to *unique* features, it is likely that alternative models have considerable applicability to the classification of learning disabilities and mental retardation. A final comment is that efforts to develop reliable and valid classifications of both learning disabilities and mental retardation have been hampered by premature attempts at the development of policy. The problem with attempts to develop definitions of both learning disabilities and mental retardation is not so much that they are never studied, but that definitions embedded in policy can hamper classification research because the definitions take on a sociopolitical reality. There is no question that policy is necessary and that definitions are necessary for policy. It is unfortunate that policy can prevent treatment of these definitions as hypotheses that need to be studied so that policy can be modified. When a policymaker complains about the increase in the number of students seen in special education, one response is that definitions of mental retardation and learning disabilities are so broad and poorly operationalized that virtually anyone doing poorly in school can be made to fit a psychometric definition if tests are employed with characteristics that fit the child. The irony is that many children defined as having learning disabilities or mental retardation for policy purposes do not meet psychometric definitions applied to unselected samples by individuals not involved in the educational process (Shaywitz, Shaywitz, Fletcher, & Escobar, 1990). This is more of a problem for learning disabilities than mental retardation because of the historical overlap of learning disabilities with behaviors involving inattention, impulsivity, and overactivity. These behaviors often produce underachievement but rarely produce IQ scores so low as to qualify the child as having mental retardation.

CLASSIFICATION OF CHILDHOOD PSYCHOPATHOLOGY

The attempt to classify behavioral disorders and childhood psychopathology in children has a long history of controversy and disagreement. In general, there are clear differences between proponents of categorical and dimensional models. Proponents of categorical models tend to rely on measurement devices dominated by structured (and unstructured) interviews (Shekim et al., 1986). These methods tend to identify multiple disorders, an approach that can be described as "splitting." The *DSM–III–R* is an example of a categorical, polythetic classification that specifies a set of core symptoms that are sufficient, but not necessary, for subgroup membership. In many respects, proponents of categorical models epitomize the notion of classification as a process and are only beginning to move toward classification as a method. These classifications represent evolutions of traditional clinical perspectives developed primarily on the basis of consensus among clinicians.

Dimensional approaches stem from a more general attempt to classify behavioral problems and childhood psychopathology in children. Proponents of these approaches tend to rely on measurement devices dominated by rating scales. Dimensional approaches derive subtypes by applying multivariate methods to large samples of children. For example, factor analysis can be used to derive sources of common variability representing a set of core dimensions. These dimensions are generally present in all children, with statistically based cutoff scores used to identify children with different disorders (Quay, Routh, & Shapiro, 1987). Whereas clinically derived classifications tend to identify many disorders, quantitative classifications tend to focus on the fewest possible reliable dimensions and, consequently, identify fewer disorders (i.e., "lumping"). One concern is the tendency to confuse test dimensions with subtypes: simply identifying a dimension does not imply existence of a disorder (Morris, 1988).

Classification efforts in childhood psychopathology have tended to evolve independently of the classification of mental retardation and learning disabilities. This is largely because the presence of mental retardation excluded children from the diagnosis of learning disabilities or childhood psychopathology, and that of childhood psychopathology excluded them from the diagnosis of learning disabilities. Classification efforts in childhood psychopathology tend not to include children with mental retardation (based solely on IQ cutoffs). Learning disabilities generally are not explicitly incorporated into the classifications despite the fact that the incidence of at least underachievement is high in populations with childhood psychopathology. When childhood psychopathology classifications are validated with cognitive measures, the failure to incorporate learning disabilities (or at least measure attributes associated with academic functioning) into the classification is of concern because of the inability to determine whether the cognitive deficit is attributable to childhood psychopathology or learning disabilities. A notable exception to this problem is the Windsor Taxonomic Research Program described by Rourke and Fuerst (1991). They reviewed several studies that specifically addressed the relationship of learning disabilities and childhood psychopathology, with careful attention to the issue of the relationship of the cognitive deficit and the problems of psychosocial functioning (Fuerst, Fisk, & Rourke, 1989; Fuerst, Fisk, & Rourke, 1990; Porter & Rourke, 1985; Rourke & Fuerst, 1991). Using a classification approach, these studies showed that reliable and valid subtypes could be obtained representing types that were relatively pure childhood psychopathology without learning disabilities as well as types that contained both. Several of these types were consistent with the hypothesis that the cognitive deficit led to the behavioral difficulties. These studies showed that children with learning disabilities are not uniform in terms of the presence or absence of childhood psychopathology; however, most children with learning disabilities do not show significant signs of childhood psychopathology. More importantly, these studies showed that there are characteristics differentiating children with learning disabilities who develop childhood psychopathology in response to those disabilities from children with learning disabilities who develop specific patterns of impaired psychosocial functioning directly related to the cognitive deficit. From a classification viewpoint, these studies provide models for future research addressing the relationships between learning disabilities and childhood psychopathology.

Similarities and Differences in the Classification of Learning Disabilities, Mental Retardation, and Childhood Psychopathology

What classification research in childhood psychopathology offers mental retardation and learning disabilities is the clearer specification of models and methods and considerable experience with both, partly because of the close relationship with adult psychopathology. Indeed, the conceptual framework underlying our work in learning disabilities classification stemmed from work in adult psychopathology. Some childhood psychopathology classifications have attempted to include learning disabilities, such as Axis II in the *DSM–III–R,* and mental retardation as an Axis I category. This is odd because the *DSM–III–R* is a categorical classification and both learning disabilities and mental retardation are presently psychometric, dimensionally based constructs.

Important issues for the learning disabilities field are: 1) whether the classification should be monothetic or polythetic, or represent another alternative model (Blashfield, chap. 2, this volume); and 2) at what level children should be classified: major subgroups or subtypes. At this point, we can see from classification efforts in childhood psychopathology, whether categorical or dimensional, that monothetic definitions are not likely to be employed with sufficient coverage or homogeneity to be useful. Consequently, some form of a polythetic or prototype classification, which specifies sufficient but not necessary attributes for membership, may be necessary. Another lesson is parsimony. The *DSM–III–R* fractionates childhood psychopathology into so many subgroups that classification methods are not likely to achieve validity. When formulating hypothetical classifications, parsimony and a bias toward lumping are probably necessary for learning disabilities. If hypothetical lumpings are not valid, classification methods will demonstrate lack of validity. The classification should evolve from fewer to more subgroups.

Classification efforts in childhood psychopathology are actually quite advanced, with progress emerging in resolving differences between categorical and dimensional approaches. For example, Achenbach, Conners, Quay, Verholst, and Howell (1989) found six dimensional syndromes among 6- to 16-year-old boys and girls that corresponded to *DSM–III–R* disorders. They were not able to find evidence for a *DSM–III–R* Oppositional Defiant Disorder independent of a dimensional aggressive disorder or a *DSM–III–R* Conduct Disorder. There were many *DSM–III–R* subdivisions and disorders that did not emerge in these dimensional analyses. However, the pressure should be on the proponents of the *DSM–III–R* to validate these disorders because dimensional approaches already possess considerable empirical support. Quay et al. (1987) concluded that

> validation is now much more in order than is further taxonomy-building. We clearly need fewer studies comparing disordered children to normal ones and more studies comparing the syndromes to one another. There is even less reason to lump children with different disorders together into a single group given some generic label such as "emotionally disturbed." (p. 524)

Similar points were made for learning disabilities by Doehring (1978) and Satz and Fletcher (1980). Unfortunately, investigations of children with learning disabilities have not consistently progressed to the point of determining precise and consensual definitions of learning disabilities, much less determining the relevant subtypes. A caveat to Quay et al.'s (1987) comments is that, until mental retardation and learning disabilities are disentangled from childhood psychopathology, validation efforts in childhood psychopathology will be quite difficult, particularly if biological correlates or treatment response is the goal. Again, progress in classification of mental retardation, childhood psychopathology, and learning disabilities may depend on the development of nosologies that incorporate overlap among these three populations (Shaywitz, Shaywitz, & Fletcher, 1992). They are not independent and cannot simply be represented as exclusionary criteria. If exclusionary criteria are used, attempts to define and classify learning disabilities will be reduced to circular definitions such as those for "dyslexia" that simply say what learning disability is not and fail to provide criteria with adequate specificity to identify the population with precision (Fletcher & Morris, 1986; Ross, 1976; Rutter, 1974).

CLASSIFICATION OF LEARNING DISABILITIES

In examining classification issues in mental retardation, childhood psychopathology, and learning disabilities, there are two important differences that characterize these areas of research. The first is that definitions are relatively straightforward for mental retardation and childhood psychopathology. Although dimensional models are used, there is disagreement about dimensions and exactly what constitutes a sufficient degree of deviance on the dimensions. There is, however, little disagreement about how deviance is defined: always relative to some age-based standard of "normality." For mental retardation and childhood psychopathology, the disorders can be defined quantitatively based on divisions of the normal distribution.

This leads directly to the second difference, which concerns the role of *discrepancy*. Definitions in all three areas of classification can be made using psychometric theory. When the discrepancy is relative to age, computation of the difference is straightforward and well understood in terms of psychometric theory. The major problems are defining the relevant dimensions and agreeing on where to place the cutoffs. The latter almost certainly must be based on consensus because divisions of the normal curve are not likely to represent subdivisions with any particular empirical validity. In other words, if the classification attributes are plotted, there will emerge no natural subdivision of these continuously distributed variables. Biological and/or treatment variables may be more likely to cluster around the more severe cases, which may represent ideal types in either polythetic or prototypic models of classification. For mental retardation and childhood psychopathology, *classification* leads directly to *definition*, which in turn produces criteria for *identification*. These are separable, but related operations.

In contrast, the notion of discrepancy is different for learning disabilities because of the use of exclusionary criteria and because of the usual practice of searching for discrepancies relative to IQ. Simply defining a child with a reading disability according to normal distribution theory (i.e., by specifying a cutoff score on an age-based reading test) is generally not an accepted practice. Somehow it must be shown that the reading score is discrepant with ability potential, which is usually operationalized by an IQ score. At the very least, it must be shown that the child has "normal intelligence."

Discrepancy and IQ

This example of discrepancy-based definitions of reading disability epitomizes many of the problems with classification research in learning disabilities. Indeed, classification, definition, and identification become muddled, so that what passes as a classification study begins by accepting a discrepancy-based definition of learning disabilities. Regardless of one's viewpoint on the relationship of IQ and learning disabilities, when a study looking for subtypes begins by ensuring the reader that the learners with disabilities all meet some IQ-based definition of learning disabilities, it is difficult to address the validity of the subtypes because the validity of the underlying classification issue is not addressed. That is, are children who are defined as having learning disabilities based on discrepancies with measured IQ different in some way from other children? In learning disabilities, the question becomes whether these children are different in meaningful ways from children with low achievement scores that are comparable to their measured intelligence. Notice how far removed we are from definitional issues in mental retardation and childhood psychopathology because we now must deal with a bivariate distribution of scores.

The issue of whether children with achievement deficiencies who meet criteria for IQ-based discrepancies are different from children with achievement deficiencies who do not meet these criteria is fundamental to the classification of learning disabilities. Definition and identification as embedded in public policy for learning disabilities are based on discrepancies with measured IQ. There is a large body of literature addressing: 1) how discrepancy is to be conceptualized and defined (Bateman, 1965; Francis et al., 1991; Kavale, 1987; Keogh, 1987); 2) the use of psychometric tests and psychometric theory (Cone & Wilson, 1981; Reynolds, 1984; Shepard, 1980; Wilson & Cone, 1984); and 3) the role of IQ tests in learning disabilities (Fletcher & Morris, 1986; Lyon, 1989; Share, McGee, & Silva, 1989; Siegel, 1989; Torgesen, 1989). Unfortunately, definition and identification have proceeded without addressing the classification issues implicit in policy-based definitions of learning disabilities involving IQ discrepancies or cutoffs. One of the few exceptions to this problem was the work of McFadden (1990), who specifically addressed the role of the IQ cutoff in studies of learning disabilities. McFadden found that: 1) children with IQs between 70 and 80 were generally represented in all clusters of children with learning disabilities; 2) many children with low IQs exhibited similar patterns of cognitive difficulties relative to children defined as having learning disabilities by discrepancy criteria; 3) although a Wechsler Intelligence Scale for Children (WISC) Full Scale IQ cutoff of 80 reduced the number of children with low IQs in learning disabilities clusters, several subtypes still contained children with approximately 20 percent lower IQs; and 4) children with low IQs were apparent in clusters of children with learning disabilities and, within such clusters, differences occurred in level but not shape. These results question the validity of differentiating learning disabilities according to IQ cutoffs of 80 and above, but do not identify appropriate cutoffs (if any). This issue remains an important topic of empirical investigation.

When the body of literature on the validity of IQ-based discrepancy definitions is examined, the issues become complex. The origins of the notion of discrepancy can be traced to early definitions of reading disabilities, which basically indicated that the disorder was not due to exclusionary problems such as mental retardation, environmental deprivation, and sensory disorders. The modern notion of discrepancy-based definitions was significantly influenced by the Isle of Wight studies by Rutter and Yule (1975). By using regression procedures, Rutter and Yule separated general reading backwardness from specific reading retardation, showing that the distribution of reading impairment was bimodal (i.e., the fabled hump). They also found differences in prevalence, reading and spelling characteristics, and neurological signs between these two types of impairment. These studies have had profound influences on the development of definitions and identification procedures for learning disabilities. They have also hindered classification efforts in learning disabilities as well as mental retardation and childhood psychopathology (Francis et al., 1991).

From a classification viewpoint, there are two levels at which definitions based on discrepancies of IQ and achievement can be addressed (see Rutter, 1989). The first is replicability of the nonnormal distribution. The second is the validity of distinguishing achievement impairments based on IQ discrepancies. Prior to discussing these issues, two precursor statements are essential. The first statement is psychometric: Discrepancies must be defined using regression procedures that correct for the correlation of IQ and achievement. Simply comparing IQ and achievement scores without these corrections may lead to considerable misidentification of children as having learning disabilities (Reynolds, 1984). The exact method of computing this discrepancy is not particularly straightforward because it is a difference score and has all the dilemmas of the difference score (Francis, Fletcher, Stuebing, Davidson, & Thompson, 1991).

The second statement is that, even if it is concluded that IQ is not a valid index of discrepancy, this does not invalidate the discrepancy hypothesis or the notion that learning disabilities are "unexpected." It only raises the issue of what alternative criterion should be used to indicate "unexpectedness" or discrepancy.

Replicability of the Nonnormal Distribution There are several epidemiological studies that have addressed the replicability of the nonnormal distribution. These studies have taken place in New Zealand (Silva, McGee, & Williams, 1985), Great Britain (Rodgers, 1983), and Connecticut (Shaywitz, Escobar, Shaywitz, Fletcher, & Makuch, 1992). Although a study of twins (Stevensen, 1988) found some evidence for nonnormality, the results were inconsistent and not replicated by other twin studies (Pennington, Gilger, Olsen, & deFries, in press). None of the other studies found clear evidence for a nonnormal distribution of reading scores. The issue is somewhat artificial. As S.E. Shaywitz et al. (1992) demonstrated, the bivariate distribution of IQ and reading scores can be shown to be distributed similarly to the univariate distribution of either IQ or reading scores. When the bivariate distribution is examined, it is also normally distributed.

This latter study, which has generated considerable controversy in the United States, explored the issue of bimodality in an epidemiological sample representing children who entered public kindergarten in the state of Connecticut in 1983. The sample ($n = 445$) was selected to ensure that the subjects met population characteristics for Connecticut schoolchildren as a whole. After enrollment in kindergarten, each child received yearly assessments of reading and mathematics achievement in grades 1 through 6 and was administered the Wechsler Intelligence Scale for Children–Revised (WISC-R) (Wechsler, 1974) in grades 1, 3, and 5. To address the issue of bimodality, regression-based definitions of reading disability were computed using this population sample. Children were identified as having reading impairment if their reading scores were at least 1.5 standard errors below their Full Scale WISC-R IQ. Empirical graphic methods, and more formal statistical tests, were used to determine whether the bivariate distribution of reading intelligence tests was normal.

Results showed no evidence of bimodality in the distribution of reading skills. The distribution of IQ, the distribution of reading, and the bivariate distribution were all normal. In addition, there was some evidence for instability in the definition of reading impairment over time. Only one sixth of the subjects identified as having dyslexia in grade 1 were so identified in grade 3; instability was also apparent from grades 3 to 5. This instability was perfectly predictable based on the hypothesis that dyslexia represents reading skills that are continuously and normally distributed in the population. Consequently, the data from S.E. Shaywitz et al. (1992) did not support the commonly held notion that reading problems as defined by discrepancy-based definition represented a discrete diagnostic entity. Rather, these data suggested that

> dyslexia goes along a continuum that blends imperceptibly with normal reading ability. These results indicate that no distinct cut-off point exists to distinguish children with dyslexia clearly from children of normal reading ability; rather, the dyslexic children simply represent a lower portion of a continuum of reading capabilities. (p. 148)

Like other studies completed subsequent to that of Rutter and Yule (1975), the study by S.E. Shaywitz et al. (1992) found no evidence for a hump in the distribution of reading skills.

Validity of Differentiating Learning Disabilities Based on IQ Discrepancies There are also several studies that address the degree to which readers with disabilities can be separated based on whether their achievement scores are discrepant with their IQs. Silva et al. (1985) compared specific reading retardation and general reading backwardness groups defined with procedures virtually identical to those used by Rutter and Yule (1975). Although both groups were predominantly male, the incidence of males was slightly higher in the specific reading retardation group. In addition, the general reading backwardness group had more neurological abnormalities than either the specific reading retardation group or the group without reading difficulties. They also showed more impairment of motor coordination. In contrast to Rutter and Yule (1975), Silva et al. (1985) found that the specific reading retardation group had better language skills than the general reading backwardness group. Reading and spelling skills were similar, but the specific reading retardation group performed better on arithmetic measures.

Jorm, Share, MacLean, and Matthews (1986) compared specific reading retardation and general reading backwardness in Australian children. The incidence of reading difficulties was generally small in these studies. The specific reading retardation group differed from the general reading backwardness group in letter copying, syntactic comprehension, receptive vocabulary, sentence memory, name writing and reading, and motor impairment. However, differences between readers with specific reading retardation and readers without difficulties occurred only on specific language and early literacy skills such as name writing, picture and color naming, phoneme segmentation, and finger localization. Jorm et al. (1986) concluded that, although the two groups appeared similar in terms of reading ability, their cognitive profiles were somewhat different. The specific reading retardation group had specific language difficulties, whereas the general reading backwardness group had more global difficulties.

More recently, Share, McGee, McKenzie, Williams, and Silva (1987) found no differences in prognosis between children with specific reading retardation and those with general reading backwardness. They also failed to replicate previous findings of earlier differences between these groups. The authors concluded that, "on the basis of the data discussed here, there appears to be no evidence to support the validity of the distinctions between specific reading retardation and general reading backwardness" (p. 42).

A previous study that did not use regression-based procedures selected children with reading problems according to whether they met exclusionary definitions (Taylor, Satz, & Friel, 1979). These authors operationally defined children as "dyslexic" poor readers or "nondyslexic" poor readers based on criteria provided by the World

Federation of Neurology (Critchley, 1970). This definition specifies that a diagnosis of dyslexia can only occur in children with an IQ test score greater than 89, average or above-average socioeconomic status, and an absence of neurological, sensory, or emotional difficulties. These two groups of readers with disabilities were compared against two groups of readers without disabilities in seven different areas. The results showed no significant differences in any of the areas assessed between "dyslexic" and "nondyslexic" readers with disabilities. However, both groups differed from readers without disabilities on measures in all seven of the comparison domains.

Our group (Fletcher, 1989; Fletcher, Francis, Rourke, Shaywitz, & Shaywitz, in press; Francis et al., 1991) has provided a series of studies addressing these definitional issues. In the most recent study, comparisons were made of 1,069 children from the Windsor Taxonomic Research Program who met one of three definitions of reading disability: 1) both raw score discrepancy and regression-based discrepancy definitions (BOTH), 2) only cutoff score discrepancy definitions (ORAW), and 3) only regression-based definitions (OREG), as well as 4) low-achieving children with poor reading but no discrepancy (LA), and 5) children who did not meet any definition of reading impairment (NRI). All of these children had Full Scale WISC IQ scores that were at least 80. Validity was determined by comparison of the 5 groups on 10 subtests from a modified version of the Halstead-Reitan Psychological Battery for Children (Rourke, Fisk, & Strang, 1986). Although comparisons among the five groups were often statistically significant, estimates of effect size were generally quite small and did not explain much of the variability separating groups. The only comparison for which effect size was large was comparison of the NRI and BOTH groups. It was also interesting that measures heavily influenced by phonological analysis, particularly speech sound perceptions and auditory closure, consistently separated the groups. Indeed, severity of reading impairment in all groups corresponded to ranked mean scores on speech sound perceptions, regardless of whether children met regression-based or low achievement definitions. Fletcher et al. (in press) also compared OREG children to LA and NRI children. This comparison corresponded most directly to the general reading backwardness–specific reading retardation difference in Rutter and Yule's (1975) study. Again, effect sizes were small and not clinically meaningful.

Other laboratories have also produced studies showing that comparison of children with learning disabilities according to discrepancy-based and low achievement criteria yields generally negative results or small effect sizes. Siegel (in press) was unable to find significant differences between children who met a 1-standard-deviation definition of differences in standard scores from IQ and decoding measures and children who met low achievement criteria. These studies are noteworthy because of the large samples involved, such that adequate power should have been available to detect reasonable differences. In addition, Pennington, Gilger, Olson, and deFries (in press) and Scarborough (1989) were unable to identify differences in the genetic heritability of reading disability between children who met discrepancy-based and those who met low achievement definitions. Finally, using children from the Connecticut Longitudinal Study, Shaywitz, Fletcher, Holahan, and Shaywitz (in press) identified differences in prognosis and outcome favoring children with reading problems based on IQ discrepancy (in contrast to Rutter & Yule, 1975), but found few IQ-independent differences between children who met discrepancy-based and low achievement definitions of reading disability.

These findings are not surprising. The groups formed when low-achievement and discrepancy-based criteria used are heterogeneous and represent arbitrary subdivisions of the IQ–achievement score distribution. In general, the classification hypothesis underlying the specific reading retardation–general reading backwardness distinction is at best weak and of questionable validity. It is interesting to note that tests such as the WISC-R do not measure phonological language skills. They generally measure language skills that are heavily dominated by measures of vocabulary, verbal reasoning and other aspects of the semantic component of language. If intelligence tests included cognitive measures of phonological awareness, the possibility of observing differences in "ability potential" and "ability achievement" would be minimized. It is possible that learning disabilities could be identified primarily by low achievement definitions (Fletcher & Morris, 1986; Siegel, 1989, in press). Additional research is needed to specify what level of severity is necessary and the coverage of a low achievement approach.

Conclusions: Validity of IQ-Based Discrepancies for Learning Disabilities If we conclude that: 1) reading skills, and the bivariate distribution of IQ and reading, are normally distributed; and 2) distinctions of slow learners and specific learning disabilities have limited validity (and even less utility), then how should learning disabilities be defined? Kavale (1987) argued that "discrepancy is best linked to underachievement and that a learning disability should be something more than underachievement. It is concluded that discrepancy is a necessary but not sufficient criterion in the identification of a learning disability" (p. 12). In contrast, Siegel (1989, in press) argued with considerable support that IQ-based discrepancies are difficult to support. Similarly, the review of literature in this chapter only weakly supports the validity of these distinctions.

Alternative Concepts of Discrepancy

It is important to recognize that there are alternatives to the use of IQ scores as indices of ability potential in defining learning disabilities. Prior to considering some of these alternatives, what are the advantages of eliminating the notion of discrepancy from definitions and classifications of learning disabilities? There are many reasons why this elimination would facilitate classifications of learning disabilities, childhood psychopathology, and mental retardation. First, elimination of the concept of discrepancy would avoid the thorny psychometric problems associated with computation of difference scores (Francis et al., 1991), including regression to the mean and other sources of temporal instability (B.A. Shaywitz et al., in press; S.E. Shaywitz et al., 1992). Second, elimination would place the descriptive classification of learning disabilities in the same framework as the descriptive classification of mental retardation and childhood psychopathology—dimensional, with major issues concerning how to define dimensions and where to place cutting scores. Third, elimination might enable development of a more general classification of school-related problems in children, partly because we could begin to incorporate those children in the 70–90 IQ range who are presently the "lost boys" (and girls) of learning disabilities classification. The implication is, of course, that more children could be identified as having either learning disabilities or mental retardation, which may raise policy concerns because of budget issues. However, the reductions in the costs of establishing eligibility could be so great that more money would be available for services to reduce the magnitude of this problem.

Prior to suggesting classifications that would more clearly integrate learning disabilities, mental retardation, and childhood psychopathology, it may be helpful to examine some alternative criteria for determining ability potential besides IQ tests. There are three possibilities that involve underachievement relative to: 1) other academic skills; 2) other cognitive skills; and 3) a variant of cognitive skills, the phonological core–variable difference model proposed by Stanovich (1988; see also chap. 13, this volume).

Discrepancy Relative to Other Academic Skills There is ample evidence that homogeneous subgroups of learners with disabilities can be defined based on discrepancies in the development of various academic skills. The assumption is that all children have equal potential for development of the eight areas outlined in the most recent policy-based learning disabilities definitions. Fletcher (1985) and Rourke (1989) reviewed evidence showing systematic cognitive, behavioral, and electrophysiological differences in children defined as having impairments in reading and spelling (RS), arithmetic (A), and reading, spelling, and arithmetic (RSA) independently of IQ-based discrepancies (i.e., low achievement definitions). Children with these academic profiles, particularly in the RS and A groups, are homogeneous and have reliably definable cognitive difficulties consistent with current research in learning disabilities and in the normal development of academic skills.

Despite these findings, several problems remain. First, this approach does not resolve the issue of how to subdivide IQ. Most of this research includes children with learning disabilities with IQs of 80 or above. What about children in the 70–80 range? Second, the RSA group is large and heterogeneous, and this classification does little to resolve the heterogeneity. Further subdivision may be possible based on hierarchical patterns of cognitive skills. However, whether these divisions are meaningful biologically (Dykman, Ackerman, & Holcomb, 1986), remedially (Lyon & Moats, 1989), or along other dimensions (Loveland, Fletcher, & Bailey, 1990; Ozols & Rourke, 1985), evidence for subtypes within the RSA subgroup remains to be established. Some of these issues can be addressed with hierarchical models in which specification of learning disabilities into academic types occurs at one level and that into cognitive types at a second level (McFadden, 1990; Satz & Morris, 1980). Certainly, studying reading disabilities without determining the status of arithmetic or attentional skills may introduce significant heterogeneity in the research findings because of correlations of cognitive skills and treatment response with the presence of these comorbid conditions (Fletcher, Morris, & Francis, 1991).

Discrepancy Relative to Other Cognitive Skills Definitions of learning disabilities that use indices of ability potential based on development of cognitive skills other than IQ scores have also been proposed. Among the skills are listening comprehension (Spring & French, 1990), visual-spatial ability (Symes & Rapoport, 1972), and phonological language skills (Stanovich, 1988). Definitions based on cognitive processing skills would be quite difficult to implement. First, such definitions would not deal with the fundamental classification problem of differentiating learning disabilities from mental retardation and childhood psychopathology because scores on processing tests are clearly impaired in these latter populations, albeit possibility for different reasons than in learning disabilities populations. For example, children with pure forms of ADHD may have problems with listening comprehension tasks because of inattention. Many children with ADHD and childhood psychopathology have problems with visual-spatial tasks. Second, processing measures are generally much lower in reliability than composite-based cognitive measures. Third, as Doehring (1978) and Stanovich (1986) suggested, processing abilities are indirectly influenced by academic development. If reading skills fail to develop, vocabulary becomes deficient because the child is not exposed to the higher order forms of language in books (Doehring, 1978). Consequently, a Matthew effect (Stanovich, 1986), in which children with reading problems show cumulative deficits over time because of lack of access to the orthography, influences development not only of academic skills but also of processing ability. This is one reason why age-standardized IQ scores in children with learning disabilities drop over time, the effect of which is often to "cure" the learning disabilities by labeling the child a slow learner and making the child ineligible for services. Processing skills may be useful for characterizing different forms of learning disabilities, but only if the presence of learning disabilities is initially meaningfully defined. In reality, substituting other cognitive measures for IQ tests simply alters the measurement domain used to define "ability potential" and is more of a patch than a solution.

Phonological Core–Garden Variety Framework From a reading perspective, there is much to commend Stanovich's (1988) formulation of reading disability. As he stated,

> The concept of dyslexia requires that the deficits displayed by such children do not extend too far into other domains of cognitive functioning. If they did, this would depress the constellation of abilities we call intelligence, reduce the reading/intelligence discrepancy, and the child would no longer be dyslexic! Indeed, he or she should have become a garden variety! (p. 601)

As the statement suggests, Stanovich is arguing for a distinction between children with reading impairment who display problems that are exclusively related to phonological awareness and children who have reading impairments and a variety of cognitive impairments, including deficits in phonological awareness. As he notes, there is substantial evidence showing that reading difficulties are directly correlated with various aspects of phonological processing (Libermann & Shankweiler, 1985; Mann & Brady, 1989). Although on the surface this argument sounds like the Rutter and Yule (1975) distinction between specific reading retardation and general reading backwardness, it is actually a distinction based on processing skills. It is also a distinction based on the assumption that reading skills are continuously distributed in the population, so that the definition of reading disability simply depends on where the severity cutoff score is placed on a reading dimension. Consequently, the classification of reading disability is a matter of defining an appropriate level of deviance from normality on a reading test, excluding other disorders, and then administering a set of processing tests to define which children have problems restricted to the phonological area and which children have more pervasive cognitive impairments.

This is a hierarchical model of classification that implicitly addresses some of the concerns that we have raised throughout this chapter. It does not clearly address distinctions between mental retardation, learning disabilities, and childhood psychopathology, but it could be expanded to do so by measuring sufficiently broad classification attributes to account for the overlap among children in these major areas. Indeed, it is likely that such an approach would identify the "lost boys and girls" who tend to fall between the cracks of learning disabilities/mental retardation classifications. Many (but not all) of these children would likely represent "garden-variety" poor readers.

Models of Learning Disabilities Classification

A final issue concerns the type of classification model implicit in this approach to classification, definition, and identification of learning disabilities. This is where distinctions between monothetic, polythetic, and prototype models become especially useful (Blashfield, chap. 2, this volume). It is likely that distinctions between learning disabilities and mental retardation will be monothetic. There will be a set of necessary and sufficient attributes that results in a child being classified as having either mental retardation or learning disabilities. However, ignoring childhood psychopathology, what type of model best fits the heterogeneity of children subsequently designated as having learning disabilities in reading, arithmetic, or other academic areas (as well as those designated as having mental retardation)? Given what is known about the cognitive correlates of various manifestations of learning disabilities, it is possible that some version of a prototype model may be most useful. Polythetic models are probably less useful because they assume that none of the classification attributes are necessary for category membership. Because phonological awareness effects are arguably an important component of most forms of reading disability, polythetic models are limited in applicability. In contrast, prototype models assume that membership is determined in part by the degree to which a particular member epitomizes the ideal type. In this respect, because phonological language skills are closely related to reading disability, a key part of any definition of reading disability may need to include problems with phonological awareness. A hierarchical definition involving both poor reading and phonological awareness deficits could be established. Other cognitive problems could characterize children with reading disabilities. However, category membership diminishes as other symptoms are obtained, leading to relationships with other forms of reading disability and mental retardation. Another way to approach this question is to ask simply what forms of reading impairment are represented by children who are at the centroid of a multivariate reading score distinction. If these children represent members who do poorly in reading and who have relatively pure phonological language disabilities, Stanovich's (1988) model would be supported.

CONCLUSIONS

The classification of learning disabilities, mental retardation, and childhood psychopathology will proceed only if operations pertinent to classification, definition, and identification are clearly separated. We have argued throughout this chapter that progress toward clarification of classification and definitional issues will be made if classifications are more broadly based and attempt to incorporate the needs of all three areas. We have also argued that these efforts will be facilitated with dimensional approaches that address the overlap among children in these three areas. It is possible to develop hypothetical classifications of children in all three areas based on the approach to classification implicit in this chapter (Shaywitz et al., 1992). This approach to classification is principally descriptive and oriented primarily toward definitional issues, which we believe involve descriptive classifications. It may be entirely desirable to develop classifications using other types of classification attributes. How classifications based on biological correlates or treatment response would overlap descriptive classifications is unclear, but it is a potentially intriguing problem.

In the learning disabilities area, we have also argued against definitions of reading disability based solely on discrepancies with IQ scores. These types of definitions are difficult to operationalize from a psychometric viewpoint. They also possess limited validity and have questionable utility when the costs of implementation are considered. In this regard, it must be recognized that it requires considerable resources to make a child eligible (or ineligible) for special education services. However, arguments against definitions of learning disabilities based on discrepancies with IQ do not invalidate either the construct of learning disabilities or the notion of discrepancy-based definitions provided the discrepancy is based on a construct other than IQ. There is support for definitions based on deviations of reading skill relative to chronological age (Siegel, 1989, in press). Classifications that simply separate children according to academic skills and that are based on dimensional versions of normal distribution theory may be all that is needed for defining children as having learning disabilities. Such developments would only be meaningful if classifications of mental retardation can be developed (using nonacademic dimensions) that will interface with learning disabilities classifications to make this initial distinction. Once the child enters the learning disabilities or mental retardation classification, definitions of learning disabilities may be possible based solely on the variations in the distribution of academic skills (Stanovich, 1988). Validation of cutoff points and determination of what type of dimension yields the most reliable classifications become the most important concerns.

Regardless of how learning disabilities is defined, there is still substantial heterogeneity within these children. That there are subgroups of learning disabilities is clear, but whether valid and reliable subtypes exist within learning disabilities subgroups is not clear. The simple fact that reading ability (and disability) is normally distributed does not mean that subtypes will not be apparent, particularly if measures of cognitive processing are used. Differentiating between phonological core and garden-variety disability in readers may be quite meaningful for understanding the reading disability. However, the other problems characterizing children with learning disabilities that make them heterogeneous may be critically important for understanding the neurobiology of learning disabilities and response to treatment.

A final comment involves another lesson from mental retardation and childhood psychopathology. Perhaps a major problem with psychometric definitions of learning disabilities is that they require children to fail in academic areas before they can be identified. Such an approach precludes early detection. The degree to which reading problems are refractory to treatment is well established (Taylor, 1989). Continuing to focus research and intervention efforts on children who must meet current psychometric definitions may not be wise. As with mental retardation and childhood psychopathology, it may be important to focus more attention on issues concerning early identification and intervention. By the time a child establishes a degree of learning disability, it may be too late to have a significant impact on the problem (Satz & Fletcher, 1988). Given the ample evidence showing that children at risk for learning disabilities can be identified at age 4 or 5, and can respond to early remediation attempts (Satz & Fletcher, 1988), the need for psychometric definitions may be less important. Indeed, it may be ultimately more useful to define learning disabilities in terms of a developmental model emphasizing growth and development as compared to definitional models that simply focus on end points.

REFERENCES

Achenbach, T.M., Conners, C.K., Quay, H.C., Verholst, F.C., & Howell, C.T. (1989). Replication of empirically derived syndromes as a basis for a taxonomy of child/adolescent psychopathology. *Journal of Abnormal Child Psychology, 17,* 299–323.

American Psychiatric Association. (1987). *Diagnostic and statistical manual of mental disorders* (3rd ed. rev.). Washington, DC: American Psychiatric Press, Inc.

Bateman, B.D. (1965). An educator's view of a diagnostic approach to learning disorders. In J. Hellmuth (Ed.), *Learning disorders* (Vol. 1, pp. 219–239). Seattle: Special Child Publications.

Blashfield, R., & Draguns, J. (1976). Evaluative criteria for psychiatric classification. *Journal of Abnormal Psychology, 85,* 140–150.

Cone, T.E., & Wilson, L.R. (1981). Quantifying a severe discrepancy: A critical analysis. *Learning Disabilities Quarterly, 4,* 359–371.

Critchley, M. (1970). *The dyslexic child.* Springfield, IL: Charles C Thomas.

Crnic, K.A., & Reid, M. (1989). Mental retardation. In E.J. Mash & R.A. Barkley (Eds.), *Treatment of childhood disorders* (pp. 247–285). New York: Guilford Press.

Doehring, D.G. (1978). The tangled web of behavioral research on developmental dyslexia. In A.L. Benton & D. Pearl (Eds.), *Dyslexia: An appraisal of current knowledge* (pp. 123–138). New York: Oxford University Press.

Dykman, R.A., Ackerman, P.T., & Holcomb, P. (1986). Hyperactive and ADD children: Similarities and differences. In D. Gray & J. Kavanagh (Eds.), *Biobehavioral measures of dyslexia* (pp. 147–162). Parkston, MD: York Press.

Fletcher, J.M. (1985). External validation of learning disability subtypes. In B.P. Rourke (Ed.), *Neuropsychology of learning disabilities: Essentials of subtype analysis* (pp. 187–211). New York: Guilford Press.

Fletcher, J.M., Espy, K.A., Francis, D.J., Davidson, K.C., Rourke, B.P., & Shaywitz, S.E. (1989). Comparisons of cut-off score and regression-based definitions of reading disabilities. *Journal of Learning Disabilities, 22,* 334–338.

Fletcher, J.M., Francis, D.J., & Morris, R.D. (1988). Methodological issues in neuropsychology: Classification, measurement, and non-equivalent group comparisons. In F. Boller & J. Grafman (Eds.), *Handbook of neuropsychology* (Vol. 1, pp. 85–110). Amsterdam: Elsevier.

Fletcher, J.M., Francis, D.J., Rourke, B.P., Shaywitz, S.E., & Shaywitz, B.A. (in press). Validity of discrepancy-based definitions of reading disabilities. *Journal of Learning Disabilities.*

Fletcher, J.M., & Morris, R.D. (1986). Classification of disabled learners: Beyond exclusionary definitions. In S. Ceci (Ed.), *Handbook of cognitive, social, and neuropsychological aspects of learning disabilities* (Vol. 1, pp. 55–80). Hillsdale, NJ: Lawrence Erlbaum Associates.

Fletcher, J.M., Morris, R.D., & Francis, D.J. (1991). Methodological issues in the classification of attention-and-related disorders. *Journal of Learning Disabilities, 24,* 65–79.

Fletcher, J.M., & Satz, P. (1985). Cluster analysis and the search for learning disability subtypes. In B.P. Rourke (Ed.), *Neuropsychology of learning disabilities: Essentials of subtype analysis* (pp. 40–64). New York: Guilford Press.

Forness, S.R., & MacMillan, D.L. (1989). Mental retardation and the special education system. *Psychiatric Annals, 19,* 190–196.

Francis, D.J., Espy, K.A., Rourke, B.P., & Fletcher, J.M. (1991). Validity of intelligence test scores in the definition of learning disability: A critical analysis. In B.P. Rourke (Ed.), *Validity issues in learning disabilities* (pp. 12–40). New York: Guilford Press.

Francis, D.J., Fletcher, J.M., Stuebing, K.K., Davidson, K.C., & Thompson, N.M. (1991). Analysis of change: Modeling individual growth. *Journal of Consulting and Clinical Psychology, 59,* 27–37.

Fuerst, D.R., Fisk, J.L., & Rourke, B.P. (1989). Psychosocial functioning of learning-disabled children: Replicability of statistically derived subtypes. *Journal of Consulting and Clinical Psychology, 57,* 275–280.

Fuerst, D.R., Fisk, J.L., & Rourke, B.P. (1990). Psychosocial functioning of learning-disabled children: Relations between WISC Verbal IQ-Performance IQ discrepancies and personality subtypes. *Journal of Consulting and Clinical Psychology, 58,* 657–660.

Fuerst, D.R., & Rourke, B.P. (1991). Validation of psychosocial subtypes of children with learning disabilities. In B.P. Rourke (Ed.), *Neuropsychological validation of learning disability subtypes* (pp. 160–179). New York: Guilford Press.

Golden, R.R., Galob, H.S., & Watt, N.S. (1983). Bootstrapsing conjectural indicators of vulnerability for schizophrenia. *Journal of Consulting and Clinical Psychology, 51,* 937–939.

Goodall, D.W. (1966). Hypothesis-testing in classification. *Nature, 211,* 329–330.

Jorm, A.F., Share, D.L., MacLean, R., & Matthews, R. (1986). Cognitive factors at school entry predictive of specific reading retardation and general backwardness: A research note. *Journal of Child Psychology and Psychiatry, 27,* 45–54.

Kavale, K.A. (1987). Theoretical issues surrounding severe discrepancy. *Learning Disabilities Research, 3,* 12–20.

Keogh, B.K. (1987). Learning disabilities: In defense of a construct. *Learning Disabilities Research, 3,* 4–9.

Liberman, I., & Shankweiler, D. (1985). Phonology and the problems of learning to read and write. *Remedial and Special Education, 6,* 8–17.

Loveland, K.A., Fletcher, J.M., & Bailey, V. (1990). Verbal and non-verbal communication of events in learning disability subtypes. *Journal of Clinical and Experimental Neuropsychology, 12,* 433–447.

Lyon, G.R. (1989). IQ is irrelevant to the definition of learning disabilities: A position in search of logic and data. *Journal of Learning Disabilities, 22,* 504–512.

Lyon, G.R., & Moats, L.C. (1989). Critical issues in the instruction of the learning disabled. *Journal of Consulting and Clinical Psychology, 56,* 830–835.

MacMillan, D.L. (1988). Issues in mild mental retardation. *Education and Training in Mental Retardation, 23,* 273–284.

MacMillan, D.L., Hendrick, I.G., & Watkins, A.V. (1988). Impact of Diana, Larry P., and PL-142 on minority students. *Exceptional Children, 54,* 426–432.

Mann, V.A., & Brady, S. (1989). Reading disability: The role of language differences. *Journal of Consulting and Clinical Psychology, 56,* 811–816.

McFadden, G.T. (1990). *Determination of the subtypal composition of several samples of learning disabled children selected on the basis of WISC FSIQ IQ level: A neuropsychological, multivariate approach.* Unpublished doctoral dissertation, University of Windsor, Ontario, Canada.

Morris, R., Blashfield, R., & Satz, P. (1981). Neuropsychology and cluster analysis: Potentials and problems. *Journal of Clinical Neuropsychology, 3,* 79–99.

Morris, R.D. (1988). Classification of learning disabilities: Old problems and new approaches. *Journal of Consulting and Clinical Psychology, 56,* 789–794.

Morris, R.D., & Fletcher, J.M. (1988). Classification in neuropsychology: A theoretical framework and research paradigm. *Journal of Clinical and Experimental Neuropsychology, 10,* 640–658.

Ozols, E.J., & Rourke, B.P. (1985). Dimensions of social sensitivity in two types of learning-disabled children. In B.P. Rourke (Ed.), *Neuropsychology of learning disabilities: Essentials of subtypes analysis* (pp. 281–301). New York: Guilford Press.

Pennington, B.F., Gilger, J.W., Olson, R.K., & deFries, J.C. (in press). External validity of age versus IQ discrepant definitions of reading disability: Lessons from a twin study. *Journal of Learning Disabilities.*

Porter, J., & Rourke, B.P. (1985). Socioemotional functioning of learning-disabled children: A subtype analysis of personality patterns. In B.P. Rourke (Ed.), *Neuropsychology of learning disabilities: Essentials of subtype analysis* (pp. 257–279). New York: Guilford Press.

Quay, H.C., Routh, D.K., & Shapiro, S.K. (1987). Psychopathology of childhood: From description to validation. *Annual Review of Psychology, 38,* 491–532.

Reynolds, C.R. (1984). Critical measurement issues in learning disabilities. *Journal of Special Education, 18,* 451–476.

Rodgers, B. (1983). The identification and prevalence of specific reading retardation. *British Journal of Educational Psychology, 53,* 369–373.

Ross, A.D. (1976). *Psychological aspects of learning disabilities and reading disorders.* New York: McGraw-Hill.

Rourke, B.P. (1982). Central processing deficiencies in children: Toward a developmental neuropsychological model. *Journal of Clinical Neuropsychology, 4,* 1–18.

Rourke, B.P. (Ed.). (1985). *Neuropsychology of learning disabilities: Essentials of subtype analysis.* New York: Guilford Press.

Rourke, B.P. (1989). *Nonverbal learning disabilities: The syndrome and the model.* New York: Guilford Press.

Rourke, B.P. (1991a). Neuropsychological validation studies in perspective. In B.P. Rourke (Ed.), *Neuropsychological validation of learning disability subtypes* (pp. 3–11). New York: Guilford Press.

Rourke, B.P. (1991b). *Neuropsychological validation of learning disability subtypes.* New York: Guilford Press.

Rourke, B.P., Fisk, J., & Strang, J. (1986). *Neuropsychological assessment of children.* New York: Guilford Press.

Rourke, B.P., & Fuerst, D.R. (1991). *Learning disabilities and psychosocial functioning: A neuropsychological perspective.* New York: Guilford Press.

Rutter, M. (1974). Emotional disorder and educational underachievement. *Archives of Diseases in Childhood, 49,* 249–256.

Rutter, M. (1989). Isle of Wight revisited: Twenty-five years of child psychiatric epidemiology. *Journal of the American Academy of Child and Adolescent Psychiatry, 29,* 633–653.

Rutter, M., & Yule, W. (1975). The concept of specific reading retardation. *Journal of Child Psychology and Psychiatry, 16,* 181–197.

Sattler, J. (1988). *Assessment of children's intelligence and special abilities* (2nd ed.). Philadelphia: W.B. Saunders.

Satz, P., & Fletcher, J. (1980). Minimal brain dysfunctions: An appraisal of research concepts and methods. In H.E. Rie & E.D. Rie (Eds.), *Handbook of minimal brain dysfunctions: A critical review* (pp. 669–714). New York: John Wiley & Sons.

Satz, P., & Fletcher, J.M. (1988). Early identification of learning disabilities: An old problem revisited. *Journal of Consulting and Clinical Psychology, 56,* 824–829.

Satz, P., & Morris, R. (1981). Learning disability subtypes: A review. In F.J. Pirozzolo & M.C. Wittrock (Eds.), *Neuropsychological and cognitive processes in reading* (pp. 109–141). New York: Academic Press.

Scarborough, H.D. (1989). Prediction of reading disability from familial and individual differences. *Journal of Educational Psychology, 81,* 101–108.

Share, D.L., McGee, R., McKenzie, D., Williams, S., & Silva, P.D. (1987). Further evidence relating to the distinction between specific reading retardation and general reading backwardness. *British Journal of Developmental Psychology, 5,* 35–44.

Share, D.L., McGee, R., & Silva, P.D. (1989). I.Q. and reading progress: A test of the capacity notion of I.Q. *Journal of the American Academy of Child and Adolescent Psychiatry, 28,* 97–100.

Shaywitz, B.A., Fletcher, J.M., Holahan, J., & Shaywitz, S.E. (in press). Discrepancy compared to low achievement definitions of reading disability: Results from the Connecticut Longitudinal Study. *Journal of Learning Disabilities.*

Shaywitz, B.A., Shaywitz, S.E., & Fletcher, J.M. (1992). The Yale Center for the Study of Learning and Attention Disorders. *Learning Disabilities, 3,* 1–12.

Shaywitz, S.E., Escobar, M.D., Shaywitz, B.A., Fletcher, J.M., & Makuch, R. (1992). Distribution and temporal stability of dyslexia in an epidemiological sample of 414 children followed longitudinally. *New England Journal of Medicine, 326,* 145–150.

Shaywitz, S.E., Shaywitz, B.A., Fletcher, J.M., & Escobar, M.D. (1990). Prevalence of reading disability in boys and girls: Results of the Connecticut Longitudinal Study. *Journal of the American Medical Association, 264,* 998–1002.

Shekim, W.O., Cantwell, D.P., Kashani, J., Beck, N., Martin, J., & Rosenberg, J. (1986). Dimensional and categorical approaches to the diagnosis of attention deficit disorder in children. *Journal of the American Academy of Child Psychiatry, 25,* 653–658.

Shepard, L. (1980). An evaluation of the regression discrepancy method for identifying children with learning disabilities. *Journal of Special Education, 14,* 79–91.

Siegel, L. (1989). I.Q. is irrelevant to the definition of learning disabilities. *Journal of Learning Disabilities, 22,* 469–478.

Siegel L. (in press). Dyslexic vs. poor readers: Is there a difference? *Journal of Learning Disabilities.*

Silva, P.A., McGee, R., & Williams, S. (1985). Some characteristics of nine year old boys with general reading backwardness or specific reading retardation. *Journal of Child Psychology and Psychiatry, 20,* 407–421.

Silverstein, A.B., Lozano, G.C., & White, J.F. (1989). A cluster analysis of institutionalized mentally retarded individuals. *American Journal of Mental Retardation, 94,* 1–5.

Skinner, H.A. (1981). Toward the integration of classification theory and methods. *Journal of Abnormal Psychology, 90,* 68–87.

Spring, C., & French, L. (1990). Identifying reading-disabled children from listening and reading discrepancy scores. *Journal of Learning Disabilities, 23,* 53–58.

Stanovich, K.E. (1986). Matthew effects in reading: Some consequences of individual differences in the acquisition of literacy. *Reading Research Quarterly, 21,* 360–406.

Stanovich, K.E. (1988). Explaining the differences between the dyslexic and the garden-variety poor reader: The phonological core variable difference model. *Journal of Learning Disabilities, 21,* 590–604.

Stevensen, J. (1988). Which aspects of reading ability show a "hump" in their distribution? *Applied Cognitive Psychology, 2,* 77–85.

Still, G.F. (1902). Some abnormal psychological conditions in children. *Lancet, i,* 1077–1082.

Strauss, A.A., & Lehtinen, L.E. (1947). *Psychopathology and education of the brain-injured child.* New York: Grune & Stratton.

Symes, J.S., & Rapoport, J.L. (1972). Unexpected reading failure. *American Journal of Orthopsychiatry, 42,* 82–91.

Taylor, H.G. (1989). Treatment of learning disabilities. In L. Mash & E. Terdel (Eds.), *Behavioral treatment of childhood disorders.* New York: Guilford Press.

Taylor, H.G., Satz, P., & Friel, J. (1979). Developmental dyslexia in relation to other childhood reading disorders: Significance and clinical utility. *Reading Research Quarterly, 15,* 84–101.

Torgesen, J.K. (1989). Why I.Q. is relevant to the definition of learning disabilities. *Journal of Learning Disabilities, 22,* 484–486.

Wechsler, D. (1974). *Wechsler Intelligence Scales for Children—Revised.* New York: Psychological Corporation.

Wilson, L., & Cone, T. (1984). The regression equation method of determining academic discrepancy. *Journal of School Psychology, 22,* 95–110.

Zigler, E. (1969). Developmental versus difference theories of mental retardation and the problem of motivation. *American Journal of Mental Deficiency, 73,* 536–556.

4

BROADENING THE SCOPE OF CLASSIFICATION RESEARCH
Conceptual and Ecological Perspectives

Deborah L. Speece

The focus of this chapter is on extending the discussion of classification research to broader conceptual issues of what this type of research represents and how it may be recast to address difficult problems in learning disabilities. The methodological aspects of empirical classification are also critical to a thorough understanding of this work, but this ground has been covered from a variety of perspectives (e.g., Adams, 1985; Blashfield & Aldenderfer, 1988; Lyon & Risucci, 1988; Morris & Fletcher, 1988; Speece 1990b). An analysis of conceptual issues may assist understanding of the potential of classification research and how it fits into the larger framework of investigations of learning disabilities. To this end, two themes are developed: 1) classification activities are fundamental to the understanding of school failure generally and learning disabilities specifically, and 2) ecological factors play a powerful role in the etiological, predictive, and treatment aspects of learning disabilities that must be acknowledged and incorporated in the design of our research.

CLASSIFICATION IS FUNDAMENTAL
TO UNDERSTANDING LEARNING DISABILITIES

The assumption that classification is critical to progress in learning disabilities has been met with some resistance that is both healthy and necessary in providing perspective on the strengths and limitations of the approach. An analysis of two conceptual issues is helpful here: What is subtyping, and what is a subtype?

What Is Subtyping?

Empirical subtyping represents a set of procedures designed to identify more homogeneous groups of subjects across a multivariate data set. However, this response has not been accepted as valid by some. To elaborate, Speece and Cooper (1991) identified four positions in the literature that were decidedly antisubtyping. These positions were: 1) subtyping is a senseless heuristic because it does not address intervention; 2) subtypes equal aptitudes, with the corollary that subtyping will meet the same supposedly disappointing fate as has research on aptitude by treatment interactions; 3) subtyping does not contribute to the description of learning disabilities and thus should be held in abeyance until learning disabilities are adequately described; and 4) subtyping is reductionistic and therefore dangerous.

Each of these positions was countered with logical and empirical evidence that is not repeated here. The salient points for the present purposes are that there is not unanimous agreement on the value of subtyping and that the first two antisubtyping sentiments represent a sense of frustration regarding what classification research has not provided as opposed to what it is. With appropriate attention to methodological detail, the results of subtyping research *may* lead to investigations that add precision to intervention (e.g., Cross & Paris, 1988; Lyon, 1985). To suggest that subtyping research must be synonymous with intervention is a value, not a prerequisite. Other equally important goals include understanding the etiology (Lyon & Risucci, 1988) and the developmental course (Speece & Cooper, 1991) of learning disabilities. Subtyping simply represents a method of seeking order in a heterogeneous collection of entities. To be sure, an investigator interested in classification must do more than produce subtypes (e.g., establish external validity), but this decision rests on the theoretical orientation of the research and is not dictated by the decision to pursue classification.

What Is a Subtype?

If it can be agreed that the point of subtyping is to identify groups that may serve several purposes, then it becomes important to consider what a subtype represents. Two additional points of contention in the literature are germane to this discussion and deserve careful consideration in deliberations on the value of subtyping. The first concerns the wisdom of assuming that the clusters of subjects that result from empirical subtyping are discrete—that is, nonoverlapping. This point has been raised by Ellis (1985) and Stanovich (1989). The second has to do with the difficulty of using group data to inform decisions on the classification of individuals. This issue has been raised by Deno (1990) in a discussion of the role of individual differences in special education, and I suspect it underlies several of the arguments against subtyping outlined earlier.

Homogeneity of Subtypes　With regard to the assumption that subtypes are discrete, it is a mistake to either require or assume that subjects can be placed unambiguously into homogeneous clusters. In addition, failure to identify discrete clusters is not reason to abandon classification efforts. Investigators who have engaged in empirical classification research are probably the most acutely aware that absolutely discrete subtypes do not exist, regardless of the variables used to form the subtypes, a point also discussed by Lyon and Flynn (1991). We may have been led astray by becoming too enamored with the Monte Carlo studies designed to test the strength of clustering algorithms in identifying data that fall into compact, well-separated clusters that are visually obvious (e.g., Milligan & Cooper, 1985). Given this mind set, investigators examine their own data and anticipate the same type of cluster clarity.

Familiarity with the literature and "real" data suggest this separation is rare, as Figure 1 implies. These data represent a plot of the canonical discriminant functions of a three-cluster solution based on the performance of 112 first-grade children across a multiple-domain data set (D.H. Cooper & D.L. Speece, unpublished data). As can be seen, these children were not as obedient as the manufactured data points of the Monte Carlo studies, even though the clusters were replicated and validated (Speece & Cooper, 1990).

Medin (1989) provided evidence to support a shift from viewing categories as discrete to viewing categories as "fuzzy" or "ill-defined." He did not view this shift as providing negative evidence on the existence of categories, but rather as providing a better fit with the reality of conceptual structure. Instead of requiring that all instances of a category share some fundamental common characteristic, it is more likely "that categories are organized around a set of properties or clusters of correlated attributes" (Medin, 1989, p. 1470). Medin's distinction between these two types of conceptual structure and preference for the latter, "probabilistic" view of categories free us from the restrictive requirement that categorization must be exhaustive and mutually exclusive. It also helps us understand the nature of our data in a realistic manner.

Medin (1989) offered an additional point relevant to categorization in learning disabilities. He suggested that categories are a prod-

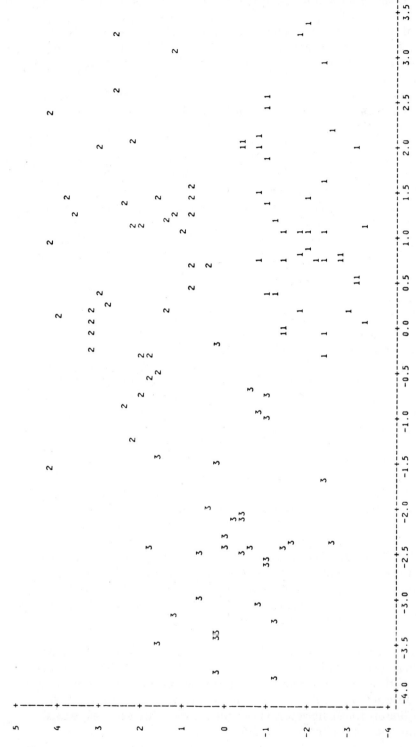

Figure 1. Two-dimensional representation of a three-cluster solution based on the performance of 112 first-grade children.

uct of the organizer's knowledge base and theories rather than a strict function of similarity (see also Lakoff, 1987). An example may assist understanding. Imagine a 5-year-old child sorting store coupons into three categories: food (cereal, spaghetti sauce, soup), kitchen supplies (sandwich bags, dishwashing liquid, trash bags), and cleaning supplies (sponges, cleanser, disinfectant). She hesitates when considering the proper placement of the coupon for charcoal and then confidently places it with kitchen supplies. When asked to explain her reasoning, she notes that charcoal is packaged in a bag so she put it in the bag category. Medin's incorporation of theories as fundamental to classification and the reasoning of our young taxonomist should give us pause as we set about the business of identifying subtypes of children.

What does it mean for classification efforts if we abandon the notion that subjects must fall into discrete groups? Does it imply that classification cannot inform the goals of etiology, prediction, and treatment that are viewed as the scientific impetus behind classification endeavors? I think not. Rather, the acceptance of probabilistic categories propels us to consider even more carefully the circumstances under which any particular classification scheme is useful where "useful" is informed by theory and data as opposed to conjecture. The acknowledgment that subtypes are "fuzzy" does not undermine the importance of the activity but provides an opportunity to investigate the differences in explanatory power that accrue as a result of studying only the best exemplars of a subtype versus including entities that are more distant relatives (see Blashfield, chap. 2, this volume; Fletcher, Francis, Rourke, Shaywitz, & Shaywitz, chap. 3, this volume; and Morris, chap. 5, this volume for further discussion of this issue).

Usefulness of Group Data in Individual Classification The acceptance of clusters as probabilistic rather than definitive provides problems for those who wish certitude at the level of application. This raises the second argument against classification, the limited usefulness of categories for the individual case. Deno (1990) summarized the basic conflict between the goals of science and the goals of education: "this emphasis on classification actually contradicts the assertion of individual uniqueness; it suggests that different individuals can be placed together in a group where their individual uniqueness does not interact with different sets of learning experiences" (p. 161). Thus, Deno (1990) is pessimistic about the usefulness of classification in informing practice because of the child's interaction with the environment and the moment-by-moment nature of this interaction.

Medin (1989), however, views the relationship between classification and treatment quite differently:

Categorization involves treating two or more distinct entities as in some way equivalent in the service of accessing knowledge and making predictions. . . . The need to access relevant knowledge explains why clinical psychologists do not (or could not) treat each individual as unique. Although one would expect treatment plans to be tailored to the needs of individuals, absolute uniqueness imposes the prohibitive cost of ignorance. (p. 1469)

The difference between Deno's and Medin's positions is the level of abstraction with which each is comfortable. Deno (1990) asserted that environmental variation may wash out any benefit of categorical knowledge, whereas Medin (1989) acknowledged individual differences, but posited that categories are basic for human thought and behavior.

Although we may conclude that classification is a necessary but not sufficient activity for understanding learning disabilities, the criticism that classification is not useful because it inevitably loses the essence of the individual is challenged by Meehl (1954):

All macroscopic events are absolutely unique. It is a further mistake to exaggerate the degree to which this lack of concreteness reflects a special failing of the scientist, since there is *no* kind of human knowledge which exhaustively characterizes direct experience by a set of propositions. No set of percentile ranks, no graphical representation of personality components, and *no paragraph of characterological description* can contain all the richness of our immediate experience. The abstractive or summarizing character of descriptions is shared by differential equations, maps, gossip, and novels alike. So-called scientific description, however, abstracts those things which are most relevant in terms of causal-analytic and predictive aims; and secondly, employs a language which minimizes ambiguity. (p. 130)

If the words of noted psychologists such as Meehl and Medin can be invoked to support classification research, what accounts for the lack of interest in some research circles? It appears that research in classification magnifies methodological problems that are not as blinding, but still evident in most studies on learning disabilities. The major problem that can no longer be ignored is the resistance to investigating the role of ecological factors in learning disabilities, which represents the second theme of this chapter. The examination of this phenomenon is restricted to instructional environments, but the argument extends to family and other influences as well.

ROLE OF ECOLOGICAL
FACTORS IN LEARNING DISABILITIES

The call for the analysis of instructional environments is not new (e.g., Corno & Snow, 1986; Eder, 1981; Ehri, 1989; Heller, Holtzman,

& Messick, 1982; MacMillan, Keogh, & Jones, 1986; Speece, 1990a), nor is the extension that subtype-by-treatment interactions should be pursued (e.g., Ellis, 1985; Forness, 1990; Lyon, 1985, 1988; Speece & Cooper, 1990). Whereas the list of scientists who promote this view is quite long, the corresponding list of appropriate studies of learning disabilities is almost nonexistent. Decades of research on the influence of the environment continue to be ignored, and the field remains entrenched with the notion that learning disabilities are due to within-child deficits. As Fletcher and Morris (1986) have noted, current definitions of learning disabilities as intrinsic disorders are simply assumptions in need of empirical validation.

Perhaps it is believed that the environmental disclaimers in the subject description sections of research papers take care of the issue. I am referring to statements that the children identified as having learning disabilities received "usual instruction," that the learning problem could not be due to environmental differences because the school system's definition of learning disabilities excludes such children, that the children were members of middle-class families, and so forth. It is difficult to take seriously arguments that suggest these types of markers reflect homogeneity of environment. The situation is reminiscent of the early work with time-on-task that demonstrated reliable correlations between school attendance and achievement. Although the wags could quip that those results demonstrated that showing up is indeed 90% of the achievement battle, no one would seriously suggest that walking into a school is more than just a surrogate for more important micro-level variables. The theme here is that casual dismissal of learning ecologies will result in the field of learning disabilities continuing to chase its tail.

The argument goes beyond subtype-by-treatment interaction research as a validation of the subtypes to an examination of the role ecological factors may play in producing learning disabilities. Certainly it has been established that environmental events can have a direct impact on the functioning of the organism. Situational depression brought on by a tragic life event responds to antidepressant drugs, indicating a physiological response to an environmental variable. Hanshaw and colleagues (1976) studied the relationship between congenital cytomegalovirus (CMV) infection, a relatively common problem, and low intelligence scores in school-age children.[1] Cytomegalovirus-positive children in lower socioeconomic status (SES) families had significantly lower IQ scores than did control children within the same social class, and there were no IQ differ-

[1]I thank Roger Blashfield and Donald MacMillan for bringing these examples to my attention.

ences between CMV-positive and CMV-negative children in higher SES families. Hanshaw et al. suggested these findings demonstrated that more favorable environmental conditions may offset the possible increased risk associated with CMV.

It may be argued that these examples are extreme, or that everyone "knows" the impact of environmental variables, or that the intrinsic deficit notion of learning disabilities does not preclude environmental explanations of the deficits. The point to be emphasized, however, is that ecological factors have rarely been acknowledged, much less systematically investigated, in learning disabilities. This extreme trait view (i.e., intrinsic deficits) is rare in psychology currently (Altman & Rogoff, 1987), but analysis of definitions of learning disabilities demonstrates it is alive and well in the learning disabilities field.

Effects of Instructional Environment

There are ample data to suggest that the instructional environment is more than a nuisance variable in failure to learn. Turnure, Buim, and Thurlow (1976) presented paired associates to groups of children of average intelligence and children identified as having mental retardation matched on mental age. They systematically varied the type of instructions given to induce learning of the pairs by modeling instructions typical of memory experiments. The instructions included labeling, sentence repetition, and sentence generation. There were no recall differences between the two groups, suggesting that young children and children with retardation are victims of a production deficiency.

However, Turnure et al. also included three interrogative conditions based on the reasoning that young children are adept at handling this form of discourse. The results showed that both groups of children recalled almost twice as many pairs as in the previous conditions and that there were no differences between the groups. That such a simple instructional change resulted in meaningful memory differences led Turnure et al. to conclude that the children's performance under the usual experimental conditions may be better attributed to "instructional deficiencies" than to production deficiencies.

Yoder, Kaiser, and Alpert (1991) examined differential responses of children with language delay to two types of language training. One instructional package was similar to direct instruction and the second was similar to mediated instruction that was child centered and emphasized verbal elaboration. Yoder et al. identified subject-by-treatment interactions *within* this group such that children with lower language functioning benefited most from the direct instruction model. Similar findings were reported by Dale (1990).

A further example of instructional effects is contained in a subtype-by-treatment study reported by Cross and Paris (1988). In this study, third- and fifth-grade students were separately subtyped according to scores on reading performance and reading skills awareness measures. The children were given intensive instruction in the use of reading strategies, with changes measured via transitional analysis of pre- and posttest measures. Of interest here is the finding that the subtype-by-treatment methodology was able to detect for whom the intervention was useful. Specifically, only third graders in subtypes with good or average pretest skills benefited, whereas, at the fifth-grade level, only subtypes with poor or average skills benefited.

Subtype-by-Environment
Effects on School Placement

A final example of the effects of environmental factors comes from research aimed at the prediction of school failure through analysis of the heterogeneity of both child characteristics and learning environments (Cooper & Speece, 1988). We did not implement interventions, but rather described the existing classroom environments. Our subjects were two groups of first-grade children. One group was considered average achieving and the other was considered at risk for school failure by virtue of their referral to a Teacher Assistance Team by their first-grade teachers. Thus, these children were beginning to exhibit signs of school failure, but had not been identified as having disabilities by the schools.

The methodology of this study was sufficiently different from most subtyping investigations to warrant its discussion in some detail. A major departure was the selection of variables from multiple domains for the cluster analysis of child characteristics. Table 1 lists the variables used in the study. Measures were selected from a variety of domains and included achievement, intelligence, teacher ratings of classroom behavior, classroom discourse skills, and learning potential. Another difference was the clustering of both control and at-risk children to examine whether profiles existed that were unique to either group (see Speece, 1990b, for further elaboration).

Six clusters were identified that were both reliable and valid (Speece & Cooper, 1990). Figure 2 depicts the mean profiles of the clusters. Clusters 2, 3, and 5 were interpreted as representing meaningful different variations of normal performance, whereas clusters 1, 4, and 6 were associated with atypical patterns of behav-

Table 1. Summary of measures used for cluster analysis

Measures	Variables	Abbreviation
Diagnostic Achievement Battery	Reading composite	RDG
	Math composite	MTH
Cognitive abilities	Verbal IQ	VIQ
	Nonverbal IQ	NIQ
Cooper-Farran Behavioral Rating Scale	Work-related skills	WRS
	Interpersonal skills	IPS
Preschool language assessment instrument	Level 1 (matching perception)	PL1
	Level 2 (analysis of perception)	PL2
	Level 3 (reordering perception)	PL3
	Level 4 (reasoning about perception)	PL4
Dynamic assessment task	Total training prompts	TLP
	Residual posttest gain	RPT

ior. Cluster 1 resembled learning disabilities, cluster 4 was reminiscent of mild mental retardation, and cluster 6 suggested language difficulties.

The learning environment was described by classroom observations that focused on the teacher and the target child (Code for Instructional Structure and Student Academic Response [CISSAR]; Stanley & Greenwood, 1981). The observation system captured classroom activity, task, structure, teacher behavior, and student behavior. From these data we constructed 16 composite ecological arrangements (CEAs) that represented variations of the activity, task, structure, and teacher behavior components (Cooper & Speece, 1990a). Table 2 presents a narrative description of the eight most frequently occurring CEAs as well as the percentage of occurrence in the at-risk group.

Of interest to the present discussion was the association between clusters and school placement decisions during a 3-year period and the initial findings with respect to subtype-by-environment effects on school placement (Cooper & Speece, 1990b). Separate analyses of the child characteristic clusters and classroom ecological variables indicated relationships with placement in special education. Of the entire at-risk sample ($n = 103$), 27% had special placements during a 3-year period. Cluster 6, the language problem sub-

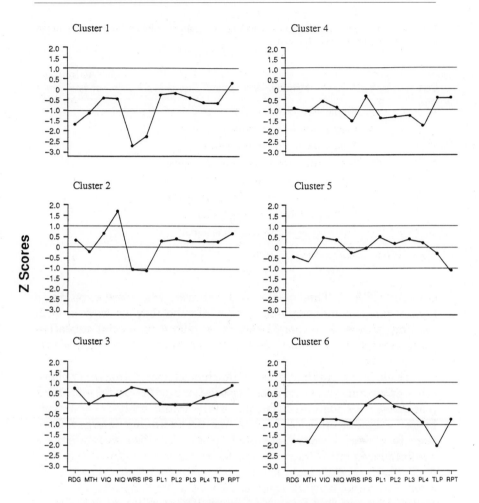

Child Characteristic Variables

Figure 2. Mean profile of clusters. (RDG = reading achievement; MTH = math achievement; VIQ = verbal IQ; NIQ = nonverbal IQ; WRS = rating of work-related skills; IPS = rating of interpersonal skills; PL1 through PL4 = level scores on Preschool Language Assessment Instrument [see Table 1]; TLP = total prompts of Dynamic Assessment Task; RPT = residual posttest gain score on Dynamic Assessment Task.) (From Speece, D.L., & Cooper, D.H. [1990]. Ontogeny of school failure: Classification of first grade children. *American Educational Research Journal, 27,* 119–140. Copyright 1990 by the American Educational Research Association. Reprinted by permission of the publisher.)

type, had a significantly higher risk of special placement, whereas cluster 1, interpreted as a learning disabilities profile, exhibited a marginally significant association with special placement. Analysis of the association between the instructional environments (CEAs) and placements for the at-risk sample yielded a significant relation-

Table 2. Descriptions of composite ecological arrangements and mean percentage of occurrence for at-risk children

CEA	Narrative description	Mean percentage of occurrence
1	Whole class dictation task	6
2	Class independently working; paper	7
3	Target student in reading group	13
4	Independent work during reading group	29
5	Teacher-class discussion	11
6	Class independently working; nonpaper	4
7	Skill instruction in reading group	10
8	Free time with instructional material	9

Adapted from Cooper and Speece (1990b).

ship for CEA 4. This means that children who were exposed to higher rates of independent work while the teacher worked with reading groups were more likely to be placed in special education than were children who were exposed to lower frequencies of this arrangement.

Thus, by examining either child characteristic clusters or classroom environmental variables, associations with special education placement were identified. Turning to the initial analysis of subtype-by-environment interactions, one significant finding emerged. Children in cluster 1 were more likely to be identified as requiring a special placement if they received lower rates of reading group time (CEA 3). Marginally significant results were found for clusters 1 and 6 and independent work time (CEA 4) (Cooper & Speece, 1990b). It could be argued that finding a few significant relations is not justification to pursue the difficult task of identifying ecological effects. However, what should be emphasized is that ecological measures derived from relatively brief classroom observations were powerful enough to index associations with child characteristic clusters and school placement outcomes.

With respect to the instructional environments of the first-grade classrooms, there were no differences between the classroom ecologies encountered by the average achieving and at-risk samples, and levels of active academic engagement were low (23%–30%). That is, the children deemed by their teachers as presenting initial school difficulties did not appear to experience anything different from children who were not at risk, and neither group was particularly active. These findings are of interest in light of research by

Rogoff and her colleagues on instructional interaction between mothers and their school-age children (Rogoff, Ellis, & Gardner, 1984; Rogoff & Gardner, 1984).

Rogoff's analysis of children's level of participation in the instructional setting revealed a significant correlation (.62) between performance on a memory test and a variable composed of "large and constant participation" and increased role of the child in the learning activity (Rogoff & Gauvain, 1986). An earlier study comparing test performances of 7- and 9-year-old children revealed that mothers of the younger children adjusted their instruction to compensate for the perceived difficulty of a school-related task such that the instructional adjustment was related to significantly better test performance by the younger children (Rogoff et al., 1984).

Both the results and the methodology of these studies should be of interest to researchers interested in learning disabilities. As summarized by Rogoff et al. (1984), "our results suggest that the natural ecology of child development compensates for children's differential readiness to learn specific material by adjusting learning experiences" (p. 199). A parallel examination of classroom learning environments in schools would provide an additional and potentially powerful element to consider in the developmental analysis of learning disabilities. Methodologically, this may require the blending of descriptive, experimental, and ethnographic approaches as explained and demonstrated by Rogoff and her associates (e.g., Rogoff & Gardner, 1984).

Final Comments

It may seem that we have strayed considerably from a conceptual analysis of empirical classification research by suggesting that microanalyses of learning environments may hold important insights for the field of learning disabilities, especially given the few studies in the realm of subtype-by-treatment interaction designs. Although this latter approach continues to be an important item on the research agenda, it does not logically follow that interaction effects must be identified before a more fine-grained analysis may proceed. The potential of classification research is not limited to specific types of designs. An interpretive analysis of child-classroom effects in the context of subtype membership (e.g., the language problem subtype described by Speece & Cooper, 1990) is not difficult to imagine.

To summarize, there appears to be much to gain by expanding research paradigms to an examination of the effects of environmental factors on the course of learning failure as a means of broadening the theoretical underpinnings of learning disabilities. This task demands extensive knowledge of various design and analysis strategies. However, it is important not to be constrained by knowledge of methodology in the search for understanding of the phenomenon of learning disabilities. It would be to our advantage to consider carefully Cornfield's (1959) perspective on the relation between method and theory:

> The investigator who does not familiarize himself with every tool that might contribute to his progress is foolhardy. But expeditions into new territory must travel light, and the art of investigation often consists of knowing what can be left behind. Enthusiasm for the newer statistical tools, while deserved, should be tempered with recognition of the importance of insight, imagination, and intimate knowledge of one's field. (p. 251)

REFERENCES

Adams, K.M. (1985). Theoretical, methodological, and statistical issues. In B.P. Rourke (Ed.), *Neuropsychology of learning disabilities* (pp. 17–39). New York: Guilford Press.

Altman, I., & Rogoff, B. (1987). World views in psychology and environmental psychology: Trait, interactional, organismic, and transactional perspectives. In D. Stokols & I. Altman (Eds.), *Handbook of environmental psychology* (Vol. 1, pp. 7–40). New York: John Wiley & Sons.

Blashfield, R.K., & Aldenderfer, M.S. (1988). The methods and problems of cluster analysis. In J.R. Nesselroade & R.B. Cattell (Eds.), *Handbook of multivariate experimental psychology* (2nd ed., pp. 447–473). New York: Plenum.

Cooper, D.H., & Speece, D.L. (1988). A novel methodology for the study of children at risk for school failure. *The Journal of Special Education, 22,* 186–197.

Cooper, D.H., & Speece, D.L. (1990a). Instructional correlates of students' academic responses: Comparisons between at-risk and control students. *Early Education and Development, 1,* 279–299.

Cooper, D.H., & Speece, D.L. (1990b). Maintaining at-risk children in regular education settings: Initial effects of individual differences and classroom environments. *Exceptional Children, 57,* 117–126.

Cornfield, J. (1959). Principles of research. *American Journal of Mental Deficiency, 64,* 240–252.

Corno, L., & Snow R.E. (1986). Adapting teaching to individual differences among learners. In M.C. Wittrock (Ed.), *Handbook of research on teaching* (3rd ed., pp. 605–629). New York: Macmillan.

Cross, D.R., & Paris, S.G. (1988). Developmental and instructional analyses of children's meta cognition and reading comprehension. *Journal of Educational Psychology, 80,* 131–142.

Dale, P.S. (1990, April). *Cognitively and academically focussed programs for young children: A re-examination of learner characteristics and program structure.* Paper presented at the annual meeting of the American Educational Research Association, Boston.

Deno, S.L. (1990). Individual differences and individual difference: The essential difference of special education. *The Journal of Special Education, 24,* 160–173.

Eder, D. (1981). Ability groupings as a self-fulfilling prophecy: A microanalysis of teacher-student interaction. *Sociology of Education, 54,* 151–162.

Ehri, L.C. (1989). The development of spelling knowledge and its role in reading acquisition and reading disability. *Journal of Learning Disabilities, 22,* 356–365.

Ellis, A.W. (1985). The cognitive neuropsychology of developmental (and acquired) dyslexia: A critical survey. *Cognitive Neuropsychology, 2,* 169–205.

Fletcher, J.M., & Morris, R. (1986). Classification of disabled learners: Beyond exclusionary definitions. In S.J. Ceci (Ed.), *Handbook of cognitive, social, and neuropsychological aspects of learning disabilities* (pp. 55–80). Hillsdale, NJ: Lawrence Erlbaum Associates.

Forness, S.R. (1990). Subtyping in learning disabilities: Introduction to the issues. In H.L. Swanson & B.K. Keogh (Eds.), *Learning disabilities: Theoretical and research issues* (pp. 195–200). Hillsdale, NJ: Lawrence Erlbaum Associates.

Heller, K., Holtzman, W., & Messick, S. (1982). *Placing children in special education: A strategy for equity.* Washington, DC: National Academy Press.

Hanshaw, J.B., Scheiner, A.P., Moxley, A.W., Gaev, L., Abel, V., & Scheiner, B. (1976). School failure and deafness after "silent" congenital cytomegalovirus infection. *The New England Journal of Medicine, 295,* 468–470.

Lakoff, G. (1987). *Women, fire, and dangerous things: What categories reveal about the mind.* Chicago: The University of Chicago Press.

Lyon, G.R. (1985). Educational validation studies of learning disabilities subtypes. In B.P. Rourke (Ed.), *Neuropsychology of learning disabilities* (pp. 228–256). New York: Guilford Press.

Lyon, G.R. (1988). Subtype remediation. In K. Kavale, S. Forness, & M. Bender (Eds.), *Handbook of learning disabilities* (Vol. 2, pp. 33–58). San Diego: College-Hill Press.

Lyon, G.R., & Flynn, H.M. (1991). Assessing subtypes of learning disabilities. In H.L. Swanson (Ed.), *Handbook on the assessment of learning disabilities: Theory, research, and practice* (pp. 60–74). Austin, TX: PRO-ED.

Lyon, G.R., & Risucci, D. (1988). Classification of learning disabilities. In K. Kavale (Ed.), *Learning disabilities: State of the art and practice* (pp. 44–70). San Diego: College-Hill Press.

MacMillan, D.L., Keogh, B.K., & Jones, R.L. (1986). Special education research on mildly handicapped learners. In M.C. Wittrock (Ed.), *Handbook of research on teaching* (3rd ed., pp. 686–724). New York: Macmillan.

Medin, D.L. (1989). Concepts and conceptual structure. *American Psychologist, 44,* 1469–1481.

Meehl, P.E. (1954). *Clinical versus statistical prediction.* Minneapolis: University of Minnesota Press.

Milligan, G.W., & Cooper, M.C. (1985). An examination of procedures for determining the number of clusters in a data set. *Psychometrika, 50,* 159–179.

Morris, R., & Fletcher, J.M. (1988). Classification in neuropsychology: A theoretical framework and research paradigm. *Journal of Clinical and Experimental Neuropsychology, 10,* 640–658.

Rogoff, B., Ellis, S., & Gardner, W. (1984). The adjustment of adult-child instruction according to child's age and task. *Developmental Psychology, 20,* 193–199.

Rogoff, B., & Gardner, W.P. (1984). Guidance in cognitive development: An examination of mother–child instruction. In B. Rogoff & J. Lave (Eds.), *Everyday cognition: Its development in social context* (pp. 95–116). Cambridge, MA: Harvard University Press.

Speece, D.L. (1990a). Aptitude-treatment interaction: Bad rap or bad idea? *The Journal of Special Education, 24,* 139–149.

Speece, D.L. (1990b). Methodological issues in cluster analysis: How clusters become real. In H.L. Swanson & B.K. Keogh (Eds.), *Learning disabilities: Theoretical and research issues* (pp. 201–213). Hillsdale, NJ: Lawrence Erlbaum Associates.

Speece, D.L., & Cooper, D.H. (1990). Ontogeny of school failure: Classification of first grade children. *American Educational Research Journal, 27,* 119–140.

Speece, D.L., & Cooper, D.H. (1991). Retreat, regroup, or advance? An agenda for empirical classification research in learning disabilities. In L. Feagans, E.J. Short, & L. Meltzer (Eds.), *Subtypes of learning disabilities* (pp. 33–52). Hillsdale, NJ: Lawrence Erlbaum Associates.

Stanley, S.V., & Greenwood, C.R. (1981). *CISSAR: Code for instructional structure and student academic response: Observer's manual.* Kansas City: University of Kansas, Juniper Gardens Children's Project, Bureau of Child Research.

Stanovich, K.E. (1989). Various varying views on variation. *Journal of Learning Disabilities, 22,* 366–369.

Turnure, J.E., Buim, N.E., & Thurlow, M.L. (1976). The effectiveness of interrogatives for promoting verbal elaboration productivity in young children. *Child Development, 47,* 851–855.

Yoder, P.J., Kaiser, A.P., & Alpert, C. (1991). An exploratory study of the interaction between language teaching methods and child characteristics. *Journal of Speech and Hearing Research, 34,* 155–167.

5

ISSUES IN EMPIRICAL VERSUS CLINICAL IDENTIFICATION OF LEARNING DISABILITIES

Robin Morris

Very little evidence suggests that the current classifications and definitions used to identify (diagnose) children with learning disabilities are either logically consistent, easily operationalized, or empirically valid (Fletcher & Morris, 1986; Morris, 1988). More importantly, these classifications and definitions provide clinicians and researchers little useful information in terms of enhanced communications or improved predictions, the two primary reasons for using any classification system in science (Blashfield & Draguns, 1976). In many situations, the standardized inclusionary and exclusionary criteria developed by researchers or governmental agencies have been accepted without debate. In truth, these standardized criteria should be viewed as hypotheses requiring evaluation. Any valid classification and diagnostic system for children with learning disabilities should, at minimum, be both standardized and reliable. It should predict developmental courses or treatment requirements for different types of children, and it should yield etiological information that can be used for developing prevention strategies (Morris & Fletcher, 1988).

Sokal (1974) has stated that:

> The paramount purpose of a classification is to describe the structure and relationship of the constituent objects to each other and to similar objects and to simplify these requirements in such a way that general statements can be made about classes of objects. (p. 1115)

This work was supported by a grant from the National Institute of Neurological Disorders (NS 20489), "Nosology of Higher Cerebral Function Disorders in Children."

Most research on the classification of children with learning disabilities has focused on generating objective criteria for placing children into homogeneous diagnostic groups that are meaningfully different. Even within a theoretical orientation that considers all children with learning disabilities to be alike, such that there are no separate homogeneous diagnostic groups or subtypes, the question remains as to how such children are different from, or similar to, children without disorders or children who have other types of childhood disorders.

One of the most significant limitations of previous classification studies is that they have been isolated from a more general classification framework that includes other childhood disorders. This isolation has created a wide range of debates within the field, including those focused on the relationship between learning disabilities and attention deficit disorders or different forms of childhood psychopathology and behavior disorders. So that they would not have to address such issues directly, researchers have typically used exclusionary criteria. Such exclusionary criteria represent classification system attributes, but they rarely have been validated. Because of this history, practitioners in the field of learning disabilities have debated intensely whether children have disorders that co-occur (comorbidity of multiple independent disorders) or whether homogeneous groups of children have a single disorder with attributes of both learning and psychological disabilities. Such debates could be addressed more directly by the appropriate inclusion in classification research designs of groups of children with a wide range of childhood disorders, especially those groups that do not meet the typical criteria by which a child is considered to have learning disabilities. It should be remembered that the concept of learning disabilities is as much a hypothesis as are other concepts, such as attention deficit disorders or depression. As Rutter (1974) clearly stated, "we should not presuppose either the existence of any particular condition or the scientific value of the concept."

The use of a broader array of children is clearly more typical of what clinicians and teachers deal with on a day-to-day basis. One can conceptualize the typical clinician's job as one of classification/identification, with the implicit null hypothesis being that a specific child comes from the normal population. This orientation is very closely related to the null hypothesis in most classification studies, whether they be clinically/rationally or empirically/statistically based, which suggests that there are no homogeneous groups (Goodall, 1966) within one's sample of data.

The clinical/rational and empirical/statistical approaches to classification research are much more similar than many in the field would suggest. In fact, the basic methodological framework and practical problems involved in each approach are almost identical. The methodological models underlying all classification research are more encompassing than the use of any particular statistical tool. Statistics are, after all, only the tools used to assist researchers in their search for objectivity.

The design and implementation of any methodologically sophisticated classification study of children with learning disabilities requires input from both the clinical and the empirical orientations. Unfortunately, clinicians and empirical researchers, who approach the classification problem from slightly different perspectives, regard each other's methods with suspicion. Thus, they have not accepted each other's classification study results, even though the findings are frequently congruent and the limitations are similar (Satz & Morris, 1981).

COMPARING CLINICAL AND EMPIRICAL APPROACHES

In many ways, classification problems, whether developed via clinical/rational or empirical/statistical approaches, can be thought of as an attempt to integrate both the ipsative (individual differences) and the normative (group differences) approaches to understanding a child's abilities and attributes. When clinicians or researchers focus on specific attributes or combinations of attributes in some children but not all, they begin the basic process of developing a classification system. This framework, which forms the foundation of the clinician's job, is very similar to the process of partitioning variance, which forms the foundation of the researcher's job. Clinicians make an implicit assumption, much like their peers in research, that the more variance they can explain and understand, the better their descriptions and predictions.

Most clinical and empirical approaches typically build classification systems from the bottom up rather than from the top down; the top-down method is used in some empirical approaches focusing on partitioning variance (Q-type factor analysis, hierarchical divisive clustering methods). Many clinical classification systems begin with the identification of a "classic" or "prototypic" child who is qualitatively different from other types of children. Using this child and his or her attributes, the clinician can identify other children who are similar, although not exactly the same (polythetic classification approach). Most of the classical cluster analytic and multivariate methods used for classification research also use a similar bottom-up approach. Many of the hierarchical agglomerative methods, based on a complete similarity/dissimilarity matrix between all subjects, group children who are the most similar with each other. Interestingly, the iterative partitioning clustering methods, which require the clinical identification of prototypic or centroid cases to represent each group, can represent a hybrid approach to classification. Once such cases are identified, the basic empirical clustering process groups together those children who are most similar to these prototypes based on metrics of association.

Most alternative classification systems for learning disability have been developed through the clinical/rational approach (Bannatyne, 1971; Boder, 1973; Denckla, 1972; Johnson & Myklebust, 1967; Kinsbourne & Warrington, 1966; Mattis, French, & Rapin, 1975). In many ways, clinicians have provided the earliest and most important alternative classification models available to us. No studies using empirically based classification approaches have provided such theoretically useful and face-valid descriptions and, at times, usable operational definitions of groups of children with learning disabilities (for examples, see Boder, 1973; Denckla, 1972). This is partly because most of the empirically based classification studies have been performed in a post hoc manner on previously acquired data, thus limiting hypothesis testing (Satz & Morris, 1981). Most of the studies using the empirical/statistical approaches have been attempts to make clinical models more explicit and objective, or to develop statistical classification methods, or to explore theoretical issues of special relevance to the field of learning disabilities.

Unfortunately, these alternative clinically derived classification systems have not been extensively validated (Fletcher, 1985) or widely accepted, except in a few notable instances (Lyon; 1985). Most of these clinical classification systems have been available for more than 15 years; few others have appeared in more recent years, despite increasing concern over the inadequacies of the current diagnostic systems (Morris, 1988).

Although he or she may not be able to explicate it, each clinician has an internal classification model that he or she has been taught or has modified or developed through clinical experiences. Most of the clinicians in the field typically use a more global classification framework that includes children with other psychological, behavioral, cognitive, or learning problems. They therefore have a more global perspective on the possible heterogeneity of children in general, and they have a broader understanding of the covariation of the children's attributes.

In contrast, many empirical researchers go to the other extreme by focusing on only one group of children (e.g., those with learning disability), or on one attribute of such children (e.g., phonological segmentation skills). Applebee (1971) pointed out years ago the significant limitations of these traditionally myopic empirical studies by stating that, if one looks only at one attribute or at one group of children, the subsequent findings will be limited. This lack of a more global perspective is a clear limitation of many empirical approaches to the classification and identification of children with learning disabilities.

Most experienced clinicians understand the type of classification model that they are using and the purpose of it. Although they may use dimensional data to assist in diagnosis, most clinicians are more comfortable using categorical or hierarchical classification models. They also typically have an a priori model of all the possible hypothesized groups within their classification system (i.e., the *Diagnostic and Statistical Manual of Mental Disorders,* 3rd ed. [*DSM–III*]). In addition, they understand the attributes that a child must have or not have in order to be grouped within their classification system. Most of the time they implicitly use a polythetic or hybrid attribute grouping approach to identify which children belong to which group.

Empirical researchers typically evaluate and further develop the many alternatives within the clinical/rational approach to classification and diagnosis. For example, empirical models could focus on true multidimensional classification models, selecting more sensitive attributes for the identification of groups and evaluating monothetic grouping models. Through this process, empirical researchers can evaluate the "weaknesses" of the classical clinical processes and can decide whether alternative models may be more useful and valid. Any objective evaluative research, however, must be undertaken within a currently used clinical classification system. Otherwise, the research would not be widely accepted by those who would actually put the classification into practice—the clinicians (Blashfield & Draguns, 1976). Truly independent and novel classification models developed via empirical approaches, if such are actually possible, would need to be significantly more valid than the current clinical models in order to gain wide acceptance by clinicians and researchers. In the area of learning disabilities, this has clearly not happened.

The clinical process of developing classification and diagnostic systems is not without problems. The first difficulty arises with the realization that all clinicians must have some underlying theoretical framework and classification model before they ever evaluate their first child. Without such a system, they would not know which of the overwhelming number of possible attributes on which to focus, how to assess them, or how to classify/diagnose a specific child into a specific group. These initial theoretical models and classification systems differ greatly among different professional groups. In fact, one of the biggest differences between various professional groups is the breadth and depth of their theoretical and classification models. For example, few speech and language pathologists are trained to assess and diagnose children who may have internalized psychopathology or other non–language-based disorders. However, their theoretical and classification frameworks related specifically to language disabilities are of greater depth and sophistication than are those of most other professional groups. Although such depth is valuable, limiting breadth in theoretical perspectives increases the likelihood that observer biases will occur. Observer bias is not restricted to clinicians; it also arises when empirical researchers focus only on children with learning disabilities and know little about other types of children. How they know when they have included another type of child in their sample is unclear.

Another problem that occurs is that persons of different theoretical orientations, either clinical or empirical in approach, focus on different attributes of the child for classification purposes. In this scenario, for example, two different clinicians may evaluate the same child and classify him or her completely differently, even though they obtained congruent information. This occurs frequently even when both state that one attribute of significance in their models is the same (e.g., verbal memory) but then assess it differently because their theoretical conceptualization and operationalization of the attribute are different. Clearly, both clinical and empirical researchers must specify their theoretical model and how it is operationalized. Professionals in the field should also consider developing classification systems that are usable by clinicians and researchers from very different theoretical backgrounds. This would require the development of different ways to operationalize any primary classification system using the evaluative tools and abilities of each involved group.

Any theoretical classification model clearly biases a clinician's observations of a child and a researcher's interpretation of empirical results. What they observe as significant in their evaluations is typically implicit in their working classification model. In other words, they find what they propose to find, and they typically fail to find any information that does not fall within their working model. Because of this, many persons not knowledgeable about the issues involved in classification research suggest that such studies are circular. It must be remembered, however, that methodology developed for classification research is designed only to provide a systematic and replicable approach to the problem. It does not guarantee reality. Probably a more important issue is that it is very difficult for a clinician or empirical researcher to modify his or her working theoretical or classification model or to develop a new one. Morris and Fletcher (1988) stated:

> In general, any classification system sets some limits on the theories that may evolve. On the one hand, theories also determine the characteristics of the classification. Neither theory nor classification systems can develop rapidly when they are independent of each other. (p. 644)

Classification systems change more frequently in the clinical arena. Many clinical researchers are less knowledgeable about the advances and changes in the theoretical literature than are their empirical peers. They are more knowledgeable, however, about the reality and the limitations of the classification systems they use on a day-to-day basis. In contrast, empirical researchers are frequently more aware of the theoretical models involved and the methodology useful in evaluating the models. At times, however, they are unaware of the specific limitations in the definitions and criteria they use for the identification of children with learning disabilities. Of course, there is always the possibility that clinicians are overinterpreting the structure and covariation expected among subjects and variates within any group, that they are influenced by their patient referral biases, or that they are artificially grouping children in a manner that is not useful or valid either for clinical purposes or for research. These potential biases in clinical models represent one of the primary concerns of more empirically oriented researchers, who would prefer to develop more objective classification systems. Unfortunately, there are no empirical methods that can generate theoretical models or ideas. These methods are only tools for evaluating a set of hypotheses or ideas in some replicable and systematic manner. Thus, many empirical researchers have in some ways been dependent on the clinical researchers for initially generating and specifying such models and ideas, as has been the case since the first clinical description of a child with learning disabilities at the turn of the century. This conceptualization does not suggest that empirical researchers cannot develop alternative ideas and models based on their own findings or findings of other researchers to further their independent classification studies. Clearly it is in the integration and translation of any ideas and models between the clinicians and empirical researchers where synergy can be obtained that will assist the field to develop more valid classification models that will benefit both groups.

Skinner (1981) provided a methodology for incorporating clinical/rational and empirical/statistical approaches within a similar framework. Both approaches have similar strengths and limitations—

more so than most practicing clinicians and researchers would admit. Both clinicians and researchers have their "blind spots," and both are required to make numerous subjective decisions when developing any classification system. Clinicians deal with real-world children and classification problems day after day; empirical researchers operationalize and evaluate the theoretical constructs in an objective and systematic way. Clearly, the field of learning disabilities needs both approaches, and their interaction should be more encouraged.

A CLASSIFICATION RESEARCH MODEL

Skinner's (1981) classification model has been described in great detail in previous work on the classification of learning disabilities (Fletcher & Morris, 1986; Morris, 1988; Morris & Satz, 1984) and so this chapter does not expand on it. The three major components of the Skinner (1981) model include: 1) the a priori specification of a theoretical classification model, 2) its internal validation following its operationalization, and 3) its external validation. These three components represent the theoretical issues and methodological steps within any classification research or resulting diagnostic system, no matter what its orientation is (clinical/rational, empirical/statistical, or a combination of the two).

The Theoretical Model

The theoretical classification model component requires the clinician or the researcher to describe explicitly the purpose and type (i.e., categorical, hierarchical, dimensional, or hybrids) of the proposed classification system. The investigators also are required to develop a priori descriptions of the hypothesized groups that will comprise the classification model. These hypothesized groups may be represented by a theoretical description of their makeup or by a classic example (prototype) of a child who would be found within the group. Cattell and Coulter (1966) considered such "types" as providing "the most representative pattern in a group of individuals located by a high relative frequency, a mode, in the distribution of persons in multidimensional space" (p. 239). The investigators next identify the a priori conceptual attributes required to include or exclude children from the hypothesized groups. In other words, they must identify and describe the characteristics for assessing the similarity and differences among members of the various hypothesized groups. This assessment involves an understanding of the theoretical distinction (Sneath & Sokal, 1973) between monothetic groups (in which a set of attributes are both necessary and sufficient for an individual to be included), polythetic groups (in which a set of attributes are shared but no single one is essential or sufficient for membership), and hybrid groups (in which some attributes are required while others are not essential or sufficient). In addition, the investigators must specify, a priori, the relations expected between the hypothesized groups and external attributes that are not used to define them.

The investigators should also identify alternative classification models that could be used for comparison purposes. Numerous clinically and empirically derived classification models can be used as alternative classification hypotheses (Satz & Morris, 1981). By comparing the proposed model with such alternatives on indices of internal and external validity (described later), the investigators can clearly identify the more useful of the models. This approach is similar to the testing of different conceptual models, using the same data, in structural equation modeling approaches to factor analysis. These latter two tasks, identifying external variates for validation studies and comparing alternative classification models for "goodness of fit," are critical to the evaluation of any newly proposed classification model. The a priori nature of these tasks is essential; post hoc comparisons are limited in power.

The proposed theoretical classification model then requires operationalization. This necessitates the development of an adequate strategy for sampling those children who might be considered to have learning disabilities and those children who would represent the appropriate contrast groups. Without adequate sampling strategies, it is possible to generate groups that do not represent the true nature of the population of children with learning disabilities. Such sampling must ensure that sample sizes are ample enough to identify the a priori groups. Particular problems in sampling include how to guarantee that low-base-rate groups are included and how to define and handle outliers (subjects who are atypical).

The next step is the operationalization of the theoretical classification attributes, which should differentiate the hypothesized groups, into a practical evaluation battery (i.e., clinical ratings or psychometric tests). Then decisions about the procedures by which the groups will be identified or formed are made. It is this step of the methodological classification model wherein the clinical/rational and empirical/statistical approaches appear to differ the most, although both have the same methodological goal: to identify the groups within the samples. Typically, clinical/rational investigators review evaluation profiles or assessment data to find children who belong in the a priori groups or are most similar to each other. The empirical/statistical investigators have traditionally used multivariate classification procedures, such as cluster analysis (Morris, Blashfield, & Satz, 1981), to place children into appropriate groups. Such multivariate procedures may use as starting points prototypical subjects identified a priori. Conversely, the procedures may also identify the groups post hoc.

The varying methods for creating groups have generated great debate. Clinical/rational approaches are considered overly biased by clinicians' idiosyncratic interpretations of their data, which they frequently cannot share with others in any explicit manner. They are also considered overly simplified because clinicians frequently do not grasp all the complexities of multivariate data, which typically require conceptualization in multidimensional spaces. However, clinicians maintain that, because of their significant experiential data base, they are better able to identify the most important attributes in a child's data. They contend that they are able to consider numerous nonevaluated factors, such as the child's motivation, in interpreting a specific pattern of results. Empirical approaches are typically considered limited because they do not adequately reflect all of the available information about a child. They are also considered atheoretical in nature. In addition, empirical researchers must make numerous subjective decisions while carrying out these approaches. Clearly, naive empiricism has prevailed at times among researchers using empirical approaches. There have also been situations in which statistical methods have guided the questions being addressed rather than vice versa. Empirical researchers, however, suggest that their approach is more objective and that some of their methods more adequately address the complexities of multivariate data. Each of the two approaches requires many subjective decisions. The more explicit these decisions can be made prior to developing groupings, the more acceptable the results will be to critics. Regardless of which approach is taken, replicability is an important goal.

Another primary decision concerns the number of groups in the data sample. Because this decision should be made a priori, when the theoretical model is being formulated, it should not be much of an issue. Nonetheless, many empirical researchers would prefer that the data analysis indicate the number of groups the sample contains. Unfortunately, the available analytic methods cannot determine the appropriate number of groups with any reliability (Morris et al., 1981). Both the clinical/rational and empirical/statistical approaches require subjective decisions regarding how many groups are predicted or found. Thus, neither approach is particularly pristine.

Although the sets of independent groups, developed by either approach, conform to the a priori classification model, they do not necessarily reflect the actual underlying structure of the children or data involved. Therefore, both internal and external validation procedures are required. Once the groups are identified, regardless of the approach, the validation procedures are nearly identical, at least conceptually. This allows for the direct comparison and unbiased evaluation of clinically and empirically derived classification results. As Morris and Fletcher (1988) have suggested, the "derivation of groups is not the endpoint of classification research, it is just the beginning" (p. 644).

Internal Validation

The internal validation component of the Skinner (1981) model, which many refer to as the evaluation of a classification's consistency and reliability, has numerous subcomponents. These include the evaluation of each group's reliability, homogeneity, and coverage. The evaluation of the current discrepancy definitions of children with learning disabilities shows that, as the criteria for identification become more strict (i.e., more reliable), the definitions coverage decreases, although group differences may emerge. Under less strict criteria, group differences are less possible because of the increasing variance. To address the possibility that any such groups are the result of some random or methodologically egocentric process, some investigators have relied on Monte Carlo (Morris et al., 1981) and Expert System modeling of the original multivariate data or clinical decision processes, respectively. It is at this level of evaluation that alternative classification systems can be compared so that only the more reliable are evaluated further. A classification system cannot be more valid than it is reliable. Note, however, that the problems of unreliability in classification and diagnostic systems for learning disabilities are endemic to many medical-diagnostic areas, including better developed procedures such as reading radiographs for broken bones (Koran, 1975).

External Validation

The external validation procedures are directly related to more traditional between-group data analysis designs (Fletcher, Francis, & Morris, 1988). This phase of Skinner's (1981) classification research model is considered the most important (Morris & Fletcher, 1988) but is frequently omitted from many classification studies. It includes the identification of group differences in terms of external descriptors, developmental outcomes, treatment effectiveness, or etiological bases for the disorders. Without such differences, the most standardized and reliable classification system is of no clinical, empirical, or predictive use. It is at this level of evaluation that many classification investigators have questioned the validity of traditional definitions of children with learning disabilities, including traditional discrepancy-based definitions (Fletcher & Morris, 1986; Fletcher et al., 1990; Reynolds, 1981; Taylor, Satz, & Friel, 1979), and have found them wanting. When such shortcomings appear, investigators must start the entire process over again and attempt to develop more valid alternative classifications and definitions. It is this developmental process, from both clinical/rational and empirical/statistical viewpoints, that is described next.

SIMILARITIES AND PROBLEMS IN THE CLINICAL AND EMPIRICAL OPERATIONALIZING OF THEORETICAL CLASSIFICATION ATTRIBUTES

Probably one of the most critical processes involved in classification research is the adequate operationalization of the classification and external attributes specified by an a priori model. Once a clinician or researcher has operationalized the model attributes (via their assessment battery or evaluation protocol), he or she is then ready to identify which children should be included or excluded from each hypothesized group, either by the clinical evaluation of the assessment results or by the empirical evaluation of the resulting data.

Although most clinicians use some basic assessment battery and model in their clinical work, their assessment models are rarely made explicit and therefore do not meet the basic needs of classification research. Often, these clinical assessments are used for general purposes and are based on commonly used measures, and do not specifically operationalize the attributes of interest for the specific classification model under development or evaluation. When assessment models are explicit, they provide a rich foundation for further evaluation and use in classification research. All clinicians should be required to make explicit their assessment model and to link it to the classification in use, or under development.

Most empirical researchers, who are not involved in ongoing general assessment duties, are more prone to develop and evaluate an assessment model and battery based on the theoretical classification model being developed and evaluated. They have a greater tendency to develop more specific experimental evaluation processes to assess those attributes for which standardized measures are not available, although they typically limit their evaluation of such measures' psychometric characteristics.

Unfortunately, both clinical and empirical researchers fail to evaluate whether the assessment tools chosen to operationalize a specific construct or attribute are independent and valid evaluations of the underlying theoretical constructs. Many times measures are chosen based on their face validity and titles rather than on their actual measurement attributes. Most assessment tools are typically designed to assist in operationalizing a more global theoretical construct (e.g., IQ) and have not been developed for the operationalization of the specific attributes required in many classification models. Unfortunately, these assessment tools assess only specific aspects of behaviors, and their limitations for classification purposes are numerous.

Problems with Standardized Assessment Instruments

Many significant constructs of theoretical importance have few technically adequate assessment instruments, with adequate ceilings and floors across the wide range of ages and ability levels typically seen in children with learning disabilities. Frequently, we have had to deal with a more theoretically complicated problem of a child for whom we cannot assess the ability, behavior, or attribute in question. If a child cannot perform any items on a measure, what does it mean? Perhaps the specific behavior cannot be assessed, and therefore the construct of interest is not a part of the child. Perhaps the measure of the construct/attribute used is not adequate and a more sensitive measure is needed. Or perhaps the child does not have the specific attribute, and therefore scores a 0. This latter situation can occur only if the conceptual scale of interest has a true 0 score, which is rare. Missing data also cause problems in classification models because the occurrence or nonoccurrence of a particular attribute may be critical in deciding to which group a child belongs.

Most of the available standardized test instruments have numerous conceptual and practical problems. The biggest problems concern measurement, scaling, and related psychometric issues. Many measures have inadequate ceilings and floors for populations with various disabilities. This is typically because they were developed based on a normal population and were not evaluated in groups with greater behavioral variability. Another problem, for both clinicians and empirical researchers, is that the tests have been developed from different theoretical orientations and normative standardization populations, therefore making within-subject comparisons of results more difficult.

The actual scaling used for classification purposes poses additional problems. Phillips and Clarizio (1988) have shown that many of the problems associated with grade-equivalent scores also occur with some scaled scores. Because of the methods used in test construction and scaled score development, scaled score differences may not always represent equal intervals. In addition, normality is typically forced on most new score distributions during test development even in the face of nonnormal distributions. These issues of normality become especially important when the problem of skewed and nonnormal distributions are identified in the population of children being evaluated. Nonnormal distributions of raw scores may actually indicate that multiple underlying groups exist within the sample being assessed. By forcing normalization and standard scores on such data, the investigator may actually obscure the variance, which could be important in differentiating the groups of interest. Clearly, we need empirical and clinical approaches for analyzing nonlinear and nonnormal data, which typically appear in assessment research.

Another potential problem in psychometrics revolves around whether the relationships among constructs change within different samples, especially over development, or in samples of children with developmental or learning disabilities. This issue is related to the multifactorial and global nature of many of the current tests used for classification purposes. Many common measures, such as IQ tests, which have the best developed psychometric properties, also have some of the most notable limitations for classification studies. Such global measures do not include an assessment of the most relevant attributes required to identify children with learning disabilities (Francis, Espy, Rourke, & Fletcher, in press). The Wechsler Intelligence Scale for Children–Revised, for example, does not contain any measure of phonological awareness or syntax; therefore, its verbal scale (VIQ) assesses only semantic aspects of a child's language functioning. Because clinicians are not aware of this limitation, they frequently misuse the verbal score as a measure of all language abilities. The other problem with almost all such tests is that there may be numerous ways to obtain the same score. It would be useful to have such tests yield different scores and outcomes based on different types of errors or styles of processing. In such qualitative or process-oriented approaches, it is not the actual score on the test that is critical for understanding the behaviors of interest, but the pattern and types of errors. Empiricists typically suggest that these qualitative approaches to assessing a child's behavior can be quantified, but this is rarely done. Few such global measures provide scoring systems that allow for the partitioning or identification of the various behavioral functions required to complete them.

An additional problem is the common practice of creating some type of composite score from multiscale measures, even in the face of wide discrepancies in a child's abilities across the scale. Such composite scores typically represent the average across the different abilities assessed and can frequently mask an area of specific strength or deficit. This is especially true when different sets of abilities and constructs are combined. In order to make a composite score from a combination of measures, the investigator must take into account sampling theory and sampling size. Inadequate or biased sampling of attributes can greatly affect any composite or average score. Most researchers understand that, in averaging a small sample of values, one discrepant value will have a significant effect on the mean of the sample. In general, such composite scores, unless theoretically required, should be avoided whenever possible.

Finally, no classification study will be any better than the degree of reliability and validity of the independent and dependent measures being used to operationalize it. Classification measures should be chosen to maximize hypothesized group differences based on the investigators' theoretical orientation and classification model.

Advantages and Disadvantages of Extensive Assessment Batteries

These and related problems have frequently been the focus of misunderstanding and debate regarding classification studies. Empiricists frequently have attacked the large test batteries used in many clinical studies of children with learning disabilities as representing a "shotgun" approach toward assessment. In other words, if the clinician assesses everything possible, he or she is bound to find something wrong, and many times the attributes identified are not related to the basic classification problem being addressed. Another group of critics has suggested that such extensive evaluations are atheoretical because they do not represent any specific theoretical model of the problems being addressed. For example, a large battery of neuropsychological measures used to assess children with reading disabilities has been criticized because it contains no model relating to reading development. Findings that nonlanguage abilities are also deficient in such children have been dismissed as theoretically irrelevant correlates. Conversely, clinicians frequently believe that such criticisms are naive and that most empirical research batteries are inadequate and insensitive for assessing the actual attributes of interest. Clinicians are frequently not interested in only reading abilities. Most of their assessment models or test batteries are developed to assess a wide variety of possible outcomes and classification models.

One of the most obvious limitations of many clinical approaches to the development of classifications is that the rationale for their assessment and test batteries is not made explicit and understandable for scientific evaluation. It is further suggested that these assessment batteries are based on an assessment model that will guarantee the identification of all possible attribute outcomes and groups of children. In other words, extensive assessment battery approaches are required to include or exclude all of the possible types of children. The extensiveness is required so that the clinician can differentiate among the complex factors involved in understanding assessment results. For example, most clinical batteries used to assess the attributes of children with learning disabilities will include some measure of phonemic segmentation or awareness skills, but they will also include some measure of auditory attention and anxiety, which are known to influence such abilities and test scores, so that these confounding factors can be ruled out. The prevalence of these confounding factors within the population of interest must be considered in order to evaluate the cost–benefit of such additional measures.

By including measures that are not expected to help discriminate between groups and that have no theoretical link to the underlying classification system, the clinician is actually able to evaluate more fully the accuracy of the model. It is not sufficient simply to show that certain attributes are identified in specific groups of children; it is also critical to show that there are other attributes, described a priori, that are not identified within such children. In many ways, these additional measures represent an alternative set of hypotheses that should also be evaluated. For example, the clinician may find, in addition to a child's phonological and semantic language weaknesses predicted by the model under evaluation, fine-motor weaknesses in a child's right hand and some evidence of visual inattention in the child's right hemispace. The hand weakness and visual inattention, which are not a part of the clinician's linguistic model of reading disabilities, might suggest a theoretical model related to brain–behavior relationships. In this alternative framework, a child's left hemisphere is hypoaroused or in some way dysfunctional, which has led to poor language system development and its correlated reading problems. Such a revised model could encompass both the original model, which focused on the relations between specific linguistic abilities and reading, and the additional data, which focused on the underlying theoretical biobehavioral mechanism that possibly links together all of the child's attributes. In this revised model, reading problems are just the tip of the iceberg. The child has a more wide-based problem than just the phonological processing weakness. Without the inclusion of the additional, non-theoretically linked variates, the possibly more complete classification model could not have been discovered.

Summary

The need for more sophisticated test and assessment measure development is one of the most complex and critical areas requiring further attention and development in classification research, whether addressed from a clinical/rational or an empirical/statistical approach. This includes the improvement of existing measures and, more importantly, the development of new and psychometrically or conceptually better measures. An investigator may have the best theoretical and conceptual model possible, but if he or she evaluates it by using inappropriate, insensitive, or conceptually invalid assessment measures, there is a high probability, because of the significant error variance involved, of making a type II evaluation error of the underlying model.

SIMILARITIES AND PROBLEMS IN THE CLINICAL AND EMPIRICAL PROCESSES OF THE GROUP FORMATION

Both clinical/rational and empirical/statistical researchers approach the grouping process by evaluating each child's attributes and deciding how similar the child is to other children. If a researcher has specified an a priori set of classification rules, it is very easy, if the rules are comprehensive, to use the rules to classify all children. For example, the rules may state that all children who have a 1-standard-deviation discrepancy between their word recognition scores and their nonverbal IQ scores are to be placed into group A and that all children who have word recognition scores within 5 points of their nonverbal IQ scores are to be placed into group B. This is the most simple approach to grouping children and is easily replicated and validated across different samples if the children are assessed appropriately. If rules are not comprehensive, the samples receive limited coverage (not all children are classified into a group).

More typically, clinical or empirical researchers are not easily able to specify a priori the exact identification rules for each group of children. This is especially true if they use a polythetic attribute classification approach in which only the attribute set can be specified, and not the exact combinations to be included within the formed groups. When exact rules are not specified, the hypothesized model provides the only guidance for evaluating and classifying children. In this situation, most clinicians use a type of profile classification and sorting. In a similar manner, most cluster-analytic and multivariate classification statistics sort each child's assessment profiles through a comparison of the child's similarities and dissimilarities, assessed via various metrics, with all other children's profiles.

A key conceptual issue for both the clinicians and the empirical researchers concerns their basic understanding of what the profiles represent. In two-dimensional space, a profile of test scores has three main attributes: elevation, pattern, and scatter (flatness). Elevation is best represented by the average score across all measures within the profile; pattern is represented by the particular interrelationships among the various measures; and scatter is represented by the variance among the measures within the profile. Most clinicians try to integrate all three characteristics when sorting their cases, although some theoretical models may require them to focus on one profile attribute, such as pattern, more than another.

Most empirical classification methods, such as cluster analysis, also use the various aspects of a child's profile for comparison with the profiles of other children. These methods typically use some statistical measure of similarity (or metric of association if nominal or dichotomous attribute data are being used) between two children's profiles. These measures of similarity are typically based on elevation or pattern information. For example, a correlation between two children's profiles can be used to assess their pattern similarity: children who have highly correlated profiles are grouped together, and those who do not are not. When this two-dimensional profile model is extended into n-dimensional space, each child is represented as a unique point in n space. An easy measure of association or similarity in this model is represented as the distance in Euclidean space between two points (children). In this measure of similarity, elevation attributes frequently account for a greater percentage of the variance than do pattern attributes.

Although this description is overly simplistic and clearly not inclusive of all the possible options, it nonetheless demonstrates the similarities between the grouping processes of both the clinical/ rational and empirical/statistical approaches to group formation. Both types of grouping processes require the measure of similarity between two children's assessment results. One is done visually and conceptually and the other is performed using statistical metrics of similarity, which also have specific underlying conceptual models. Each has limitations and biases in how similarity is assessed, and how reliably it is assessed. Obviously, measurement issues are important for each and every attribute used in a child's profile. The reliability and validity of such profiles are only as high as the average reliability across the profiles' members.

SUMMARY

Methodological issues involved in the internal and external validation of either clinical/rational or empirical/statistical classification results are identical (Fletcher et al., 1988; Morris & Fletcher, 1988). From this perspective, only three ultimate outcomes satisfy external validation criteria for any classification of children with learning disabilities: 1) the identification of a group by developmental outcome interaction, 2) the identification of a group by treatment effectiveness interaction, and 3) the identification of a group by etiology interaction. Although other descriptive differences between the groups might further improve our theoretical and assessment models or improve communication among clinicians and researchers, they do not represent the ultimate classification goals.

Once investigators develop and operationalize a classification system, they must then identify sensitive and specific tools and evaluation methods to identify (diagnose) a child as fitting within the developed groups. Although many reliable and valid measures might be available from the original group of classification attributes, they may also have very limited utility in actually diagnosing children to fit into the classification. There is no guarantee that any measure can perform both the classification development and diagnostic functions effectively. In fact, one of the biggest factors that affects a measure's sensitivity and specificity in identifying a specific type of child is the base rate of the disorder in the sample being evaluated. The base rate is frequently unknown. Therefore, each diagnostic measure must be evaluated in samples with different base rates.

Both clinical/rational and empirical/statistical approaches have been used in the development of alternative classification systems for children with learning disabilities (Satz & Morris, 1981). In fact, most published studies using such approaches actually integrate components of each to varying degrees. Regardless, they do not appear to be conceptually or practically different in any major respect when evaluated within an overriding classification research methodology (Skinner, 1981) framework. Integrated studies using the relative strengths of each approach should be encouraged. The most significant problems limiting the development of more valid classification systems of children with learning disabilities include: 1) overly limited classification studies that focus only on a priori–selected children with learning disabilities; 2) poorly developed or nonexistent assessment measures for classification purposes; 3) limited theoretical models that do not include developmental constructs; 4) limited and unsophisticated validation studies that do not evaluate the critical types of validity (i.e., prediction, treatment, etiological differences); and 5) a strong tendency for researchers not to be explicit in describing their models, decisions, and processes involved in any classification study, regardless of their approach (i.e., clinical or empirical).

REFERENCES

American Psychiatric Association. (1987). *Diagnostic and statistical manual of mental disorders* (3rd ed. rev.). Washington, DC: American Psychiatric Press, Inc.

Applebee, A.N. (1971). Research in reading retardation: Two critical problems. *Journal of Clinical Psychology and Psychiatry and Allied Disciplines, 12,* 91–113.

Bannatyne, A. (1971). *Language, reading, and learning disabilities.* Springfield, IL: Charles C Thomas.

Blashfield, R.K., & Draguns, J. (1976). Evaluative criteria for psychiatric classification. *Journal of Abnormal Psychology, 85,* 140–150.

Boder, E. (1973). Developmental dyslexia: A diagnostic approach based on three atypical reading-spelling patterns. *Developmental Medicine and Child Neurology, 15,* 663–687.

Cattell, R.B., & Coulter, M.A. (1966). Principles of behavioral taxonomy and the mathematical basis of the taxonome computer program. *British Journal of Mathematical and Statistical Psychology, 19,* 237–269.

Denckla, M.B. (1972). Clinical syndromes in learning disabilities: The case for "splitting" vs. "lumping." *Journal of Learning Disabilities, 5,* 401–405.

Fletcher, J., & Morris, R. (1986). Classification of disabled learners: Beyond exclusionary definitions. In S. Ceci (Ed.), *Handbook of cognitive, social, and neuropsychological aspects of learning disabilities* (Vol. 1, pp. 55–80). Hillsdale, NJ: Lawrence Erlbaum Associates.

Fletcher, J.M. (1985). External validation of learning disability subtypes. In B.P. Rourke (Ed.), *Neuropsychology of learning disabilities: Essentials of subtype analysis* (pp. 187–211). New York: Guilford Press.

Fletcher, J.M., Espy, K.A., Francis, D.J., Davidson, K.C., Rourke, B.P., & Shaywitz, S.E. (1990). Comparisons of cut-off score and regression-based definitions of reading disabilities. *Journal of Learning Disabilities, 22,* 334–338.

Fletcher, J.M., Francis, D.J., & Morris, R. (1988). Methodological issues in neuropsychology: Classification, measurement, and the comparison of non-equivalent groups. In F. Boller & J. Grafman (Eds.), *Handbook of neuropsychology* (Vol. 1, pp. 83–110). Amsterdam: Elsevier.

Francis, D.J., Espy, K.A., Rourke, B.P., & Fletcher, J.M. (in press). Validity of intelligence test scores in the definition of learning disability: A critical analysis.

Goodall, D.W. (1966). Hypothesis-testing in classification. *Nature, 211,* 329–330.

Johnson, D.J., & Myklebust, H.R. (1967). *Learning disabilities, educational principles and practices*. New York: Grune & Stratton.

Kinsbourne, M., & Warrington, E. (1966). Developmental factors in reading and writing backwardness. *British Journal of Psychology, 54*, 145–156.

Koran, L.M. (1975). The reliability of clinical methods, data and judgements. *New England Journal of Medicine, 293*, 642–626, 695–701.

Lyon, R. (1985). Educational validation studies of learning disability subtypes. In B.P. Rourke (Ed.), *Neuropsychology of learning disabilities: Essentials of subtype analysis* (pp. 228–253). New York: Guilford Press.

Mattis, S., French, J.H., & Rapin, I. (1975). Dyslexia in children and young adults: Three independent neuropsychological syndromes. *Developmental Medicine and Child Neurology, 17*, 150–163.

Morris, R. (1988). Classification of learning disabilities: Old problems and new approaches. *Journal of Consulting and Clinical Psychology, 56*, 789–794.

Morris, R., Blashfield, R., & Satz, P. (1981). Neuropsychology and cluster analysis: Potentials and problems. *Journal of Clinical Neuropsychology, 3*, 79–99.

Morris, R., & Fletcher, J.M. (1988). Classification in neuropsychology: A theoretical framework and research paradigm. *Journal of Clinical and Experimental Neuropsychology, 10*, 640–658.

Morris, R., & Satz, P. (1984). Classification issues in subtype research: An application of some methods and concepts. In H.A. Whitaker & R.N. Malatesha (Eds.), *Dyslexia: A global issue* (pp. 59–82). New York: Martinus Nijhoff.

Phillips, S.E., & Clarizio, H.F. (1988). Limitations of standard scores in individual achievement testing. *Educational Measurement: Issues and Practice, 7*, 8–15.

Reynolds, C.R. (1981). The fallacy of "two years below grade level for age" as a diagnostic criterion for reading disorders. *Journal of School Psychology, 19*, 350–358.

Rutter, M. (1974). Emotional disorder and educational under-achievement. *Archives of Disease in Childhood, 49*, 249–256.

Satz, P., & Morris, R. (1981). Learning disability subtypes: A review. In F.J. Pirozollo & M.C. Whitrock (Eds.), *Neuropsychological and cognitive processes in reading* (pp. 109–141). New York: Academic Press.

Skinner, H.A. (1981). Toward the integration of classification theory and methods. *Journal of Abnormal Psychology, 90*, 68–87.

Sneath, P.H.A., & Sokal, R.R. (1973). *Numerical taxonomy: The principles and practice of numerical classifications*. San Francisco: W.H. Freeman.

Sokal, R.R. (1974). Classification: Purposes, principles, progress, prospects. *Science, 185*, 1115–1123.

Taylor, H.G., Satz, P., & Friel, J. (1979). Developmental dyslexia in relationship to other childhood disorders: Significance and utility. *Reading Research Quarterly, 15*, 84–101.

II

DEFINITION
AND THEORY
IN LEARNING
DISABILITIES

The field of learning disabilities has been persistently impeded in its development because of difficulties formulating operational definitions that apply consistently to the heterogeneous types of learning disorders subsumed within the category. In many ways, the lack of definitional clarity can be attributed to the number of disciplines and advocacy groups that are interested in studying and helping children with learning disabilities. This multidisciplinary view of learning disabilities spawns definitions that appear to be written to please everyone, and to reflect all viewpoints of the disorders subsumed within this subset of disabilities. Unfortunately, by seeking to respond to all agendas and interests, writers of current definitions have not been able to provide a set of valid descriptive statements that serve to communicate the essential characteristics of a learning disability.

In addition, this limited definitional clarity is accompanied by, and probably significantly related to, limitations in the development of theories that can account for and predict the behaviors and learning characteristics observed in children with learning disabilities. Therefore, the synergistic relationship that should exist between theory and definition in the field of learning disabilities is diluted appreciably, and the field continues to define its responsibilities and charges in less than productive ways.

The chapters in this section seek to clarify these issues and to provide reasonable directions for progress in the development of robust definitions and theories. Doris initiates the discussion by providing a historical overview of the field with an eye toward the substantial relationship between past events and the field's present definitional status. MacMillan adds to this discussion through his presentation of the similarities and differences that have existed between the field of mental retardation and the field of learning disabilities in their struggles to construct valid operational definitions. By drawing these parallels, MacMillan suggests some blueprints for the development of definitions in which researchers and policymakers in the field of learning disabilities should be interested. Torgesen then provides excellent guidelines for, and examples of, theories that can reduce the ambiguity inherent in current conceptualizations and definitions of learning disabilities. Finally, Kavale challenges the field to provide a comprehensive and unified perspective about the nature of learning disabilities by constructing a multidimensional "metatheory" that can accommodate, explain, and predict the complex relationships that exist among cognitive abilities, the environment, schooling, genetics, cultural background, neuropsychological functioning, and academic underachievement.

6

DEFINING
LEARNING DISABILITIES
A History of the Search for Consensus

John L. Doris

In reviewing the reports of congenital dyslexia that appeared in medical journals around the turn of the century, one is frequently struck by the clarity and severity of the disability. Recall a few lines from Pringle Morgan's description of a 14-year-old boy:

> I then asked him to read me a sentence out of an easy child's book without spelling the words. The result was curious. He did not read a single word correctly, with the exception of "and," "the," "of," "that," etc.; the other words seemed to be quite unknown to him, and he could not even make an attempt to pronounce them.
>
> I next tried his ability to read figures, and found he could do so easily. . . . He multiplied 749 by 876 quickly and easily. He says that he is fond of arithmetic and has no difficulty with it, but that printed or written words "have no meaning for him," and my examination of him quite convinces me that he is correct in that opinion. Words written or printed seem to convey no impression to his mind, and it is only after laboriously spelling them that he is able by dint of the sound of the letters, to discover their import. . . . I may add that the boy is bright and of average intelligence in conversation. . . . The schoolmaster who has taught him for some years says that he would be the smartest lad in the school if the instruction were entirely oral. (Morgan, 1896, p. 1378)

Such reports indicate that the rare, extreme case of congenital word blindness, or whatever we choose to call it, is a serious educational disability with readily apparent face validity. The problem both then and now is, if such children are identified, how shall they be helped? The public school is by design an institution for the mass education of children. The constraints of human and economic resources prevent it from being otherwise.

Nevertheless, whenever a sufficiently large group of children with disabilities is identified as being unable to adjust themselves to the standard curriculum of our compulsory, lockstep, graded educational system, the school does make adjustments. This does not necessarily occur out of concern for the child with disabilities; as the educational administrators at the turn of the century recognized, adjustment must be made if only in order to keep the regular classroom functioning smoothly. So when a new group of children with school adjustment problems is identified, questions arise: How many of such children are there? What kind of accommodation can the school make in terms of its curriculum or organization that will meet the needs for such children without overstraining the available resources?

Within the first decade of the 20th century, the American public schools had already identified groups of children for which accommodation was needed, and it is in this period that our programs of special education took their initial shape. The accommodation was primarily in the form of segregated educational programs for children with mental retardation, physical disabilities, and behavior problems, with the larger metropolitan school districts making additional provision for the non–English-speaking immigrant children.

In contrast to these sizable groups of children filling the newly established special classes in ever-growing numbers, the early prevalence data on the extreme or pathological cases of reading disability in no way suggested a large problem in need of special accommodation by the schools. Hinshelwood (1917) decried Thomas's (1908) prevalence estimate of 1 in 1,000 as too high, and Schmitt (1917/1918) noted that her 13 cases had surfaced from a Chicago school population of 42,900 pupils. These small numbers sounded no alarm bells within the schools, and certainly elicited no general public or governmental concern. However, during succeeding decades, this narrow category of severe reading disability underwent prodigious and protean expansion with ever-changing shifts in nomenclature and definitional criteria, accompanied by more or less rational amalgamations with various other problems in the educational adjustment of children.

By 1970, the concerns of the schools, the health professions, and the general public would unite behind federally supported programs of diagnosis, remediation, and prevention for all such children then gathered together under the rubric of *learning disabilities*. In the academic year of 1988–1989, nearly 2 million children with learning disabilities received special educational services from public schools

(U.S. Department of Education, 1990). Some brief reflection on the historical development of this progression from the once rare "word-blind" child to the ubiquitous child with learning disabilities of today may serve to enhance our perspective on the hotly debated issues of research and service provision that fill our educational, behavioral, and medical journals.

THE 1920s AND 1930s:
IMPACT OF MEDICINE ON CATEGORIZATION
OF CHILDREN WITH LEARNING DISABILITIES

Beginning in the 1920s, a number of developments occurred in the interface between medicine and education that served to alter the scope and even the nature of the problem of children with reading disabilities.

Influence of Psychiatry on the Shift
from Word Blindness to a Range of Reading Disabilities

As the field of mental hygiene gained momentum and child guidance clinics began to multiply, the schools became increasingly reliant on medicine, particularly in the form of psychiatry, for direction and assistance in the management of its more difficult pupils. A small but relevant illustration of this development occurred in 1925, when Samuel Orton, director of a state psychopathic hospital, responded to a request of the Iowa Conference of Social Work by sending a visiting mental health clinic to rural Greene County. In the 2 weeks of its existence the clinic evaluated 173 referrals from all sources. Of note is the fact that the bulk of the referrals were from the county schools. Eighty-four of the children were described by their teachers as "dull, backward or retarded" and 30 were described as "nervous, peculiar, or unruly" (Lyday, 1926).

Among these referrals were 15 children, with IQs ranging from 70 to 122, whom the clinic identified as having a special difficulty in learning to read. Although Orton granted that only two of his cases fit Hinshelwood's strict criteria for "congenital word blindness," he was struck by similarities in the reading behavior of all the cases that had been identified as having a special reading problem in the Greene County schools. These similarities included such notable characteristics as the reversal of individual letters and the tendency to read letter groups or palindromic words right to left (Orton, 1925).

Given this group of cases, varying in the severity of defect but similar in their behavioral symptoms, Orton was convinced that the category of word blindness should be broadened to include a graded series of reading disabilities from such severe cases as those studied by Hinshelwood to those individuals who could in fact achieve a fair degree of facility in reading.

In addition to broadening the category, Orton rejected Hinshelwood's theory of defective embryonic development of the cerebral area subserving visual memory of words and letters. Instead, based in part on the observed letter reversals and the sinistral reading of groups of letters and words, he offered as an explanation for reading disabilities the developmental failure to establish unilateral cortical dominance, and suggested the term *strephosymbolia* as more aptly describing the entity.

On the basis of continued research on reading disabilities in Iowa schoolchildren, Orton was to assert that "children suffering from this condition in a degree sufficiently severe to be a really significant obstacle to school progress formed at least two per cent of the total school population in every community visited" (Orton, 1928, p. 1098). This 2% estimate is a marked increase over the prevalence rate of less than 1 in 1,000 offered by Hinshelwood. If it were accepted as an accurate estimate of children with a distinct disability in reading, the schools in fact would be faced with a sizable problem in need of special provisions. However, the fact was that, in the 1920s and 1930s, educators investigating reading failures in the schools, for the most part, did not conceive of these children as qualitatively different from successful readers.

William S. Gray (1921, 1922) and Clarence T. Gray (1922) may have extolled the value of the measurement of perceptual span and the tracking of eye movements in reading as part of a diagnostic evaluation, and even prescribed remedial exercises to cure such defects, but they recognized a wide variety of causal factors, such as speech and language disorders, inadequate teaching, sensory disorders, and problems in attention and attitude. Basing their work on the laboratory research and technology that had been developing in reading research since the late 19th century and the theory and practice in educational testing that had developed in the prior decade, they were able to approach systematically the problem of diagnosis and remediation. The Grays recognized word blindness as one form of extreme reading disability, but their work and the work of others who contributed to the development of remedial reading programs in the schools during the 1920s and 1930s focused on the much larger numbers of children whose disabilities were presumed to be of different cause and less severity. In fact, some of the leaders in remedial reading, such as Gates (1935), challenged the utility of the concept of word blindness in considering the reading disabilities of children. Gates pointed out that such "non-readers" were not a distinct group but merely the extreme cases of disability on a distribution of reading ability graded imperceptibly from the reader with the most difficulties to the most competent reader. To Gates, the differences that placed a child on a particular point in the distribution were of degree, not kind. Such a theoretical stance made for a close alliance between the growing field of remedial reading, with its techniques of diagnosis and instruction, and the developmental reading programs as practiced throughout the regular grades of the school.

Early in his research program, Orton became aware of the not infrequent occurrence of stuttering in children with marked reading disability and speculated that this speech difficulty was also related to a fundamental problem in the establishment of cerebral dominance. By the time of his 1937 publication, *Reading, Writing and Speech Problems in Children,* Orton considered a broader range of developmental disorders, including: 1) developmental alexia, or strephosymbolia; 2) developmental agraphia, or marked difficulty in learning to write; 3) developmental word deafness, in which auditory acuity is normal but there is a specific impairment of verbal understanding; 4) developmental motor aphasia, or motor speech delay; 5) developmental apraxia, or abnormal clumsiness; and 6) stuttering.

What is interesting from the point of view of our present day usage of the term *learning disabilities* is that this was an early attempt to classify within the same conceptual and etiological framework a range of language and motor disabilities in addition to the commonly encountered reading disabilities. Similar extension in the list of categories of learning problems by those who developed the field of learning disabilities in subsequent decades would, of course, also be a factor in causing ever-upward revision in prevalence estimates of children with learning disabilities in the public schools (Johnson & Myklebust, 1967).

Linking Neurological Lesions and Behavioral and Intellectual Impairment: The Concept of Minimal Brain Damage

In addition to Orton's contribution, a second development in the medical field during the 1920s that affected the categorization of children with learning problems and added to the prevalence rates was the introduction of the concept of minimal brain damage. The epidemic of encephalitis following the First World War played a particularly important role in the formation of this concept. Early in the 1920s, a number of medical reports indicated that children recovering from encephalitis exhibited various sequelae—physical, intellectual, and behavior deficits occurring in all degrees from the most severe to the scarcely identifiable (Happ & Mason, 1921; Patterson

& Spence, 1921). These sequelae, following on a known infection of brain tissue, provided a model of brain injury accompanied by a variety of behavioral and intellectual disturbances with or without the coexistence of gross neurological signs.

In short order, the model was extended to include the assumption that, when a patient presents with deficits identical to the sequelae of epidemic encephalitis without evidence of prior acute illness, he or she must nevertheless have suffered from brain disease. Thus in Lauretta Bender's (1942) report on the experience of her group with the evaluation and treatment of postencephalitic children, there is emphasis on hyperkinesis and other impulse disturbances and on the presence of distinctive psychometric patterns. In summary, she stated:

> The diagnostic criteria for encephalopathic behavior disorders are now considerable. Even without a history of the specific etiological factor or evidence of the specific pathology, the diagnostic methods which may be applied to fields of behavior are sufficient to establish a diagnosis. (pp. 379–380)

Reports by various clinicians and researchers on the relationship of prenatal and perinatal factors affecting subsequent development of the child also served to strengthen the hypothesis of a relationship between undetectable neurological lesions and behavioral and intellectual impairment (Gesell & Amatruda, 1941; Lilienfeld & Pasamanick, 1954).

The application of this concept of minimal brain damage to the learning problems of the school-age child was greatly fostered by the research and remedial training programs of Alfred A. Strauss and his colleagues. Within the general category of mental retardation, Strauss distinguished the child with brain injury or "exogenous" retardation, and the child whose mental subnormality was familial or unrelated to injury to the central nervous system ("endogenous" retardation). Based on his clinical work and an impressive program of research carried out with Heinz Werner, Strauss concluded that the child with brain injury was characterized by disturbances in perception, thinking, and emotional behavior that differentiated him or her from the child with endogenous or familial retardation.

Among the various criteria Strauss listed for the diagnosis of minor brain injury, the following was most influential in determining the scope of the nascent area of learning disabilities:

> When no mental retardation exists, the presence of psychological disturbances can be discovered by the use of some of our qualitative tests for perceptual and conceptual disturbances. Although the . . . [other] criteria may be negative, whereas the behavior of the child in question resembles that characteristic for brain injury, and even though the

performances of the child on our tests are not strongly indicative of brain injury, it may still be reasonable to consider a diagnosis of brain injury. (Strauss & Lehtinen, 1947, p. 112)

This criterion indicates the great importance Strauss and his coworkers assigned to behavioral patterns and to test performance; these could be diagnostic even in the absence of mental retardation.

THE 1940s THROUGH THE 1960s: FROM BIRTH INJURY TO LEARNING DISABILITY

The concept of minimal brain damage without mental retardation promulgated by Strauss and his collaborators had a heavy impact on the theoretical formulations and practice recommendations of many who defined and developed the field of learning disabilities in the following decades—especially those who emphasized the perceptual-motor and psycholinguistic processes underlying the acquisition of reading skills. In many respects, particularly in advocating the reduction of environmental stimulation within the learning environment, Cruickshank was the closest adherent to the Strauss-Lehtinen tradition. Taking a position congenial to many a practice-oriented educator, he argued "While proper diagnosis is important, the symptomology—the characteristics of the child—is more important, because it is the latter with which educators, psychologists, and others who are involved in habilitative programs and therapy must deal" (Cruickshank, 1977, p. 5).

This position of Cruickshank, that the etiology was less important than the behavioral disability, was advocated even more strongly by Samuel Kirk. With Barbara Bateman, he argued that, generally, remediation was determined by the behavioral symptoms, not by the neurological findings: "Our interest is in the kind and extent of diagnosis of learning problems, that lead directly to a formulation of what should be done about the disability" (Kirk & Bateman, 1962/1963, p. 73). In that same article appeared a definition of learning disability that Kirk had also advanced in his textbook, *Educating Exceptional Children* (1962). This definition of learning disability was to become the progenitor of a number of definitions widely prevalent in succeeding decades:

A *learning disability* refers to a retardation, disorder, or delayed development in one or more of the processes of speech, language, reading, writing, arithmetic, or other school subjects resulting from a psychological handicap caused by possible cerebral dysfunction and/or emotional or behavioral disturbances. It is not the result of mental retardation, sensory deprivation, or cultural or instructional factors. (Kirk & Bateman, 1962/1963, p. 73)

Subsequently, at the 1963 organizational meeting of the Association for Children with Learning Disabilities, Kirk (1975) contrasted etiological terms such as *minimal brain damage* or *cerebral dysfunction* with behaviorally descriptive terms such as *hyperkinetic behavior* or *perceptual disorders* in the classification of such children. Warning of the dangers inherent in all labels, but assuming that the purpose of the organization was "not to conduct research on behavior and the brain, but to find effective methods of diagnosis, management, and training of the children," he offered the term *learning disability* as a general designation for the wide range of disabilities with which the organization was concerned. Adopted in the title of this advocacy organization, the term soon became the prevailing designation.

The "functional diagnosis" of minimal brain damage or learning disability by means of behavioral indices and by performance on various psychological and educational tests, particularly the newer perceptual-motor and psycholinguistic tests specifically designed for diagnostic purposes, greatly facilitated the identification of a growing number of children with educational disabilities. The use of these efficient diagnostic tests coupled with remedial exercises devised by Strauss, Cruickshank, Kirk, Frostig, and others apparently filled a great need for frustrated educators struggling with the learning difficulties of their pupils. Critical evaluations of these instruments and remedial exercises subsequently diminished much of their popularity. Nevertheless, the decades of the 1970s and 1980s were to see phenomenal growth in the field of learning disabilities.

THE 1970s AND 1980s: HYPERACTIVITY, ATTENTION DISORDERS, AND OTHER DEFINITIONAL ISSUES

Certainly, not the least factor in the growth of the field of learning disabilities was the passage of the Education of the Handicapped Act of 1970 (P.L. 91-230), which authorized programs of research, training, and model centers addressed to the needs of "children with specific learning disabilities." In the school year of 1968–1969, just prior to the passage of this Act, some 120,000 children were enrolled in special education services under this categorical label (Martin, 1970). In 1976–1977, the year following passage of the Education for All Handicapped Children Act (P.L. 94-142), which had made further provisions for the education of children with learning disabilities, 796,000 children so designated received special educational services. By 1988–1989, the number had reached 1,987,000— accounting for 4.9% of the public school enrollment from prekindergarten through 12th grade and 43.6% of all children receiving special education services (U.S. Department of Education, 1990).

Concurrent with this growth in the number of children designated as having learning disabilities, there has been a marked drop in the number of children served in the category of mental retardation. In some instances reassignment of children has been justified on the basis of the co-occurrence of the two disorders, but it is generally conceded that many children with mild retardation are now served as having learning disabilities for other than sound diagnostic reasons. Similarly, other children with school adjustment problems have been drawn into the vortex of the ever-enlarging category of learning disabilities. Of special significance in this respect are those children characterized by attention disorders and hyperactivity.

Hyperactivity versus Attention-Deficit Disorder

Throughout the decades in which there was a focus on the perceptual-motor and psycholinguistic learning disorders of children with minimal brain damage, the attention of other investigators, such as Bradley and his colleagues, had been focused on the hyperactivity of such children. That focus was reinforced by the discovery of the effectiveness of certain psychoactive drugs in the management of hyperactivity (Bradley, 1950; Laufer & Denhoff, 1957; Laufer, Denhoff, & Solomons, 1957). Following early reports on the use of medications to control hyperactivity and incidentally to improve learning performance, the use of these drugs, particularly the stimulant methylphenidate, rapidly spread throughout the country.

By 1970, the medication of children for problems associated with school performance had become so widespread as to cause an upsurge of public concern that at times was expressed in strident journalistic exposés. The result was a congressional investigation (U.S. Congress, 1970), and professional reaction in the form of appointed committees and journal articles addressing the issues. The net result provided some reassurance to the public and professionals alike about the effectiveness of the medications, coupled with warnings about the need for diagnostic care in differentiating hyperkinetic behavioral disturbance from similar behavioral symptoms that might be due to other illness or to environmental stress (American Academy of Pediatrics Committee on Drugs, 1970; Report of the Conference, 1971).

In succeeding years, the medication of children with hyperactivity increased. The spread was monitored for one locality by the research of Safer and his colleagues. From 1971 to 1987 they undertook repeated surveys of school nurses in suburban Baltimore County to determine the number of children on medication for hyperactivity. The results indicated that in this period the number of public elementary schoolchildren so treated had increased from 1.07% of approximately 70,000 public elementary schoolchildren in 1971 to 5.96% of the approximately 36,000 enrolled in 1987 (Safer & Krager, 1988).

Based on this increased utilization rate during the 1980s and on prior estimates, Safer and Krager suggested that a conservative nationwide estimate would indicate that 750,000 school-age youth with hyperactivity/inattentiveness were being medicated for their condition. They also expressed concern that during this time period an increasing number of "inattentive, nonhyperactive, primarily learning-impaired" students had been treated with stimulants. Their concern here resulted from the fact that the vast majority of studies to date "indicate that stimulant treatment by itself does not result in maintained or long-term achievement gains, even though such drugs improve attention, grades, and the amount of completed school work by affected students" (Safer & Krager, 1988, p. 2258).

These statistical data and estimates on medicated children are of value in that they give some indication of the minimal numbers of children who have been diagnosed as hyperactive. Actual prevalence data on the disorder are, of course, difficult to ascertain because of a number of issues, not least of which are those concerned with the conceptual and operational definitions of the disorder.

Central to the attempted improvement in conceptual clarity was the shift in emphasis, during the course of the 1970s, from the hyperactivity of this group of children to their attention deficits (Douglas & Peters, 1979). By 1980, the third edition of the *Diagnostic and Statistical Manual of Mental Disorders (DSM–III)* (American Psychiatric Association, 1980) no longer categorized these children as hyperkinetic but included them under a superordinate category of attention-deficit disorder (ADD) characterized by inattention, impulsivity, and hyperactivity. This category in turn was divided into subcategories providing for attention deficits with and without hyperactivity.

More recently, the 1987 revision of the *DSM–III (DSM–III–R)* has recategorized the children (American Psychiatric Association, 1987). Children characterized by the triad of inattention, impulsiveness, and hyperactivity are categorized under the attention-deficit hyperactivity disorder, which is a subclass of the disruptive behavior disorders. Those children who would have been categorized as having attention-deficit disorder without hyperactivity under *DSM–III* are now placed in a completely separate category of undifferentiated attention-deficit disorder. The net result of these revisions is the apparent reemphasis of the importance of the hyperactivity component in what had been termed attention-deficit disorder in 1980.

Despite the significant definitional problems, and problems in the measurement of hyperactivity, Shaywitz and Shaywitz (1988) maintained that, when similar rating scales are employed and when teachers are used as raters, the prevalence of ADD appears to range between 10% and 20%. With parents as raters, the prevalence is higher. They believe the low rates of 3%–5% reported in some studies represent a very skewed portion of the ADD population so diagnosed by professionals using diagnostic criteria that are too stringent. The prevalence rate of 10%–20% advanced by Shaywitz and Shaywitz would have profound implications for the field of learning disabilities if, as some propose, changes in federal law were to include children with ADD as a category to be served under provisions designed for individuals with learning disabilities.

Although progress has been made in differentiating out of the 1960s conglomerate of minimal brain dysfunction the *DSM–III–R* category of attention-deficit hyperactivity disorder (ADHD) as distinct from learning disabilities, the generally conceded high degree of co-occurrence of these conditions still poses problems (Cantwell & Baker, 1991; Safer & Allen, 1976; Shaywitz & Shaywitz, 1988; Silver, 1990). In their discussion of methodological issues in the classification of attention-related disorders, Fletcher and his colleagues pointed out not only this problem of comorbidity of attention and learning problems, but also the overlap of both of these categories with *DSM–III–R* of Oppositional Defiant Disorder. They concluded that "any research on children with ADHD is a classification study because of the lack of precision of consensually accepted definitions of these disorders" (Fletcher, Morris, & Francis, 1991, p. 77).

Persistence of Definitional Issues in Learning Disabilities

In the mid-1970s, Freeman vigorously expressed himself on the long-standing definitional issues in learning disabilities:

> There is only one phrase for the state of the art and practice in the field of minimal brain dysfunction (MBD), hyperactivity (HA), and learning disability (LD) in children: a mess. There is no more polite term which would be realistic. The area is characterized by rarely challenged myths, ill-defined boundaries, and a strangely seductive attractiveness. These categories and their management, because of massive support from frustrated parents, professionals, government, and the drug and remedial-education industries, constitute an epidemic of alarming proportions—but is the problem the disease or its treatment? (Freeman, 1976, p. 5)

To Freeman there was in fact no epidemic in the fields of minimal brain dysfunction, learning disorders, and hyperactivity in children, "but rather, an unfortunate episode in the history of progressive medicalization of deviant or troublesome behavior" (1976, p. 22). Furthermore, he maintained that:

> Surely part of the confusion in the field is due to a lack of useful criteria to delimit these nonsynonymous groups of children: MBD, LD, and HA. "One or more" of an endless series of equivocal and often subjective characteristics is not very helpful but can open the possibility that almost any child can be labeled. (1976, p. 10)

In spite of his vigorous attack on categorical labels, equivocally defined, with presumptive etiologies and questionable therapies, it is interesting that Freeman still assumed the existence of a core subgroup of "severely and persistently impaired children." The threat of labels indiscriminately applied to ever-increasing numbers of children was that they obscured "the very important distinction between the relatively small number of children with biologically based difficulties and the larger number who are failing to meet the expectations of their families or the school system for other reasons" (1976, p. 22).

The indiscriminate application of the label of learning disabilities had been previously documented for the federally funded Child Service Demonstration Centers. These model centers were funded under the Education of the Handicapped Act (P.L. 91-230), with its specified definition of learning disabilities, and one might have supposed that their selection of children to be serviced would, for the most part, reflect the influence of that federal definition. Yet, Kirk and Elkins (1975), reporting on the characteristics of more than 3,000 children enrolled in these centers, stated that:

> It would appear from the data that the majority of children in the projects, although underachieving to some degree, would not qualify as specific learning disabled children, since (a) many of the children were retarded equally in reading, spelling, and arithmetic and were therefore not specific but general in academic retardation, and (b) a substantial proportion were minor or moderate in their degree of underachievement. (p. 636)
> Previously, many of these children would have been classified as slow learners or as mentally retarded. . . . Admittedly, these children—slow learners, disadvantaged children and others—need attention from compensatory programs . . . but one can raise the question of whether these children require the same kind of emphasis as children with specific learning disabilities. . . . (pp. 636–637).

A subsequent analysis of the reports from the Child Service Demonstration Centers, which had been funded from 1971 to 1980,

although admittedly based on less than satisfactory data, led Mann
and his associates to similar if less temperate conclusions:

> Let us then accept the facts as we find them. And they suggest that we
> adopt learning disabilities as a generic term for all "mildly" hand-
> icapped as the label to replace other stigmatizing ones. To clarify the
> term for labeling purposes we can go the DSM III route—a vague
> enough one to suit all purposes, and meeting the requirements of an
> age which does not prize diagnostic excellence. We can have: learning
> disabilities with cultural deprivation, learning disabilities with behav-
> ior disorders, learning disabilities with neurological problems, etc.
> Markers, then, of various sorts can be used to define these [learning
> disabled] groups for scientific study as Barbara Keogh has suggested
> [Keogh, Major, Reid, Gandara, & Omori, 1978]. Thus, we have [learn-
> ing disabled] with variables I, X, Y for this study, [learning disabled]
> with variables M, W, Y for that study. (Mann, Davis, Boyer, Metz, &
> Wolford, 1983, p. 17)

Although these studies of data gathered from the Child Service
Demonstration Centers have the advantage of sampling the practices of a large number of states, they have the limitation of methodological weakness recognized by their authors. Shepard and her
colleagues, focusing on the state of Colorado, gave a more solidly
based assessment of practice in the field of learning disabilities in
that setting. In one component of their work, a probability sample of
790 cases was selected from all the children served in programs for
children with learning disabilities in the state of Colorado and their
case records were analyzed for defining characteristics. Approximately 43% of the sample had characteristics associated in federal
law and professional literature with definitions of learning disabilities. Approximately another 40% consisted of children with other
disabilities and learning problems. The remaining 17% were mis-
identified for various reasons, such as poor assessment.

> The implication of these results for basic research on learning disabil-
> ities is that the label applied for the purpose of providing services
> cannot be assumed valid. If the label is taken as a dependable sign of
> the disability, then research on [learning disabilities] heritability pat-
> terns, prevalence rates, and the effectiveness of interventions will be
> confounded. The meaning or meanings of learning disabilities will re-
> main elusive. (Shepard, Smith, & Vojir, 1983, p. 328)

The indiscriminate use of the label of learning disabilities, as
documented in these studies by Kirk, Mann, Shepard, and their
colleagues, contributed to the ongoing debate in the literature on the
distinctness of the learning disabilities category in relationship to
other special education categories. In view of these concerns, the
question could obviously be raised as to the basic usefulness of
the category. Tucker, Stevens, and Ysseldyke (1983) reported on the

"experts'" perception of this issue. Of the 119 professionals respond-ing to a query on the viability of the category of learning disabilities in 1981, 83% responded positively. To the question of whether or not learning disabilities were clinically identifiable by specific symp-toms or a constellation of symptoms differentiating them from other problems associated with learning, 88% responded affirmatively. The survey also obtained estimates on the prevalence of learning disabilities and, although the range of estimates was extraordinary, most respondents gave estimates between 0% and 3%.

The results of this survey would suggest that the category of learning disabilities has a great deal of professional support. Nev-ertheless, the experts recognized that improvement in the classifica-tion of children with learning disabilities was needed and highly desirable. That was evident in the comments made by many of the respondents who had readily agreed to the viability of the category. In fact, it is apparent that, ever since Kirk first advanced the term of learning disabilities in the early 1960s, the field has repeatedly struggled to improve its conceptual and operational definitions.

In an article optimistically entitled "On Defining Learning Dis-abilities: An Emerging Consensus," Hammill (1990) identified 11 different conceptual definitions that are prominent today or have experienced a degree of popularity in the past. Within these defini-tions he identified nine important conceptual elements on which the definitions could differ. These included such components as the eti-ology, the role of psychological processes, and the specification of academic, spoken language, and/or nonlanguage skill deficits.

Calculating the percentage agreement on these components among the definitions, Hammill concluded that, contrary to popular opinion, there is considerable agreement among the definitions. This was particularly true of every important definition of learning disabilities currently enjoying any degree of popularity. Of all 11 definitions considered, 4 that have been developed since 1977 are, in Hammill's view, the only professionally viable alternatives. These definitions are those offered by the U.S. Office of Education (USOE), the National Joint Committee on Learning Disabilities (NJCLD), the Learning Disabilities Association of America (LDA), and the Interagency Committee on Learning Disabilities (ICLD). The re-maining definitions are considered to have only historical impor-tance.

Of the viable alternatives, Hammill gives special considera-tion to two, those of the USOE and the NJCLD. That of the USOE is based squarely on the definition as it appears in federal legis-lation:

"Specific learning disability" means a disorder in one or more of the basic psychological processes involved in understanding or in using language, spoken or written, which may manifest itself in an imperfect ability to listen, speak, read, write, spell, or to do mathematical calculations. The term includes such conditions as perceptual handicaps, brain injury, minimal brain dysfunction, dyslexia, and developmental aphasia. The term does not include children who have learning problems which are primarily the result of visual, hearing, or motor handicaps, of mental retardation, of emotional disturbance, or of environmental, cultural, or economic disadvantage. (U.S. Office of Education, 1977, p. 65083)

The definition of the NJCLD is in agreement with the USOE definition on seven of the nine elements examined by Hammill. It deletes the controversial phrase *basic psychological processes,* and it specifies conceptual problems (i.e., problems in reasoning or thinking) in addition to the academic and spoken language problems listed in the USOE definition.

Of these two definitions, Hammill considers the NJCLD the best (Hammill, Leigh, McNutt, & Larsen, 1987; National Joint Committee on Learning Disabilities, 1987). The inclusion of the psychological process clause is the main limitation of the USOE definition. The term lacks specificity and was not operationalized in the identification criteria that accompanied the USOE's publication of the definition. The term also carries the burden of its association with the once-popular perceptual notions advocated by Frostig, Kephart, Getman, and others during the 1960s.

Although an advocate of the NJCLD definition and believing that it has the best chance of becoming the consensus definition, Hammill concluded that:

> Political realities are such that the NJCLD definition may never replace the 1977 USOE definition in law. But this may not be important. What is important, however, is that professionals and parents unite around one definition so that we can say with assurance, "This is what we mean when we say *learning disabilities.*" (Hammill, 1990, p. 83)

The political realities Hammill refers to may be reflected in part in the utilization of the USOE's definition by state education agencies. This utilization has been tracked by a number of investigators, and the results indicate that the majority of states define learning disabilities in ways that are basically the same or only slightly different from the 1977 federal definition (Frankenberger & Harper, 1981; Mercer, Hughes, & Mercer, 1985; Mercer, King-Sears, & Mercer, 1990).

There is considerably less consensus in the ways that states choose to operationalize their identification procedures. However,

Mercer and his colleagues indicate that "Increasingly, prereferral interventions, adequate assessment instruments, and discrepancy models that emphasize the use of standard scores and regression formulas are being recommended by state departments of education in an effort to more adequately identify [learning disabled] students" (Mercer, King-Sears, & Mercer, 1990, p. 152). These authors see the need to incorporate in the definition of learning disabilities a clear statement of the existence of a discrepancy between estimated ability and academic performance. This would serve to bring definitions and criteria into greater agreement and add a unifying component to the definition.

THE 1990s: OUTLOOK FOR CONSENSUS IN DEFINING LEARNING DISABILITIES

Hammill's analysis of progress in the conceptual definition of learning disabilities and the surveys of state practices by Mercer and colleagues, especially when contrasted to the state of the field when Freeman assessed it in 1976, give the impression of considerable advance in the field of learning disabilities. However, the problems that remain—such as the need to increase the rigor of the best available definitions and to operationalize these definitions for purposes of both research and practice—are still formidable.

In facing these problems, it must be kept in mind that, under such conceptual definitions as those examined by Hammill and operationalized in state regulations examined by Mercer and colleagues, we have identified and are attempting to deliver services to approximately 2 million schoolchildren. The conceptual definitions of the field allow for heterogeneity, the criteria for operationalizing those definitions vary from state to state, and within states the guidelines for local school districts are subject to more or less ambiguity. It is no wonder that children are often misclassified and hence poorly served.

We may make further progress in reaching a consensual definition for the broad term *learning disabilities* and for agreement on specific criteria for its application. However, one wonders if the real progress will not come from disentangling groups of children from this huge conglomorate mass, rigorously specifying the nature of their difficulties, and systematically exploring appropriate educational interventions for these subgroups. If that is so, one can take satisfaction in the great vitality the field has recently shown with increasingly rigorous research not only on broad subgroups such as children with learning disabilities in different academic subjects, but also within the subgroup of specific reading disabilities, where we see a very active and constructive controversy on the underlying processes for different types of reading impediment.

REFERENCES

American Academy of Pediatrics Committee on Drugs. (1970). An evaluation of the pharmacological approaches to learning impediments. *Pediatrics, 46,* 142–144.

American Psychiatric Association. (1980). *Diagnostic and statistical manual of mental disorders* (3rd ed.). Washington, DC: American Psychiatric Press, Inc.

American Psychiatric Association. (1987). *Diagnostic and statistical manual of mental disorders* (3rd ed., rev.). Washington, DC: American Psychiatric Press, Inc.

Bender, L. (1942). Post-encephaletic behavior disorders in childhood. In J.B. Neal (Ed.), *Encephalitis* (pp. 363–384). New York: Grune & Stratton.

Bradley, C. (1950). Benzedrine and Dexedrine in the treatment of children's behavior disorders. *Pediatrics, 5,* 24–37.

Cantwell, D.P., & Baker, L. (1991). Association between attention deficit-hyperactivity disorder and learning disorders. *Journal of Learning Disabilities, 24,* 88–95.

Cruickshank, W.M. (1977). *Learning disabilities in home, school and community.* Syracuse, NY: Syracuse University Press.

Douglas, V.I., & Peters, K.G. (1979). Toward a clearer definition of the attention deficit of hyperactive children. In G.A. Hale & M. Lewis (Eds.), *Attention and cognitive development* (pp. 173–247). New York: Plenum.

Fletcher, J.M., Morris, R.D., & Francis, D.J. (1991). Methodological issues in the classification of attention-related disorders. *Journal of Learning Disabilities, 24,* 72–77.

Frankenberger, W., & Harper, J. (1981). States' criteria for identifying learning disabled children: A comparison of 1981/82 and 1985/86 guidelines. *Journal of Learning Disabilities, 20,* 118–121.

Freeman, R.D. (1976). Minimal brain dysfunction, hyperactivity, and learning disorders: Epidemic or episode? *School Review, 85,* 5–30.

Gates, A. (1935). *The improvement of reading* (rev. ed.). New York: Macmillan.

Gesell, A., & Amatruda, C.S. (1941). *Developmental diagnosis.* New York: Hoeber.

Gray, C.T. (1922). *Deficiencies in reading ability.* Lexington, MA: D.C. Health.

Gray, W. (1922, June). Remedial cases in reading: Their diagnosis and treatment. *Supplementary Educational Monographs, 22.*

Gray, W.S. (1921). Diagnostic and remedial steps in reading. *Journal of Educational Research, 4,* 1–15.

Hammill, D.D. (1990). On defining learning disabilities: An emerging consensus. *Journal of Learning Disabilities, 23,* 74–84.

Hammill, D.D., Leigh, J.E., McNutt, G., & Larsen, S.C. (1987). A new definition of learning disabilities. *Journal of Learning Disabilities, 20,* 109–112.

Happ, W.M., & Mason, V.R. (1921). Epidemic encephalitis: A clinical study. *Bulletin of The Johns Hopkins Hospital, 32,* 137–159.

Hinshelwood, J. (1917). *Congenital word-blindness.* Chicago: Medical Book Co.

Johnson, D.J., & Myklebust, H.R. (1967). *Learning disabilities: Educational principles and practices.* New York: Grune & Stratton.

Keogh, B.K., Major, S., Reid, H.P., Gandara, P., & Omori, H. (1978). Marker variables. *Learning Disabilities Quarterly, 1,* 5–11.

Kirk, S.A. (1962). *Educating exceptional children.* Boston: Houghton Mifflin.

Kirk, S.A. (1975). Behavioral diagnosis and remediation of learning disorders. In S.A. Kirk & J. McRae McCarthy (Eds.), *Learning disabilities: Selected ACLD papers* (pp. 7–10). Boston: Houghton Mifflin.

Kirk, S.A., & Bateman, B. (1962/1963). Diagnosis and remediation of learning disabilities. *Exceptional Children, 29,* 73–78.

Kirk, S.A., & Elkins, J. (1975). Characteristics of children enrolled in the child service demonstration centers. *Journal of Learning Disabilities, 8,* 630–637.

Laufer, M.W., & Denhoff, E. (1957). Hyperkinetic behavior syndrome in children. *The Journal of Pediatrics, 50,* 463–474.

Laufer, M.W., Denhoff, E., & Solomons, G. (1957). Hyperkinetic impulse disorder in children's behavior problems. *Psychosomatic Medicine, 19,* 38–49.

Lilienfeld, A.M., & Pasamanick, B. (1954). Association of maternal and fetal factors with the development of epilepsy. *Journal of the American Medical Association, 155,* 719–724.

Lyday, J.F. (1926). The Greene County Mental Clinic. *Mental Hygiene, 10,* 759–786.

Mann, L., Davis, C.H., Boyer, C.W., Metz, C.M., & Wolford, B. (1983). LD or not LD, that was the question. *Journal of Learning Disabilities, 16,* 14–17.

Martin, E.W. (1970). Programs of The Bureau of Education for the Handicapped: U.S. Office of Education. *Programs for the handicapped.* Washington, DC: U.S. Department of Health, Education, and Welfare, Secretary's Committee on Mental Retardation.

Mercer, C.D., Hughes, C., & Mercer, A.R. (1985). Learning disabilities definitions used by state education departments. *Learning Disabilities Quarterly, 8,* 45–55.

Mercer, C.D., King-Sears, P., & Mercer, A.R. (1990). Learning disabilities definitions and criteria used by state education departments. *Learning Disabilities Quarterly, 13,* 141–152.

Morgan, W.P. (1896). A case of congenital word blindness. *British Medical Journal, 2,* 1378.

National Joint Committee on Learning Disabilities. (1987). Learning disabilities: Issues on definition. *Journal of Learning Disabilities, 20,* 107–108.

Orton, S.T. (1925). "Word-blindness" in school children. *Archives of Neurology and Psychiatry, 14,* 581–615.

Orton, S.T. (1928). Specific reading disability—strephosymbolia. *Journal of the American Medical Association, 90,* 1095–1099.

Orton, S.T. (1937). *Reading, writing and speech problems in children.* New York: Norton.

Patterson, D., & Spence, J.C. (1921). The after effects of epidemic encephalitis in children. *Lancet, ii,* 491–493.

Report of the conference on the use of stimulant drugs in the treatment of behaviorally disturbed young school children. (1971). *Journal of Learning Disabilities, 4,* 523–530.

Safer, D., & Allen, R.P. (1976). *Hyperactive children: Diagnosis and management*. Baltimore: University Park Press.

Safer, D.J., & Krager, J.M. (1988). A survey of medication treatment for hyperactive/inattentive students. *Journal of the American Medical Association, 260,* 2256–2258.

Schmitt, C. (1917/1918). Developmental alexia: Congenital word-blindness, or inability to learn to read. *The Elementary School Journal, 18,* 680–700, 757–769.

Shaywitz, S.E., & Shaywitz, B.A. (1988). Attention deficit disorder: Current perspectives. In J.F. Kavanagh & T.J. Truss, Jr. (Eds.), *Learning disabilities: Proceedings of The National Conference* (pp. 369–523). Parkton, MD: York Press.

Shepard, L.A., Smith, M.L., & Vojir, C.P. (1983). Characteristics of pupils identified as learning disabled. *American Educational Research Journal, 20,* 309–331.

Silver, L.B. (1990). Attention deficit-hyperactivity disorder: Is it a learning disability or related disorder? *Journal of Learning Disabilities, 23,* 394–397.

Strauss, A.A., & Lehtinen, L.E. (1947). *Psychopathology and education of the brain-injured child*. New York: Grune & Stratton.

Thomas, C.J. (1908). The aphasias of childhood and education hygiene. *Public Health, 21,* 90–100.

Tucker, J., Stevens, L.J., & Ysseldyke, J.E. (1983). Learning disabilities: The experts speak out. *Journal of Learning Disabilities, 16,* 6–14.

U.S. Congress, House of Representatives, Committee on Government Operations, Special Studies Subcommittee. (1970). *Federal involvement in the use of behavior modification drugs on grammar school children of the right to privacy inquiry*. Washington, DC: U.S. Government Printing Office.

U.S. Department of Education, Office of Educational Research and Assessment. (1990). *Digest of education statistics*. Washington, DC: U.S. Government Printing Office.

U.S. Office of Education. (1977, December 29). Assistance to the states for education of handicapped children: Procedures for evaluating specific learning disabilities. *Federal Register, 42*(250), 65082–65085.

7

DEVELOPMENT OF OPERATIONAL DEFINITIONS IN MENTAL RETARDATION
Similarities and Differences with the Field of Learning Disabilities

Donald L. MacMillan

In this chapter, classification and definition in mental retardation and learning disabilities are contrasted. In 1941, Edgar Doll noted that "The *concept* of mental deficiency today is clear enough; the difficulty lies rather in the inadequate employment of means by which the accepted definitions are satisfied" (p. 214). Currently, I believe we are reasonably clear on what constitutes mental retardation and learning disabilities, but we, like Doll's contemporaries, have disagreements when it comes to how we satisfy the definitions. The essential difference between the two emerges when we consider whether the substantive learning problems encountered by the child are *expected* or *unexpected*. The basis for the expected level of performance may be a measure of aptitude or comparisons of performance in other areas (e.g., math versus reading, listening comprehension versus reading comprehension). When there is congruence between the severe learning deficit and the basis for expectancy, the child has mental retardation; when there is incongruence, the child has learning disabilities. As Doll noted, the concept is clear enough, whereas

The present work was supported primarily by Grants G008530208 and H023C80072 from the U.S. Office of Education to the author. Opinions expressed herein are those of the author and should not be interpreted to have agency endorsement. The critical reading of an earlier draft of this chapter by Richard Eyman, Steven Forness, and Keith Widaman is sincerely appreciated.

the criteria on which expected or unexpected learning problems are based will produce extended debate.

This chapter explores the dimensions of behavior included in definitions commonly used. In so doing, it is recognized that children who meet the definitions of mental retardation and learning disabilities constitute very heterogeneous groups differing in the severity of the disability, the generalizability of the learning problems, and the probable etiology of the learning problem. To achieve some degree of order, we have seen fit to subdivide children with mental retardation and those with learning disabilities, within disability, into more homogeneous subgroups. Again, the basis on which these subdivisions are created has generated considerable discussion. Finally, one frequently finds that children qualify for more than one disability category simultaneously. That is, a child has mental retardation *and* orthopedic disabilities or has learning disabilities *and* exhibits attention-deficit disorder (ADD). Decision rules are needed on how this comorbidity will be considered and treated. The final two sections of this chapter consider the relationship between definition and diagnosis, followed by evidence on how these have had an impact on detection rates. Before turning to these topics, however, let us consider a few fundamental issues concerning classification systems.

CLASSIFICATION SYSTEMS

Blashfield (chap. 2, this volume) summarizes various classification models, and it is instructive to note that, in mental retardation and learning disabilities, the models utilized are referred to as *monothetic models,* wherein each dimension of behavior specified is necessary and sufficient. A discussion of the wisdom of using a monothetic model instead of one of the alternatives is beyond the scope of this chapter. Of importance to the present discussion, however, is that every case of mental retardation or learning disabilities should have every defining feature.

Zigler and Hodapp (1986) observed that a well-specified classification system contains two features. The classificatory principle that establishes the rules (i.e., the criteria) for categorizing an individual into one class or another should lead to high reliability among different classifiers. That is, high agreement among different classifiers using the classificatory principle would constitute high reliability of classification. The second feature of a classification principle making it useful is the number of meaningful correlates of classification into one category (e.g., mental retardation or learning disabilities). Stated differently, this second feature concerns how much is known about members of a given category on the basis of knowing that a given individual has been classified as belonging to that category. When there are many correlates of category member-ship, one would say the classification system has greater validity. In other words, the classification system employed to categorize children as having learning disabilities or mental retardation would ideally have high agreement among classifiers as to which children should be classified in either category or as having no disabilities (i.e., it would be reliable) *and* there would be a number of correlates of each of the different classification groups (i.e., correlates of learning disabilities would be meaningful, as would the correlates of mental retardation); hence, the classification systems would be valid.

As dimensions of behavior included in the definitions of mental retardation and learning disabilities are examined, it may be useful to consider the extent to which each of these dimensions can be reliably assessed and the extent to which the classificatory principle yields high agreement among classifiers. In addition, the issue of meaningful correlates should be considered. Do we know what specific behaviors or characteristics will be associated with group membership?

Current Classification in Mental Retardation

Clausen (1967) traced the definitions of mental retardation historically, observing how successive definitions tended to broaden the concept. Those who did pioneering work on intelligence testing (e.g., Goddard, Terman) left a legacy that pervaded the field of mental retardation—the belief that IQ is fixed or immutable. In terms of mental retardation, this translated into the notion that the disability is a permanent and lifelong condition, and is illustrated in the influential definition written by Doll (1941), which, in part, states that the condition is "essentially incurable." The American Association on Mental Retardation (AAMR) first produced a classification system in 1921, which relied heavily on IQ and subdivided the population with mental retardation into three groups: moron (IQ 50–75), imbecile (IQ 25–50), and idiot (IQ < 25). As Clausen has noted, the concept expanded until it reached its zenith with publication of the AAMR manual edited by Heber (1959, 1961). In the 1961 version, mental retardation was defined as, "subaverage general intellectual functioning which originates in the developmental period and is associated with impairment in adaptive behavior" (p. 3).

Publication of the Heber (1961) manual resolved one controversy concerning *incurability* and resulted in the AAMR exerting influence and leadership in defining mental retardation. In addition, the 1961 definition was the most *inclusive* definition of mental retardation yet devised, which was intentional—it would serve to ensure that no child would be denied needed services and did so by setting a very liberal IQ criterion of −1 standard deviation as the cutoff. Diagnostic decision-making, then, concerning eligibility of specific children relied very heavily on the second criterion, adaptive behavior, in qualifying or disqualifying children as having mental retardation. As is discussed later, the adaptive behavior criterion proved elusive to measure and/or assess reliably, making it the target of much debate (Clausen, 1967, 1972; Halpern, 1968; MacMillan & Jones, 1972; Zigler, Balla, & Hodapp, 1984).

Issues surrounding the classification of children were considered in depth in the project on classification supported by nine U.S. Department of Health, Education, and Welfare (HEW) agencies, which resulted in the publication of reports edited by Hobbs of Vanderbilt University (1975a, 1975b). The high priority given to issues of classification arose largely from the heated exchanges and litigation pertaining to the classification as "mildly" or "educable mentally retarded" of children who were, in disproportionate numbers, members of ethnic minority groups (see later section, Overrepresentation). In other words, the issues raised concerning the "evils" of classification and labeling arose in the context of mental retardation—and at a time when the 1961 definition, or some version thereof, was being used by most states in defining mental retardation.

The resultant overrepresentation of minority children as "mildly/educable mentally retarded" led to disenchantment with the Heber (1961) definition, particularly after litigation (e.g., *Diana v. State Board of Education,* 1970; *Larry P. v. Riles,* 1971) challenged diagnostic practices leading to the overrepresentation. Sentiment clearly shifted against the inclusiveness of the 1961 definition and, when the AAMR revised the manual (Grossman, 1973), a more exclusive definition was drafted that excluded the *borderline* category; however, it continued, and in fact strengthened, the adaptive behavior criterion.

The most current definition[1] of mental retardation by the AAMR reads,

> Mental retardation refers to substantial limitations in present functioning. It is characterized by significantly subaverage intellectual functioning, existing concurrently with related limitations in two or more of the following applicable adaptive skill areas: communication, self-care, home living, social skills, community use, self-direction,

---

[1]On May 26, 1992, the AAMR approved a new definition of mental retardation. It is unclear at this time the extent to which other organizations (e.g., the American Psychiatric Association) and agencies (e.g., state education codes) will utilize a revised definition. IQ ranges for different levels of severity will also change.

health and safety, functional academics, leisure, and work. Mental retardation manifests before age 18. (American Association on Mental Retardation, 1992, p. 5)

Reschly (1992) noted that the criterion of IQ was predominant in the 1961 definition; however, the change in wording from "associated" to "existing concurrently" gave adaptive behavior importance equal to the general intellectual functioning dimension. This is discussed in greater detail later in this chapter.

Reschly (in press) described how the American Psychiatric Association (APA), which has published the *Diagnostic and Statistical Manual of Mental Disorders (DSM)* since 1952, brought its definition and classification scheme in line with that of the AAMR after 1960. Moreover, the most recent editions of the AAMR manual (Grossman, 1983) and the *DSM* (3rd ed., revised; *DSM–III–R*) (American Psychiatric Association, 1987) contain definitions that differ only in emphasis on dimensions of behavior when contrasted with the Heber (1961) definition. The *DSM–III–R* definition is essentially the same: "(1) significantly subaverage general intellectual functioning, accompanied by (2) significant deficits or impairments in adaptive functioning, with (3) onset before the age of 18" (American Psychiatric Association, 1987, p. 28). In terms of the diagnostic processes, the two schemes are indistinguishable. Both define general intellectual functioning in terms of individually administered tests of intelligence and adopt an IQ cutoff of 2 standard deviations below the population mean, *but* admonish clinicians to consider the flexible use of IQ scores up to 75 if noted adaptation problems appear to be due to intellectual deficits. The upper chronological age limit for both is 18 years, and adaptive behavior is defined in terms of personal independence and social responsibility.

Reschly (1992) noted differences in the amount of detail devoted to mental retardation in the respective manuals. The AAMR manual is 150 pages long and is concerned exclusively with mental retardation, whereas the *DSM–III–R* devotes 6 pages to the subject. Furthermore, Reschly commented on the fact that two members of the AAMR committee (Herbert Grossman and Dennis Cantwell) were also members of the APA Subcommittee on Mental Retardation, which, in part, explains some of the agreement. Given the greater detail of the AAMR definition and classification, subsequent discussion is based on this definition.

Current Classification in Learning Disabilities

In contrast with mental retardation, no single organization or definition is currently dominant in the field of learning disabilities.

Although there has been extensive discussion of definitions of learning disabilities over the years (e.g., Kavale & Forness, 1985), anything approaching a consensus on the classificatory principle defining learning disabilities appears lacking (Johnson, 1988). Learning disabilities continues to be somewhat vague, perhaps intentionally, in recognition of the fact that, after other disability categories are defined, there remains a group of children who do not perform adequately in the schools and who need services. This problem has been recognized for some time. Wepman, Cruickshank, Deutsch, Morency, and Strother (1975) noted these same problems and bemoaned the lack of explicit criteria for defining learning disabilities: "The lack of clear definition of this category of handicap has not only created problems in the control of special education funds; it has also vitiated much unfocused educational, psychological, and medical research" (p. 303).

Although versions of the AAMR definition of mental retardation have been dominant in the state education codes, such has not been the case in learning disabilities. Wepman et al. (1975) observed the great diversity in terms used across states (educationally handicapped, specific learning disabilities, communicative and intellectual deviations, neurologically handicapped, brain damaged, perceptually handicapped), which carried with them varied criteria for eligibility. Furthermore, in the learning disabilities field, definition and diagnostic criteria appear divorced. Johnson (1988) stated that "Most definitions and criteria include some mention of an ability-achievement discrepancy. That is, in order to be classified as learning disabled, an individual must manifest a discrepancy between potential and achievement" (p. 82).

Overrepresentation

Mild mental retardation was the subject of litigation that received wide attention because it centered on the fact that certain ethnic minority groups (i.e., blacks and Hispanics) were enrolled in classes for the "educable mentally retarded" in disproportionately high numbers, that is, they were overrepresented. Between 1979 and 1986, four federal trials took place dealing with the overrepresentation of black children and examining whether these programs constituted violations of the Education of the Handicapped Act and the equal protection clause of the 14th Amendment. The topic of minority overrepresentation is considered in detail in the writing of Reschly (1988b; Reschly, Kicklighter, & McKee, 1988a, 1988b, 1988c). Despite the fact that three of these four cases (*Marshall et al. v. Georgia*, 1984, 1985; *PASE v. Joseph P. Hannon*, 1980; *S-1 v. Turlington*, 1979, 1981, 1986) were decided in favor of the defendants, state departments of education or local school districts, the most widely known case, *Larry P. v. Riles* (1971, 1979, 1984) resulted in a decision in favor of the plaintiffs that placed a ban on the use of IQ tests with black children. Despite the fact that the courts upheld the traditional mental retardation conceptualizations, the criteria for identification, and the diagnostic procedures to assessing these criteria, the litigation exerted considerable impact on how school personnel function (Reschly, 1992).

The issues raised in these cases, along with some underlying assumptions, are not only germane to the mild mental retardation construct, but challenge some of the basic criteria for defining learning disabilities, as well. First, the issue of fairness of intelligence tests when administered to certain minority groups emerges whenever a child being assessed for mental retardation (to establish whether he or she qualifies on the "subaverage general intellectual functioning" criterion) or for learning disabilities (to establish aptitude against which achievement is compared in computing a discrepancy) is a minority child. Second, because of the use of an arbitrary IQ cutoff to define mental retardation, different proportions of white and black children fall above and below that cutoff as a result of different distributions of IQ. Third, to what extent do current identification procedures yield ethnic proportions of children with mental retardation and learning disabilities that are comparable to each ethnic group's proportions in the general school population? Finally, what is the rationality of expecting such proportionate representation?

The rate of overrepresentation in mental retardation has been confused and misunderstood (Reschly, 1988b). Typically, the proportion of a given ethnic group in a special education program (e.g., one for children labeled "educable mentally retarded" or who have learning disabilities) is contrasted with the proportion of that ethnic group in the general school population. For example, in 1968–1969 in California, black students constituted approximately 9% of the school population and slightly more than 25% of the "educable mentally retarded" enrollments. Yet, Reschly (1988b) reported that, in the same school year, 3.2% of black students in California were classified as "educable mentally retarded." Distinctions such as these are important in estimating the magnitude of the overrepresentation by providing different perspectives.

Fairness of IQ Tests for Minority Students Although this issue has generated extended discussion and debate in the context of mental retardation, the challenge to tests of intelligence when used with minority children has not received comparable attention in the learning disabilities field, even when the child being assessed is a minority child. When discrepancy scores are used to establish eligibility, the intelligence test becomes a major source of data on which eligibility decisions will be made.

Arbitrary Cutoff Scores: Impact on Black and White Children As noted above, establishing the cutoff at −1 or −2 standard deviations is an arbitrary decision that, nevertheless, has rather substantial consequences. Clearly, the definition of a disability group and the identification criteria employed have an impact on the prevalence of that condition. Moreover, if the criteria are known to include more males than females, more blacks than whites, and so forth, they can lead to overrepresentation of particular groups of children. Let us consider the relationship of the IQ criterion to both mental retardation and learning disabilities identification criteria.

As an example, the standardization data on the Wechsler Intelligence Scale for Children–Revised (WISC-R) reported the distributions of IQs for black and white subjects to differ in rather important ways. These data are plotted in Figure 1 and are based on data reported by Kaufman and Doppelt (1976). Whereas the mean IQ for whites is 102.26 (*SD* = 14.04), the mean IQ for blacks is 86.43 (*SD* = 12.70). As a result, different proportions of the two populations fall below the cutoffs established at various times as the upper limit

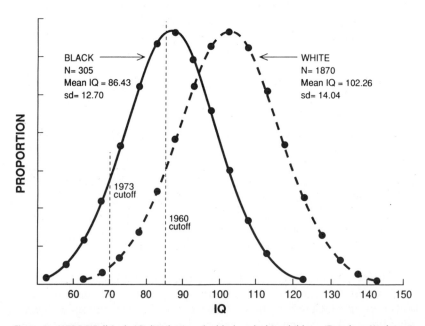

Figure 1.   WISC-R Full Scale IQ distributions for black and white children. (Data from Kaufman & Doppelt [1976], Table 1.)

defining mental retardation (note the dotted lines at IQs 70 and 85), with a far greater proportion of black subjects being eligible for mental retardation classification on the IQ criterion alone. Conversely, a far smaller percentage of black subjects are eligible for learning disabilities classification when exclusionary criteria are utilized (i.e., the learning problem cannot be due to mental retardation).

By subtracting the mean value for each ethnic group from the IQ cutoff score and dividing by that ethnic group's standard deviation, one derives Z scores that permit estimating the percentage of each group falling above and below the arbitrary cutoff points. The results of these calculations using IQ 85 as the cutoff indicate that approximately 10.9% of white subjects achieved IQs below that point, whereas 45.6% of blacks had IQs of 85 or below. Using IQ 70 as the cutoff, 9.85% of blacks would be psychometrically eligible for mental retardation classification, whereas only 1.07% of whites would be eligible. The remaining percentage of each ethnic group is eligible for learning disabilities classification in the sense that they do not qualify as having mental retardation and therefore are in the eligible pool *if* one can demonstrate the necessary discrepancy. Under IQ 70 guidelines, approximately 90% of blacks are eligible for learning disabilities classification and almost 99% of whites are eligible.

Overrepresentation of black children in the categories of learning disabilities and mental retardation, then, takes on different significance. In mental retardation, the detection rate–to–classification eligible ratio for blacks would be lower than for whites if the same percentages of the *total* (not IQ-eligible) population were detected. However, in learning disabilities, the detection rate–to–classification eligible ratio would be dramatically higher for blacks than whites if the same proportion of the total population were detected as having learning disabilities.

Ethnic Variations in Detection Enrollment of students with disabilities in special education classes has been monitored by the Office of Civil Rights (OCR). A major report (Heller, Holtzman, & Messick, 1982) noted projected enrollments in various special education categories by ethnic group. The data on which these initial projections were made were collected in 1978. Subsequently, the OCR 1986 data were reported by the National Council of Advocates for Students. Reschly (1992) summarized these data in a table modified here as Table 1. The most recent data suggest approximately the same proportion of all three ethnic groups as having learning disabilities and a disproportionately high number of black students as having mild mental retardation and emotional disturbance. How-

Table 1. Percentages of students classified as having mild mental retardation (MMR), learning disabilities (LD), and emotional disturbance (ED) by ethnic group

Category	1978 OCR[a] data			1986 OCR data		
	Black	Hispanic	White	Black	Hispanic	White
MMR	3.46	0.98	1.07	2.30	0.56	0.87
LD	2.23	2.58	2.32	4.43	4.31	4.29
ED	0.50	0.29	0.29	1.04	0.46	0.57
Total	6.19	3.85	3.68	7.77	5.33	5.73

From Reschly, D. J., & Wilson, M. S. (1990). Cognitive processing vs. traditional intelligence: Diagnostic utility, intervention implications, and treatment validity. *School Psychology Review 26*, 120–142; reprinted by permission.
[a] Office of Civil Rights.

ever, between 1978 and 1986 the proportion of all three ethnic groups identified as having learning disabilities rose substantially. Comparisons of these proportions to the proportion of each group psychometrically eligible for learning disabilities classification (i.e., those with IQs above the current mental retardation cutoff) might suggest a different conclusion: that black students with learning disabilities are, in fact, overrepresented.

Whereas the national data reported by the OCR appear to indicate that black and Hispanic students are not overrepresented in the learning disabilities classification, studies conducted in particular parts of the country have reported overrepresentation in learning disabilities of black and Hispanic children (Ortiz & Yates, 1983). Some have interpreted the increase in the number of minority children in learning disabilities as emerging from an "EMR-for-LD shift"; in other words, some of the minority children formerly labeled as "educable mentally retarded" are being classified as having learning disabilities today in certain states (see Chinn & Hughes, 1987). Tucker (1980), for example, reported on the increase in identification in school districts in the Southwest. He noted the dramatic increase between 1970 and 1977 in the placement of minority children in learning disabilities programs, and wrote: "It does not take much imagination to infer that there is at least the possibility that when it was no longer socially desirable to place black students in ['educable mentally retarded'] classes, it became convenient to place them in the newly provided [learning disabilities] category" (pp. 103–104).

In summary, the linkage between definition and diagnostic procedures and the magnitude of the mental retardation and learning disabilities populations is apparent. At present, less attention has been paid to the ethnic mix in learning disabilities than has been devoted to the issue of overrepresentation in mental retardation. Nevertheless, balancing individual need and ensuring services for every child in need with the goal of achieving racial balance may, at times, cause trouble. Both fields ought seriously to consider the rationality of the assumption underlying the overrepresentation issue. That is, should one expect proportionate representation in programs designed to serve children with learning problems? Reschly (1988b) observed, however, that overrepresentation per se may not be the problem. He noted that overrepresentation of minority children in Chapter 1 and Head Start programs is at least as great, if not greater than, that in "educably mentally retarded" classes, yet it has never been the subject of litigation. Similarly, there may be reasons concerned with the perceptions of programs, their effectiveness, and the degree of stigmatization experienced by students that could mitigate against overrepresentation in learning disabilities being a cause for concern.

ISSUES CONCERNING THE CONSTRUCTS
OF MENTAL RETARDATION AND LEARNING DISABILITIES

This section considers several issues concerning the construct of mental retardation raised by Reschly (1992). Although it is impossible to exhaustively consider each issue, it is hoped that each serves as a basis for considering learning disabilities definitions and the extent to which the issues are similar or different. The questions to be addressed are:

What dimensions of behavior should be included in the definition?
How can more homogeneous subcategories be defined?
How should comorbidity, or overlap with other conditions, be considered?

Selection of Dimensions
of Behavior To Be Included in the Definition

Two dimensions of behavior are included in the definition of mental retardation—intellectual functioning and adaptive behavior. Moreover, the person must evidence deficits in these two areas before age 18. Intellectual functioning is to be assessed by means of individually administered tests such as the Stanford-Binet, Wechsler scales, and Kaufman Assessment Battery for Children, or other standardized scales. The upper cutoff for defining mental retardation is −2 standard deviations (roughly IQ 70), but can go as high as IQ 75. Intellectual level is viewed as determinative of mental retardation along with impaired adaptive behavior and chronological age.

Hence, there are three dimensions of behavior included in the dominant AAMR definition of mental retardation, and an individual's failure to qualify on *any one of these criteria* should lead to a failure to diagnose the individual. There are some problems with assessing IQ in certain individuals with mental retardation (see Reschly, in press), including the problems in establishing level of retardation using IQ scores because IQs below 55 have a very tenuous psychometric foundation.

Adaptive behavior as determinative of mental retardation poses a series of problems. The inclusion of adaptive behavior as a defining parameter of mental retardation has been criticized by several influential scholars (Clausen, 1967, 1968, 1972; Zigler, Balla, & Hodapp, 1984; Zigler & Hodapp, 1986) as introducing error into the classification system. Primarily, these scholars contend that the construct of adaptive behavior is elusive and that extant scales are inadequate for assessing adaptive behavior, particularly in cases of mild mental retardation. The problems primarily arise in the diagnostic process when decisions regarding eligibility are being made. If the individual's IQ is sufficiently low to warrant classification as having mental retardation, and he or she is under 18 years of age, the decision hinges on whether or not there is evidence of impaired adaptive behavior. This problem is revisited as we consider the linkage between definition and diagnosis.

It strikes me that the definitions of learning disabilities developed in 1968 by the National Advisory Committee on Handicapped Children (NACHC), that of the National Joint Committee for Learning Disabilities (NJCLD) in 1981, and the proposed revisions suggested by the Interagency Committee (Kavanagh & Truss, 1988) are less clear in specifying which dimensions of behavior are to be included in defining and diagnosing learning disabilities. The 1968 NACHC definition implies a single and homogeneous disorder in one or more *basic psychological processes* and contains the "exclusionary" component, by which impaired performance should not be due to other disabling conditions (e.g., mental retardation, emotional disturbance, economic disadvantage). The 1981 NJCLD definition acknowledges that learning disabilities is a generic term referring to a heterogeneous group of disorders; presumes the etiology to be central nervous system dysfunction; and notes that, although learning disabilities may exist concomitantly with other disorders, they are not the direct result of these other disorders. The proposed revisions by the Interagency Committee include "social skills" as an area in which the difficulties may be manifested (see Kavanagh & Truss, 1988, pp. 549–551, for a discussion of this topic).

Using Zigler and Hodapp's (1986) notions regarding reliability and validity of classification, the learning disabilities definitions proposed to date seem to be sorely lacking. For example, the exclusionary clauses make the definition of learning disabilities dependent on the mental retardation definition. When the intellectual functioning criterion in the definition of mental retardation shifted from −1 to −2 standard deviations below the mean (Grossman, 1973), those individuals with IQs between 70 and 85 became ineligible for mental retardation classification and eligible for learning disabilities classification. Moreover, the presumption of central nervous system dysfunction underlying the learning problem is not a definitional parameter; yet, it is reminiscent of the presumed organic basis for mental retardation evident in early definitions (e.g., Doll, 1941), which was subsequently dropped because it could not be assessed. Listing features *presumed* to be associated with learning disabilities in the definition fails to specify the essence of a learning disability and simply clutters the issue (e.g., gender might be assumed to be related). The number of correlates of learning disabilities, or what Skinner (1981) referred to as the evidence on which the descriptive validity is established, would seem to be few given the heterogeneity of the learning disabilities population. A search for relevant attributes (i.e., symptoms, personality constructs, biographical data) shared by children with learning disabilities would, in my opinion, yield very few. Shepherd (1988) stated that, although classification of learning disabilities implies a diagnosis, the term initially was intended to obtain needed services in the public schools, and is not a diagnosis as such. She wrote: "When a child is described as 'learning disabled,' we typically think that we know a lot about the child. When we stop to think about it, though, we are not exactly sure of what we do know" (p. 165). The validity issue concerning classification in learning disabilities might require further attention and empirical examination.

Defining More Homogeneous Subcategories

Both mental retardation and learning disabilities definitions subsume individuals who vary markedly on any number of parameters—degree of disability, etiology of the disability, specialized needs that require treatment, and so forth. The AAMR classification scheme attempts to create more homogeneous subgroups by classifying individuals with mental retardation by degree or level of retardation—defined almost exclusively by IQ ranges. Four levels of mental retardation are currently delineated, although there were five recognized in the 1961 scheme. The levels are defined in terms of IQ ranges as mild (IQ 50–55 to approximately 70), moderate (IQ 35–40 to 50–55), severe (IQ 20–25 to 35–40), and profound (IQ below 20–25). (However, see the footnote on p. 120.) The AAMR system provides some description of the upper levels of adaptive behavior associated with each of the four levels of mental retardation, but no decision rules and little guidance are provided to guide clinicians and/or researchers in assigning individual cases to subgroups. (The *DSM–III–R* makes no use of adaptive behavior in classifying.) The 1961 definition (Heber, 1961) also included an additional level, *borderline mental retardation,* with a corresponding IQ range of approximately 70–85.

Educators traditionally have employed a subgrouping that differs from the AAMR scheme (see MacMillan, 1982), yet is also essentially a scheme using degree or level as the basis for classification. The categories used by educators are educable mentally retarded (EMR), trainable mentally retarded (TMR), and severely and profoundly mentally retarded (SPMR). Decision rules are usually clinical impressions of the "best fit" between programs and the child's needs and prognosis for independent functioning.

Reschly (1992) noted that currently available tests of intelligence do not provide scores in the lower range (those defining severe and profound mental retardation) and went on to suggest that, with improvements in the measurement of adaptive behavior, consideration should be given to defining levels of retardation with adaptive behavior milestones rather than IQ. As is discussed subsequently, others would be vehemently opposed to such a suggestion.

The AAMR and the *DSM–III–R* both recognize two etiological patterns: mental retardation attributable to biological factors and that attributable to psychosocial factors. Reschly (1992) noted that the *DSM–III–R* lists five classes of etiological influences, whereas the AAMR provides a more elaborate system for reporting etiological factors. It must be stressed, however, that precise etiology cannot be specified in the majority of cases. An extended discussion of the importance of organic versus nonorganic etiologies has emerged in the mental retardation literature over the years, including the writings of Alfred Strauss (Strauss & Kephart, 1955; Strauss & Lehtinen, 1947), who was so influential in the early work in learning disabilities. Let us consider the utility of differentiation on the basis of etiology.

Zigler and his colleagues (Zigler, 1967; Zigler, Balla, & Hodapp, 1984; Zigler & Hodapp, 1986) have repeatedly stressed the importance of recognizing two distinctly different groups of people classified as having mental retardation, which they termed a "two-group approach." Zigler and Hodapp (1986) noted that empirical work has repeatedly shown that there are many more cases of IQs less than

50 than would be predicted from theory. The generally accepted explanation for this excess of cases derives from the observation that

> there are really two separate distributions of intelligence: one for those whose intelligence is the product of some interaction between heredi- tary and environmental components; and the other for those whose intellectual apparatus has been physically damaged, thus altering the biological side of the formula. (Zigler & Hodapp, 1986, p. 72)

Zigler and Hodapp (1986) described the distribution obtained for individuals with organic damage as being asymmetrical and be- ginning at IQ 0 (cases of anencephaly), peaking at IQ 30, and then having a long tail that extends well into the high-IQ range (thereby encompassing the occasional individual with brain damage who evi- dences no intellectual retardation). This is shown in Figure 2. Zigler, Balla, and Hodapp (1984) proposed a classification scheme for men- tal retardation based on etiology and defined by an IQ of 2 standard deviations or more below the population mean, which would remove adaptive behavior from being determinative of mental retardation and utilize it as a correlate rather than as a classificatory principle.

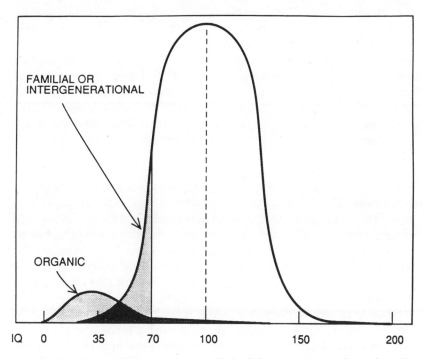

Figure 2. Distributions of IQ among persons with familial or intergenerational mental retarda- tion and those with organic mental retardation. (From Zigler, E., & Hodapp, R.M. [1986]. *Under- standing mental retardation* [p. 73]. New York: Cambridge University Press; reprinted by permis- sion.)

The proposed classification system (see Figure 3) employs etiology as a classificatory principle. That is, an IQ of -2 standard deviations or lower would define the child as having mental retardation, and that child would then be classified by etiology into one of three subgroups—organic, familial, and undifferentiated. This classification would proceed based on the classificatory principle listed in Figure 3 under each of the three etiological groups, which would employ known correlates in guiding the application of this principle. In subsequent writings (Burack, Hodapp, & Zigler, 1988; Zigler & Hodapp, 1986) this approach is extended and the case is made for further refinement within the familial and organic groups. For example, in the categories of unknown familial and etiology, Zigler and Hodapp (1986), hypothesized several subgroups: 1) familial mental retardation, with at least one parent who also has mental retardation; 2) "polygenic isolates," with parents of average intelligence and a nurturant environment; that is, those who received a poor "genetic draw"; and 3) "socio-culturally retarded"—persons who have mental retardation as a result of prolonged exposure to an extremely impoverished environment.

Burack et al. (1988) divided the organic branch into specific etiologies: 1) chromosomal abnormalities, 2) metabolic imbalances, 3) neurological insults, 4) congenital defects, and 5) perinatal complications and infections. They then illustrated differences in the stability of IQ over time for individuals with Down syndrome, cerebral palsy, and fragile X syndrome. By designing research to treat etiologically formed groups as factors, one can explain greater proportions of variance when etiology is related to behavioral outcomes (see Burack, 1990, for a dramatic example comparing children with Down syndrome and Williams syndrome). Should these authors be correct, failure to differentiate could lead to confounding of etiology by level of retardation, which will obscure existing relationships. In concluding, Burack et al. (1988) observed that their proposal was intended to increase precision and thereby improve the science concerned with mental retardation; the differentiation of organic retardation is an extension of the original two-group formulation designed to further increase precision in the research conducted.

What means of achieving greater precision in subdividing subjects with learning disabilities are available, and what is the utility of these approaches? Certainly, various approaches to reducing subject heterogeneity in learning disabilities research samples have been explored. Keogh and colleagues have developed procedures for describing empirically defined subgroups (Keogh, Major, Reid, Omori, & Gandara, 1980), and Torgeson (1982) has employed rationally defined subgroups; Lyon and Watson (1981), McKinney and Fisher (1982), and Cooper and Speece (1990) have utilized cluster

	Organic (0–70)	Familial (50–70)	Undifferentiated (0–70)
CLASSIFICATORY PRINCIPLE	Demonstrable organic etiology	No demonstrable organic etiology. Parents have this same type of retardation	Cannot reliably be placed in either of the other two classes
CORRELATES	Found at all SES levels	More prevalent at SES levels	
	IQs most often below 50	IQs rarely below 50	
	Siblings usually of normal intelligence	Siblings often at lower levels of intelligence	
	Often accompanied by severe problems	Health within normal range	
	Appearance often marred by physical stigmata		
	Mortality rate higher (more likely to die at a younger age than the general population)	Normal mortality rate	
	Often dependent on care from others throughout life	With some support can lead an independent existence as an adult	
	Unlikely to marry and often infertile	Likely to marry and produce children of low intelligence	
	Unlikely to experience neglect in their homes	More likely to experience neglect in their homes	
	High prevalence of other physical disabilities (e.g., epilepsy, cerebral palsy)	Less likely to have other physical disabilities	

Figure 3. A three-group model for the classification of persons with mental retardation. (From Zigler, E., & Hodapp, R.M. [1986]. *Understanding mental retardation* [p. 53]. New York: Cambridge University Press; reprinted by permission.)

analysis to create subtypes of children with learning disabilities; and Weller and Strawser (1987) have suggested "consensus subtypes" as a means of creating more homogeneous groups of children with learning disabilities. These approaches, however, have been experimental efforts to reduce sample heterogeneity for purposes of research. Parallel schemes linked to learning disabilities definitions have not been forthcoming as classification principles to create more homogeneous subgroups within the broad rubric of learning disabilities.

As is discussed later, the increase in the prevalence of learning disabilities between 1977, when P.L. 94-142 was fully implemented, and the present has been described as epidemic. It seems that there might be utility in a two-group approach applied to learning disabilities. That is, children served in programs for children with learning disabilities include a "hard core" of children resembling those constituting Strauss's exogenous subgroup, the original children with dyslexia, and the children for whom Cruickshank (1967; Cruickshank, Bentzen, Ratzeberg, & Tannhauser, 1961) developed classroom environments and instructional strategies. These children encountered such severe academic failure that the need for special education was obvious to all. However, in the 1960s and early 1970s youngsters with less obvious disorders, who nevertheless had school learning problems, came to be subsumed under the learning disabilities description provided by Kirk in 1963 (see Weiderholt, 1974). Gradually, learners with more mild disabilities were qualified under the learning disabilities guidelines, until learning disabilities becomes the largest category of students with disabilities according to the Office of Special Education Programs (OSEP) child counts, including a segment described by some as having "garden variety" learning disabilities (see Stanovich, chap. 13, this volume), a group hard to distinguish from those who are simply low achievers.

Efforts paralleling those of Zigler and colleagues in the learning disabilities area might impose greater precision on research and treatment. There exists a minority of children with learning disabilities with clear, or highly suspected, organic etiologies, and a second group with uncertain (unlikely organic) etiologies. These two branches might be further divided on the basis of some classificatory principle that can be reliably applied. For example, degree of discrepancy between aptitude and achievement might be used to classify a student by degree of learning disability. Further classification could proceed on the basis of evidence of basic underlying processes, recognizing that some children with considerable discrepancies exhibit processing problems, whereas others do not and yet are eligible for learning disabilities classification under state guidelines using discrepancy formulas. It is difficult at this writing to presume to know the dimensions on which such a classification system should be developed, but I am confident that the current state (i.e., a learning disability is a learning disability is a learning disability) is far too imprecise (see Blashfield, chap. 2, this volume; Fletcher, Francis, Rourke, Shaywitz, & Shaywitz, chap. 3, this volume; Stanovich, chap. 13, this volume for further discussion). The imprecision in classification that exists currently in the learning disabilities field appears to encourage research that will frequently yield great error variance because of the failure to control for differences in subgroups of children with learning disabilities.

A word of caution is in order regarding the validity of determining etiology among individuals with mental retardation. Chaney and Eyman (1982) contrasted the accuracy of etiological classifications based on clinical diagnosis (which used clinical history, physical examination, and laboratory tests) of clients when they were admitted to a large state institution with findings from autopsies performed when those clients died. A total of 1,025 cases were admitted between 1927 and 1975, and they died between 1944 and 1976. Comparison of clinical diagnosis (made at time of admission) with anatomical diagnosis (made at time of autopsy) resulted in agreement in 47% of cases of prenatal etiology, 32% of perinatal etiology, and 47% of postnatal etiology. The point pertinent to the present discussion is that clinical diagnosis of etiology is imprecise, and one must not assume that such classification is necessarily valid. In the learning disabilities area, wherein etiological classification is even more problematic than in mental retardation, the error rate will probably be even higher.

**Consideration of Comorbidity,
or Overlap with Other Conditions**

In mental retardation, the classification schemes of the AAMR and the APA both recognize that mental retardation can, and does, occur in conjunction with other disorders. Having decided in 1961 that mental retardation refers to an individual's current functioning, these schemes permit diagnosing other disorders that exist concurrently, and this does nothing to suggest that the diagnosis of mental retardation is inappropriate. Reschly (1992) noted that decision rules for such cases are provided in the *DSM–III–R*, but are lacking in the AAMR scheme. Hence, dual diagnosis of an individual as having mental retardation and exhibiting certain mental disorders (e.g., schizophrenia) is not an unusual situation in the field of mental retardation.

In the learning disabilities area, the definition of the NACHC (1968) failed to recognize that learning disabilities could coexist with other disabilities such as emotional disturbance or mental retardation. The NJCLD (1981) modified the definition concerning the issue of comorbidity and acknowledged that a learning disability "may occur concomitantly with other disabling conditions," but went on to state that "it is not the direct result of those conditions or influences." This latter emphasis would require diagnostic skills beyond those currently employed, particularly since the wording implies the intent to establish which disability caused the other. The proposed modified definition by the Interagency Committee (Kavanagh & Truss, 1988) is particularly sensitive to comorbidity of learning disabilities with ADD, but still provides no decision rules to guide the identification processes.

INTERFACE OF DEFINITION AND IDENTIFICATION PROCESSES

Definitions of mental retardation and learning disabilities should specify parameters to be assessed in the identification and/or diagnostic process that establishes whether or not a given child meets the definition and thereby warrants classification in either category. In practice, the linkage between definition and identification practices has been troublesome.

Linkage Between Definition and Identification Practices

The Issue of Adaptive Behavior   An awkward situation was described by Clausen (1968, 1972) concerning the inclusion of adaptive behavior as one of the defining parameters of mental retardation. In essence, Clausen argued that no adequate instruments existed with which to evaluate adaptive behavior—meaning that a central criterion for defining mental retardation could not be assessed. This state of affairs led Clausen to advocate use of a psychometric definition, with an IQ of 70 constituting the upper limit of mental retardation. One argument advanced in support of this position was that clinicians used IQ alone in identifying cases of mental retardation, and the proposed definition would be made consistent with prevailing practice. In responding to Clausen's (1967) original paper on the concept of mental deficiency, Halpern (1968) suggested that the adaptive behavior clause remain in the definition while diagnostic practices utilize a single psychometric criterion. Clausen responded that Halpern's proposal could result in the diagnosis of mental deficiency in a person who did not meet the definition. MacMillan and Jones (1972) agreed with Clausen, noting that diagnosis establishes whether or not a child qualifies (i.e., meets the definition) as having mental retardation. Failure to evaluate all parameters or criteria defining the condition in the identification process would, in fact, lead to the situation Clausen described: children qualified as having mental retardation who do not meet the definition and children judged unqualified who would meet the definition were reliable assessment of all parameters available.

Another critic of including adaptive behavior as a defining criterion has been Edward Zigler, who has repeatedly expressed concern over the unreliability of the classification scheme for mental retardation introduced by including adaptive behavior in the definition. For example, Zigler and Hodapp (1986) observed that a simple definition of social adaptation for an adult is whether or not he or she is employed. They go on to question whether a "65 IQ man who holds a job is not retarded. Yet if he is laid off, on the day his employment terminates he becomes retarded" (p. 66). In other words, including adaptive behavior in the definition of mental retardation reduces the reliability of classification and results in a classification system that, in the words of Zigler, is "inadequate and unacceptable."

The problem is clinically deciding whether an individual's adaptive behavior is sufficiently impaired to warrant that classification as having mental retardation occurs primarily in cases of mild mental retardation. That is, when the degree of intellectual impairment is sufficiently great that a person scores below IQ 50, the corresponding adaptive behavior is almost invariably impaired. Conversely, as one approaches the upper limit of IQ used to define "subaverage general intellectual functioning" (particularly when that upper limit was −1 standard deviation), the probability is less that both IQ and measured or clinically determined adaptive behavior will be low.

Congruence Between Definition and Diagnostic Process The situation regarding definition–diagnostic process congruence appears even more problematic in the learning disabilities field (see Mercer, Hughes, & Mercer, 1985; Mercer, King-Sears, & Mercer, 1990), as illustrated by the following statement: "lack of agreement among professionals and educators on who is learning disabled (i.e., definition) as well as appropriate assessment instruments and procedures (i.e., criteria) is widespread" (Mercer et al., 1990, p. 142). Similarly, Kavale and Forness (1985), after tracing the history of disagreement in terms of learning disabilities definitions, proposed that a definition of learning disabilities might profit by being modeled after the mental retardation definition. Such a definition would stress "significantly subaverage academic impairment," IQ in the normal range, and exclusion of certain conditions (i.e., gross physical and neurological disabilities, uncorrected impairments in auditory or visual acuity, serious emotional disturbance, and sustained lack of environmental or instructional opportunities). Although decision rules would have to be adopted as identification criteria for these dimensions of behavior stressed in the definition, such a definition would avoid some of the vexing problems confronting the employment of other definitions that specify as parameters psychological processing variables, central nervous system impairment, and other criteria impossible to assess reliably given the state of the art/science.

Mercer et al. (1990) surveyed all states and Washington, DC, regarding their definitions of learning disabilities and the identification criteria. Table 2 summarizes the criteria. Note that 57% of the states have a definition identical to, or very similar to, the 1977 NACHC definition that appears in P.L. 94-142. However, two states do not even have a definition, and the remaining 20 states use definitions that differ substantially from the NACHC definition. Whereas only 14 states have definitions that mention aptitude–achievement discrepancy as a population parameter, 86% of the states use such a discrepancy as a criterion for identifying children as having learning disabilities! Recall Clausen's (1972) point regarding the possibility of identifying children as a member of a class when they do not meet the definition of the population. Furthermore, the majority of state definitions are silent regarding level of intelligence and do not include it as a criterion; yet 94% of the states exclude cases of mental retardation from being classified as having learning disabilities. Nationally, and in most states, mental retardation is defined and diagnosed in terms of subaverage general intellectual functioning as a determinative criterion.

Mercer et al. (1990) noted that definitions and criteria are often incongruent, as in the case in which a state definition includes a psychological process component while that process component is not included among the eligibility criteria. Although 47 states incorporate psychological processes in their definitions, only 14 states include it in the identification criteria. Although the NACHC definition and the definition of learning disabilities provided in the regulations of P.L. 94-142 do not mention a discrepancy, the discrepancy component is included in the definitions of 14 states and the criteria of 44 states. Such inconsistency precludes study of a population with known parameters and generalizations from research conducted in one state to "students with learning disabilities" in another.

In considering the discrepancy construct (see also Stanovich, chap. 13, this volume), which is so widely employed in the diagnosis of learning disabilities, I do not wish to go into the psychometric issues regarding discrepancy formulas (e.g., the various formulas for regression of achievement on IQ, use of grade-equivalent scores). Instead, I wish to highlight a subject vehemently argued in mental retardation circles that has not arisen in learning disabilities. Influential in the testimony presented to the court in *Larry P. v. Riles* (1971) was the concept introduced by Jane Mercer that tests of intel-

Table 2. Definition components and related criteria included in state definitions by number of states and respective percentages

Components and related criteria	Definition		Criteria		Criteria and/or definition	
	N	%	N	%	N	%
Definition type						
1977 only	20	39	—	—	—	—
1977 with variation	9	18	—	—	—	—
Different	20	39	—	—	—	—
No definition used	2	4	—	—	—	—
Intelligence						
Average or above average	3	6	6	12	9	18
Above mental retardation criteria	1	2	5	10	6	12
Not stated	48	94	36	71	34	67
Process						
Process disorder	47	92	14	27	47	92
Language disorder	46	90	41	80	49	96
Academic						
Reading	47	92	41	80	49	96
Writing	47	92	41	80	49	96
Spelling	41	80	10	20	42	82
Arithmetic	47	92	41	80	48	94
Exclusion—primary						
Visual impairment	44	86	39	76	48	94
Auditory impairment	44	86	39	76	48	94
Motor impairment	42	82	38	75	46	90
Mental retardation	44	86	39	76	48	94
Emotional disturbance	42	82	39	76	47	92
Environmental disadvantage	43	84	38	75	48	94
Neurological impairment						
Included	32	64	2	4	32	64
Discrepancy						
Included	14	27	44	86	45	88
Operationalization of discrepancy						
Standard scores	—		18		18	
Standard deviation	—		23		23	
Regression formula	—		13		13	
WISC-R verbal V performance	—		1		1	
40%–50% or more discrepancy	1		2		3	
Grade level discrepancy	—		2		2	
No statement about operationalization	1		10		11	

ligence and standardized achievement tests "autocorrelate"; that is, they measure the same thing. Reschly (1988b, p. 24) described three conclusions reached by Judge Peckham in his written opinion after finding in favor of the plaintiffs: 1) IQ tests are biased, 2) IQ and standardized achievement tests autocorrelate, and 3) the customary use of achievement tests is acceptable. Such logic is troubling; yet, it led to prohibitions in using IQ for establishing special education eligibility for black children in California. MacMillan and Balow (1991) speculated on the assessment incongruities in California following the *Larry P.* decision, one being:

> The criteria for qualifying children as mentally retarded require establishing "subaverage general intellectual functioning" and for LD students one must establish a severe discrepancy between aptitude and achievement. Yet, the scales which are conventionally used to assess "intellectual functioning" or "aptitude" are the subjects of the ban. (p. 11)

They went on to consider the notion of autocorrelation vis-à-vis learning disabilities. If IQ tests and standardized achievement tests measure the same thing, the meaning of a "severe discrepancy" between two measures of the same thing suggests that error measurement is the essence of a learning disability. The scant attention given to the autocorrelation concept, considering the attention it received in the *Larry P.* case, is indeed surprising.

Arbitrary Criteria in Identification   Both the mental retardation and learning disabilities fields employ criteria that are arbitrary in the decision rules for identifying cases. This is not necessarily bad, but those working in the field should be aware of this fact and its consequences. No where has this been more apparent than when the AAMR shifted the upper IQ limit from −1 to −2 standard deviations in 1973. There is nothing sacred about an IQ of 85, 70, or 75. Nevertheless, if an exclusion component exists in a definition (i.e., children with learning disabilities cannot also be classified as having mental retardation), the fact that learning disabilities eligibility is intimately linked to mental retardation eligibility must be recognized and the consequences of a definition of learning disabilities being at the mercy of any changes in the mental retardation definition must be considered. Take, for example, the impact of the upper limit IQ shift in the mental retardation definition on learning disabilities. When the AAMR shifted from −1 to −2 standard deviations for the upper cutoff of mental retardation, the learning disabilities definition suddenly included as potentially eligible for learning disabilities certification all children whose IQs fell between approximately 70 and 85 because these cases were no longer eligible for classification as having mental retardation.

Zigler and Hodapp (1986) noted that the rationale for selecting a particular IQ cutoff (85 or 70) is not to be found as a result of sound classification procedures; rather, it derives from a statistical formula. They noted that it has been customary to set the IQ cutoff for mental retardation at 2 standard deviations below the mean. In describing how arbitrary and confusing it can be to use statistical formulas, they pointed out how shifting the upper limit from -1 to -2 standard deviation immediately changed the percentage of the population eligible for mental retardation classification by IQ criterion from 3 to 16. With publication of the Grossman (1973) manual, the cutoff was placed at 2 standard deviations below the mean, permitting the classification of individuals with IQs as high as 75 as having mental retardation in an attempt to suggest that IQ be used as a rough guideline (Grossman, 1983).

Because the portion of the IQ curve between 50 or 55 and 85 is rapidly accelerating, small changes in the IQ cutoff scores alter rather dramatically the proportion of the population falling at, or below, that score. Reschly (1992) noted that using a cutoff of 75 and below results in *twice as many people being eligible* as using IQ 70 and below (see Table 3). Furthermore, there are more cases that fall in the IQ interval of 71 and 75 than in the entire range associated with mild mental retardation (approximately IQ 55–70).

In the field of learning disabilities, arbitrariness appears specifically as discrepancy components are discussed. That is, how discrepant should aptitude and achievement be before defining a child as having a learning disability? Clearly, the decision is arbitrary. Furthermore, the decision will have implications for the prevalence of learning disabilities: the smaller the discrepancy required, the higher the prevalence. Perhaps, in some places, reasoning proceeded in the other direction, in which the question was asked, "What kind

Table 3. Percentages of the population falling below certain IQ cutoffs and falling within certain IQ intervals

IQ	Normal curve percentage
Below 70	2.28
70 and below	2.68
Below 75	4.75
75 and below	5.48

IQ Interval	Percentage within IQ interval
56–60	0.30
61–65	0.69
66–70	1.52
71–75	2.80

These estimates assume no distortion in the curve, and an IQ score (e.g., IQ 75) is treated as an interval (74.5–75.5). This table is based on Table 3 in Reschly (in press).

of prevalence rate do you want?" Knowing the desired prevalence rate, one could then select the magnitude of the discrepancy that would result in the desired prevalence. Mercer et al. (1990) reported that 23 states use a discrepancy of 1–2 standard deviations and 12 states recommend the use of regression formulas. Mercer et al. further illustrated the variability between states by noting that one state recommends comparisons of verbal and performance scales on the WISC-R, three states suggest a discrepancy between aptitude and achievement of 40%–50%, and two states recommend the use of grade-level discrepancy. Although 45 states include the discrepancy component in their definitions and/or criteria, 11 did not indicate how the discrepancy is operationalized. Hence, although the discrepancy component is commonly used, the method for establishing a discrepancy is certainly not standardized and the magnitude of the discrepancy required for eligibility for learning disabilities classification varies from state to state.

System Identification

Clearly, the linkage between definition and identification processes is problematic in both mental retardation and learning disabilities. The inconsistencies noted above do not even include discussion of the specific instruments used to assess dimensions of adaptive behavior, intelligence, achievement, and other basic psychological processes. Ample evidence exists on the psychometric inadequacies of many scales used by those charged with the identification process. Before leaving this broad area, however, I would like to discuss briefly how children come to the attention of authorities through the referral process, which has been referred to as *system identification* (Keogh & MacMillan, 1983; MacMillan, Meyers, & Morrison, 1980; Morrison, MacMillan, & Kavale, 1985) in the context of mental retardation and learning disabilities.

Although one can specify definitional parameters of mental retardation and learning disabilities and prescribe scales to be used in identifying cases, in fact, the diagnosis of these disorders must be understood as it naturally occurs (see Zigmond, chap. 12, this volume), which is usually in the public schools. In fact, mild mental retardation and learning disabilities are largely school-manifested phenomena, and those factors increasing, or reducing, the likelihood of identification and formal labeling explain, in part, why prevalence figures based on epidemiological surveys have never approached estimates of mental retardation based on the percentage of the population scoring below the operative cutoff IQ. No one would survey all individuals, using individual tests of intelligence, to detect all cases with IQs that satisfy the subaverage general intellectual functioning criterion for mental retardation. Similarly, school personnel do not administer individual tests of intelligence and then compute discrepancy scores in comparison to scores on standardized achievement tests to "find" students with learning disabilities. In truth, only cases initially referred by parents or teachers, in most instances, to those responsible for establishing eligibility are formally evaluated. Zigler and Hodapp (1986) used the term *detection rates* in recognition of the fact that one cannot equate detection rates with the actual prevalence (this topic is discussed in detail later in this chapter). Furthermore, they noted that the ratio of detected to undetected cases may (and probably does) vary by age, IQ level, racial group, gender, and socioeconomic status.

Implicit in understanding detection rates of mental retardation and learning disabilities in the context of the public schools is consideration of the referral process. MacMillan et al. (1980) described the complex set of factors that affects the likelihood of a given child being identified as having mild mental retardation in the public schools. Variations in teacher tolerance for deviant behavior (academic or deportment), availability of support for low-achieving students in the school, the philosophy of the principal regarding referral of problem students, and the modal achievement level in a given classroom all operate to influence teacher referral behavior, which, in turn, has an impact on detection rates.

In the system identification of students with learning disabilities, the variations in prevalence and/or detection by age, gender, IQ level, socioeconomic status, and racial group have received substantially less attention than the same variations in mental retardation; nevertheless, they have been examined (see Keogh & MacMillan, 1983; Morrison, MacMillan, & Kavale, 1985). It is evident that the schools are not in the business of providing "clean research samples" for researchers and that the referral process is every bit as germane in learning disabilities as it is in mental retardation. Variability in referral behavior of teachers has an impact on the ratio of detected to undetected cases of learning disabilities, which, in turn, precludes establishing the true prevalence of learning disabilities.

What is crucial to recognize in consideration of definitions and identification processes is that there are some cases that *would* qualify as having mental retardation or learning disabilities according to operative criteria, but are never referred, and, therefore, not evaluated. In the field of mental retardation, the predominant view is that such cases occur more frequently in the higher IQ ranges (i.e., potential cases of mild mental retardation) (MacMillan, 1988, 1989). Estimates of true prevalence in both fields, however, probably are impossible given the fact that the process depends on parents and teachers employing unreliable and somewhat idiosyncratic criteria for deciding whether to initiate the referral–assessment–placement sequence.

Paradox: Neither Learning Disabilities Nor Mental Retardation

Efforts to define which students have mental retardation and learning disabilities and what criteria shall be used to establish eligibility have, in some states, resulted in the isolation of a segment of children who are ineligible in either category despite having serious learning problems (MacMillan, 1989; see also Fletcher et al., chap. 3, this volume). Forness (1985) described the situation in California, where mental retardation was defined as -2 standard deviations below the mean in IQ, whereas learning disabilities classification eligibility was based on the demonstration of a severe discrepancy between IQ and achievement. Tables were published by the California State Department of Education (1983) for establishing cutoff points when specific combinations of intelligence and achievement tests were used. Forness described how use of the WISC-R and either the Wide-Range Achievement Test or Peabody Individual Achievement Test results in a situation in which the lowest IQ band that would permit establishing a severe discrepancy averaged 82.7. In other words, students with IQs below about 82 could not demonstrate a severe discrepancy regardless of how low their achievement test scores dropped; those low scores could be explained in terms of low aptitude. The result was that students with IQs above 70 and below 82 were ineligible for special education programs for children with either mental retardation or learning disabilities.

IMPACT OF DEFINITION
AND DIAGNOSIS ON DETECTION RATES

The magnitude of the problem to society posed by mental retardation and learning disabilities is usually estimated by the number of cases of individuals receiving services. Epidemiologists use the concepts of *incidence* and *prevalence* to reflect how widespread a condition, usually a disease, is in a given population. These terms have been used in the context of mental retardation (see MacMillan, 1982), with incidence referring to the number of *new cases* identified during some time frame (e.g., 6 months) while prevalence refers to the percentage of the population affected (total number of cases identified) at some point in time. Because most identified cases of mental retardation are not disease entities (i.e., a person is not infected with mental retardation), but rather qualify on the basis of behavioral characteristics, it may stretch these concepts to describe identification rates as incidence or prevalence indices. Hence, Zigler's term *detection rates* will be used when referring to the number of cases being served in programs for children with mental retardation or learning disabilities, recognizing that undetected cases exist in which the individual would qualify if assessed, but, because he or she has not been referred, that individual avoids classification as having mental retardation or learning disabilities.

Epidemiological research in mental retardation has consistently found detection rates far below the rates one would predict from a normal distribution of IQ. There has been a rather consistent finding of 0.3%–0.4% of the general population falling into the IQ less than 50 range (Abramowicz & Richardson, 1975; McLaren & Bryson, 1987). For this segment of the population, one would expect that detection of most cases does, in fact, occur. In cases with IQs above 50, but below extant cutoff scores, detection is far more problematic. When researchers use case registration data, the prevalence rates reported vary considerably for this IQ 50–70 range. For example, Baird and Sadovnick (1985) estimated 0.17% of the general population are detected as having mild mental retardation, whereas others (e.g., Fishbach & Hull, 1982; Frost, 1977) reported 0.37% and 0.59% rates—well below the percentage one would predict from normal curve estimates. Such estimates, however, are based on case registration data (i.e., cases actually detected). The study by Granat and Granat (1973) illustrates the problems of extrapolating from these findings: they reported more undetected than detected cases in a survey of 19-year-old males.

Variations in the rate of mental retardation have been noted by age, gender, IQ range, socioeconomic status, and ethnicity (MacMillan, 1982; McLaren & Bryson, 1987; Richardson, Katz, & Koller, 1986). Although some of the variation by age occurs as a result of higher mortality rates in persons with severe and profound retardation and there are cases of mental retardation that are X-linked, the majority of such variation exists because of detection practices, not because of true changes in prevalence. Moreover, it appears to occur most frequently in cases of mild mental retardation, and it occurs in the context of the public schools (Mercer, 1973). As a result, the number of children served in public school programs for children with mental retardation provides some insight into the changing nature of mild mental retardation.

The growth of public school programs for students with mental retardation increased dramatically during the 1950s and 1960s. Between 1948 and 1966 there was a 400% increase in the number of students served in such programs (Mackie, 1969). At the time President Ford signed into law P.L. 94-142 in 1975, mild mental retardation had the highest incidence of the exceptional child diagnoses (Reschly, 1988a). However, litigation and definitional changes, discussed previously, reversed the trend, and mild mental retardation, as reflected in detection rates, was on its way to disappearing as a clinical entity (MacMillan, 1988; Polloway & Smith, 1988). Reports prepared by the U.S. Department of Education for Congress include child count data by disability category, and these data are revealing in terms of what has happened in the areas of mental retardation and learning disabilities since 1976–1977, the first year of full implementation of P.L. 94-142. In the case of mental retardation, keep in mind the rather stable estimate of 0.4% for cases with IQs less than 50; the change in child counts in mental retardation has occurred in the cases of IQs greater than 50, and one can subtract 0.4 from the percentage figures reported for total mental retardation child counts to estimate detection rates of mild mental retardation in the schools.

Table 4 shows the changes that occurred since 1976–1977 for total special education (all disabilities), mental retardation, and learning disabilities. Note that in the first year of full implementation of P.L. 94-142, 2.16% of all schoolchildren were served in programs for children with mental retardation and 1.80% in programs for children with learning disabilities. By the next year, learning disabilities had surpassed mental retardation, and since that time the gap between the two has dramatically increased. These national figures, however, obscure substantial variations among states. For example, the percentage of schoolchildren served in programs for children with mental retardation in 1987–1988 ranged from 0.41% in New Jersey and 0.42% in California to 3.32% in Alabama. For learning disabilities, the figures ranged from 2.11% in Georgia to 7.70% in Rhode Island. Nationally, between 1976–1977 and 1987–1988, there has been a reduction in mental retardation of 34.3%, while learning disabilities has increased by 144.7% (Office of Special Education Programs, *Eleventh Annual Report*, 1989, Table AA20).

Some perplexing issues arise as one considers how detection rates of mental retardation and learning disabilities could have fluctuated so markedly. Is mental retardation somehow being "cured," while an epidemic in learning disabilities occurs? If the definitions of these conditions specify parameters and the diagnostic process is administered systematically, how can one condition decrease by almost 35% while another increases by almost 145%? Moreover, how can we explain the variability among states in the percentage of total school populations served in programs for children with mental retardation and learning disabilities? Clearly, these enormous variations exist because of the influence of system identification factors,

Table 4. National trends from 1976–1977 to 1987–1988 in children served in programs for children with learning disabilities and mental retardation[a]

	76-77	77-78	78-79	79-80	80-81	81-82	82-83	83-84	84-85	85-86	86-87[b]	87-88
Number served (in 1,000s)												
Total special education	3,692	3,751	3,889	4,005	4,142	4,198	4,255	4,298	4,315	4,317	4,422	4,128
LD	796	964	1,230	1,276	1,462	1,622	1,741	1,806	1,823	1,862	1,926	1,942
MR	959	933	901	869	829	786	757	727	708	661	664	601
Percentage of total population												
LD	1.80	2.21	2.66	3.06	3.57	4.05	4.39	4.62	4.72	4.73	4.49	4.41
MR	2.16	2.14	2.12	2.09	2.02	1.96	1.91	1.86	1.84	1.68	1.22	1.37
Percentage of special education population												
LD	21.5	25.7	29.1	31.9	35.3	38.6	40.9	42.0	42.2	43.1	43.6	47.0
MR	26.0	24.9	23.2	21.7	20.0	18.7	17.8	16.9	16.4	15.3	15.0	14.6

[a]Figures through 1985–1986 are from Singer and Butler (1987).
[b]In the Tenth Annual Report and thereafter, percentages by disabling condition are not available for ages 3–5. Estimates for 1986–1987 for total population were computed by taking the number of children 3–21 (Table BA2), subtracting those ages 18–21 (Table BA6) and those ages 3–5 (Table BA3), and dividing by enrollment for ages 5–17 (Table BH5).

discussed above, on the detection process. In addition, sociopolitical factors have influenced identification in mental retardation directly (i.e., through litigation and legislation) and indirectly (i.e., attempts to balance ethnic proportions).

REFERENCES

Abramowicz, H.K., & Richardson, S.A. (1975). Epidemiology of severe mental retardation in children: Community studies. *American Journal of Mental Deficiency, 80,* 18–39.

American Association on Mental Retardation. (1992). *Mental retardation: Definition, classification, and systems of supports* (Special 9th Edition). Washington, DC: American Association on Mental Retardation.

American Psychiatric Association. (1987). *Diagnostic and statistical manual of mental disorders* (3rd ed., rev.). Washington, DC: American Psychiatric Press.

Baird, P.A., & Sadovnick, A.D. (1985). Mental retardation in over half a million consecutive livebirths—An epidemiological study. *American Journal of Mental Deficiency, 89,* 323–330.

Burack, J.A. (1990). Differentiating mental retardation: The two-group approach and beyond. In R.M. Hodapp, J.A. Burack, & E. Ziegler. (Eds.), *Issues in the developmental approach to mental retardation* (pp. 27–48). New York: Cambridge University Press.

Burack, J.A., Hodapp, R.M., & Zigler, E. (1988). Issues in the classification of mental retardation: Differentiating among organic etiologies. *Journal of Child Psychology and Psychiatry, 29,* 765–769.

California State Department of Education, Office of Program Evaluation and Research. (1983). *A manual for determination of a severe discrepancy.* Sacramento: State Department of Education.

Chaney, R.H., & Eyman, R.K. (1982). Etiology of mental retardation: Clinical vs. neuroanatomic diagnosis. *Mental Retardation, 20,* 123–127.

Chinn, P.C., & Hughes, S. (1987). Representation of minority students in special education classes. *Remedial and Special Education, 8*(4), 41–46.

Clausen, J.A. (1967). Mental deficiency: Development of a concept. *American Journal of Mental Deficiency, 71,* 727–745.

Clausen, J. (1968). A comment on Halpern's note. *American Journal of Mental Deficiency, 72,* 950.

Clausen, J. (1972). Quo vadis, AAMD? *The Journal of Special Education, 6,* 51–60.

Cooper, D.H., & Speece, D.L. (1990). Maintaining at-risk children in regular education settings: Initial effects of individual differences and classroom environments. *Exceptional Children, 57,* 117–126.

Cruickshank, W.M. (1967). The development of education for exceptional children. In W.M. Cruickshank & G.O. Johnson (Eds.), *Education of exceptional children and youth* (pp. 6–22). Englewood Cliffs, NJ: Prentice-Hall.

Cruickshank, W.M., Bentzen, F., Ratzeberg, F., & Tannhauser, M.A. (1961). *Teaching method for brain-injured and hyperactive children.* Syracuse, NY: Syracuse University Press.

Diana v. State Board of Education, Civil Action No. C-70-37 (N.D. Cal. 1970).

Doll, E.A. (1941). The essentials of an inclusive concept of mental deficiency. *American Journal of Mental Deficiency, 46,* 214–219.

Fishbach, M., & Hull, J.T. (1982). Mental retardation in the province of Manitoba. *Canada's Mental Health, 30,* 16–19.

Forness, S.R. (1985). Effects of public policy at the state level: California's impact on MR, LD, and ED categories. *Remedial and Special Education, 6*(3), 36–43.

Frost, J.B. (1977). Prevalence of mental handicap in the west of Ireland. *Irish Medical Journal, 70,* 263–265.

Granat, K., & Granat, S. (1973). Below-average intelligence and mental retardation. *American Journal of Mental Deficiency, 78,* 27–34.

Grossman, H.J. (Ed.). (1973). *Manual on terminology and classification in mental retardation.* Special Publication Series No. 2. Washington, DC: American Association on Mental Deficiency.

Grossman, H.J. (Ed.). (1973). *Manual on terminology and classification* (rev. ed.). Washington, DC : American Association on Mental Deficiency.

Grossman, H.J. (Ed.). (1983). *Classification in mental retardation* (3rd rev.). Washington, DC: American Association on Mental Deficiency.

Halpern, A. (1968). A note on Clausen's call for a psychometric definition of mental deficiency. *American Journal of Mental Deficiency, 72,* 948–949.

Heber, R. (1959). A manual on terminology and classification in mental retardation. *American Journal of Mental Deficiency, 56,* Monograph Supplement (Rev.).

Heber, R. (1961). Modifications in the manual on terminology and classification in mental retardation. *American Journal of Mental Deficiency, 65,* 499–500.

Heller, K.A., Holtzman, W.H., & Messick, S. (Eds.). (1982). *Placing children in special education.* Washington, DC: National Academy Press.

Hobbs, N. (Ed.). (1975a). *Issues in the classification of children, Vol. 1.* San Francisco: Jossey-Bass.

Hobbs, N. (Ed.). (1975b). *Issues in the classification of children, Vol. 2.* San Francisco: Jossey-Bass.

Johnson, D.J. (1988). Review of research on specific reading, writing, and mathematics disorders. In J.F. Kavanagh & T.J. Truss, Jr. (Eds.), *Learning disabilities: Proceedings of the national conference* (pp. 79–163). Parkton, MD: York Press.

Kaufman, A.S., & Doppelt, J.E. (1976). Analysis of WISC-R standardization data in terms of the stratification variables. *Child Development, 47,* 165–171.

Kavale, K.A., & Forness, S.R. (1985). *The science of learning disabilities.* San Diego, CA: College-Hill Press.

Kavanagh, J.F., & Truss, T.J., Jr. (Eds.). (1988). *Learning disabilities: Proceedings of the national conference.* Parkton, MD: York Press.

Keogh, B.K., & MacMillan, D.L. (1983). The logic of sample selection: Who represents what? *Exceptional Education Quarterly, 4,* 136–153.

Keogh, B.K., Major, S.M., Reid, H.P., Omori, H., & Gandara, P. (1980). Proposed markers in learning disabilities research. *Journal of Abnormal Child Psychology, 8*(1), 21–31.

Larry P. v. Riles. Civil Action No. 71-2270 (N.D. Cal. 1971). 495 F. Supp. 926 (N.D. Cal. 1979); Decision on Merits, United States Court of Appeals, Ninth Circuit, No. 80-427, January 23, 1984, Trial Court Decision Affirmed.

Lyon, G.R., & Watson, B.L. (1981). Empirically derived subgroups of learning disabled readers: Diagnostic characteristics. *Journal of Learning Disabilities, 14,* 256–261.

Mackie, R. (1969). *Special education in the United States: Statistics 1948–1966.* New York: Teachers College Press.

MacMillan, D.L. (1982). *Mental retardation in school and society* (2nd ed.). Boston: Little, Brown.

MacMillan, D.L. (1988). Issues in mild mental retardation. *Education and Training in Mental Retardation, 23,* 273–284.

MacMillan, D.L. (1989). Equality, excellence, and the EMR populations: 1970–1989. *Psychology in Mental Retardation and Developmental Disabilities, 15*(2), 1, 3–10.

MacMillan, D.L., & Balow, I.H. (1991). Impact of Larry P. on educational programs and assessment practices in California. *Diagnostique, 17,* 57–69.

MacMillan, D.L., & Jones, R.L. (1972). Lions in search of more Christians. *The Journal of Special Education, 6,* 81–91.

MacMillan, D.L., Meyers, C.E., & Morrison, G.M. (1980). System-identification of mildly mentally retarded children: Implications for interpreting and conducting research. *American Journal of Mental Deficiency, 85,* 108–115.

Marshall et al. v. Georgia. U.S. District Court for the Southern District of Georgia, CV482-233, June 28, 1984; Affirmed (11th Cir. No. 80-8771), October 29, 1985.

McKinney, J.D., & Fisher, L. (1982, April). *The search for subtypes of specific learning disabilities.* Paper read at the Gatlinburg Conference on Research in Mental Retardation/Developmental Disabilities, Gatlinburg, TN.

McLaren, J., & Bryson, S.E. (1987). Review of recent epidemiological studies of mental retardation: Prevalence, associated disorders, and etiology. *American Journal of Mental Retardation, 92,* 243–254.

Mercer, C.D., Hughes, C., & Mercer, A.R. (1985). Learning disabilities definitions used by state education departments. *Learning Disabilities Quarterly, 8,* 45–55.

Mercer, C.D., King-Sears, P., & Mercer, A. (1990). Learning disabilities definitions and criteria used by state education departments. *Learning Disabilities Quarterly, 13,* 141–152.

Mercer, J.R. (1973). *Labeling the mentally retarded.* Berkeley: University of California Press.

Morrison, G.M., MacMillan, D.L., & Kavale, K.A. (1985). System identification of learning disabled children: Implications for research sampling. *Learning Disabilities Quarterly, 8,* 1–10.

National Advisory Committee on Handicapped Children. (1968). *Special education for handicapped children: First annual report.* Washington, DC: U.S. Department of Health, Education and Welfare.

National Joint Committee on Learning Disabilities. (1981). A new definition of learning disabilities. *Learning Disabilities Quarterly, 4,* 336–342.

Office of Special Education Programs, U.S. Department of Education. (1989). *Eleventh annual report to Congress on the implementation of The Education of the Handicapped Act.* Washington, DC: U.S. Department of Education.

Ortiz, A., & Yates, J.R. (1983). Incidence of exceptionality among Hispanics: Implications for manpower planning. *National Association of Bilingual Education Journal, 7*(3), 41–53.

PASE (Parents in Action on Special Education) v. Joseph P. Hannon, U.S. District Court, Northern District of Illinois, Eastern Division, No. 74 (3586), July, 1980.

Polloway, E.A., & Smith, J.D. (1988). Current status of the mild mental retardation construct: Identification, placement, and programs. In M.C. Wang, M.C. Reynolds, & H.J. Walberg (Eds.), *Handbook of special education: Research and practice* (Vol II, pp. 7–22). Oxford, England: Pergamon Press.

Reschly, D.J. (1988a). Introduction. In M.C. Wang, M.C. Reynolds, & H.J. Walberg (Eds.), *Handbook of special education: Research and practice* (Vol. 2, pp. 3–5). Oxford, England: Pergamon Press.

Reschly, D.J. (1988b). Minority mild mental retardation: Legal issues, research findings, and reform trends. In M.C. Wang, M.C. Reynolds, & H.J. Walberg (Eds.), *Handbook of special education: Research and practice* (Vol. 2, pp. 23–41). Oxford, England: Pergamon Press.

Reschly, D.J. (1992). Mental retardation: Conceptual foundation, definitional criteria, and diagnostic operations. In S.R. Hooper, G.W. Hynd, & R.E. Mattison (Eds.), *Developmental disorders: Diagnostic criteria and clinical assessment* (pp. 23–67). Hillsdale, NJ: Lawrence Erlbaum Associates.

Reschly, D.J., Kicklighter, R.H., & McKee, P. (1988a). Recent placement litigation, Part I: Regular education grouping: Comparison of *Marshall* (1984, 1985) and *Hobson* (1967, 1969). *School Psychology Review, 17,* 7–19.

Reschly, D.J., Kicklighter, R.H., & McKee, P. (1988b). Recent placement litigation: Part II: Minority EMR overrepresentation: Comparison of *Larry P.* (1979, 1984, 1986) with *Marshall* (1984, 1985) and *S-1* (1986). *School Psychology Review, 17,* 20–36.

Reschly, D.J., Kicklighter, R.H., & McKee, P. (1988c). Recent placement litigation, Part III: Analysis of differences in *Larry P., Marshall,* and *S-1* and implications for future practices. *School Psychology Review, 17,* 37–48.

Richardson, S.A., Katz, M., & Koller, H. (1986). Sex differences in number of children administratively classified as mildly mentally retarded. An epidemiological review. *American Journal of Mental Deficiency, 91,* 250–256.

Shepherd, M.J. (1988). Discussion. In J.F. Kavanagh & T.J. Truss, Jr. (Eds.), *Learning disabilities: Proceedings of the national conference* (pp. 164–167). Parkton, MD: York Press.

Singer, J.D., & Butler, J.A. (1987). The Education for All Handicapped Children Act: Schools as agents of social regard. *Harvard Educational Review, 57*(2), 125–152.

Skinner, H.A. (1981). Toward the integration of classification theory and methods. *Journal of Abnormal Psychology, 90,* 68–87.

S-1 v. Turlington, preliminary injunction, U.S. District Court, Southern District of Florida, Case No. 79-8020-Div-CA WPB, June 15, 1979; Affirmed United States Court of Appeals, 5th Circuit, January 26, 1981, 635 F. 2nd 342 (1981); Trial on Merits, May 19–June 4, 1986; Order on Motion to Dismiss, No. 79-9020-Civ-Atkins, U.S. District Court, Southern District of Florida, October 9, 1986.

Strauss, A.A., & Kephart, N.C. (1955). *Psychopathology and education of the brain-injured child, Vol. 2.* New York: Grune & Stratton.

Strauss, A., & Lehtinen, L. (1947). *Psychopathology and education of the brain-injured child.* New York: Grune & Stratton.

Torgeson, J.K. (1982). The use of rationally defined subgroups in research on learning disabilities. In J.P. Das, R.F. Mulcahy, & A.E. Wall (Eds.), *Theory and research in learning disabilities* (pp. 111–132). New York: Plenum.

Tucker, J.A. (1980). Ethnic proportions in classes for the learning disabled: Issues in nonbiased assessment. *Journal of Special Education, 14,* 93–105.

Weiderholt, J.L. (1974). Historical perspectives on the education of the learning disabled. In L. Mann & D. Sabatino (Eds.), *The second review of special education* (pp. 103–152). Philadelphia: JSE Press.

Weller, C., & Strawser, S. (1987). Adaptive behavior of subtypes of learning disabled individuals. *Journal of Special Education, 21,* 101–116.

Wepman, J.M., Cruickshank, W.M., Deutsch, C.P., Morency, A., & Strother, C.R. (1975). Learning disabilities. In N. Hobbs (Ed.), *Issues in the classification of children* (Vol. 1, pp. 300–317). San Francisco: Jossey-Bass.

Zigler, E. (1967). Familial mental retardation: A continuing dilemma. *Science, 155,* 292–298.

Zigler, E., Balla, D., & Hodapp, R. (1984). On the definition and classification of mental retardation. *American Journal of Mental Deficiency, 89,* 215–230.

Zigler, E., & Hodapp, R.M. (1986). *Understanding mental retardation.* New York: Cambridge University Press.

8

VARIATIONS ON THEORY IN LEARNING DISABILITIES

Joseph K. Torgesen

One point on which almost everyone can agree concerning learning disabilities is that it is a concept surrounded by ambiguity. Thus, it is important at the beginning of a discussion of theories in this area to clarify the range of possible content that such theories might address. What should a theory of learning disabilities be about? As I show later, this question really has a variety of legitimate answers. However, within this chapter, I focus on only one kind of theory—causal—while recognizing the importance of multiple theoretical approaches to this field.

In the remainder of the chapter, I first suggest a number of points that causal theories of learning disabilities need to address, and then outline the two currently best developed theories of learning disabilities, showing how each of them either addresses or fails to address, the critical aspects of learning disabilities theory. I conclude with a comparison of the two theories in terms of their relative strengths and weaknesses. Part of this discussion addresses the role of general intelligence as it relates to the concept of learning disabilities (see also Stanovich, chap. 13, this volume).

As a first step in narrowing the focus of the chapter, I take as a starting point the definition of learning disabilities offered recently by the National Joint Committee on Learning Disabilities (NJCLD). This definition appears to enjoy a broad current consensus in the field (Hammill, 1990). The definition states:

> Learning disabilities is a general term that refers to a heterogeneous group of disorders manifested by significant difficulties in the acquisition and use of listening, speaking, reading, writing, reasoning, or mathematical abilities. These disorders are intrinsic to the individual,

presumed to be due to central nervous system dysfunction, and may occur across the life span.

Problems in self-regulatory behaviors, social perception, and social interaction may exist with learning disabilities but do not by themselves constitute a learning disability.

Although learning disabilities may occur concomitantly with other handicapping conditions (for example, sensory impairment, mental retardation, serious emotional disturbance) or with extrinsic influences (such as cultural differences, insufficient or inappropriate instruction), they are not the result of those conditions or influences. (NJCLD, 1988, p. 1)

The important elements of this definition, for present purposes, are: 1) recognition that the term *learning disabilities* refers to more than a single type of learning disorder, 2) the assumptions that these learning disorders are intrinsic to the individual and the result of central nervous system (CNS) dysfunction, and 3) the assertion that they are different from those disorders caused by pervasive or general mental deficiency. These elements direct our attention to learning disabilities that are specific, or limited, in their impact on cognitive development and that are caused by differences in cognitive functioning that are intrinsic to the individual. Taken at face value, this definition suggests that theories of learning disabilities should attempt to understand the impact of specific disabilities in cognition on learning and development. Additionally, these theories should also establish links between specific information-processing limitations and patterns or loci of brain dysfunction.

LEARNING DISABILITIES
AS A SCIENCE AND SOCIAL MOVEMENT

The first point of confusion for theory development arises because the NJCLD definition has been used in at least two significantly different ways. First, it has helped to demarcate an area of research on special kinds of individual differences in learning and performance. Ideally, researchers in this field are entitled to limit systematically the scope of their inquiry and make very tight and consistent operational definitions to specify the population of interest. Following these basic principles of scientific procedure, the field might have a real hope of successfully describing and explaining the limited range of phenomena identified by the definition.

However, this definition has also stimulated the development of the field of learning disabilities in special education, which is more similar to a political/social movement than a field of scientific study (Torgesen, 1992; see also MacMilllan, chap. 7, this volume). This field started with a conceptualization of the child with learning disabilities similar to the one in the present definition and, through a persistent process of bold overstatement and political pressure, has created laws and processes that now identify 5% of all schoolchildren as having learning disabilities. It is unlikely that even exhaustive study of this school-identified 5% will result in coherent and useful theories of learning disabilities. It is a group defined by shifting political realities, local expediencies, and questionable psychometrics. Thus, if we are interested in explaining learning problems encompassed by the present definition, our theories should not depend on data taken from groups of school-identified children with learning disabilities. Additionally, we should never view data taken from samples of such school-identified children as an adequate test of the core assumptions about learning disabilities made in the definition.

For example, the concept of learning disabilities is not threatened by our inability to show that every school-identified child with learning disabilities has a specific processing disability resulting from neurological impairment. It is true, however, that if only a minuscule percentage of children being served in programs for children with learning disabilities actually fit the assumptions of the definition, this would create problems for the learning disabilities movement. As troublesome as these problems might be for learning disabilities as a political/social/educational movement, they only affect the scientific integrity of the concept to the extent that rhetoric from the learning disabilities movement has been borrowed by scientists to justify their research programs!

Given that school-identified children with learning disabilities do not provide a proper reference group for the validation of scientific theories about learning disabilities, they are, nevertheless, an appropriate subject for theories about the sociology and politics of learning disabilities. Theories that help us understand referral and evaluation processes, service delivery mechanisms, or labeling and stigmatizing effects might all be informed by studies of schoolidentified children with learning disabilities. Although these theories can contribute in important ways to the improvement of practices relevant to children with learning disabilities, they would not have a direct impact on our understanding of the basic concept described in the definition.

THEORIES ABOUT DEVELOPMENT
OF SECONDARY CHARACTERISTICS

Another way to approach the question of what theories of learning disabilities might be about is to make a distinction between primary and secondary characteristics of children with learning disabilities. Historically, most of our efforts have focused on causal theories that attempt to understand the development and effects of specific processing disabilities. This is understandable because it is these specific, and primary, cognitive limitations that are the core concept of the definition. However, we also know that early failure in school has, itself, profound effects on the child's continuing development (Stanovich, 1986; Torgesen, 1990b). That is, the early and consistent failure caused by a primary, or intrinsic, learning disorder frequently results in the development of secondary characteristics that further interfere with the child's ability to perform successfully in school, on the job, or in social situations (Kistner & Torgesen, 1987; Schumaker, Deshler, & Ellis, 1986). Although such characteristics as a limited knowledge base, low self-esteem, or a confused and inactive learning style might be secondary consequences of early reading failure, they could easily be primary causes of school dropout, delinquency, or even poor grades in middle school.

A conference was recently convened in which both the primary and secondary characteristics of children with learning disabilities were discussed extensively (Torgesen, 1990a). The proceedings of this conference suggested that effective intervention for children with severe learning disabilities may have its major impact on secondary characteristics, whereas the primary, and specific, disability is less affected. Findings from several long-term follow-up studies (Gottfredson, Finucci, & Child, 1982; Horn, O'Donnell, & Vitulano, 1983) have shown that children with learning disabilities who receive intensive intervention often make quite successful adjustments to adult life in spite of retaining obvious limitations in certain academic skills. In one study (Gottfredson et al., 1982), interviews with adults with learning disabilities showed that they ascribed their success to characteristics that are frequently impaired in children with learning disabilities, such as motivation, perseverance, and social skills.

Our present knowledge of the development of secondary characteristics in learning disabilities is at least as primitive as our knowledge of the primary causes of the learning difficulty. Preliminary work has begun on such topics as attributional styles (Licht, 1983), self-efficacy (Schunck, 1989), social behavior (McKinney, 1990), knowledge base deficits (Ceci & Baker, 1990), and schooling changes (Brown, Palincsar, & Purcell, 1986) that can help us understand the development of secondary characteristics in children with learning disabilities. However, the area is ripe for the development of systematic theories to guide further study. Such theories promise to be equally important to those focusing on primary characteristics in helping us to understand the development of children with learning disabilities.

Thus far, two general classes of phenomena that are appropriate for the development of theories about learning disabilities have been suggested. We certainly need better theories to help us understand the politics, sociology, and practices of learning disabilities as a social/educational movement. Our understanding of learning disabilities, particularly from a life span perspective, would also be dramatically enhanced by better theories about the development and effects of the secondary characteristics of these children. Although both of these areas are important candidates for scientific study, by far the largest amount of effort, both historically and presently, is going to the development of causal theories of learning disabilities. These theories attempt to describe and account for the development of intrinsic processing limitations that have their basis in some kind of CNS dysfunction. Development and evaluation of this type of theory is fundamental to the validation of the concept.

IMPORTANT ELEMENTS
OF LEARNING DISABILITIES THEORY

Any complete causal theory of learning disabilities must address at least four crucial points. My organization of these points is functional; they are described in the order in which they should probably be addressed in theory development.

The first requirement is a clear specification of the academic or behavioral outcome to be explained by the theory. The more specific and detailed this description, the more likely the next steps in theory development will proceed successfully. Such descriptions as "learning problems," "reading difficulties," "learning disability," or "math problems" are obviously inadequate as starting points for good causal theories of learning disabilities. Rather, if the theory is to explain difficulties acquiring reading or math skills, the description of the problem should take full advantage of all we know about the task in order to specify a coherent family of skill deficits to be explained (Brown & Campione,1986).

The next step in theory development should be the formulation of an information-processing model to identify the "intrinsic" processing limitations that underlie failure on the academic or developmental learning task. This model should be useful to further theory development because it would help to pinpoint the phenomena to be explained by deeper layers of theory involving brain–behavior relationships. That is, a specific academic difficulty might potentially be caused by several different factors. Having a well-validated conceptualization of the specific processing limitations responsible for the learning problem would provide substance and specificity to the behavior side of the brain–behavior link.

The information-processing model within a causal theory of learning disabilities must have explanatory power in two critical areas. First, and most obviously, it must explain in what specific ways the processing limitation or limitations on which it focuses can lead to problems in acquiring the academic or developmental skills identified in the first stage of theory development. Second, it must also show how these particular processing limitations exercise only a limited, or specific, effect on cognitive performance. Because, by definition, learning disabilities are not the result of pervasive, or general, learning problems, any processing limitation identified as a core disability must be shown to have a strictly limited impact on intellectual functioning. Ideally, the processing limitations used in theories of learning disabilities should be embedded within more general models of intellectual functioning so that their theoretical relationships to other types of processes can be adequately described (see Stanovich, chap. 13, this volume, for a detailed discussion of this issue).

The third element required in causal theories of learning disabilities is identification of the locus or pattern of brain abnormality that is responsible for the processing limitations described earlier. Much of the current excitement in the study of learning disabilities is being generated by the development of new technologies that will allow collection of better data relevant to theory development at this level.

Finally, a fully adequate causal theory of learning disabilities should address the etiology of the CNS dysfunction that is part of the theory. It is crucial to show that the dysfunction itself could not be caused by the learning failure it is used to explain. That is, in explaining specific kinds of reading disability by reference to CNS dysfunction, we must be sure that the failure to learn to read was not itself the cause of the apparent CNS abnormality (Coles, 1987).

In addition to covering these four specific points, a theory of learning disabilities in children should also have a developmental orientation. That is, the theory should explain the developmental course of the disability, including the way it is manifested at different ages, and its ultimate prognosis.

TWO CAUSAL THEORIES OF LEARNING DISABILITIES

The two most completely developed current causal theories of learning disabilities are the nonverbal learning disabilities syndrome, primarily described in the work of Byron Rourke (1989), and the theory of reading disabilities involving limitations in phonological processing. Space limitations do not allow an evaluation of the evidence on which these theories are based. However, the completeness of each theory is discussed in terms of the four points I have just outlined.

Theory of Nonverbal Learning Disabilities

Children with nonverbal learning disabilities (NLD) were originally identified from among heterogeneous groups of children with learning disabilities because of their particularly poor performance on mechanical arithmetic tasks (Rourke & Finlayson, 1978; Rourke, Young, & Flewelling, 1971). In a series of studies since 1973, Rourke and his colleagues have extended this description of these children's academic difficulties to include early difficulties with graphomotor skills, problems in reading comprehension, mathematical reasoning, and science tasks that involve problem solving and complex concept formation. Areas of academic strength in these children include word identification skills in reading, spelling, and verbatim memory for oral and written verbal material. Children with NLD have also been shown to have social/behavioral problems, including difficulties adapting to novel situations, low levels of social competence, and a high risk for development of internalized forms of psychopathology.

Rourke's theory does not identify specific processing deficits of children with NLD within an information-processing model of mechanical arithmetic. However, he does provide extensive discussion of these children's intrinsic cognitive limitations from a neuropsychological perspective. The theory describes how a core of primary processing difficulties involving tactile perception, visual–spatial organizational skills, complex psychomotor functions, and problems in overassimilation of novel events leads to a variety of higher level cognitive deficits. These deficits include problems in complex concept formation, reasoning, and problem solving, as well as difficulty with the pragmatics of oral language. The theory contains explicit links between these higher level cognitive deficits and many of the academic deficits experienced by children with NLD involving complex reasoning and problem solving. Rourke also provides explicit discussion of the ways that the cognitive limitations of children with NLD lead to their social/behavioral problems (Rourke, Young, & Leenaars, 1989).

It is clear in Rourke's model that several important areas of mental functioning are relatively undisturbed in children with NLD. At a primary neuropsychological level, these include auditory perception, simple motor behaviors, and rote memory abilities. At higher levels of development, these basic neuropsychological strengths produce relatively high levels of skill in phonological processing, receptive language, verbal knowledge and associations, and verbal output.

Rourke's theory concerning the neurological impairment of children with NLD focuses on disturbances of function within the right cerebral hemisphere. Specifically, he states that

> the necessary condition for the production of the NLD syndrome is the destruction or dysfunction of white matter that is required for intermodal integration. For example, a significant reduction of callosal fibers or any other neuropathological state that interferes substantially with "access" to right hemispheral systems (and thus, to those systems that are necessary for intermodal integration) would be expected to eventuate in the NLD syndrome. (Rourke, 1988, p. 312)

Further theoretical elaboration indicates that the particular manifestations of the NLD syndrome present within a specific individual depend both on the total amount of white matter that is affected and on the location and stage of development at which the white matter is lesioned, removed, or rendered dysfunctional.

Rourke views the NLD syndrome as the "final common pathway" for a variety of conditions that produce white matter disease or dysfunction (Rourke, 1987). Symptoms of NLD are associated with conditions that produce shearing, removal, or absence of white matter from the right hemisphere. Examples of such conditions include head injury involving shearing of white matter, hydrocephaly, treatment of acute lymphocytic leukemia with large doses of x-ray irradiation over a long period of time, congenital absence of the corpus callosum, or significant tissue removal from the right cerebral hemisphere. Other etiologies for the white matter dysfunction underlying the NLD syndrome include teratogenic effects between conception and birth and extremely low birth weight itself. Any condition that leads to shearing or destruction of white matter, or low levels of myelination in these fibers, is a potential cause of NLD in young children. There is no evidence, or theoretical speculation, at present about a genetic mechanism for the transmission of NLD, except to say that specific diseases that produce white matter dysfunction may be genetically determined (B. P. Rourke, personal communication, September 19, 1990).

Strengths of the Theory As currently conceptualized, the theory of NLD has a number of significant strengths. It is embedded within a comprehensive model of brain–behavior relationships that has a strong developmental emphasis and that provides a clear rationale for both intellectual strengths and weaknesses. The goals and the scope of the theory are grand. In Rourke's words, "the clear aim was to develop and refine a comprehensive theoretical model of brain–behavior relationships that would be capable of encompassing the life-span developmental/adaptive dimensions of learning abilities and disabilities in all of their complex manifestations" (Rourke, 1988, p. 327).

Another strength of the theory is its focus on both the intellectual and social development of children with NLD. The theory contains extensive analyses of ways in which the primary cognitive limitations of the syndrome alter the normal developmental sequence. Although it is a causal theory of learning disabilities, Rourke's model contains careful elaborations of the ways that secondary characteristics develop from the primary disabilities. In particular, the model contains explicit mechanisms by which cognitive limitations can lead to serious social/behavioral problems in children with NLD.

Weaknesses of the Theory A major weakness of the theory at present is the failure to clearly elaborate the ways that the cognitive limitations of children with NLD produce the primary academic symptom, difficulties with mechanical arithmetic tasks. A potentially fruitful area of investigation with these children would be development of a more complete information-processing model of their arithmetic difficulties. This model would not only help to refine our understanding of their specific difficulties in acquiring arithmetic skills, but might also help to clarify or validate descriptions of their underlying cognitive limitations. Clearly, such a model is necessary if tight theoretical links are to be established between the academic performance problem and the intrinsic intellectual disabilities of children with NLD.

Phonological Theory of Reading Disabilities

This theory of a specific form of learning disabilities derives centrally from the work of Isabelle Liberman and her colleagues at Haskins Laboratories (Bradey & Shankweiler, 1991; Shankweiler & Liberman, 1989), although numerous contributors have made, and continue to make, important contributions to its development (see Bradley & Bryant, 1985; Lundberg, Frost, & Peterson, 1988; Morais, Alegria, & Content, 1987; Perfetti, 1985; Stanovich, 1988; Vellutino & Scanlon, 1987; Wagner & Torgesen, 1987; see also Stanovich, chap. 10, this volume). The central academic problem for children with phonological reading disabilities (PRD) involves difficulties acquiring fluent word identification skills in reading. In particular, these children have great difficulty learning to apply the "alphabetic principle" to take advantage of grapheme–phoneme correspondences in reading unfamiliar words. They are often unable to attain fully alphabetic (Frith, 1985) reading skills. Through consistent practice, they can frequently acquire a useful vocabulary of familiar words they recognize as wholes, but their speed of reading for these words usually remains impaired. In contrast with their difficulties in the acquisition of word reading skills, children with PRD often have average to high levels of general intelligence and are relatively unaffected in ability to learn mathematics and other academic content.

In attempting to explain reading difficulties of the sort outlined above, Liberman and associates began by asking the question, "What is required of the child in reading a language but not in speaking or listening to it?" (Liberman, Shankweiler, & Liberman, 1989, p. 4). Their answer was that the child must master the alphabetic principle:

> This entails an awareness of the internal phonological structure of words of the language, an awareness that must be more explicit than is ever demanded in the ordinary course of listening and responding to speech. If this is so, it should follow that beginning learners with a weakness in phonological awareness would be at risk. (p. 5)

Research following this general hypothesis has indeed found that many children who experience difficulties in early stages of reading acquisition are delayed in the development of phonological awareness. Other lines of research have also shown that children with PRD have subtle difficulties in speech perception, speech production, and naming. Furthermore, these children also frequently show difficulties in short-term memory tasks involving verbal materials. Although there are unresolved questions about whether these processing difficulties actually derive from a common source (Wagner & Torgesen, 1987), they are generally regarded as symptomatic of a general, and intrinsic, disability in processing the phonological structures of language.

There are very close theoretical ties between phonological processing disabilities and early reading failure (Liberman et al., 1989). In fact, each aspect of phonological processing difficulty identified as part of the general syndrome has a plausible causal role leading to word reading difficulties. In suggesting that processing difficulties are limited to the phonological structures of language, the theory also allows for broad areas of normal intellectual development. For example, the theory suggests that ability to process the semantic aspects of language is unaffected. In addition, all information processing of nonverbal stimuli should be relatively normal in children with PRD.

The Haskins group attributes the information-processing difficulties associated with PRD to isolated difficulties in one aspect of the uniquely human language capabilities. This type of processing skill is usually located in the left temporal region of the brain (Damasio & Geschwind, 1984). Thus, the locus of brain dysfunction responsible for PRD is placed in this region. At least one theoretical strand (Galaburda, 1988) suggests that the particular anomalies in this area of the brain that are most closely associated with PRD arise very early in development, and thus could not be the result, rather than the cause, of reading problems. In contrast to NLD, the brain dysfunction of children with PRD is localized to gray, rather than white, matter.

The primary etiological factor for the kinds of brain anomalies associated with PRD is thought to be genetic transmission. There is good evidence that phonological processing ability is highly heritable (Olsen, Wise, Conners, Rack, & Fulker, 1989).

Strengths of the Theory   At present, a major strength of the theory of PRD is the close links it has forged between intrinsic limitations in phonological processing ability and early word reading problems. Already, this information-processing analysis of early reading tasks has suggested intervention procedures that are effective in both a preventive (Bradley & Bryant, 1985; Lundberg, Frost, & Peterson, 1988) and a remedial (Alexander, Anderson, Voeller, & Torgesen, 1990) role. That is, explicit training in phonological awareness can help to reduce the number of children who show reading problems in the early grades, and it can also help children with severe reading disabilities learn to read words more effectively.

Weaknesses of the Theory   A major weakness of the theory is that it has only recently begun to acquire a developmental perspective. Very little is known about the course of development of phonological processing problems. For example, although such problems may be relatively widespread in young children with reading difficulties, it is possible that a much smaller proportion of older children retain significant problems in this area (Torgesen, 1991). Possible changes in symptoms with development is also an area in need of further study and theoretical elaboration. For example, delays in development of phonological awareness may be the most noticeable symptom of PRD in very young children. As children grow older, other kinds of phonological processing disabilities, such as naming or short-term memory problems, may be more characteristic of the syndrome.

THE THEORIES CONSIDERED TOGETHER

Both of these important theories address all the points of concern for complete causal theories of learning disabilities. They identify specific academic difficulties in their populations of interest, and they contain explanations for these difficulties in terms of intrinsic cognitive limitations. Furthermore, they propose specific mechanisms of CNS dysfunction to explain the cognitive deficits, and both offer hypotheses about a range of possible etiologies for these neural pathologies. Of course, the same could be said for a variety of other theories of learning disabilities that are no longer accepted as plausible.

Undoubtedly, various aspects of these theories will be modified by subsequent research findings. However, what separates these theories from earlier ones is the broad range of data that they encompass. Both of the theories are the product of extensive empirical research that has employed more sophisticated methodologies than were available to pioneering theorists in the field. Both also are embedded within more fully developed scientific paradigms than have been available until recently (Torgesen, 1986).

The relative strengths of each theory reflect the predominant paradigm within which each was developed. Most of the research supporting the development of NLD theory has been conducted within the neuropsychological paradigm. As a consequence, the theory is relatively strong and complex in its conceptualization of the brain–behavior relationships that produce the disorder. The theory itself is embedded within a more complete neuropsychological framework than is the theory about phonologically based reading disabilities.

In contrast, most of the research on PRD has utilized methods and concepts from information-processing psychology. Thus, it is relatively rich in its analysis of the academic tasks on which failure occurs, and the links between intrinsic cognitive deficits and academic failure are relatively more explicit than in NLD theory. With the explosion of information-processing research on reading within the past 20 years, the theory of PRD has been able to draw on an increasingly coherent body of psychological theory to support its explanation for a specific type of reading disability.

Although basic differences in assumptions, concepts, and methods frequently make it difficult for researchers operating within different paradigms to communicate with one another, learning disabilities theory is clearly a place where such communication is vital to the success of the enterprise. The NLD theory can clearly profit from more attention to information-processing analysis of academic and cognitive tasks, and the theory of PRD can benefit from more complete utilization of developmental neuropsychological concepts in its formulation.

One problem for which NLD theory may have a clearer solution at present than PRD theory involves the question of intellectual strengths in children with learning disabilities. The theory of NLD is much more explicit about which particular intellectual strengths are associated with the syndrome than is the PRD theory. The NLD theory has conceptualized the entire range of intellectual strengths and weaknesses that are part of the syndrome within a coherent neuropsychological framework. In contrast, PRD theory has been much more explicit about cognitive weaknesses than cognitive strengths associated with the syndrome. Descriptions of children with PRD rely essentially on statements about "IQ in the average range" to document that the children have a reading disability that is not caused by general mental retardation. As Stanovich (1989) has documented, the concept of general intelligence is fundamentally inadequate as a benchmark of the intellectual strengths of children with learning disabilities.

Issues in Using IQ as a Benchmark for Cognitive Strengths

The problem with remaining vague about descriptions of intellectual strengths in children with PRD is that it makes it very difficult to determine if these children are actually different in important ways from children whose reading problems are consistent with their level of general intelligence. Clearly, the specificity of reading disorders varies along a continuum (see Stanovich, chap. 13, this volume). At one end of the continuum, we may have children with phonological disabilities who also have broad mental deficiencies. In the middle, we might have children with phonological problems in the context of broadly deficient verbal skills but nonverbal abilities in the average range. At the other end of the continuum, we might have children with difficulties in phonological processing, but whose other verbal and nonverbal abilities are not affected. It is this continuum that creates problems when we try to test the important assumption that children with PRD can profit from different kinds of educational interventions than those helpful to children with more pervasive cognitive limitations.

Assume, for the moment, that the reading problems of children with both specific and general learning problems are caused by their difficulties in processing phonological information (Siegel, 1989). Whether one finds the groups to be meaningfully different in an educational sense will depend on at least two factors. First, it will depend on the range of learning tasks one studies. If one examines only the way in which single word decoding skills are learned, the groups may not appear importantly different from one another. They are both deficient on the essential abilities required for this task. However, if one also examines a broader range of learning tasks (acquiring vocabulary, learning comprehension strategies, assimilating background knowledge) that are also important to reading as a whole, differences between groups may more easily emerge. The differences identified in this broader search of learning tasks may be very important for instruction because they may be helpful in identifying ways for children to compensate for their basic processing difficulties (Torgesen, Dahlem, & Greenstein, 1987).

The second factor that is crucial in determining functional learning differences between PRD and "garden-variety" poor readers involves the specific intellectual strengths of the PRD group. If, as is sometimes the case, this group is defined by the fact that performance IQ is in the average range (with verbal IQ being allowed to vary across a broader continuum), one might not predict any meaningful academic differences between children with PRD and the "garden-variety" group. This is because performance IQ does not correlate highly with academic achievement. The strengths it identifies are not those that typically aid children to learn better on most school tasks (see Stanovich, chap. 13, this volume, for a detailed discussion of this issue).

This latter example illustrates that, in formulating a theory of learning disabilities, we must pay as much attention to specific intellectual strengths as to weaknesses. If the subgroup defined by our theory is shown not to be meaningfully different in functional learning abilities than more broadly impaired groups, it might be because we are not studying children with the right strengths. If the strengths of children with learning disabilities are defined too narrowly, or are irrelevant to school success, these children will not appear different in many school settings from children with general mental deficiencies. Any complete conceptualization of learning disabilities must include both clear identification of the cognitive deficits of these children and a clear specification of the strengths that make them meaningfully different from children with other types of learning problems.

Prevalence of These Subgroups

A final point of interest and concern to both theories is the extent to which they describe problems that are characteristic of significant numbers of children in school. At present, the safest assumption about the problems described in each theory is that they are continuously distributed in a multidimensional space (Stanovich, 1988; see also chap. 13, this volume). Thus, answers to questions about incidence will depend completely on the degree of severity, or specificity, with which we are concerned. However, as a point of departure, it seems probable that children who are clearly described by each theory are relatively rare in populations of school-identified children with learning disabilities. For example, my own research (Torgesen, 1988) suggests that, among children in the middle elementary grades, only about 15% continue to show severe problems with representation of phonological information in short-term memory. Two relatively large-scale classification studies found that about 15% of samples of children with learning disabilities had highly specific problems in phonological representation, and another 15% had similar problems associated with broader intellectual impairment (Lyon & Watson, 1981; Speece, 1987).

Byron Rourke (personal communication, September 19, 1990) has indicated informally that, for every 20 children with PRD referred to his clinic, he sees one child with NLD. Although this makes these problems very rare indeed, Rourke also indicated that this incidence rate has doubled in the last 20 years. He ascribed the change in rate to increased survival of children with a variety of problems associated with white matter disease and injury.

Although both of these incidence estimates are extremely preliminary, they do suggest that learning disabilities of the kind described in the NJCLD definition may be rarer than is commonly estimated. It seems clear that both scientific integrity and advancement of theory in this area will be served by careful discipline in our claims about the extent of these problems among children.

REFERENCES

Alexander, A., Anderson, H., Voeller, K.S., & Torgesen, J.K. (1990). *Phonological awareness training and remediation of analytic decoding deficits in a group of severe dyslexics.* Unpublished manuscript, University of Florida, Gainesville, and Florida State University, Tallahassee.

Bradey, S., & Shankweiler, D. (1991). *Phonological processes in literacy: A tribute to Isabelle Y. Liberman.* Hillsdale, NJ: Lawrence Erlbaum Associates.

Bradley, L., & Bryant, P. (1985). *Rhyme and reason in reading and spelling.* Ann Arbor: University of Michigan Press.

Brown, A.L., & Campione, J.C. (1986). Psychological theory and the study of learning disabilities. *American Psychologist, 14,* 1059–1068.

Brown, A.L., Palincsar, A. S., & Purcell, L. (1986). Poor readers: Teach, don't label. In U. Neisser (Ed.), *The school achievement of minority children: New perspectives* (pp. 105–143). Hillsdale, NJ: Lawrence Erlbaum Associates.

Ceci, S.J., & Baker, J.G. (1990). On learning . . . more or less: A knowledge × process × context view of learning disabilities. In J.K. Torgesen (Ed.), *Cognitive and behavioral characteristics of children with learning disabilities.* Austin, TX: PRO-ED.

Coles, G.S. (1987). *The learning mystique: A critical look at "learning disabilities."* New York: Pantheon.

Damasio, A.R., & Geschwind, N. (1984). The neural basis of language. *Annual Review of Neurosciences, 7,* 127–147.

Frith, U. (1985). Beneath the surface of developmental dyslexia. In K. Patterson, J. Marshall, & M. Coltheart (Eds.), *Surface dyslexia* (pp. 301–330). London: Lawrence Erlbaum Associates.

Galaburda, A.M. (1988). The pathogenesis of childhood dyslexia. In F. Plum (Ed.), *Language, communication, and the brain* (pp. 127–137). New York: Raven Press.

Gottfredson, L.S., Finucci, J.M., & Child, B. (1982). *The adult occupational success of dyslexic boys: A large-scale, long-term follow-up* (Report No. 334). Baltimore: The Center for Social Organization in the Schools, Johns Hopkins University.

Hammill, D.D. (1990). On defining learning disabilities: An emerging consensus. *Journal of Learning Disabilities, 23,* 74–84.

Horn, W.F., O'Donnell, J.P., & Vitulano, L.A. (1983). Long-term follow-up studies of learning disabled persons. *Journal of Learning Disabilities, 16,* 542–555.

Kistner, J., & Torgesen, J.K. (1987). Motivational and cognitive aspects of learning disabilities. In A.E. Kasdin & B.B. Lahey (Eds.), *Advances in clinical child psychology* (pp. 289–334). New York: Plenum Press.

Licht, B.G. (1983). Cognitive-motivational factors that contribute to the achievement of learning disabled children. *Journal of Learning Disabilities, 16,* 483–493.

Liberman, I.Y., Shankweiler, D., & Liberman, A. M. (1989). The alphabetic principle and learning to read. In D. Shankweiler & I.Y. Liberman (Eds.), *Phonology and reading disability: Solving the reading puzzle* (pp. 1–33). Ann Arbor: University of Michigan Press.

Lundberg, I., Frost, J., & Peterson, O. (1988). Effects of an extensive program for stimulating phonological awareness in pre-school children. *Reading Research Quarterly, 23,* 263–284.

Lyon, R., & Watson, B. (1981). Empirically derived subgroups of learning disabled readers: Diagnostic characteristics. *Journal of Learning Disabilities, 14,* 256–261.

McKinney, J.D. (1990). Longitudinal research on the behavioral characteristics of children with learning disabilities. In J. Torgesen (Ed.), *Cognitive and behavioral characteristics of children with learning disabilities* (pp. 115–138). Austin, TX: PRO-ED.

Morais, J., Alegria, J., & Content, A. (1987). The relationships between segmental analysis and alphabetic literacy: An interactive view. *Cahiers de Psychologie Cognitive, 7,* 414–438.

National Joint Committee on Learning Disabilities. (1988). Letter to NJCLD member organizations.

Olsen, R., Wise, B., Conners, F., Rack, J., & Fulker, D. (1989). Specific deficits in component reading and language skills: Genetic and environmental influences. *Journal of Learning Disabilities, 22,* 339–348.

Perfetti, C.A. (1985). *Reading ability.* New York: Oxford University Press.

Rourke, B.P. (1987). Syndrome of nonverbal learning disabilities: The final common pathway of white-matter disease/dysfunction? *The Clinical Neuropsychologist, 1,* 209–234.

Rourke, B.P. (1988). The syndrome of nonverbal learning disabilities: Developmental manifestations in neurological disease, disorder, and dysfunction. *The Clinical Neuropsychologist, 2,* 293–330.

Rourke, B.P. (1989). *Nonverbal learning disabilities: The syndrome and the model.* New York: Guilford Press.

Rourke, B.P., & Finlayson, M.A.J. (1978). Neuropsychological significance of variations in patterns of academic performance: Verbal and visual-spatial abilities. *Journal of Abnormal Child Psychology, 6,* 121–133.

Rourke, B.P., Young, G.C., & Flewelling, R.W. (1971). The relationships between WISC Verbal-Performance discrepancies and selected verbal, auditory-perceptual, and problem-solving abilities in children with learning disabilities. *Journal of Clinical Psychology, 27,* 475–479.

Rourke, B.P., Young, G.C., & Leenaars, A.A. (1989). A childhood learning disability that predisposes those afflicted to adolescent and adult depression and suicide risk. *Journal of Learning Disabilities, 22,* 169–175.

Schumaker, J.B., Deshler, D.D., & Ellis, E.S. (1986). Intervention issues related to the education of learning disabled adolescents. In J.K. Torgesen & B.Y.L. Wong (Eds.), *Psychological and educational perspectives on learning disabilities* (pp. 329–365). New York: Academic Press.

Schunk, D.H. (1989). Self-efficacy and cognitive achievement: Implications for students with learning problems. *Journal of Learning Disabilities, 22,* 14–22.

Shankweiler, D., & Liberman, I.Y. (1989). *Phonology and reading disability.* Ann Arbor: University of Michigan Press.

Siegel, L.S. (1989). IQ is irrelevant to the definition of learning disabilities. *Journal of Learning Disabilities, 22,* 469–479.

Speece, D.L. (1987). Information processing subtypes of learning disabled readers. *Learning Disabilities Research, 2,* 91–102.

Stanovich, K.E. (1986). Matthew effects in reading: Some consequences of individual differences in the acquisition of literacy. *Reading Research Quarterly, 21,* 360–406.

Stanovich, K.E. (1988). Explaining the differences between the dyslexic and the garden-variety poor reader: The phonological-core variable-difference model. *Journal of Learning Disabilities, 21,* 590–604.

Stanovich, K.E. (1989). *Discrepancy definitions of reading disability: Has intelligence led us astray?* Paper presented at the joint NICHD and IARLD Conference on Learning Disabilities, June, Ann Arbor, Michigan.

Torgesen, J.K. (1986). Learning disabilities theory: Its current state and future prospects. *Journal of Learning Disabilities, 19,* 399–407.

Torgesen, J.K. (1988). Studies of children with learning disabilities who perform poorly on memory span tasks. *Journal of Learning Disabilities, 21,* 605–612.

Torgesen, J.K. (Ed.). (1990a). *Cognitive and behavioral characteristics of children with learning disabilities.* Austin, TX: PRO-ED.

Torgesen, J.K. (1990b). Concluding comments. In J. Torgesen (Ed.), *Cognitive and behavioral characteristics of children with learning disabilities.* Austin, TX: PRO-ED.

Torgesen, J.K. (1991). Cross-age consistency in phonological processing. In S. Bradey & D. Shankweiler (Eds.), *Phonological processes in literacy* (pp. 187–194). Hillsdale, NJ: Lawrence Erlbaum Associates.

Torgesen, J.K. (1992). Learning disabilities: Historical and conceptual issues. In B.Y.L. Wong (Ed.). *Learning about learning disabilities* (pp. 3–38). San Diego: Academic Press.

Torgesen, J.K., Dahlem, W.E., & Greenstein, J. (1987). Using verbatim text recordings to enhance reading comprehension in learning disabled adolescents. *Learning Disabilities Focus, 3,* 30–38.

Vellutino, F., & Scanlon, D.M. (1987). Phonological coding, phonological awareness, and reading ability: Evidence from longitudinal and experimental study. *Merrill-Palmer Quarterly, 33,* 321–364.

Wagner, R.K., & Torgesen, J.K. (1987). The nature of phonological processing and its causal role in the acquisition of reading skills. *Psychological Bulletin, 101,* 192–212.

9

A SCIENCE AND THEORY OF LEARNING DISABILITIES

Kenneth A. Kavale

At first glance, this chapter's title may appear inappropriate, inconsequential, or perhaps a bit presumptuous, but the purpose is to argue that the lack of science and theory is a primary contributor to the almost perpetual state of chaos in learning disabilities. Many of the most basic problems in the learning disabilities field are intellectual and can only be resolved through greater attention to science and theory.

THE LEARNING DISABILITIES FIELD AND ITS PROBLEMS

No other area of special education is marked by so much controversy, conflict, and crisis (Haight, 1980). Although the learning disabilities field is an ongoing concern and has managed to become the largest category in special education, it cannot continue to be the dumping ground for all children who are experiencing learning problems (Gallagher, 1986; Kavale, 1988b). Although the service expansion in learning disabilities continues, the intellectual core of the field seems trapped. The learning disabilities field appears to be boxed in by several forces that have created conceptual tensions but permit expansion. The tensions are illustrated in Figure 1. One side of the box, advocacy, is composed of federal, state, and local policies that bear little resemblance to available knowledge or available notions about acceptable practice. The second side, ideology, is found in the many political and ideological squabbles that tend to characterize professional dialogue and relationships. The third side, policy, is found in the many advocacy groups who call for more services that will eventually strain resources, even under the best of circumstances. The fourth side, research, is found in the context of re-

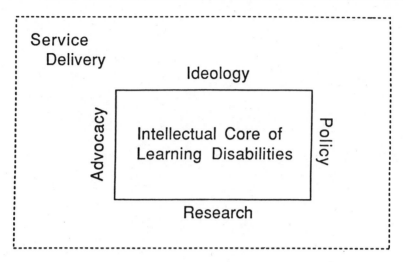

Figure 1. The intellectual trap of learning disabilities.

search in learning disabilities that has been, in effect, a limiting tradition not providing a solid core on which to build a science of learning disabilities.

It is at this fourth side that this chapter is directed. Almost any problem, be it definition, identification, prevalence, assessment, intervention, or policy, stems from the same source—a failure to provide a comprehensive and unified perspective about the nature of learning disabilities. Although it is easy to point out this limitation, its resolution is difficult and the obstacles real and formidable. Two problems will serve to illustrate the difficulties. The first is found in the fact that the learning disabilities phenomenon is probably even more complex than is realized currently. In a meta-analysis of more than 1,000 studies, Kavale and Nye (1985–86) attempted to determine if there was some area or areas where performance differences between groups with and without learning disabilities would be great enough to serve as the basis for more focused conceptualizations. A first aggregation of study results (see Figure 2) across four domains (linguistic, achievement, neuropsychological, social/ behavioral) found no differences, indicating that no domain could be singled out as a more important contributor. The next aggregation (see Table 1) was across 38 individual variables, but again no differences emerged and levels of differentiation were remarkably similar. Thus, no single variable could be identified as a primary source of learning disabilities. The conclusion was that learning disability is a complex and multivariate problem that may not be profound, but appears to be valid.

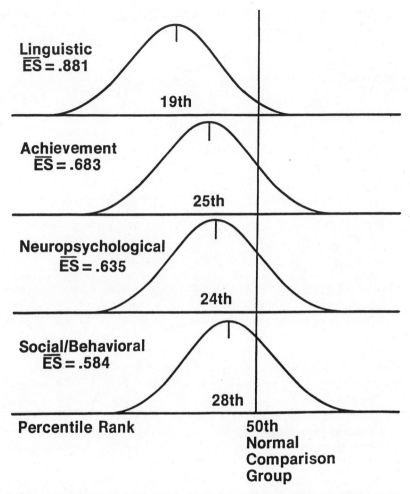

Percentile Rank

Linguistic
$\overline{ES} = .881$

19th

Achievement
$\overline{ES} = .683$

25th

Neuropsychological
$\overline{ES} = .635$

24th

Social/Behavioral
$\overline{ES} = .584$

28th

50th
Normal
Comparison
Group

Figure 2. Level of differentiation between groups with and without learning disabilities for four primary domains.

The second problem is found in the measurement problems associated with learning disabilities. The source of these problems is found in the fact that most learning disabilities measurement is not theory based (Kavale & Mundschenk, 1990). A theory represents the necessary link between operational measures and physical properties (Zebrowski, 1979). Although such association is commonplace in the physical sciences, it is not often attempted in learning disabilities. To demonstrate why this is the case and how complicated the associations may become, suppose that learning disabilities are measured through an assumed consequence such as underachieve-

Table 1. Average effect sizes for outcome categories in linguistic, achievement, neuropsychological, and social/behavioral domains

Domain	n	Mean	SE	%
Linguistic				
Semantic	37	.790	.153	79
Syntactic	32	.879	.099	81
Phonological	8	1.192	.481	88
Pragmatic	15	.824	.357	80
Achievement	9	1.143	.238	87
Achievement				
Reading achievement	46	.757	.096	78
Word attack	16	.597	.104	73
Reading comprehension	47	.714	.085	76
Word recognition	52	.736	.080	77
Reading rate	6	.332	.115	63
Math achievement	19	.607	.096	73
Computation	30	.503	.102	69
Reasoning	5	.280	.134	61
Spelling	38	.726	.202	77
Handwriting	9	.951	.186	83
Neuropsychological				
Intelligence (IQ)	71	.457	.055	68
Attention	37	.639	.111	74
Vigilance	10	.603	.120	73
Selective attention	4	.570	.215	72
Concentration	14	.718	.089	76
Cognitive style	9	.588	.087	72
Memory	60	.759	.092	78
Short term	31	.759	.079	78
Long term	18	.710	.101	76
Rehearsal strategies	11	.838	.128	80
Conceptual processes	44	.702	.129	76
Problem solving	17	.765	.169	76
Concept formation	24	.669	.099	75
Learning rate	3	.640	.178	74
Perceptual functioning	155	.677	.075	75
Visual perception	64	.675	.079	75
Auditory perception	40	.660	.081	75
Auditory-visual integration	19	.886	.147	81
Perceptual-motor	32	.576	.017	72
Neurophysiological	27	.530	.111	70
Social/behavioral				
Interpersonal behavior	52	.653	.086	74
Interpersonal perception	41	.604	.071	73
Intrapersonal perception	38	.535	.069	70

ment and a residual or error term that can be reduced by aggregating over a large sample (Figure 3). Unfortunately, there are other causes of underachievement including cognitive abilities, environ-

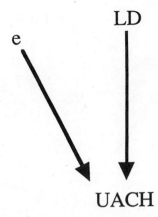

Figure 3. Simple model of underachievement (UACH) as an assumed consequence of learning disabilities (LD). (e, error term.)

ment, and schooling. However, these variables, in turn, do not operate in isolation and are intercorrelated with each other and learning disabilities, as illustrated in Figure 4. Further complication is found in antecedent variables such as neuropsychological functioning and history (i.e., genetics and cultural background). Soon the model looks like that shown in Figure 5, a far cry conceptually from the version in Figure 3.

The implications are clear. First, what may have started as a relatively straightforward problem of measuring a phenomenon in terms of its presumed effects is soon broadened into the difficult

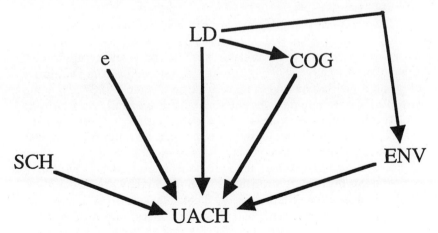

Figure 4. Model incorporating additional causes of underachievement (UACH)—schooling (SCH), cognitive abilities (COG), and environment (ENV)—and their intercorrelations with learning disabilities (LD). (e, error term.)

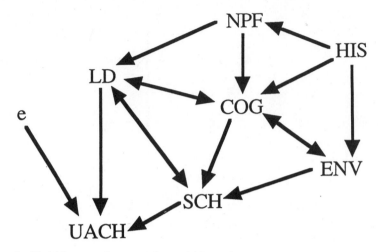

Figure 5. Model incorporating antecedent variables such as neuropsychological functioning (NPF) and history (HIS) into the measurement of learning disabilities (LD) by an assumed consequence: underachievement (UACH), which has other interrelated causes. (e, error term; COG, cognitive abilities; SCH, schooling; ENV, environment.)

theoretical problem of accounting for the complexly related causes of underachievement (Zeller & Carmines, 1980). Thus, theoretical and measurement issues are almost inextricably intertwined. Second, it is obvious that the measurement process may become highly technical and conceptual. It becomes much more than Stevens's (1951) classic definition of measurement as the assignment of numbers to objects or events according to rules. Measurement must also be seen as serving a theoretical function, with the goal being the clarification of basic concepts.

These complicating factors are compounded by the characteristics of learning disabilities researchers themselves. As a group, these researchers reveal differences in attitudes and temperament that introduce heterogeneity among them as well as the population of students with learning disabilities (see Grinnell, 1987). In a survey of attitudes among learning disabilities researchers, for example, there might be groups who assume either a "hard science" stance, a more phenomenological approach, or a more humanistic orientation. Other learning disabilities researchers view themselves primarily as critics whose task is to point out assets and liabilities.

The intellectual differences are complicated by the fact that the field of learning disabilities is lodged between a natural science (i.e., the study of students with learning disabilities) and a human science (i.e., a helping profession) (Winch, 1958). Within this context, the role of theory is subject to debate. The human science side of learning disabilities demands application in the form of methods and materials, and consequently theory is not seen as integral to that process. Because a majority of the learning disabilities field is concerned with applied problems (e.g., teaching students with learning disabilities), it is not difficult to understand why theory development is not viewed as a primary activity.

The human side of learning disabilities also questions the desirability of natural science models for the study of human behavior (Gibson, 1960; Lundberg, 1961). The absence of theory and laws about human behavior is considered to be the result of two obstacles: complexity of the subject matter, and social and moral impediments to experimentation on human subjects. These assumptions are based on the dubious premise that, as complexity and impediments to experimentation increase, the rate of progress in scientific understanding cannot increase (Scriven, 1956).

The subject matter of, for example, particle physics has increased in complexity over time and has become more difficult to deal with experimentally; yet, progress in systematically explaining the nature of matter has accelerated. Thus, to explain the failure of behavioral science by stating that increases in complexity and experimental difficulty have reduced the rate of theoretical progress requires that it be shown how perceived obstacles operate for human behavior but not elsewhere (Bunge, 1963). What is it about human behavior that logically or metaphysically exempts it from scientific study? What difference in kind is there between a child experiencing school failure and matter in motion that results in the impossibility of lawlike functioning? Appeals to complexity and experimental recalcitrance provide unsatisfactory explanations (Turner, 1976). They are false beliefs that are, unfortunately, central in learning disabilities thinking and highly ramified in their influence on research.

THE LIMITING TRADITION OF LOGICAL EMPIRICISM

The limiting tradition alluded to earlier surrounds the positivist approaches that have dominated most of the behavioral sciences in this century (Achinstein & Barker, 1969). Most research efforts in learning disabilities are cast in a logical empiricist format, and have produced fundamentally sound data without the metaphysical contamination so assiduously avoided (Hanfling, 1981). The problem is that, although data collection is adequate, there is difficulty in putting the data together in some coherent and unified form. The reason is that "theory" in a positivist sense does not possess a formal character that can be determined to be either true or false (Stegmuller, 1976). A theory is viewed primarily as a conceptual tool for arranging data (Carnap, 1969; Hempel, 1952). The nomological network (see Cronbach & Meehl, 1955) believed to be the theoretical underpinning of positivism is not satisfactory because it represents no more than a more formal and systematic redescription of the obtained data. Hence, data collected within a logical empiricist format tend to remain isolated, and theoretical development tends to remain limited (Toulmin & Leary, 1985).

The difficulty with the positivist position is that rigor in data collection is no guarantee of scientific knowledge. Alchemy, astrology, and phrenology, for example, placed a premium on controlled observation, measurement, and prediction, but all were recognized as exercises in charlatanism because they lacked any semblance of theoretical development (Andreski, 1972). Although it was claimed that theory was not essential, the lack of theory is best attributed to the fact that it was ultimately impossible to achieve. The strong positivist tradition in learning disabilities, with a deemphasis on theoretical development and emphasis on data collection, places the field philosophically closer to phrenology than physics (Weimer, 1979).

Even with theory development viewed as a secondary activity, some areas of learning disabilities do possess quite well-developed theoretical foundations. These areas include attention (Shaywitz & Shaywitz, 1988), memory (Brainerd, Kingsma, & Howe, 1986), reading (Stanovich, 1982a, 1982b), language (Wallach & Butler, 1984), phonological processing (Stanovich, 1988; Wagner, 1986), semantic knowledge (Kail & Leonard, 1986), information processing (Swanson, 1987), cognitive processes (Morrison & Manis, 1982), neurophysiological functioning (Cotman & Lynch, 1988; Martin, 1986), motivation (Licht & Kistner, 1986), social factors (Bryan & Bryan, 1990; Weiner, 1980), problem solving (Swanson, 1988a), general cognitive ability (IQ) (Wong, 1989), strategic behavior (Rabinowitz & Chi, 1986), neuropsychological functioning (Hynd, Obrzut, Hayes, & Becker, 1986), rule learning (Manis & Morrison, 1985), and metacognition (Wong, 1985). Additionally, Torgesen (1986) outlined the contributions from three paradigms for the study of learning disabilities: neuropsychological, information processing, and applied behavior analysis. The past has seen theories related to brain lateralization (Orton, 1937), minimal brain dysfunction (Strauss & Lehtinen, 1947), psycholinguistic deficits (Kirk & Kirk, 1971), perceptual-motor functioning (Kephart, 1960), sensory integration (Ayres, 1968), and neurological organization (Delacato, 1966).

THEORETICAL DILEMMAS IN LEARNING DISABILITIES

Although these theories differ with respect to their validity and verification, they all suffer from the same problem: They are undimensional conceptualizations that have incorporated only a narrow and circumscribed context for learning disabilities. Learning disability does not possess its own character as such. Rather, it is an assortment of correlative conditions that influence the phenomenon in varying degree, as illustrated in Figure 6.

Because all students with learning disabilities do not manifest, for example, attention deficits or memory problems, explanations must be appropriate for a range of possible behaviors in the sense of explaining how their difficulties relate to the phenomenon of learning disabilities (see Achinstein, 1983). In a Gestalt sense, learning disabilities is probably more than the sum of its parts, and it becomes necessary to possess a view of the whole phenomenon.

If it is agreed that the basic aims of theory are to explain and to predict (Toulmin, 1961), current theories of learning disabilities possess the basic flaw of not explaining a sufficient number of cases and probably predicting even fewer. The goal should be to explain learn-

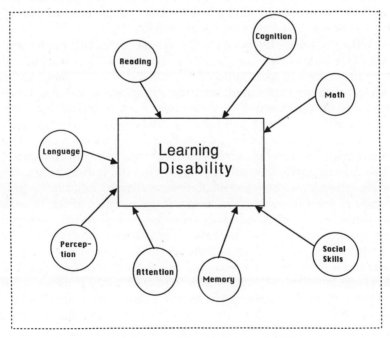

Figure 6. The state of theory in learning disabilities.

ing disabilities in general rather than learning disability in particular (see Coleman, 1986, for a discussion related to sociology). This generality requires macro-level theory wherein individual theoretical notions are combined into a larger superstructure encompassing the entire phenomenon (Stegmuller, 1976). These macro-level theories ultimately enhance explanation by permitting a greater degree of generality than that which is to be explained. Explanation consists of subsuming whatever is to be explained under higher order (i.e., inclusive and comprehensive) principles (Braithwaite, 1955). The implication is that theory should be looked on as a more general notion that comprises of two elements: 1) a population of models, and 2) hypotheses linking those models with systems in the real world (Giere, 1988). It is possible, for example, to speak about "the kinetic theory of gases" or "the theory of evolution," where reference is not to a single theory, but to a spectrum of individual notions falling under a general rubric. The "theory of evolution," for example, does not refer to any single notion; rather, it suggests a number of models for evolutionary change that are all based on the hypothesis that organic species possess common lines of descent (Brooks & Wiley, 1986). The learning disabilities field must take these larger theoretical structures seriously because it has been argued that general theories are the primary tool for both understanding and appraising scientific progress (Laudan, 1977).

Without larger theoretical units, it will be difficult to identify a single learning disabilities discipline (Barnes, 1977). Although the same phenomenon is presumably investigated, it is now studied with tremendous variation in attitudes, techniques, and judgmental standards that makes it difficult to observe commonality. For example, consider the divergence between those with a developmental view of learning disabilities and those who work within a behavioral framework. Research on social variables tends to be as narrowly focused as research on medical aspects. How do we best incorporate reading theory into learning disabilities research? What is the proper role of neuropsychological research in learning disabilities as compared and contrasted with information-processing research? How do we best resolve the role of intelligence in discussions of learning disabilities? How is research focused on schooling made compatible with efforts examining extraschool influences? Where does learning disabilities fit within the traditional spectrum of special education, especially with regard to mental retardation and behavior disorders? Where does the strong psychometric tradition in learning disabilities fit? Such questions are interrelated and demand answers within a framework of a larger structural unit. The learning disabilities phenomenon should not be seen as a series of discrete and isolated entities even though it has been more easily handled this way through historical tradition and conceptual parsimony (Toulmin, 1972).

All of this is to suggest that the learning disabilities field must focus its efforts on more generalized theories that promote understanding of learning disabilities in general, and demonstrate how previously independent and isolated aspects of learning disabilities can be coordinated into a larger framework. The micro-theories of learning disabilities must now be combined into a macro-level theory that is descriptive of learning disabilities in a comprehensive, ordered, and unified context (Collins & Pinch, 1982). A representation of the form of such theory is illustrated in Figure 7. This exercise seems critical if closure for the learning disabilities phenomenon is ever to be achieved.

Using the data presented earlier, one possibility can be illustrated. Because no single domain or area emerged as a primary source of learning disabilities, a heuristic representation of the relationships among factors contributing to learning disabilities was proposed and tested with path analysis (Wright, 1921). Two models were developed; the first includes the four primary domains and the second incorporates a number of individual variables. These models are presented in Figures 8 and 9, respectively. The idea is to represent a "weak causal ordering" among variables and paths that can be judged on the criterion of meaningfulness (Pedhazur, 1982). Almost all paths in both models are meaningful, which confirms the

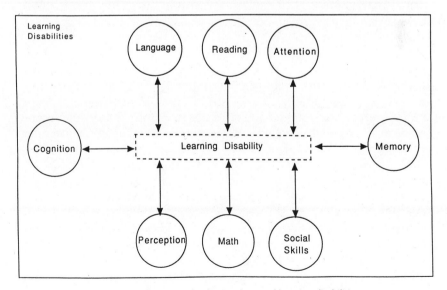

Figure 7. A coherent and cohesive theory of learning disabilities.

Model I

$R^2 = .513$

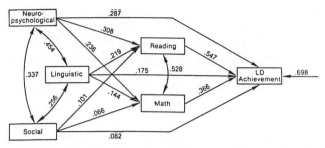

Figure 8. Model developed by path analysis of four primary domains of learning disabilities.

necessity of including all variables for a comprehensive description. Probably the most important point is that these two models do not exhaust the number of possible structural arrangements for depicting the relationships among learning disabilities variables. The development of such models is a conceptual process and, consequently, they are neither "right" nor "wrong," but only useful (Kenny, 1979).

KNOWLEDGE ACCUMULATION AND LEARNING DISABILITIES

The development of heuristic representations of the relations among variables contributing to learning disabilities is contingent on how

Model II

$R^2 = .592$

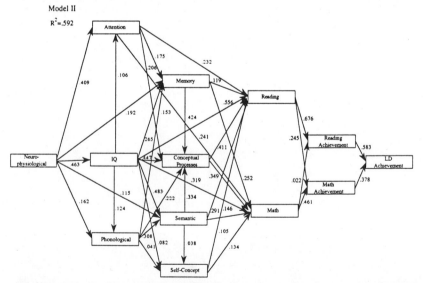

Figure 9. Model developed by path analysis of several individual variables of learning disabilities.

well knowledge has been accumulated. The accumulation of knowledge is essential because the outcomes provide the building blocks for theoretical development and significant breakthroughs in understanding (Kuhn, 1970). The learning disabilities field has probably not paid sufficient attention to synthesizing available research information and, consequently, knowledge has not been incorporated into larger structural units (Hanson, 1958).

The development of comprehensive and unified theories requires knowledge accumulation that must be approached as a formal systematic process (Cooper, 1984). Knowledge accumulation should be based not on questions that address specific functioning, but rather on broadly conceived questions (Strike & Posner, 1983). These questions ask things such as: What are the critical and invariant properties of learning disabilities, and what are their operative dynamics? Too often, it is assumed that there are no invariant properties, that subjectivity makes the learning disabilities field interpretive and provisional; hence, a science of learning disabilities is out of the question (see Kavale & Forness, 1985). One reason for this view is the lack of attention to knowledge accumulation, which can take several forms (Polkinghorne, 1983).

The first accumulation technique is testing the plausibility of theoretical ideas with research findings (Taveggia, 1974). This is perhaps the most typical approach, but it is often taken too seriously and too literally. When the research process, in its classical, logical, empiricist form, does not proceed as expected (Feigl, 1956), then increased skepticism about the prospects for a science of learning disabilities develops. When it is discovered that the learning disabilities field is also inundated with political considerations, special interests, ideological differences, and so on, there is even more disillusionment (Greene, 1981).

This pessimism is partially the result of a rather idealized view of how knowledge accumulation occurs in the "hard" sciences (Churchland & Hooker, 1985). In fact, the same accumulation difficulties are found in these sciences; yet, they muddle along in building "scientific" knowledge. In general, most sciences proceed by examining some intriguing ideas, usually not stated with great precision (at least initially), by negotiating and arguing with those who hold different ideas, and by marshaling, often selectively, evidence to bear on various positions (Knight, 1976). The point is that, over time, this intellectual and sociopolitical process produces knowledge about which scientists agree.

The process, even in this less than idealized state, is viewed as science (Brown, 1984). It thus appears that learning disabilities will never appear to be a science until it, at least, adopts scientific attitudes. It is important to note that scientific status should not necessarily imply physics or chemistry as the models (Scriven, 1956). Geology and meteorology are examples of sciences not as well developed because their predictions are far from precise. There is little need to slavishly imitate the physical sciences to gain prestige. The learning disabilities field need only aspire to become more of a science at this time. This will then orient thinking toward better problem selection, better methods, and better interpretation (Smart, 1968).

A second means of knowledge accumulation is conceptual, wherein scholars build on others' ideas, as suggested in Newton's phrase, "If I have seen further it is by standing on the shoulders of giants" (Merton, 1965). The process is one in which the ideas of others are selectively chosen and extended in some way, producing a theoretical argument that is more powerful than the original one (Churchman, 1971). Unfortunately, this type of activity is not often attempted in learning disabilities and, if attempted, is too often not an extension, but only a retracing of the history of ideas (Merton, 1957). In the learning disabilities field, to paraphrase, "we stand in the shadow rather than on the shoulders of giants." It, therefore, must be realized that conceptual understanding is facilitated by adapting, synthesizing, developing, and extending the ideas of others.

A third type of knowledge accumulation is based on creativity (Bunge, 1962). Knowledge accumulation should be viewed not as merely a lockstep, mechanical process, but also as a creative process in which new ideas are inserted, often with surprising and revolutionary implications, into the corpus of knowledge (Reason & Rowan, 1981). Too often, creativity is discounted because it does not take into account a strictly empirical approach (Nagel, 1980). The problem is that most fields proceed with intellectual traditions, styles, or (to use the overworked word) paradigms that act like conceptual blinders, and prevent the synthesis, consolidation, and extension of ideas into some creative juxtaposition.

METATHEORETICAL DEVELOPMENT AND LEARNING DISABILITIES

The many different "theories" about learning disabilities currently available represent a loosely organized picture of the nature of learning disabilities. The comprehensive and unified perspective suggested earlier in the form of a macro-level theory is contingent not only on a better information base provided by enhanced knowledge accumulation, but also on the development of metatheory (Bunge, 1959). Swanson (1988b) provided a rationale and framework for metatheoretical development in learning disabilities. The reactions to the paper (see e.g., Blachman, 1988; Kavale, 1988a; Scruggs & Mastropieri, 1988) revealed fundamental differences about the roles of basic and applied research in the learning disabilities field, and a recurrent theme questioning the necessity for basic research in an applied field. The bias toward applied research reflects again the natural versus human science tension discussed earlier. The less than enthusiastic view of basic research suggests that a term such as *metatheory* is likely to raise many "red flags." However, metatheory should be viewed as the means by which a field is bound together and focuses on core ideas, assumptions, and procedures (Marx, 1964). Metatheory thus can serve a practical purpose and should not be allowed to wander into the philosophical stratosphere (Newton-Smith, 1981). Too often, metatheoretical treatises are simply statements about "theories" and become distracting because the emphasis on philosophy does little to suggest how theoretical developments can be synthesized into a comprehensive and unified pragmatic scheme (Morgan, 1983).

Metatheory should deal with the most fundamental and general questions about learning disabilities: What is the nature of learning disability? Is there an essence of learning disability? What is the appropriate level of analysis in learning disabilities? What are the goals of learning disabilities description? With answers to these questions, metatheory becomes the "glue" for developing a unified picture of learning disabilities. Metatheory thus becomes critical for theoretical development; it provides a framework for considering theoretical questions, it guides the construction of theoretical arguments, and it provides criteria for evaluating the relevance, reliability, and consistency of the outcomes (Bunge, 1959).

THEORY BUILDING IN LEARNING DISABILITIES

How, then, can macro-theory development in learning disabilities occur? It would seem that macro-theory development should begin with an (explicit or implicit) adoption of a metatheoretical position. Whatever its rationality, the proposed metatheory is then used to construct a comprehensive and unified picture of learning disabilities. Evaluation of this schema then serves as a basis for revision and reformulation of the original metatheoretical position adopted. In this sense, macro-theory growth becomes a reflexive process involving the use of metatheories to construct, compare, and assess theoretical arrangements (Giere, 1984).

The lack of metatheoretical development in learning disabilities may be explained partially by the fact that the learning disabilities field is now structured in ways that divide theory and methods and partition the field into a large number of subspecialties (Senf, 1986). The result is that those individuals concerned with theories and those concerned with methodology hardly communicate, that much research activity ignores theory, and that the primary learning disabilities players operate in considerable ignorance of, and unconcern about, each others' work. It is necessary that these artificial divisions and partitions end. They are counterproductive because attention is deflected away from the primary question: What is learning disability? It should not be considered disorder X, Y, or Z, but a complex amalgam of many deficits. A primary means to produce that amalgam is conceptual—synthesis and consolidation of existing knowledge and theories (Rescher, 1977a). It appears that too much time is spent talking *about* theories, when what is required is rational discussion about the assets and liabilities of particular theories (Mitroff & Mason, 1981). The learning disabilities field then can be restructured with a more comprehensive and unified theory. It is only when this process is complete that the learning disabilities field may realize its full potential in explaining the particular school failure of a selected group of students experiencing school difficulties.

The primary problem becomes one of deciding how to choose and coordinate different views about a phenomenon such as learning disabilities. The decision processes used by individuals can be viewed as a dichotomy (see Hull, 1988). On one side are those termed "internalists," who believe that new ideas are accepted, rejected, or ignored because of the weight of the evidence and cogency of arguments. On the other side are "externalists," who believe that a wide variety of other factors, including diverse social forces and idiosyncratic personal motives, cause the acceptance or rejection of new ideas.

An internalist position may possess a more logical and objective rendering, but it is difficult to ignore externalist views. For example, the learning disabilities field has become fertile ground for ideological debate, as evidenced by the Marxist analyses presently available (e.g., Carrier, 1986; Sigmon, 1987). Although subject to debate (see Kavale & Forness, 1987), a larger question exists about the validity of such analyses: Are they really about learning disabilities or do they simply reflect the application of a political point of view to a content area? The learning disabilities field may have come to include social manifestations, but its scientific status should have little to do with sociopolitical views. Too much externalism in the decision process tends to reduce objectivity because it tends to introduce too much emotion (Scheffler, 1967). The likely outcome is ideological squabbles that ultimately end with the espousal of some form of social relativism with respect to empirical truth (Gellner, 1985). To avoid this situation, reason, argument, and evidence become crucial elements in the decisions made with respect to the determinants of learning disabilities (Shapere, 1984). The learning disabilities field should, therefore, adopt a more internalist position even though it is understood that an externalist position is likely to exert some influence. Such a position is termed *naturalistic* and assumes "that theories come to be accepted (or not) through natural processes involving individual judgment and social interaction" (Giere, 1988, p. 144).

The learning disabilities field must focus its efforts on developing more general, macro-level theory. The goal should be to pull together into a grand scheme the patchwork quilt of conceptualizations now characterizing learning disabilities (Menard, 1971). Figure 10 presents a schematic model for the steps necessary to achieve such a theory for learning disabilities. The most important compo-

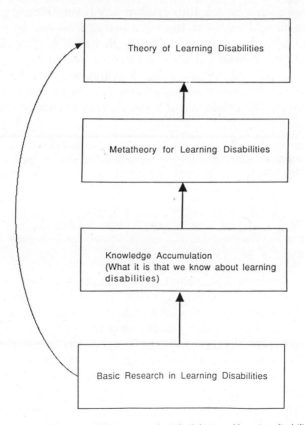

Figure 10. Building a comprehensive and unified theory of learning disabilities.

nents are the middle two, dealing with knowledge accumulation and metatheory because they have been the most neglected. To this point, most basic research in learning disabilities has been used to formulate theory directly. Although reasonably effective, the resulting theory has been too narrowly focused and has remained isolated and unincorporated into a larger framework. By adding the middle two components, the scope can be expanded and, ultimately, a more comprehensive and unified picture of learning disabilities can be achieved.

EVOLUTIONARY EPISTEMOLOGY
FOR LEARNING DISABILITIES

Kuhn (1970), in *The Structure of Scientific Revolutions,* presented the well-known idea that science progresses through revolutions. Although the idea is not universally accepted (e.g., Lakatos & Musgrave, 1970), it seems certain that Kuhn was not using learning disabilities as his model. Rather than any revolutionary paradigm shifts, learning disabilities has been marked instead by paradigm drifts wherein ideas possess only an ephemeral quality (Kavale & Forness, 1985). It seems clear that learning disabilities will not experience any paradigm shifts in the Kuhnian sense. Kuhn did, however, allude to a different sort of process that is analogous to biological evolution. The resolution of revolutions in science is a matter of:

> Selection by conflict within the scientific community of the fittest way to practice future science. The net result of a sequence of such revolutionary selections, separated by periods of normal research, is the wonderfully adapted set of instruments we call modern scientific knowledge. Successive stages in that development process are marked by an increase in articulation and specialization. And the entire process may have occurred, as we now suppose biological evolution did, without benefit of a set goal, a permanent fixed scientific truth, of which each stage in the development of scientific knowledge is a better exemplar. (Kuhn, 1970, pp. 171–172)

Later, Toulmin (1972) emphasized that both biological and conceptual evolution are special instances of a more general selection process. For biology, the process that selects genes is termed *natural selection.* For concepts, the process akin to biology can be termed *rational selection* (Rescher, 1977b). Popper (1972) referred to this process as evolutionary epistemology. In an analysis of selection processes, Popper (1972) suggested that they result from the interplay of two factors—replication (in terms of methodology) and interaction (in terms of cooperation). The selection processes are necessary when there is conceptual heterogeneity that results in competition among concepts. It is this requirement for conceptual heterogeneity that makes an evolutionary approach to learning disabilities an attractive alternative for theory building. The reason: conceptual heterogeneity is a hallmark of the learning disabilities field (Kavale, 1987).

An evolutionary approach to learning disabilities may also be a particularly appropriate mechanism because learning disabilities is a relatively small field that can constrain competition to a manageable level (Boyd & Richerson, 1985). Terms such as *scientific community* are facilely tossed about, but, in reality, the selection process occurs in relatively small groups (Andrews, 1979). It has been shown, for example, that, even in a narrowly defined subject area such as high-energy particle physics, there is no genuine research group (Blau, 1978). Instead, about one half of those involved were organized into small "cliques" or research teams and the rest worked primarily alone. The isolates, however, usually did not make significant contributions. About half the cliques were also organized loosely into a federation or "invisible college" that was the most productive (Crane, 1972). Thus, cliques should be the unit of "hereditary" transmission, and learning disabilities should not include a significant number of isolated researchers. The problem with isolation is that investigators must start anew each generation, so there is no transgenerational accumulation (Hull, 1988).

If the idea of scientific progress as a selection process among competing concepts is accepted, the lack of harmony in learning disabilities is not necessarily a hindrance to development. Analyses of science have demonstrated that the relationships among participants show a mix of cooperation and competition, camaraderie and animosity, as well as varying allegiances and alliances (Taubes, 1987; Ziman, 1968). These analyses also demonstrate that such factionalism need not frustrate the selection process (Hull, 1988). After studying the behavior of the Apollo project scientists (see Mitroff, 1974a), it was remarked that the "problem is how objective knowledge results in science not despite bias and commitment but because of them" (p. 591). The study showed that objective knowledge was obtained through bias, jealousy, and irrationality. It was also found that the least productive scientists tended to behave the most admirably, whereas those who made the greatest contributions just as frequently behaved the most deplorably (Mitroff, 1974b). Thus, the learning disabilities field appears to possess all the elements for an evolutionary epistemology for learning disabilities: conceptual heterogeneity; a relatively small population of researchers; and, as even a cursory examination would reveal, many who have made significant contributions.

CONCLUSION

Theoretical development is an important and necessary activity for the learning disabilities field. Although individual theories about learning disabilities are available, they are often too circumscribed to explain a full range of learning disability–associated behaviors. Therefore, a need exists for macro-level theory that will coordinate individual theories into a structure providing a more comprehensive and unified perspective about the learning disabilities phenomenon. A focus in macro-level theory will permit understanding of learning disabilities in general rather than learning disability in particular. The development of more generalized theory appears to be contingent on two activities: knowledge accumulation and metatheoretical development. The former is concerned with synthesizing available knowledge into a usable form, and the latter focuses on core ideas and assumptions to provide a blueprint for theory growth. The process of theory construction should be part of an evolutionary epistemology that will result in sustained scientific progress in the learning disabilities field.

REFERENCES

Achinstein, P. (1983). *The nature of explanation*. New York: Oxford University Press.

Achinstein, P., & Barker, F. (1969). *The legacy of logical positivism*. Baltimore: The Johns Hopkins University Press.

Andreski, S. (1972). *Social sciences as sorcery*. London: Andre Deutsch.

Andrews, F.M. (Ed.). (1979). *Scientific productivity: The effectiveness of research groups in six countries*. Cambridge, England: Cambridge University Press.

Ayres, A.J. (1968). Sensory integrative processes and neuropsychological learning disabilities. In J. Hellmuth (Ed.), *Learning disorders* (Vol. 3, pp. 43–58). Seattle, WA: Special Child Publications.

Barnes, B. (1977). *Interests and the growth of knowledge*. London: Routledge & Kegan Paul.

Blachman, B. (1988). The futile search for a theory of learning disabilities. *Journal of Learning Disabilities, 21*, 286–288.

Blau, J.R. (1978). Sociometric structures of a scientific discipline. *Research in Sociology of Knowledge, Sciences, and Art, 1*, 91–206.

Boyd, R., & Richerson, Y.J. (1985). *Culture and the evolutionary process*. Chicago: The University of Chicago Press.

Brainerd, C.J., Kingsma, J., & Howe, M.L. (1986). Long-term memory development and learning disability: Storage and retrieval loci of disabled/nondisabled differences. In S. Ceci (Ed.), *Handbook of cognitive, social, and neuropsychological aspects of learning disabilities* (Vol. 1, pp. 161–184). Hillsdale, NJ: Lawrence Erlbaum Associates.

Braithwaite, R.B. (1955). *Scientific explanation*. Cambridge, England: Cambridge University Press.

Brooks, D.R., & Wiley, E.O. (1986). *Evolution and entropy: Toward a unified theory of biology*. Chicago: University of Chicago Press.

Brown, J.R. (Ed.). (1984). *Scientific rationality: The sociological turn*. Dordrecht: Reidel.

Bryan, T., & Bryan, J. (1990). Social factors in learning disabilities: An overview. In H.L. Swanson & B.K. Keogh (Eds.), *Learning disabilities: Theoretical and research issues* (pp. 131–138). Hillsdale, NJ: Lawrence Erlbaum Associates.

Bunge, M. (1959). *Metascientific queries*. Springfield, IL: Charles C Thomas.

Bunge, M. (1962). *Intuition and science*. Englewood Cliffs, NJ: Prentice Hall.

Bunge, M. (1963). *The myth of simplicity*. Englewood Cliffs, NJ: Prentice Hall.

Carnap, R. (1969). *The logical structure of the world and pseudoproblems in philosophy*. Berkeley: University of California Press.

Carrier, J.G. (1986). *Learning disability: Social class and the construction of inequality in American education*. Westport, CT: Greenwood Press.

Churchland, P.M., & Hooker, C.A. (Eds.). (1985). *Images of sciences*. Chicago: The University of Chicago Press.

Churchman, C.W. (1971). *The design of inquiring systems*. New York: Basic Books.

Coleman, J.S. (1986). Micro foundations and macrosocial theory. In S. Lindenberg, J. Coleman, & S. Nowak (Eds.), *Approaches to social theory* (pp. 345–363). New York: Russell Sage Foundation.

Collins, H.M., & Pinch, T.J. (1982). *Frames of meaning*. London: Routledge & Kegan Paul.

Cooper, H. (1984). *The integrative research review: A systematic approach*. Beverly Hills: Sage Publications.

Cotman, C.W., & Lynch, G.S. (1988). The neurobiology of learning and memory. In J. Kavanagh & T. Truss (Eds.), *Learning disabilities: Proceedings of the national conference* (pp. 1–69). Parkton, MD: York Press.

Crane, D. (1972). *Invisible colleges: Diffusion of knowledge in scientific communities*. Chicago: The University of Chicago Press.

Cronbach, L.J., & Meehl, P.E. (1955). Construct validity in psychological tests. *Psychological Bulletin, 52*, 281–301.

Delacato, C.H. (1966). *Neurological organization and reading*. Springfield, IL: Charles C Thomas.

Feigl, H. (1956). Some major issues and developments in the philosophy of science of logical empiricism. In H. Feigl & M. Scriven (Eds.), *Minnesota studies in the philosophy of science* (Vol. 1, pp. 1–46). Minneapolis: University of Minnesota Press.

Gallagher, J.J. (1986). Learning disabilities and special education: A critique. *Journal of Learning Disabilities, 19*, 595–601.

Gellner, E. (1985). *Relativism and the social sciences*. New York: Cambridge University Press.

Gibson, Q. (1960). *The logic of social enquiry*. London: Routledge & Kegan Paul.

Giere, R.N. (1984). Toward a unified theory of science. In J. Cushing, C. Delaney, & G. Gutting (Eds.), *Science and reality* (pp. 5–31). Notre Dame, IN: University of Notre Dame Press.

Giere, R.N. (1988). *Explaining science: A cognitive approach*. Chicago: The University of Chicago Press.

Greene, J.C. (1981). *Science, ideology, and world view.* Berkeley: University of California Press.

Grinnell, F. (1987). *The scientific attitude.* Boulder, CO: Westview Press.

Haight, S.L. (1980). Learning disabilities—the battered discipline. *Journal of Learning Disabilities, 13,* 452–455.

Hanfling, O. (1981). *Logical positivism.* Oxford, England: Blackwell.

Hanson, N.R. (1958). *Patterns of discovery.* Cambridge, England: Cambridge University Press.

Hempel, C. (1952). *Fundamentals of concept formation in empirical science.* Chicago: The University of Chicago Press.

Hull, D.L. (1988). *Science as a process.* Chicago: The University of Chicago Press.

Hynd, G.W., Obrzut, J.E., Hayes, F., & Becker, M.G. (1986). Neuropsychology of childhood learning disabilities. In D. Wedding, A. Horton, & J. Webster (Eds.), *The neuropsychology handbook: Behavioral and clinical perspectives* (pp. 456–485). New York: Springer-Verlag.

Kail, R.V., & Leonard, L.B. (1986). Sources of word-finding problems in language impaired children. In S. Ceci (Ed.), *Handbook of cognitive, social, and neuropsychological aspects of learning disabilities* (Vol. 1, pp. 195–202). Hillsdale, NJ: Lawrence Erlbaum Associates.

Kavale, K.A. (1987). Theoretical quandaries in learning disabilities. In S. Vaughn & C. Bos (Eds.), *Research in learning disabilities: Issues and future directions* (pp. 19–33). Boston: Little, Brown/College-Hill.

Kavale, K.A. (1988a). Epistemological relativity in learning disabilities. *Journal of Learning Disabilities, 21,* 215–218.

Kavale, K.A. (1988b). Status of the field: Trends and issues in learning disabilities. In K.A. Kavale (Ed.), *Learning disabilities: State of the art and practice* (pp. 1–21). Boston: Little, Brown/College-Hill.

Kavale, K.A., & Forness, S.R. (1985). *The science of learning disabilities.* San Diego, CA: College-Hill Press.

Kavale, K.A., & Forness, S.R. (1987). History, politics, and the general education initiative: Sleeter's reinterpretation of learning disabilities as a case study. *Remedial and Special Education, 8,* 6–12.

Kavale, K.A., & Mundschenk, N.A. (1990). A critique of assessment methodology. In H.L. Swanson (Ed.), *Handbook on the assessment of learning disabilities* (pp. 407–432). Austin, TX: PRO-ED.

Kavale, K.A., & Nye, C. (1985–1986). Parameters of learning disabilities in achievement, linguistic, neuropsychological, and social/behavior domains. *Journal of Special Education, 19,* 443–458.

Kenny, D.A. (1979). *Correlation and causality.* New York: John Wiley & Sons.

Kephart, N.C. (1960). *The slow learner in the classroom.* Columbus, OH: Charles E. Merrill.

Kirk, S.A., & Kirk, W.D. (1971). *Psycholinguistic learning disabilities: Diagnosis and remediation.* Urbana: University of Illinois Press.

Knight, D.M. (1976). *The nature of science.* London: Andre Deutsch.

Kuhn, T.S. (1970). *The structure of scientific revolutions* (2nd ed.). Chicago: The University of Chicago Press.

Lakatos, I., & Musgrave, A. (Eds.). (1970). *Criticism and the growth of knowledge.* Cambridge, England: Cambridge University Press.

Laudan, L. (1977). *Progress and its problems: Toward a theory of scientific growth.* Berkeley: University of California Press.

Licht, B.G., & Kistner, J.A. (1986). Motivational problems of learning-disabled children: Individual differences and their implications for treatment. In J. Torgesen & B. Wong (Eds.), *Psychological and educational perspectives on learning disabilities* (pp. 225–255). Orlando, FL: Academic Press.

Lundberg, G.A. (1961). *Can science save us?* (2nd ed.). New York: Longmans.

Manis, F.R., & Morrison, F.J. (1985). Reading disability: A deficit in role learning? In L. Siegel & F. Morrison (Eds.), *Cognitive development in atypical children* (pp. 1–26). New York: Springer-Verlag.

Martin, L.J. (1986). Assessing current theories of cerebral organization. In S. Ceci (Ed.), *Handbook of cognitive, social, and neuropsychological aspects of learning disabilities* (Vol. 1, pp. 425–439). Hillsdale, NJ: Lawrence Erlbaum Associates.

Marx, M.H. (1964). The general nature of theory construction. In M. Marx (Ed.), *Theories in contemporary psychology* (pp. 3–46). New York: Macmillan.

Menard, H.W. (1971). *Science: Growth and change.* Cambridge, MA: Harvard University Press.

Merton, R.K. (1957). *Social theory and social structure.* New York: Free Press.

Merton, R.K. (1965). *On the shoulders of giants: A Shandean postscript.* New York: Free Press.

Mitroff, I.I. (1974a). Norms and counter-norms in a select group of the Apollo moon scientists: A case study of the ambivalence of scientists. *American Sociological Review, 39,* 579–595.

Mitroff, I.I. (1974b). *The subjective side of science.* Amsterdam: Elsevier.

Mitroff, I.I., & Mason, R.O. (1981). *Creating a dialectical social science: Concepts, methods, and models.* Dordrecht, Holland: Reidel.

Morgan, G. (Ed.). (1983). *Beyond method: Strategies for social research.* Beverly Hills: Sage Publications.

Morrison, F.J., & Manis, F.R. (1982). Cognitive processes and reading disability: A critique and proposal. In C. Brainerd & M. Pressley (Eds.), *Verbal processes in children* (pp. 59–93). New York: Springer-Verlag.

Nagel, T. (1980). *The limits of objectivity.* Salt Lake City: University of Utah Press.

Newton-Smith, W.H. (1981). *The rationality of science.* London: Routledge & Kegan Paul.

Orton, S.T. (1937). *Reading, writing, and speech problems in children.* New York: Norton.

Pedhazur, E.J. (1982). *Multiple regression in behavioral research: Predictions and explanation* (2nd ed.). New York: Holt, Rinehart & Winston.

Polkinghorne, D. (1983). *Methodology for the human sciences: Systems of inquiry.* Albany: State University of New York Press.

Popper, K.R. (1972). *Objective knowledge: An evolutionary approach.* Oxford, England: Clarendon Press.

Rabinowitz, M., & Chi, M.T.J. (1986). An interactive model of strategic processing. In S. Ceci (Ed.), *Handbook of cognitive, social, and neuropsychological aspects of learning disabilities* (Vol. 1, pp. 83–102). Hillsdale, NJ: Lawrence Erlbaum Associates.

Reason, P., & Rowan, J. (Eds.). (1981). *Human inquiry: A sourcebook of new paradigm research.* New York: John Wiley & Sons.

Rescher, N. (1977a). *Dialectics: A controversy-oriented approach to the theory of knowledge.* Albany: State University of New York Press.

Rescher, N. (1977b). *Methodological pragmatism.* Oxford, England: Blackwell.

Scheffler, I. (1967). *Science and subjectivity.* Indianapolis, IN: Bobbs-Merrill.

Scriven, M. (1956). A possible distinction between traditional scientific disciplines and the study of human behavior. In H. Feigl & M. Scriven (Eds.), *Minnesota studies in the philosophy of science* (Vol. 1, pp. 330–339). Minneapolis: University of Minnesota Press.

Scruggs, T.E., & Mastropieri, M.A. (1988). Legitimizing the field of learning disabilities: Does research orientation matter? *Journal of Learning Disabilities, 21,* 219–222.

Senf, G.M. (1986). LD research in sociological and scientific perspective. In J. Torgesen & B. Wong (Eds.), *Psychological and educational perspectives on learning disabilities* (pp. 27–53). Orlando, FL: Academic Press.

Shapere, D. (1984). *Reason and the search for knowledge.* Dordrecht, Holland: Reidel.

Shaywitz, S.E., & Shaywitz, B.A. (1988). Hyperactivity/attention deficits: Current perspectives. In J. Kavanagh & T. Truss (Eds.), *Learning disabilities: Proceedings of the national conference* (pp. 369–523). Parkton, MD: York Press.

Sigmon, S.B. (1987). *Radical analysis of special education: Focus on historical development and learning disabilities.* London: The Falmer Press.

Smart, J.J.C. (1968). *Between science and philosophy.* New York: Random House.

Stanovich, K.E. (1982a). Individual differences in the cognitive processes of reading I: Word decoding. *Journal of Learning Disabilities, 15,* 485–493.

Stanovich, K.E. (1982b). Individual differences in the cognitive processes of reading II: Text-level processes. *Journal of Learning Disabilities, 15,* 549–554.

Stanovich, K.E. (1988). Explaining the differences between the dyslexic and the garden-variety poor reader: The phonological-core variable-difference model. *Journal of Learning Disabilities, 21,* 590–612.

Stegmuller, W. (1976). *The structure and dynamics of theories.* New York: Springer-Verlag.

Stevens, S.S. (1951). Mathematics, measurement, and psychophysics. In S.S. Stevens (Ed.), *Handbook of experimental psychology* (pp. 1–49). New York: John Wiley & Sons.

Strauss, A.A., & Lehtinen, L.E. (1947). *Psychopathology and education of the brain-injured child.* New York: Grune & Stratton.

Strike, K., & Posner, G. (1983). Types of synthesis and their criteria. In S. Word & L. Reed (Eds.), *Knowledge structure and use: Implications for synthesis and interpretation* (pp. 343–362). Philadelphia: Temple University Press.

Swanson, H.L. (1987). Information processing theory and learning disabilities: An overview. *Journal of Learning Disabilities, 20,* 3–7.

Swanson, H.L. (1988a). Learning disabled children's problem solving: Identifying mental processes underlying intelligent performance. *Intelligence, 12,* 261–278.

Swanson, H.L. (1988b). Toward a metatheory of learning disabilities. *Journal of Learning Disabilities, 21,* 196–208.

Taubes, G. (1987). *Nobel dreams: Power, deceit and the ultimate experience.* New York: Random House.

Taveggia, T. (1974). Resolving research controversy through empirical cumulation. *Sociological Methods and Research, 2,* 395–407.

Torgesen, J.K. (1986). Learning disabilities theory: Its current state and future prospects. *Journal of Learning Disabilities, 19,* 399–407.

Toulmin, S. (1961). *Foresight and understanding.* New York: Harper & Row.

Toulmin, S. (1972). *Human understanding.* Princeton: NJ: Princeton University Press.

Toulmin, S., & Leary, D.E. (1985). The cult of empiricism in psychology, and beyond. In S. Koch & D. Leary (Eds.), *A century of psychology as science* (pp. 594–617). New York: McGraw-Hill.

Turner, M.B. (1976). *Philosophy and the science of behavior.* New York: Appleton-Century-Crofts.

Wagner, R.K. (1986). Phonological processing abilities and reading: Implications for disabled readers. *Journal of Learning Disabilities, 19,* 623–630.

Wallach, G.P., & Butler, K.G. (Eds.). (1984). *Language learning disabilities in school-age children.* Baltimore: Williams & Wilkins.

Weimer, W. (1979). *Notes on the methodology of scientific research.* Hillsdale, NJ: Lawrence Erlbaum Associates.

Weiner, J. (1980). A theoretical model of the acquisition of peer relationships of learning disabled children. *Journal of Learning Disabilities, 13,* 42–47.

Winch, P. (1958). *The idea of a social science and its relation to philosophy.* London: Routledge & Kegan Paul.

Wong, B.Y.L. (1985). Metacognition and learning disabilities. In T.G. Waller, D. Forrest-Pressley, & E. MacKinnon (Eds.), *Metacognition, cognition and human performance* (pp. 137–180). New York: Academic Press.

Wong, B.Y.L. (1989). Is IQ necessary in the definition of learning disabilities? Introduction to the special series. *Journal of Learning Disabilities, 22,* 468–520.

Wright, S. (1921). Correlation and causation. *Journal of Agricultural Research, 20,* 557–585.

Zebrowski, E. (1979). *Fundamentals of physical measurement.* North Scituate, MA: Duxbury Press.

Zeller, R.A., & Carmines, E.G. (1980). *Measurement in the social sciences: The link between theory and data.* Cambridge, England: Cambridge University Press.

Ziman, J.M. (1968). *Public knowledge: An essay concerning the social dimension of science.* Cambridge, England: Cambridge University Press.

III

PERSPECTIVES ON RESEARCH AND CLINICAL PRACTICE IN LEARNING DISABILITIES

Two major hypotheses currently undergird the concept of learning disabilities. The first hypothesis is that the learning disabilities observed in children are the result of neither emotional and/or physical factors nor an inadequate opportunity to learn. Instead, they are due to specific disorders in psychological processes. The second major hypothesis is that these processing deficits are a reflection of neurobiological and/or constitutional factors. Of significant interest to researchers and clinicians in the field of learning disabilities is how to conceptualize, measure, and test these two basic assumptions, particularly with respect to operationalizing the idea of a specific processing deficit. More specifically, what theories and perspectives are available that can organize the enormous amount of complex information relevant to the child, the school, the teacher, and the content to be learned as well as serve to help formulate descriptions and predictions of the phenomena under study?

In this third section, the authors have been charged with the task of explaining how particular theoretical and conceptual perspectives can stimulate important questions, guide the development of hypotheses, inform the process of task development, and provide a context for interpreting data for research and clinical purposes. Within this context, four theoretical and conceptual perspectives are presented and discussed. First, Swanson provides us with an overview and then a detailed discussion of how principles derived from cognitive psychology can serve to illuminate the reasons for the performance discrepancies observed in children with learning disabilities. Swanson also employs cognitive theory to support his argument that current static assessment practices using traditional psychometric measures lead to an inadequate and ecologically invalid diagnostic data base. In contrast, Swanson explains that dynamic assessment models that reflect complex forms of learning are significantly more sensitive to individual differences and substantially more robust with respect to guiding intervention. In a different vein, Levine and his colleagues contend that rich clinical descriptions based on an interactive developmental paradigm serve the diagnostic and teaching processes for the child with learning disabilities in a much more ecologically valid way. Within Levine's interactive developmental approach, an emphasis is placed on observation and a rigorous analysis of the interactions among neurocognitive operations (e.g., language, memory, attention), production components (e.g., single word decoding skill), and school-related outcomes (e.g., reading failure).

In contrast, Zigmond approaches the study, diagnosis, and teaching of children with learning disabilities from a perspective that focuses on how the school, as a system, conceptualizes and addresses the issue of learning disabilities. Zigmond argues that our understanding of learning disabilities is dependent on how schools are organized to address the needs of all children, and more specifically on understanding how schools provide for difficult-to-teach youngsters and how these youngsters adapt to different kinds of schools (and teachers). Finally, Stanovich helps us conceptualize learning disabilities not as a general area of study, but as a number of specific domain deficits. From the perspective of a scientist interested in the domain of reading and reading disorders, Stanovich contends that our ability to understand, define, and treat learning disabilities and differences in children is highly related to operationalizing the specific problem. Stanovich, using the domain of reading disability, also makes a convincing argument against the use of intelligence–achievement discrepancies in the identification of learning disabilities in general, and reading disorders in particular.

10

LEARNING DISABILITIES FROM THE PERSPECTIVE OF COGNITIVE PSYCHOLOGY

H. Lee Swanson

The purpose of this chapter is to provide a general perspective on learning disabilities from the field of cognitive psychology. Because of the vastness of this topic, I limit my applications to the assessment of performance discrepancies and research related to cognitive instruction. Before I outline these applications, however, three issues must be addressed. These relate to how cognitive psychology and learning disabilities interact in terms of: 1) definition, 2) paradigm, and 3) research focus.

INTERACTION OF COGNITIVE PSYCHOLOGY AND LEARNING DISABILITIES

Issue of Definition

Cognitive psychology is defined as a scientific endeavor to "understand the nature of human intelligence and how people think" (Anderson, 1990, p. 1). As such, the main focus of cognitive psychology is on human intellectual processes. Research is consistent in showing that human intelligence is the result of an interaction of an accumulated knowledge base with special capabilities for processing certain kinds of information (Ceci & Liker, 1986; Hunt, 1983; Keating, 1982; Sternberg, 1987). Thus, by application, to understand learning disabilities from a cognitive perspective, the field should be grounded in research about the processes that underlie human intelligence. Unfortunately, a review of the research literature indicates that the learning disabilities field has no defined model or conceptual framework linking a child's knowledge base to specific processing abilities (Ceci, 1990; Farnham-Diggory, 1986). In addition, only a few systematic attempts have been made to relate cognitive explanations of intelligence to the field of learning disabilities (e.g., Borkowski, Estrada, Milstead, & Hale, 1989; Brown & Campione, 1986; Ceci, 1990; Kolligian & Sternberg, 1987; Swanson, 1984b).

One major reason for the undeveloped link between cognitive-based models of intelligence and learning disabilities is the poor operationalization of the term *learning disabilities* (Morrison & Siegel, 1991; Swanson, 1992). A traditional account of learning disabilities is one that suggests there is only a limited aspect of contextually appropriate behavior that is depressed. This depression of contextually appropriate behavior is described in terms of a discrepancy between some aspect of academic performance and intellectual behavior (Forness, Sinclair, & Guthrie, 1983; Stanovich, 1991). For example, a child is identified as learning disabled if he or she displays reading performance 2 or more years below grade level even if he or she has an IQ within the average range. Although this conception seems like one that would easily lend itself to operationalization, there are immense problems with such an approach. One issue relates to the generality of the performance of children with learning disabilities.

At the outset, I would suggest that the term *learning disabilities* itself is a misnomer, especially if one attempts to distinguish the child with learning disabilities from the child with mental retardation (see Sternberg, 1987, for a related discussion). The difference between learning disabilities and mental retardation cannot be described adequately in terms of mentality or learning (or in terms of retardation or disabilities, for that matter [see MacMillan, chap. 7, this volume]). Rather, the only meaningful distinction that has emerged in the literature between children with learning disabilities and children with mental retardation is in terms of the generality of their performance deficit. Unfortunately, the generality of the deficits of children with learning disabilities is not easy to distinguish or conceptualize.

For example, which aspects of these children's cognitive functioning are general to all environments, and which are limited to more specific environmental situations? In addition, how does one conceptualize ability outside of the classroom context? One can, of course, skirt these issues by focusing on one contextual behavior (i.e., academic behavior in the classroom). However, even if the researcher limits himself or herself to the study of the classroom context (reading tasks), several perplexing issues emerge. For example, what constitutes intelligent behavior when the academic deficits of children with learning disabilities are in tasks highly correlated with global intelligence (i.e., problem solving; however, see Siegel, 1989, 1990; Stanovich, 1991)? That is, youngsters with learning disabilities have deficits related to a common pool of cognitive resources that permeate all intellectual tasks (Swanson, 1984a, 1989, in press-a, in press-b; Swanson, Cochran, & Ewers, 1989). For example, working memory deficits related to executive activities have been found in children with learning disabilities (e.g., Siegel & Ryan, 1989; Swanson, Cochran, & Ewars, 1989), and working memory is a generic construct to most academic tasks (e.g., Baddeley, 1986; Larson & Saccuzzo, 1989; Turner & Engle, 1989). Given these findings, how does one determine processes that are primary or secondary, given the highly intercorrelational nature of various processes to a general system? Quite simply, how can the intellectual functioning of children with learning disabilities be specific when they perform poorly on a multitude of cognitive tasks? Answers to these fundamental questions in the literature are unclear. In fact, because of these aforementioned conceptual ambiguities, some researchers have begun to question the utility of intelligence (at least as a psychometric construct) as an appropriate construct for the field of learning disabilities (Siegel, 1988, 1989a; Stanovich, 1990).

One reasonable approach to isolate specific processing deficits from a general cognitive system (intelligence) focuses on the concept of modularity, or the idea that psychological processes act independently of one another (Fodor, 1983; Stanovich, 1990). Within the context of modularity, an effort is made to focus on processes that are "encapsulated," or controlled by functionally autonomous mechanisms that are impervious to a general system. Tentative support for the concept of modularity would be found when processes that are most directly related to general intelligence (e.g., metacognition) are weakly correlated with lower level processes in a particular academic domain. There are, in fact, interesting results that suggest that isolated reading processes, such as phonological coding, are independent of intelligence (Siegel, 1988). In addition, within the domain of reading, it has been suggested that high-level comprehension or discourse, such as the predictability of events (e.g., words), does not influence lexical access (Balota, Pollatsek, & Rayner, 1985). To establish modularity, however, one would have to show that components related to intelligence (e.g., executive processing, prediction, self-monitoring) do not affect certain low-order processes during an ongoing cognitive activity. As an example, one would have to show that high-level reading strategies, such as word or content predictability, remain completely independent of phonological access. It seems unlikely, however, that one would be able to show that a person's knowledge base, reasoning ability, and/or general processing ability remain completely independent of his or her ability to read. Thus, a more fruitful line of research would be to focus on the coordination of mental processes (Borkowski & Muthukrishna, 1991; Paris & Oka, 1989; Swanson, 1984b). This notion is discussed later.

Assuming for a moment that the aforementioned issues can be put aside, one obvious strategy to begin understanding the generality (as well as specificity) of the intellectual functioning of children with learning disabilities would be to combine all the relevant cognitive dimensions of their adaptive and nonadaptive behavior (e.g., classroom functioning) into an overall test or index. No doubt, such a test would be arbitrary in the items selected, but in principle it might provide some device to separate children with learning disabilities from those without such disabilities. Unfortunately, this ideal is unattainable because many of the relevant dimensions of the cognitive behavior of children with learning disabilities, such as poor strategy use (Palincsar, Brown, & Campione, 1991), executive functioning (Swanson, in press-b), metacognitive deficiencies (Wong, 1991), and phonological awareness (Shankweiler & Crain, 1986), are not standardized or even identified. Furthermore, the poor adaptive characteristics of the child with learning disabilities would have to include not only measures of vocabulary, analogical reasoning, social judgment, and general information, but also creativity, flexibility of thinking, the learning of wit, and common sense. Some of these latter characteristics exhibit themselves only in unique situations, and others cannot be evaluated except by observing the child over an extended period of time. Thus, the research is seemingly left with two possibilities: to forget about measuring intelligence altogether or to measure it inadequately. In relation to civil rights, economics, and social biases concerning who gets labeled as "learning disabled" (Adelman & Taylor, 1991), much could be said for the first alternative, but for various reasons researchers have adopted the second. Because the second alternative characterizes the field of learning disabilities, the position taken in this chapter is to direct the measurement of the intelligence of students with learning disabilities in terms of cognitive models of intelligence.

For cognitive models of learning disabilities to be fruitful, however, research efforts must be directed toward explaining the interaction between high- and low-order processing across various operations and stages of cognitive development (Swanson, 1984b, 1988, 1989). At the beginning stages of such model development, a prototype of efficient intellectual processing must be put forth. No doubt, a testing of this prototype must be linked to neuropsychological indices (Swanson, 1991). Cognitively speaking, however, a prototype of efficient intellectual functioning reflects some selection of a repertoire of cognitive routines (executive functioning) that has a plan of action (strategy) relevant to a problem. In addition, an intellectually proficient student has the necessary information (knowledge base) and knowledge of his or her own cognitive resources (metacognition) to be able to transfer and efficiently refine (strategy abstraction) his or her learning processes. These students also have a number of low-order skills that are well developed and that can be accessed without making demands on other cognitive resources.

From these assumptions, as well as taking into consideration the previous literature, a person with learning disabilities may be defined as a child or adult with average general academic aptitude in some domains (consistent with Siegel's and Stanovich's work, an IQ test is not obligatory) who *unexpectedly* has difficulty performing certain cognitive processes and/or operations. His or her performance patterns on general academic aptitude measures may reflect a factor structure comparable to that of counterparts without disabilities on tests that load high on "g." His or her problems with the effective use of certain cognitive processes, however, are reflected on tasks that make heavy demands on specific low-order processes (e.g., selective attention to auditory stimulus, nonword reading tasks that rely on phonological codes), and/or specific high-order processes (e.g., problem-solving tasks that rely on components of executive and metacognitive functioning of cognitive resources), and/or isolated processes that are sensitive to academic domains such as reading, mathematics, and writing. This discrepancy between average global processing potential and impairment in isolated processing is assumed to be due to a cognitive or neurological constraint or inefficiency. Thus, this constraint or inefficiency manifests itself in specific low-order processing (e.g., attention, phonological coding), in specific processes of a higher order system (e.g., awareness and monitoring of attentional resources), and/or in terms of an interaction between or coordination of lower and higher order processes.

Unfortunately, the literature is unclear about how specific high- and low-order processes interact or remain functionally independent while a student with learning disabilities performs an academic task. One possible model to understand the dependence or independence among processes is to consider how the knowledge of children with learning disabilities about various situations or contexts (e.g., a reading context) influences their cognitive processing.

The importance of one's knowledge of context is well documented (Lindsay & Norman, 1977). Context provides a structural representation of how information is to be processed. This structural representation influences top-down and bottom-up processing. In top-down processing there is a concept that directs processing, whereas in bottom-up, or data-driven, processing the individual is operating without a clear hypothesis about context. Greeno (1978) stated that "information processing systems are never exclusively top-down or bottom-up in nature . . . but differ in the extent of control based on general concepts and expectations rather than on specific information" (p. 48). It is possible that the poor coordination of low- and high-order processes does not allow the child with learning disabilities "flexibility" in altering the type of processing demanded by an academic situation. For example, the reader without disabilities employs top-down processing for reading comprehension, but unconsciously and/or automatically switches to bottom-up processing whenever incongruous data (patterns of information that do not match those expected) are detected. In contrast, the child with learning disabilities lacks such flexibility or efficiently coordinated processing. Because of a lack of successful reading experience, there are few exceptions or hypotheses in mind; most of the processing is bottom up, with incoming data (e.g., letters, words) perceived separately rather than in patterns. That is, incongruities and pattern mismatches in the reading of a word or sentence do not serve as "cognitive cues" and allow the child with learning disabilities to switch processing efficiently. No doubt, whether students with learning disabilities can make smooth switches between top-down and bottom-up processing in isolated domains must be fleshed out in subsequent studies.

Paradigm Issue

The second issue to be considered when looking at learning disabilities from a cognitive perspective is the paradigm that is used to study intelligence. Cognitive psychology is dominated by the information-processing paradigm (Anderson, 1983, 1990). Such a framework assumes that three general components underlie intellectual functioning:

1. A constraint or structural component, similar to the hardware of a computer, that defines those parameters within which information can be processed at a particular stage (e.g., short-term memory, working memory, long-term memory)
2. A control or strategy component, similar to the software of a computer system, that describes the operations of the various stages

3. An executive process, by which the learner's activities (e.g., strategies) are overseen and monitored (Campione & Brown, 1984)

It is assumed that the flow of information occurs in stages, and each stage operates on the information available to it. Thus, at a global level, information-processing theory consists of stages and components (Sternberg, 1985).

The information-processing paradigm provides data on the functioning of children with learning disabilities. The major application of this paradigm to the learning disabilities field has primarily been to the area of memory, and more specifically to short-term memory (Cooney & Swanson, 1987; Swanson & Cooney, 1991). Minimal research has been directed to subcomponents related to executive processing and long-term memory. (It is also important to note that the information-processing paradigm has not been used traditionally in the learning disabilities field to study or measure intelligence.) Regardless, several researchers are in agreement that what we know about the memory of children with learning disabilities is consistent with our knowledge about the differences between older and younger children's memory (Cooney & Swanson, 1987; Swanson & Cooney, 1991). That is, the memory performance of children with learning disabilities, in most cases, has been likened to younger (or immature) children's memory performance. The parallels between memory research with samples of children with learning disabilities and age-related memory research are apparent in: 1) the distinctions made between automatic and effortful processing, 2) the focus on effortful processing or cognitive strategies (e.g., rehearsal and organization), 3) the development of a knowledge base, and 4) children's awareness of their own processes (metacognition). A summary of memory literature suggests that students with learning disabilities have difficulty on tasks that require deliberate, effortful processing (Ceci, 1986). There is also some evidence that indirectly suggests that such children may suffer from a limited knowledge base and metacognitive deficiencies (Swanson, 1983, 1986; Wong, 1991).

There are several positive aspects to the memory strategy research that have originated from the information-processing perspective. Two such advantages are noteworthy. First, a focus is placed on what is modifiable. Second, cognitive strategy approaches provide a context for conscious and active rule creation and rule following.

Focus on What Is Modifiable Differences between ability groups are conceptualized in terms of cognitive processes that are susceptible to instruction, rather than to fundamental or general differences in ability. Thus, instead of focusing on isolated elementary processing deficiencies, the types of questions that are addressed by cognitive research are more educationally relevant. Specifically, a focus is placed on what students with learning disabilities do *without* strategy instruction, what they do *with* strategy instruction, and what can be done to modify existing classroom materials to improve instruction. For example, in the area of reading, Paris and Oka (1989) argued that, although learning disabilities are traditionally conceptualized in terms of "specific" deficits, there are benefits to focusing on strategy instruction because such children's learning has been diminished in terms of the acquisition of knowledge in the content areas. Strategy instruction provides a focus on what reading strategies are important because they are usually not associated with instruction in the classroom. Understanding how to select, deploy, and monitor appropriate strategies enables readers with learning disabilities to regulate the quality of their reading performance (Brown & Palincsar, 1988; Palincsar & Brown, 1984; Pressley, 1991; Pressley, Symons, Snyder, & Cariglia-Bull, 1989). In fact, there is some preliminary evidence that relatively high levels of metacognition can compensate for relatively low levels of academic aptitude on problem-solving measures (Hasselhorn & Korkel, 1986; Swanson, 1990b).

Paris and Oka (1989) reported two additional benefits to students with learning disabilities who receive cognitive strategy instruction. First, strategies promote skills that enable effective learning because they effectively use the students' existing mental resources. Second, strategies are constructed by the students to fit their own learning styles and needs. Paris and Oka further stated that effective strategy instruction includes: 1) a focus on processes and content, 2) demonstration in the use of particular strategies, 3) recognition of the need to see strategies as useful, 4) dialogues about strategies between the student and teacher, 5) the development of meaningful goals, and 6) instruction that promotes generalization.

Related to the issue of what is modifiable, Borkowski et al. (1989) presented a model of metacognition that has relevance to the understanding of higher order deficits in students with learning disabilities. These authors' analysis of the literature suggests that, no matter how extensively strategy-specific knowledge is ingrained, the generalization of strategies to new stimuli and novel situations is difficult for the student with learning disabilities. The implication is that, although extensive training in strategies is useful, it is not sufficient. Children with learning disabilities require direct instruction in analyzing task demands, monitoring the effectiveness of strategy use, and developing a personal belief about the use of demanding strategies. Borkowski et al. (1989) proposed that the maintenance and generalization of newly acquired strategies require the presence of higher order executive processes such as strategy selection and monitoring. In their cognitive-instructional model, two components are highlighted that are modifiable for instruction. The first component focuses on executive processes required for efficient learning and integration of new information. These processes are typically deficient in children with learning disabilities. The second component focuses on the attributional beliefs of students with learning disabilities. This focus is important because Borkowski's group hypothesizes that specific strategy knowledge and executive processing may prove insufficient if such students' attributional beliefs are resistant to change (see also Borkowski, Weyhing, & Carr, 1988).

Cognitive Strategy Approaches and Rule Creation and Following Cognition involves planned activities, and a focus on strategies allows one to search for underlying "plans" that influence behavior. Also, a cognitive strategy approach allows for a counterperspective on the instructional needs of children with learning disabilities when contrasted with simplistic stimulus–response, direct instruction, and/or rote drill and practice approaches to instruction. Pressley et al. (1989) suggested comprehensive strategy programs made up of a number of factors that support active rule creation and rule following. First, it is necessary that one has an understanding of the processing that is required to do the task. For example, to write an essay, the student must plan the essay, translate the plan into a narrative, and review and revise the various steps. Second, one must have a complete model of strategy use. Pressley et al. (1989) have identified a good strategy user as one who: 1) has a variety of strategies to accomplish a task, 2) has integrated specific strategies into high-order sequences that accomplish complex cognitive tasks, 3) has a reliance on metacognitive factors to regulate competent performance, 4) has appropriate beliefs about the payoffs in the strategies he or she uses, and 5) processes an adequate knowledge base.

In sum, memory research suggests that strategy instruction must entail: 1) information about a number of strategies, 2) methods of controlling and implementing those procedures, and 3) ways to gain recognition of the importance of effort and personal causality in producing successful performance. Any one of these components taught in isolation is likely to have diminished value in remediation and/or compensatory training for students with learning disabilities.

Issue of Research Focus

The third issue is related to the topical or research focus of cognitive psychology, in contrast to the research focus within the learning disabilities field. There may be some paradigm matches between cognitive psychology and learning disabilities, at least in the area of memory, but the topical focus of contemporary research carried out in the learning disabilities field in the area of cognition does not appear to match the current topical focus of cognitive psychology. Although it is difficult to document the flow of research in cognitive psychology versus that which is occurring in the learning disabilities field, one method is to compare major texts within the fields. For example, a very important event in the field of cognitive psychology was the publication of Ulric Neisser's text entitled *Cognitive Psychology* in 1967. This book consisted of six chapters on perception and attention and four chapters on memory, language, and thought. A more recent cognitive psychology text by John Anderson (1990) contrasts sharply with Neisser's text. Specifically, only 1 chapter focuses on perception and attention, whereas 11 chapters address language, memory, and thought. As stated by Anderson (1990), this change in chapter emphasis reflects a major concern in cognitive psychology with higher mental processes. This contrast between texts in cognitive psychology may be generalized to the work in learning disabilities. It appears that basic research in the learning disabilities field reflects concentrated effort on lower order processing, such as short-term memory and attention, reminiscent of the earlier foundations of the field of cognitive psychology. This implies that research in learning disabilities lags behind (or is uninterested in) the current focus in the field of cognitive psychology. As indirect evidence for this inference, the research focus in cognitive psychology, as indicated by the titles of articles published in the journals *Cognitive Psychology* and *Intelligence,* does not coincide with the majority of topical considerations in learning disabilities journals.

Another point of contrast, as mentioned earlier, is how the field of learning disabilities attempts to study *intellectual* behavior directly. The major instrument to measure the potential of children with learning disabilities is an IQ test, which can hardly be considered a measure of potential in any dynamic sense (Brown & French, 1979; Embretson, 1987; Palincsar et al., 1991). Thus, in contrast to memory research, the measurement of the intelligence of children with learning disabilities has been characterized predominantly by differential or psychometric approaches. Differential approaches are related to mathematically derived factors as a basis for the interpretation of task performance (e.g., simultaneous and successive factors on the Kaufman ABC test [K-ABC], verbal and performance factors on the Wechsler Intelligence Scale for Children [WISC] III). Although interpretations of factor analysis are sometimes equivocal (Carroll, 1983), the goal of such procedures is to isolate global constellations of the functioning of children with learning disabilities. In a practical sense, this approach assumes that standardized intelligence tests can assess individual differences along some continuum, and that the test items reflect some meaningful construct. Otherwise, the test would be of little interest or value as a descriptive and/or predictive instrument. An important goal of the differential orientation is the accurate prediction of task performance. This is an important goal in that appropriate placement of children with learning disabilities constitutes a serious problem in public school assessment procedures (Adelman & Taylor, 1991). Unfortunately for the learning disabilities field, the differential approach tends to focus on a global range of predictors, of which only the products of performance are measured (e.g., a battery of tests is given, such as the WISC III and K-ABC, and scores are recorded). In addition, the focus on such product (i.e., test score) information, derived from measures of narrowly defined attitudes (e.g., school success), is questionable (e.g., Messick, 1984). For example, children identified as having learning disabilities by the use of psychometric procedures often may not be reliably distinguished from other low-achieving children. More importantly, there are emerging data that suggest that such an approach has difficulty: 1) defining the mental processes necessary for effective learning, 2) identifying the subprocesses required for school learning, and 3) providing a link between cognitive-instructional theory and educational practices.

Perhaps the most serious limitation of the differential approach to the diagnosis of learning disabilities is that such an orientation obscures the specific learning disability one is trying to find. For example, several reviews have suggested that children with learning disabilities perform less well than students without such disabilities on a multitude of psychometric measures. Recognizing this, researchers have typically focused on a differential deficit; that is, a greater deficit in one or more subtests than in others. Unfortunately, poor subtest performance does not necessarily represent a differential deficit in ability. It may instead reflect the generalized performance deficits of children with learning disabilities (Stanovich [1986; see also Stanovich, chap. 13, this volume] refers to these deficits as "Matthew effects"). Thus, low scores on various test items cannot be interpreted as indicating a "specific" learning disability.

In support of these inferences, two related arguments are brought to bear. First, although factor analyses indicate general abilities needed on these tests, they have not provided insight into the intellectual functioning of students with learning disabilities. One reason for this state of affairs is the fact that intelligent behavior is typically organized into problem-solving skills or cognitive strategies, which are, in turn, composed of subskills and substrategies (Bereiter & Scardamalia, 1985; Campione, Brown, Ferrara, Jones, & Steinberg, 1985; Chi, Glaser, & Farr, 1988). Thus, the intellectual factors derived from psychometric measures are constructed from *interrelated* cognitive skills. The implication for understanding the intellectual functioning of students with learning disabilities is that much of their cognitive behavior reflects their ability to access various cognitive subroutines, as well as their ability to apply strategies to an increasing range of tasks (Brown & Campione, 1986; Ceci, 1990; Palincsar & Brown, 1987).

Second, psychometric research is limited by its parochial focus on isolated *academic* skills. The assumption of many psychometric studies is that specific, independent, and identifiable clusters of skills or abilities (e.g., reading, math) are involved in the learning impairments of children with learning disabilities. However, even if such skill deficits are identified, it may be argued that such skills do not represent isolated difficulties in specific processes, but interact with another (higher order) system that influences the efficient use of these processes.

In support of these arguments, consider the research on cognitive strategy instruction. Strategy use is a higher order cognitive skill that influences and/or directs the effective use of lower order skills. Data derived from research on cognitive strategies indicate that children with learning disabilities experience difficulty with such self-regulatory mechanisms as checking, planning, testing, revising, and evaluating during an attempt to learn or solve problems (Bos & Anders, 1990; Palincsar & Brown, 1984; Short & Ryan, 1984; Wong, Wong, Perry, & Sawatsky, 1986). Furthermore, children with learning disabilities have been found to perform poorly on a variety of tasks that require the use of general control processes or strategies for solution (Borkowski et al., 1988; Swanson, in press-b; Swanson & Cooney, 1991). With respect to cognitive intervention research, the data suggest that, under some conditions, well-designed strategy training improves performance (Borkowski et al., 1988; Graves, 1986; Hasselhorn & Korkel, 1986; Short & Ryan, 1984; Wong et al., 1986), whereas at other times some general cognitive constraints prevent the effective use of control processes (Ceci, 1990; Cohen, 1981; Gelzheiser, Cort, & Shephard, 1987; Schneider, 1986; Swanson, 1989). However, when training of information-processing components includes self-evaluation (e.g., predicting outcomes, organizing strategies, using various forms of trial and error), attributions are related to effective strategy use (Short & Ryan, 1984; Licht, Kistner, Ozkaragoz, Shapiro, & Clausen, 1985), and certain subprocesses are automized (Kolligian & Sternberg, 1987; Pellegrino & Goldman, 1990; Samuels, 1987), training attempts are generally successful (Borkowski et al., 1988; Palincsar & Brown, 1984; Scruggs & Mastropieri, 1989).

Thus, a differential approach that focuses primarily on academic skill deficiencies does not present a comprehensive or complete picture of the integrative or higher order nature of the intellectual functioning of children with learning disabilities. That is, learning disabilities may be the result of a unique coordination of multiple processes that include higher, as well as lower, order activities, rather than just a specific type of processing deficiency isolated to a particular academic domain (Ceci, 1990; however, see Stanovich, 1990, for a contrasting view).

It is not the intent of the foregoing comments, however, to suggest that the differential or domain-specific models of learning disabilities be abandoned, but rather to suggest that they be put into perspective. Although the "notion of specificity" is a critical assumption to the field of learning disabilities (Stanovich, 1986), this orientation has generated a number of competing hypotheses. Furthermore, even if a specific deficit is isolated, the problem is pervasive over time in its influence on higher order cognition and the acquisition of knowledge. Without denying a specific etiology of learning disabilities, there are both theoretical and practical benefits of higher order processes when one attempts to understand the intellectual functioning of such children (Paris & Oka, 1989).

APPLICATIONS OF COGNITIVE PSYCHOLOGY TO LEARNING DISABILITIES

Within the context of the three issues discussed above, I attempt to apply principles derived from cognitive psychology to the study of learning disabilities. I first attempt to sketch some major concepts from cognitive psychology that seem particularly relevant to our understanding of performance discrepancies in children with learning disabilities. I then provide some guidelines from the cognitive intervention literature for the instruction of students with learning disabilities. The majority of these concepts are couched within the information-processing paradigm. The role I see for cognitive theories is not to overthrow differential models, but to provide a more comprehensive and elaborate understanding of learning disabilities.

Applications to Assessment

Knowledge Representation and Accessibility One major contribution of cognitive psychology to the measurement of human behavior has been its focus on knowledge representation (Anderson, 1983, 1990; Messick, 1984). A knowledge representation may be defined as the way in which a person organizes relationships among concepts. As Anderson (1990) pointed out, knowledge representations are how we relate and organize information—how we understand information. As knowledge representations develop in children, they go beyond the representations of simple facts (that are called for on the majority of standardized tests) to include complex systems of multiple relationships organized for interpretation and action.

Consistent with the assumption that the measurement of human behavior must focus on how children represent knowledge (e.g., either declaratively or procedurally, a measurement of human behavior must also consider the accessibility of that knowledge (Brown & Campione, 1981; Prawat, 1989; Wertsch, 1979). Accessibility refers to the notion that the information necessary for task performance resides within the child. Some children are able to access this information flexibly; that is, a particular behavior is not limited to a constrained set of circumstances. In addition, some children are "aware" of these processes and are able to describe them consciously and discuss their own cognitive activities that allow them to access information (Brown & Campione, 1981). As indicated previously, researchers in the learning disabilities field have converged on the notion that the ability of children with learning disabilities to access knowledge remains inert, unless they are explicitly prompted to use certain cognitive strategies.

Based on these assumptions related to knowledge representation and accessibility, what insights can be gleaned from cognitive psychology to enhance our research on performance discrepancies of children with learning disabilities? I suggest three possibilities that focus on discrepancies between general intellectual functioning and depressions in certain isolated contextual behaviors (e.g., the typical discrepancies between IQ and achievement).

A Framework for Covariation First, a focus on knowledge representations provides a basis for explaining covariation (response consistency) in intellectual test performance. That is, knowledge representation may provide a basis for explaining specific processing (variance) deficits that emerge across tasks. Messick (1984) has argued that a major problem of test score interpretation is in our accounting of response consistency. One of the many reasons the cognitive abilities of children with learning disabilities are not accurately revealed by standardized tests is because of the tests' inability to account reliably for variance.

One possible way to explain this covariation is to focus on the interaction between the two forms of knowledge: declarative and procedural (Pellegrino & Goldman, 1990). The declarative form focuses on facts (as possibly measured by IQ tests), whereas procedural knowledge represents how the child encodes knowledge as *rules* or procedures, and not as an enumeration of the entire data base of facts. In a discrepancy context, the missed facts on a series of tasks on which students with learning disabilities are having difficulty may reflect errors in declarative knowledge. However, to conceptualize the discrepancy between tests would require an understanding of the *rules* that give rise to these errors. That is, the cognitive perspective focuses on an *array of rules* that may account for the observed errors in child performance within and between standardized tests. My point is that one may argue that the covariations between IQ and achievement scores are due not only to inadequate knowledge (i.e., declarative knowledge), but also to inadequate or inappropriate assembly of control processes and/or ineffective mobilization or organization of complex relevant abilities (i.e., procedural knowledge).

To avoid post hoc theorizing of reasons why covariation (discrepancies) occurs across various intellectual measures of students with learning disabilities, however, efforts must be made toward restructuring current research tasks. This does not refer to making intelligence tests used to determine child discrepancies progressively more difficult at low and intermediate levels, but rather to constructing test items that are sensitive to processes operative with the various forms of knowledge representations. One means to accomplish this is to fashion tests that capture the development of expertise in a particular domain (e.g., reading).

Domain Expertise Several cognitive studies allow us to characterize, albeit tentatively, some complexities of developed knowledge that constitute the power of expertise (Bereiter & Scardamalia, 1986; Chi, 1985; Schoenfeld & Herrmann, 1982). It appears from recent work that experts (children without disabilities in this case) not only know more than novices (i.e., children with learning disabilities) and have a vastly richer store of relevant knowledge in long-term memory (i.e., declarative knowledge), but they also structure and continually restructure their procedural knowledge representations that combine some of the dimensions and simpler schemes used by novices into integrated functional patterns while discarding as redundant or irrelevant other dimensions to which novices attend. The challenge for research purposes in assessing the performance discrepancies in children with learning disabilities is to fashion tasks that capture the functional dimensions of developing competence or expertise. These dimensions go beyond the traditional standard test measures of performance accuracy, speed, and fluency in an academic domain to include the measurement of the restructuring, fine tuning, and automatization of cognitive processes.

Determining Competence   Second, a focus on knowledge accessibility would refine our understanding of performance discrepancies. To do this, one must distinguish between competence and performance. The assessment of competence indicates what the child knows and can do under ideal circumstances, whereas performance refers to what may be done under existing circumstances. Competence embraces a child's knowledge representation, whereas performance subsumes a host of affective, motivational, attentional, and stylistic factors that influence the ultimate response. Thus, the competence of a student with learning disabilities (in terms of IQ or achievement–performance) might not be revealed in test performance because of the personal or circumstantial factors that affect behavior. The fact that children with learning disabilities have normal intelligence, however, means that they learn some information well. Why, then, are there so many discrepancies with respect to how these children perform relative to what other information suggests they are capable of doing? One could argue that the problem is one of accessing an organized knowledge system rather than a "true" discrepancy in performance. If this is the case, what methodology does cognitive psychology have to offer for determining a true discrepancy? It is in this area that dynamic assessment has a number of benefits (Embretson, 1987).

Dynamic Assessment   Palincsar, Brown, and Campione (1991) have considered the understanding of performance discrepancies that occur when one attempts to improve performance. Using Vygotsky's (1978) notion of the "zone of proximal development," Brown and French (1979) distinguished between a child's potential and actual level of performance (see also Ferrara, Brown, & Campione, 1986). That is, a distinction is made between a child's actual level of performance (e.g., as might be measured on a standardized test) and potential level of performance (the degree of competence the child can achieve with aid). In research terms, dynamic assessment may include giving the child a task in the standardized fashion. If the child fails to determine a problem solution (answer) or concept, the researcher provides progressive cues to help the child. The number of cues or prompts needed is considered the "width" of his or her zone potential. Another similar problem is given to the child, and the examiner notes if fewer cues are needed. The transfer test is especially important in conceptualizing a performance discrepancy because it reflects the child's attempts to implement a strategy. The ability of the child to benefit from cues given by the examiner allows one to infer the child's competence. Within the context of learning disabilities, one can make the argument that a "large" difference is indicative of a "lesser" discrepancy (or disability). Children who have a wide zone of potential (competence) are those who have a reduction in the number of cues needed from problem to problem and who show effective transfer to new solutions across similar problems. Thus, a performance discrepancy reflects the difference between performance as measured by standardized tests and performance when assisted by prompts or hints. Dynamic assessment cannot be implemented by merely comparing two scores (IQ and achievement), as is currently done in determining performance discrepancies; instead, all test scores (standardized and nonstandardized) must be compared under favorable and nonfavorable conditions.

Covert Discrepancies Finally, because the focus of cognitive psychology is to determine underlying cognitive structures in performance, it is possible that meaningful, as well as subtle, discrepancies in processing may exist when none have been identified on psychometric measures (Swanson, 1988). That is, one may argue that the traditional means of procedures for determining performance discrepancies in children with learning disabilities may ignore true underlying patterns of processing strengths and deficiencies. For example, two learners who earn the same test scores may have very different information-processing strengths and weaknesses. Psychometric tasks may not separate children with and without learning disabilities in terms of overt performance; yet, actual processes used in such tasks may be complex and the differences between ability groups subtle. That is, children with learning disabilities use inefficient processes that would *not be expected* based on their "normal" test scores. To illustrate this point, consider a cognitive theory that views the human system as highly adaptive and says that individuals have at their disposal a large number of alternative routes for achieving normal performance on any particular task (Newell, 1980). Suppose the task is to remember a short list of visually presented nouns that are orthographically and phonemically distinct. Some children might use primarily phonemic or semantic information, others might remember the global shapes of words and their referents, and still others might use a combination of strategies; yet, the final levels of performance are due to different processing strategies and hence subsets of resources that are quite distinct.

Applications to Intervention

Strategy Intervention When one attempts to convert some of the assumptions of the cognitive psychology to intervention, it is usually in terms of inducing learners with disabilities to become aware of their own cognitive processes (i.e., a focus is placed on metacognition). For example, the training mechanisms favored are those that mediate learning via the teacher, who provides hints, clues, counterexamples, probes, and the like. Adequate learners are those who pose questions to themselves, practice strategies, question their assumptions, provide counterstrategies, and so forth. However, the reader should be aware that cognitive strategy instruction is a broad instructional continuum.

At one end of the instructional continuum, the teacher is viewed as one who acts as a model and interrogator of the child's strategic thinking, as well as one who engineers instructional activities that influence the child's strategic use of mental resources. As the learners' self-regulatory controls eventually become more internalized, the teachers' level of participation diminishes (Brown & Palincsar, 1988). It is assumed that these instructional activities influence the learners' executive control (monitoring) functions. For example, Palincsar and Brown (1987) suggested the possibility of enhancing the metacognitive knowledge about learning of students with learning disabilities as a means of further influencing executive control skills that monitor strategies across various tasks. Metacognitive knowledge (i.e., the learners' awareness and knowledge of their own learning processes) is viewed as providing mental input to the executive control system, which in turn organizes and mobilizes relevant information-processing skills and subskills.

At the other end of the instructional continuum, a focus is placed on processing skills and subskills that must be performed automatically (Samuels, 1987). It is assumed that the ability to perform deliberate and effortful tasks, such as reading, mathematics, and spelling, requires the automatic and rapid deployment of relevant subskills (Pellegrino & Goldman, 1990). Within this context, instruction that includes, for example, computer-based drill and practice is viewed as a possible medium capable of training subskills, such as phonological coding.

When combining both ends of the continuum, instruction for the student with learning disabilities may be conceptualized as moving through a metacognitive training phase in which the learning environment consciously directs, encourages, or elicits learning strategies toward a more automatic and less controlled form of processing. This continuum from highly effortful, conscious processing to processing that occurs without awareness, effort, or intention appropriately represents the continuum of difficulties experienced by the student with learning disabilities. In short, improvement in the learning ability of these children necessitates not only the deployment of strategies, but also an executive mechanism that automatically accesses and combines learning skills (i.e., information-processing components) when they are needed.

Given these assumptions related to strategy instruction, I now briefly outline some principles of cognitive strategy instruction derived from the experimental literature. Some of these principles have been outlined elsewhere (Levin, 1986; Swanson, 1990a; Swanson & Cooney, 1991), but are summarized here with particular application to learning disabilities.

Principles of Strategy Instruction

1: Strategies Serve Different Purposes   As can be seen in a number of studies, research in learning disabilities seeks the best strategy to teach students with learning disabilities. A number of studies, for example, have looked at enhancing such children's performance through the use of advanced organizers, skimming, asking, questioning, taking notes, summarizing, and so forth. However, apart from the fact that students with learning disabilities have been exposed to various types of strategies, the question of which strategies are the most effective is unanswered. We know in some situations, such as remembering facts, that the key word approach appears to be more effective than direct instruction models (Scruggs & Mastropieri, 1989), but, of course, the rank ordering of different strategies changes in reference to the different types of learning outcomes expected (Moely et al., 1986). Certain cognitive strategies are better suited to enhancing students' understanding of academics, such as what they have previously read, whereas other strategies are better suited to enhancing students' memory of words or facts. As yet, however, research is unclear about which strategies are best within and across particular academic domains.

2: Strategy Instruction Must Operate on the Law of Parsimony   There are a number of "multiple component packages" of strategy instruction that have been suggested for improving the functioning of children with learning disabilities. These components have usually encompassed some of the following: skimming, imagining, drawing, elaborating, paraphrasing, mnemonics, accessing prior knowledge, reviewing, and orienting to critical features. The difficulty of such packages, however, at least in terms of cognitive intervention, is that little is known about which components best predict student performance, nor do they readily permit one to determine why the strategy worked. The multiple component approaches that are typically found in a number of strategy intervention studies for students with learning disabilities must be carefully contrasted with a *component analysis* approach that involves the systematic combination of instructional activities known to have an additive effect on performance. As stated by Pressley (1986), good strategies are "composed of the sufficient and necessary processes for accomplishing their intended goal, consuming as few intellectual processes as necessary to do so" (p. 140).

3: Good Strategies for Students without Disabilities Are Not Necessarily Good Strategies for Students with Learning Disabilities Strategies that enhance access to procedural and/or declarative knowledge for students without disabilities will not, in some cases, be well suited for the child with learning disabilities. For example, in a study by Swanson and Cooney (1991), it was discovered that students who do well in mathematics benefit from strategies that enhance the access of procedural knowledge, whereas children who do poorly in mathematics benefit from strategies that enhance declarative knowledge. To further illustrate, Wong and Jones (1982) taught self-questioning strategies to monitor reading comprehension to adolescents with and without learning disabilities. Results indicated that, although the strategy training benefited those with learning disabilities, it actually lowered the performance of those without learning disabilities (see also Swanson, Cooney, & Overholser, 1989, for a related study).

4: Use of Effective Strategies Does Not Necessarily Eliminate Processing Differences It is commonly assumed that, if children with learning disabilities are presented a strategy that allows for the efficient processing of information, improvement in performance occurs because the strategies are affecting the same processes as in students without learning disabilities. This assumption has emanated primarily from studies that have imposed organization on seemingly unorganized material. The notion that readers with disabilities process the organizational features of information in the same fashion as do students without disabilities is questionable. For example, Swanson and Rathgeber (1986) found in categorization tasks that readers with disabilities, even after organizational instruction, can retrieve information without interrelating superordinate, subordinate, and coordinate classes of information as do children without disabilities. It is possible that the sorting of multiple categories, as required in previous studies, reflects an interactive process between a knowledge base and organizational strategies.

5: Comparable Performance Does Not Mean Comparable Strategies Although the previous principle suggests that different processes may be activated *during* intervention, it is also likely that subjects with learning disabilities use different strategies on tasks in which they seem to have little difficulty, and it is likely that these tasks will be overlooked in research. As discussed earlier, it is commonly assumed that, although children with learning disabilities have isolated processing deficits and require general learning strategies to compensate for these deficits, they process information in ways comparable to their normal counterparts on tasks with which they have little trouble. Yet, several authors suggest that there are a number of alternative ways for achieving comparable performance. There is research suggesting that children with learning disabilities use qualitatively different mental operations (Shankweiler & Crain, 1986) and processing routes (Swanson, 1986) compared to their counterparts without disabilities.

For example, a study (Swanson, 1988) found that children with learning disabilities may use qualitatively different processes on tasks with which they have little difficulty. Evidence in support of this finding was provided when comparing the "think-aloud protocols" of children with and without learning disabilities on picture arrangement problem-solving tasks. Think-aloud responses were divided into heuristics and strategies. Although both types of students were *comparable* in the total number of mental components used to solve the task and the number of problems solved, children with learning disabilities had difficulty in using isolated *heuristics* related to problem representation and deleting irrelevant information. In addition, children without disabilities were superior to children with learning disabilities in using strategies that relate to evaluation, systematic problem solving, feedback, and pattern extraction. Furthermore, a stepwise regression analysis suggested that the overall mental processing of children with learning disabilities was best predicted by heuristics, whereas the overall mental processing of children without disabilities was best predicted by a specific strategy.

6: Strategies Must Be Considered in Relation to a Student's Capacity There must be a match between cognitive strategy and learner's processing capacity. One important variable that has been overlooked in the learning disabilities intervention literature is the notion of processing capacity (Swanson, 1984a; Swanson, Cochran, & Ewers, 1989). Unfortunately, most learning disabilities strategy research, either implicitly or explicitly, has considered cognitive capacity to be a confounding variable and has made very little attempt to measure its influence. The importance of cognitive capacity has been illustrated in a few studies. For example, Swanson (1984b) has conducted three experiments related to the performance of students with learning disabilities on a word recall task. In these experiments, an intentional free-recall task (children informed of the secondary memory test) was presented after subjects correctly matched to-be-remembered words to a series of anagrams organized semantically, phonemically, or in an uncategorized fashion. The anagram problem-solving task of the to-be-remembered words involved two degrees of effort. In the low-effort condition, anagrams were scrambled for only the first and second letters; in the high-effort condition, all letters were rearranged. The results were unequivocal in showing the individual variations in the facilitative effects of cognitive effort on later retrieval. The reduced capacity of readers with learning disabilities was related to their failure to activate distinctive features of words from long-term memory, to allocate attention capacity to elaborate those features, and to activate a critical number of word features to fill the allocated attention capacity. In contrast, the successful recall of skilled readers apparently represents some critical number of word features activated during encoding that matched allocated attention capacity. Therefore, it is clear that any general relationship between cognitive effort and distinctive word encoding must be qualified by the child's capacity.

Thus, in some cognitive intervention studies, processing inefficiencies related to strategy use may provide an adequate, but not necessarily comprehensive, explanation of learning disabilities. This is because the learning characteristics, such as deficits in cognitive capacity, have not been taken into consideration. Before a processing inefficiency (in contrast to a processing constraint) explanation can provide a comprehensive account of effects of cognitive instruction related to the performance of children with learning disabilities, the majority of the following predictions must be supported:

1. Students with learning disabilities who use strategies should show minimal variation in their performance across tasks that *demand the use of such strategies*. That is, if these children are using systematic approach, their performance should be relatively constant.
2. Students with learning disabilities should be specifically prone to disruption of their performances that make demands on higher order processes.
3. Students with learning disabilities should be influenced minimally by task parameters that are irrelevant to strategy formation.
4. Students with learning disabilities should be specifically influenced by strategy components of instruction, such as feedback.

5. Students with learning disabilities should show markedly improved performance when they discover definite strategies for coping with the task.

6. Residual performance and differences between ability groups should be eliminated when effective strategies are acquired and learned.

The point that is being stressed here is that cognitive processing inefficiencies may not be a sufficient explanation of the instructional performance of children with learning disabilities. What is needed is instructional research that provides a framework for considering how both processes and structures interact during instructional interventions.

7: Comparable Strategy Use May Not Eliminate Performance Differences Several studies have indicated that residual differences remain between ability groups even when ability groups are instructed in strategy use. For example, in a study by Gelzheiser (1984), children with and without learning disabilities were compared on their ability to use organizational strategies. After instruction in organizational strategies, the children were compared on their ability to recall information on a posttest. The results indicated that children with learning disabilities were comparable in strategy use to those without disabilities, but were deficient in overall performance. These results basically support the notion that groups of children with different learning histories may continue to learn differently, even when the groups are equated in terms of strategy use.

8: Strategies Taught Do Not Necessarily Become Transformed into Expert Strategies One mechanism that promotes expert performance is related to strategy transformation (Chi et al., 1988). It often appears that children who become experts at certain tasks have learned simple strategies and, through practice, discover ways to modify them into more efficient and powerful procedures. In particular, the proficient learner uses higher order rules to eliminate unnecessary or redundant steps in order to hold increasing amounts of information. The child with learning disabilities, in contrast, may learn most of the skills related to performing an academic task and perform appropriately on that task by carefully and systematically following only prescribed rules or strategies. Although children with learning disabilities can be taught strategies, recent evidence suggests that the differences between children with learning disabilities and those without disabilities (experts in this case) are that the latter have modified such strategies to become more efficient (Swanson & Cooney, 1985). It is plausible that the child with learning disabilities remains a novice because he or she fails to transform simple strategies into more efficient forms (Swanson & Rhine, 1985).

SUMMARY

In this chapter I have presented three ways in which cognitive psychology can provide a perspective on performance discrepancies in children with learning disabilities and several principles related to cognitive strategy intervention. In terms of performance discrepancies, one application is to provide a framework for explaining covariation in test performance, another is to focus on competence rather than performance, and a final way is to help us uncover processing discrepancies when the overt performance of children with learning disabilities is comparable to that of their counterparts without disabilities. It is suggested that current assessment procedures used to determine performance discrepancies in children with learning disabilities are insensitive to how such children represent knowledge and access that knowledge. Although several authors have suggested that a discrepancy can be inferred from task performance on ability and achievement measures, especially if these performance discrepancies are consistently demonstrated across related tasks, as a general rule it is dangerous to make inferences about discrepancies from test performance scores. To do that requires discounting a variety of plausible sources of poor performance (e.g., generalized performance deficit, test- or task-wiseness). These variables are hopelessly confounded in current assessment practices used to determine performance discrepancies in children with learning disabilities. Yet, individuals who take the psychometric perspective continue to focus on the statistical aspects of discrepancy measurement (e.g., factors considered important are the reliability of tests, their correlations, size of score difference involved). Unfortunately, several authors (e.g., Thorndike, 1972) have concluded that the development of an accurate diagnostic interpretation of score differences is unlikely. It seems, therefore, that the problem of the psychometric approach will always be in the error of single numbers (i.e., the presence of measurement error in each score). A contrasting approach, the one suggested here, is to focus on an array of rules that account for errors in performance. It was also suggested that the field consider abandoning existing psychometric procedures used to determine performance discrepancies and begin investigating complex models of learning that are sensitive to the development of domain expertise and performance competence.

The cognitive principles are consistent with many of the points made by other authors (e.g., Levin, 1986) who have summarized the cognitive literature. I have merely highlighted some of the major steps and components that enhance cognitive processing in students with learning disabilities. It is clear that the knowledge and beliefs of students with learning disabilities about the how, where, and why of strategy use are important if they are to take control of their cognitive processing. Such information should be included in an instruction program designed to enhance cognition. However, researchers must also follow certain guidelines and principles in their selection of strategies to be taught to students. Strategies are never applied in isolation of person, process, and context. Strategies are always applied to specific materials, in a specific context, with a specific student. When these factors are kept in mind, a cognitive model of instruction has much to offer the learning disabilities field.

REFERENCES

Adelman, H.S., & Taylor, L. (1991). Issues and problems related to the assessment of learning disabilities. In H.L. Swanson (Ed.), *Handbook on the assessment of learning disabilities: Theory, research, and practice* (pp. 21–46). Austin, TX: PRO-ED.

Anderson, J.R. (1983). *The architecture of cognition*. Cambridge, MA: Harvard University Press.

Anderson, J.R. (1990). *Cognitive psychology and its implications*. New York: W.H. Freeman.

Baddeley, A.D. (1886). *Working memory*. Oxford, England: Clarendon Press.

Balota, D.A., Pollatsek, A., & Rayner, K. (1985). The interaction of contextual constraints and parafoveal visual information in reading. *Cognitive Psychology, 17*, 364–390.

Bereiter, C., & Scardamalia, M. (1985). Cognitive coping strategies and the problem of "inert" knowledge. In S. Chipman, J.W. Segal, & R. Glaser (Eds.), *Thinking and learning skills. Volume 2. Research and open questions* (pp. 65–80). Hillsdale, NJ: Lawrence Erlbaum Associates.

Bereiter, C., & Scardamalia, M. (1986). Educational relevance of the study of expertise. *Interchange, 17*(2), 10–19.

Borkowski, J.G., Estrada, M.T., Milstead, M., & Hale, C. (1989). General problem-solving skills: Relations between metacognition and strategic processing. *Learning Disabilities Quarterly, 12*, 57–70.

Borkowski, J.G., & Muthukrishna, N. (1991). Moving metacognition into the classroom: Working models and effective strategy teaching. In M. Pressley, K. Harris, & J. Guthrie (Eds.), *Promoting academic literacy*. Orlando, FL: Academic Press.

Borkowski, J.G., Weyhing, R.S., & Carr, M. (1988). Effects of attributional retraining on strategy-based reading comprehension in learning-disabled students. *Journal of Educational Psychology, 80*, 46–53.

Bos, C., & Anders, P.L. (1990). Toward an interactive model: Teaching text-based concepts to learning disabled students. In H.L. Swanson & B.K. Keogh (Eds.), *Learning disabilities: Theoretical and research issues* (pp. 247–261). Hillsdale, NJ: Lawrence Erlbaum Associates.

Brown, A., & Campione, J.C. (1981). Inducing flexible thinking: The problem of access. In M. Friedman, J. Das, & N. O'Connor (Eds.), *Intelligence and learning* (pp. 515–530). New York: Plenum.

Brown, A., & French, L. (1979). The zone of potential development: Implications for intelligence in the year 2000. *Intelligence, 4*, 255–273.

Brown, A.L., & Campione, J.C. (1986). Psychological theory and the study of learning disabilities. *American Psychologist, 41*, 1059–1068.

Brown, A.L., & Palincsar, A.S. (1988). Reciprocal teaching of comprehension strategies: A natural history of one program for enhancing learning. In J. Borkowski & J.P. Day (Eds.), *Intelligence and cognition in special children: Comparative studies of giftedness, mental retardation, and learning disabilities* (pp. 81–132). Norwood, NJ: Ablex.

Campione, J., & Brown, A. (1978). Toward a theory of intelligence: Contributions from research with retarded children. *Intelligence, 2*, 279–304.

Campione, J.C., & Brown, A.L. (1984). Learning ability and transfer propensity as sources of individual differences in intelligence. In P.H. Brooks, R. Sperber, & C. McCauley (Eds.), *Learning and cognition in the mentally retarded* (pp. 265–294). Hillsdale, NJ: Lawrence Erlbaum Associates.

Campione, J.C., Brown, A.L., Ferrara, R.A., Jones, R.S., & Steinberg, E. (1985). Breakdown in flexible use of information: Intelligence related differences in transfer following equivalent learning performances. *Intelligence, 9*, 297–315.

Carroll, J.B. (1983). Studying individual difference in cognitive abilities: Through and beyond factor analysis. In R. Dillon & R. Schneck (Eds.), *Individual differences in cognition* (pp. 1–28). New York: Academic Press.

Ceci, S.J. (1986). Developmental study of learning disabilities and memory. *Journal of Experimental Child Psychology, 38*, 352–371.

Ceci, S.J. (1990). A sideways glance at this thing called LD: A context × process × person from work. In H.L. Swanson & B.K. Keogh (Eds.), *Learning disabilities: Theoretical and research issues* (pp. 59–74). Hillsdale, NJ: Lawrence Erlbaum Associates.

Ceci, S.J., & Liker, J.K. (1986). A day at the races: A study of IQ, expertise, and cognitive complexity. *Journal of Experimental Psychology: General, 115*, 225–266.

Chi, M.T.H. (1985). Interactive roles of knowledge and strategies in the development of organized sorting and recall. In S.F. Chipman, J.W. Segal, & R. Glaser (Eds.), *Thinking and learning skills* (Vol. 2, pp. 457–484). Hillsdale, NJ: Lawrence Erlbaum Associates.

Chi, M.T.H., Glaser, R., & Farr, M. (1988). *The nature of expertise*. Hillsdale, NJ: Lawrence Erlbaum Associates.

Cohen, R.L. (1981). Short-term memory deficits in reading disabled children in the absence of opportunity for rehearsal strategies. *Intelligence, 5*, 69–76.

Cooney, J.B., & Swanson, H.L. (1987). Memory and learning disabilities: An overview. In H.L. Swanson (Ed.), *Memory and learning disabilities* (pp. 1–40). Greenwich, CT: JAI Press.

Embretson, S.E. (1987). Toward development of a psychometric approach. In C. Lidz (Ed.), *Dynamic assessment* (pp. 141–172). New York: Guilford Press.

Farnham-Diggory, S. (1986). Time, now, for a little serious complexity. In S. Ceci (Ed.), *Handbook of cognitive, social, and neuropsychological aspects of learning disabilities* (pp. 123–158). Hillsdale, NJ: Lawrence Erlbaum Associates.

Ferrara, R.A., Brown, A.L., & Campione, J.C. (1986). Children's learning and transfer of inductive reasoning rules: Studies of proximal development. *Child Development, 52,* 1087–1089.

Fodor, J.A. (1983). *Modularity of mind.* Cambridge, MA: MIT Press.

Forness, S.R., Sinclair, E., & Guthrie, D. (1983). Learning disabilities discrepancy formulas: Their use in actual practice. *Learning Disabilities Quarterly, 6,* 107–114.

Gelzheiser, L.M. (1984). Generalization from categorical memory tasks to prose in learning disabled adolescents. *Journal of Educational Psychology, 20,* 1128–1138.

Gelzheiser, L.M., Cort, R., & Shephard, M.J. (1987). Is minimal strategy instruction sufficient for learning disabled students? *Learning Disabilities Quarterly, 10,* 267–275.

Graves, A. (1986). Effects of direct instruction and metacomprehension on finding main ideas. *Learning Disability Research, 1,* 90–100.

Greeno, J.G. (1978). A study in problem solving. In R. Glaser (Ed.), *Advances in instructional psychology* (pp. 13–75). Hillsdale, NJ: Lawrence Erlbaum Associates.

Hasselhorn, M., & Korkel, J. (1986). Metacognitive versus traditional reading instructions: The mediating role of domain-specific knowledge on children's text-processing. *Human Learning, 5,* 75–90.

Hunt, E. (1983). On the nature of intelligence. *Science, 219,* 141–146.

Keating, D.P. (1982). The emperor's new clothes: The new look in intelligence research. In R. Sternberg (Ed.), *Advances in the psychology of human intelligence* (Vol. 2, pp. 1–45). Hillsdale, NJ: Lawrence Erlbaum Associates.

Kolligian, J., & Sternberg, R.J. (1987). Intelligence, information processing, and specific learning disabilities: A triarchic synthesis. *Journal of Learning Disabilities, 20,* 8–17.

Larson, G.E., & Saccuzzo, D.P. (1989). Cognitive correlates of general intelligence: Toward a process theory of G. *Intelligence, 14,* 389–433.

Levin, J.R. (1986). Four cognitive principles of learning strategy instruction. *Educational Psychologist, 21,* 3–17.

Licht, B.G., Kistner, J.A., Ozkaragoz, T., Shapiro, S., & Clausen, L. (1985). Causal attributions of learning disabled children: Individual differences and implications for persistence. *Journal of Educational Psychology, 77,* 208–216.

Lindsay, P.H., & Norman, D.A. (1977). *Human information processing: An introduction to psychology* (2nd ed.). New York: Academic Press.

Messick, S. (1984). The psychology of educational measurement. *Journal of Educational Measurement, 21,* 215–237.

Moely, B.E., Hart, S.S., Santulli, K., Leal, L., Johnson, T., & Rao, N. (1986). How do teachers teach memory skills? *Educational Psychologist, 21,* 55–57.

Morrison, S.R., & Siegel, L.S. (1991). Learning disabilities: A critical review of definitional and assessment issues. In J. Obrzut & G.W. Hynd (Eds.), *Neuropsychological foundation of learning disabilities* (pp. 79–95). New York: Academic Press.

Neisser, U. (1967). *Cognitive psychology.* New York: Appleton-Century-Crofts.

Newell, A. (1980). Reasoning, problem solving and decision processes: The problem space as a fundamental category. In R. Nickerson (Ed.), *Attention and performance VIII* (pp. 1–64). Hillsdale, NJ: Lawrence Erlbaum Associates.

Palincsar, A.M., & Brown, A.L. (1984). Reciprocal teaching of comprehension-fostering and comprehension-monitoring activities. *Cognition and Instruction, 1,* 117–175.

Palincsar, A.M., & Brown, A. (1987). Enhancing instructional time through attention to metacognition. *Journal of Learning Disabilities, 20,* 66–76.

Palincsar, A., Brown, A., & Campione, J. (1991). Dynamic assessment. In H.L. Swanson (Ed.), *Handbook on the assessment of learning disabilities: Theory, research, and practice* (pp. 75–94). Austin, TX: PRO-ED.

Paris, S.G., & Oka, E.R. (1989). Strategies for comprehending text and coping with reading difficulties. *Learning Disabilities Quarterly, 12,* 32–42.

Pellegrino, J.W., & Goldman, S.R. (1990). Cognitive science perspectives on intelligence and learning disabilities. In H.L. Swanson & B.K. Keogh (Eds.), *Learning disabilities: Theoretical and research issues* (pp. 41–58). Hillsdale, NJ: Lawrence Erlbaum Associates.

Prawat, R.S. (1989). Promoting access to knowledge, strategy, and disposition in students: A research synthesis. *Review of Educational Research, 59,* 1–41.

Pressley, M. (1986). The relevance of the good strategy user model to the teaching of mathematics. *Educational Psychologist, 21,* 139–161.

Pressley, M. (1991). Can learning disabled children become good information processors? How can we find out? In L. Feagans, E. Short, & L. Meltzer (Eds.), *Subtypes of learning disabilities* (pp. 137–162). Hillsdale, NJ: Lawrence Erlbaum Associates.

Pressley, M., Johnson, C.J., & Symons, S. (1987). Elaborating to learn and learning to elaborate. *Journal of Learning Disabilities, 20,* 76–91.

Pressley, M., Symons, S., Snyder, B.L., & Cariglia-Bull, T. (1989). Strategy instruction research is coming of age. *Learning Disabilities Quarterly, 12,* 54–63.

Samuels, S.J. (1987). Information processing and reading. *Journal of Learning Disabilities, 20,* 18–22.

Schneider, W. (1986). The role of conceptual knowledge and metamemory in the development or organizational processes in memory. *Journal of Experimental Child Psychology, 42,* 318–336.

Schoenfeld, A.H., & Herrmann, D.J. (1982). Problem perception and knowledge structure in expert and novice mathematical problem solvers. *Journal of Experimental Psychology: Learning, Memory, and Cognition, 8,* 484–494.

Scruggs, T.E., & Mastropieri, M.A. (1989). Mnemonic instruction of LD students: A field-based evaluation. *Learning Disabilities Quarterly, 12,* 119–125.

Shankweiler, D., & Crain, S. (1986). Language mechanisms and reading disorder: A modular approach. *Cognition, 24,* 139–168.

Short, E.J., & Ryan, E.B. (1984). Metacognitive differences between skilled and less skilled readers: Remediating deficits through story grammar and attribution training. *Journal of Educational Psychology, 76,* 225–235.

Siegel, L.S. (1988). Evidence that IQ scores are irrelevant to the definition and analysis of reading disability. *Canadian Journal of Psychology, 42,* 201–215.

Siegel, L.S. (1989). IQ is irrelevant to the definition of learning disabilities. *Journal of Learning Disabilities, 22,* 469–478.

Siegel, L.S. (1990). IQ and learning disabilities: R.I.P. In H.L. Swanson & B. Keogh (Eds.), *Learning disibilities: Theoretical and research issues* (pp. 111–128). Hillsdale, NJ: Lawrence Erlbaum Associates.

Siegel, L.S., & Ryan, E.B. (1989). The development of working memory in normal achieving and subtypes of learning disabled children. *Child Development, 60,* 973–981.

Sinclair, E., & Alexson, J. (1986). Learning disability discrepancy formulas: Similarities and differences among them. *Learning Disability Research, 1,* 112–118.

Stanovich, K. (1986). Matthew effects in reading: Some consequences of individual differences in the acquisition of literacy. *Reading Research Quarterly, 21,* 360–387.

Stanovich, K.E. (1990). Concepts in developmental theories of reading skill: Cognitive resources, automaticity, and modularity. *Developmental Review, 10,* 72–100.

Stanovich, K.E. (1991). Discrepancy definition of reading disability: Has intelligence led us astray? *Reading Research Quarterly, 26,* 8–29.

Sternberg, R.J. (1985). *Beyond IQ: A triarchic theory of human intelligence.* Cambridge, England: Cambridge University Press.

Sternberg, R.J. (1987). A unified theory of intellectual exceptionality. In J.D. Day & J.G. Borkowski (Eds.), *Intelligence and exceptionality: New directions for theory, assessment, and instructional practices* (pp. 135–172). Norwood, NJ: Ablex.

Swanson, H.L. (1983). Relations among metamemory, rehearsal activity and word recall in learning disabled and nondisabled readers. *British Journal of Educational Psychology, 53,* 186–194.

Swanson, H.L. (1984a). Effects of cognitive effort and word distinctiveness on learning disabled readers recall. *Journal of Educational Psychology, 76,* 894–908.

Swanson, H.L. (1984b). Process assessment of intelligence in learning disabled and mentally retarded children: A multidirectional model. *Educational Psychologist, 19,* 149–162.

Swanson, H.L. (1986). Do semantic memory deficiencies underlie learning disabled readers' encoding process? *Journal of Experimental Child Psychology, 41,* 461–488.

Swanson, H.L. (1988). Learning disabled children's problem solving: Identifying mental processes underlying intelligent performances. *Intelligence, 12,* 261–278.

Swanson, H.L. (1989). Central processing strategy differences in gifted, learning disabled and mentally retarded children. *Journal of Experimental Child Psychology, 47,* 370–397.

Swanson, H.L. (1990a). Instruction derived from the strategy deficit model. In T. Scruggs & B.Y.L. Wong (Eds.), *Intervention research in learning disabilities* (pp. 34–66). New York: Springer-Verlag.

Swanson, H.L. (1990b). The influence of metacognitive knowledge and aptitude on problem solving. *Journal of Educational Psychology, 82,* 306–314.

Swanson, H.L. (1991). An information processing approach to neuropsychology. In J. Obrzut & G.W. Hynd (Eds.), *Handbook on the neuropsychology of learning disabilities* (pp. 241–280). San Diego, CA: Academic Press.

Swanson, H.L. (1992). Operational definitions of learning disabilities: An overview. *Learning Disabilities Quarterly, 14,* 242–254.

Swanson, H.L. (in press-a). Executive processing in learning disabled readers. *Intelligence.*

Swanson, H.L. (in press-b). The modifiability and predictability of skilled and less-skilled readers' working memory. *Journal of Educational Psychology.*

Swanson, H.L., Cochran, K., & Ewers, C. (1989). Working memory and reading disabilities. *Journal of Abnormal Child Psychology, 17,* 145–156.

Swanson, H.L., & Cooney, J. (1985). Strategy transformations in learning disabled children. *Learning Disabilities Quarterly, 8,* 221–231.

Swanson, H.L., & Cooney, J.B. (1987). *Procedural and declarative knowledge in arithmetic transformations.* Paper presented at the annual meeting of the American Educational Research Association, Washington, DC.

Swanson, H.L., & Cooney, J.B. (1991). Memory and learning disabilities. In B.Y.L. Wong (Ed.), *Learning about learning disabilities* (pp. 104–122). Orlando, FL: Academic Press.

Swanson, H.L., Cooney, J.D., & Overholser, J.D. (1989). The effects of self-generated visual mnemonics on adult learning disabled readers' word recall. *Learning Disability Research, 4,* 26–35.

Swanson, H.L., & Rathgeber, A. (1986). The effects of organizational dimensions on learning disabled readers' recall. *Journal of Educational Research, 74,* 155–162.

Swanson, H.L., & Rhine, B. (1985). Strategy transformation in learning disabled children's math performance: Clues to the development of expertise. *Journal of Learning Disabilities, 18,* 596–603.

Thorndike, R.L. (1972). Dilemmas in diagnosis. In W.H. MacGinitie (Ed.), *Assessment problems in reading* (pp. 57–67). Newark, DE: International Reading Association.

Turner, M.L., & Engle, R.W. (1989). Is working memory capacity task dependent? *Journal of Memory and Language, 28,* 127–154.

Vygotsky, L.S. (1978). *Mind in society: The development of higher psychological processes* (M. Cole, V. John-Steiner, S. Schribner, & E. Souberman, Eds. and Trans.). Cambridge, MA: Harvard University Press.

Wertsch, J.V. (1979). From social interaction to higher psychological processes. A clarification and application of Vygotsky's theory. *Human Development, 22,* 1–22.

Wong, B.Y.L. (1991). Assessment of metacognitive research in learning disabilities. In H.L. Swanson (Ed.), *Handbook of the assessment of learning disabilities* (pp. 265–284). Austin: Pro Ed.

Wong, B.Y.L., & Jones, W. (1982). Increasing metacomprehension in learning disabled and normally achieving students through self-questioning training. *Learning Disability Quarterly, 5,* 228–240.

Wong B.Y.L., Wong, R., Perry, N., & Sawatsky, D. (1986). The efficacy of a self-questioning summarization strategy for use by underachievers and learning disabled adolescents. *Learning Disability Focus, 2,* 20–35.

11

LEARNING DISABILITIES
An Interactive Developmental Paradigm

Melvin D. Levine, Stephen Hooper,
James Montgomery, Martha Reed,
Adrian Sandler, Carl Swartz, and Thomas Watson

This chapter presents a conceptual framework for the study of learning disabilities. This interactive developmental paradigm represents the fusion of established principles emanating from clinical investigation and studies of normal developmental processes. The first section of the chapter offers a brief historical view of past and existing models and definitions of learning disabilities. There is an emphasis on the limitations imposed by research efforts using single-deficit models for learning disability. There follows a general description of the interactive developmental paradigm. The most salient characteristics of the paradigm are addressed, along with consideration of how it compares to earlier models of learning disabilities. The third section provides a detailed presentation of the interactive developmental paradigm. This section makes use of written output disorders to illustrate and elucidate the paradigm. The final section focuses on the theoretical and practical implications of the interactive developmental paradigm. Suggestions are presented for future research, both basic and applied, using this paradigm.

HISTORICAL AND CURRENT
PERSPECTIVES OF LEARNING DISABILITIES

Since the first case study descriptions of learning disabilities were published in the late 1800s (see Hinshelwood, 1895; Kussmaul, 1877), conceptualizations of learning disability have undergone significant development and refinement. Shifts in theories of human learning and cognitive development have contributed to changing theoretical perspectives concerning learning disabilities (Kavanagh & Truss, 1988).

Although the early case studies presented varied manifestations of learning problems, the first efforts to develop a conceptual model of learning disability, beginning with Orton's (1928) theory of delayed cerebral dominance were based on single-factor deficit conceptualizations (Hooper & Willis, 1989). Unitary explanations of learning disabilities and research in treatment methods based on such conceptualizations continued through the 1970s, as represented by the perceptual deficit theories of Bender (1956, 1957) and Frostig (1964), the visual-motor formulation of Kephart (1971) and Getman (1965), and the auditory-perceptual deficit model of Wepman (1960). In addition, considerable attention was given to the patterning/neurological organization theory of Delacato (1966) and the sensory integration deficit models of Ayres (1978, 1981) and Birch and Belmont (1964, 1965).

The single-deficit models of learning disabilities were questioned increasingly because they failed to account for the clinical heterogeneity of learning disabilities. Furthermore, studies of the efficacy of treatment techniques targeting the training of single processes (e.g., visual perception) resulted in little or no amelioration of academic performance (Kavale, 1990; chap. 9, this volume).

The trend since the 1970s has been toward conceptualizations of learning disabilities that reflect multidimensional mechanisms. At present, the multidimensional approach is evident in research efforts to subtype learning disabilities. Such studies deploy either a priori methods, in which groups are generated based on particular patterns of performance before intervention or analysis of dependent measures, or a posterior techniques, in which groups are formed using cluster-analytic techniques that generate subtypes through empirical analyses of descriptive profiles (Hooper & Willis, 1989; Rourke, 1983). As yet, however, theoreticians have been unable to agree on a conceptual model of learning disabilities that fully encompasses the striking heterogeneity of inter- and intraindividual differences found among students with learning disabilities.

Definitions of Learning Disabilities

Definitions of learning disabilities remain controversial. The first national definition of a learning disability was presented in the Elementary and Secondary Amendments of 1969 and the Education of the Handicapped Act, Title VI, of 1970 (P.L. 91-230). In P.L. 91-230, a learning disability was defined as a single disorder with a variety of vaguely described manifestations. The current federal definition, contained in the Individuals with Disabilities Education Act Amendments (P.L. 102-119), an updating of the Education for All Handicapped Children Act of 1975 (P.L. 94-142) and its amendment in 1986 to include the preschool population (P.L. 99-457), reflects little change over its predecessor (P.L. 91-230). The underlying unitary disorder conceptualization of learning disabilities has led to the mistaken belief that the population with learning disabilities represents a homogeneous group (Kavanagh & Truss, 1988).

The definition of learning disability proposed by the National Joint Committee for Learning Disabilities (Hammill, Leigh, McNutt, & Larsen, 1981) was the first to recognize formally the heterogeneous condition of learning disabilities. It also allowed for co-morbidity with other handicapping conditions (see MacMillan, chap. 7, this volume, for a contrasting point of view). More recent proposed formulations (Association for Children with Learning Disabilities, 1985; Interagency Committee on Learning Disabilities, 1987) have further broadened the definition of learning disabilities by acknowledging their chronicity as well as their potential impacts on nonacademic functioning (e.g., social skills).

As yet, no definition has produced a consensus regarding what constitutes a learning disability. All definitions of learning disabilities remain relatively vague descriptive generalizations that tend to emphasize what a learning disability *is not* while failing to delineate operational criteria by which to specify what a learning disability *is* and to identify its presence.

The inability to reach agreement on a definition of learning disabilities has led to several difficulties, including: 1) trouble in interpreting and generalizing basic and applied research that uses samples of "learning-disabled" students (Torgesen, 1986); 2) problems evaluating the efficacy of interventions for improving the achievement of students with learning disabilities (Bryan, Bay, & Donahue, 1988); 3) serious difficulty reducing the number of students who comprise false positives receiving special services (Algozzine & Ysseldyke, 1986); and 4) confusion among professionals as to the future direction of the field (Adelman & Taylor, 1986a). Dissatisfaction and frustration with the current state of affairs, and vehement expression of the need for a uniform definitional construct of learning disabilities, have been forcefully voiced by leaders in learning disabilities theory, research, and intervention (Adelman & Taylor, 1986a; Blachman, 1988; Cannon, 1991; Gavelek & Palincsar, 1988; Harris, 1988; Kavanagh & Truss, 1988; Keogh, 1986; Scruggs & Wong, 1990; Siegel, 1988; Silver, 1988; Swanson, 1988; Torgesen, 1986, 1988).

These authors at the same time ardently lament the lack of conceptual consensus that characterizes the field. Kavale (1990) stated, "Even within the context of evaluation, intervention 're-search' in LD has been contentious. Little agreement has emerged about the value of an intervention much less insight in how or why it works" (p. 6). Kavale (1990; see also chap. 9, this volume) described the shortcomings of past theoretical models, related intervention research, and areas of ongoing debate, including the philosophical basis of learning disabilities practice, process training, placement efficacy, and variance in response to treatment.

The results of a survey of prominent researchers in the field of learning disabilities suggested that, for the field to advance, theoreticians must arrive at a "conceptual and operational definition of just what constitutes a learning disability" (Adelman & Taylor, 1986b, p. 391). The respondents to the survey believed that a universally agreed on operational definition of what comprises a learning disability will advance theory and research (Adelman & Taylor, 1986b), which in turn will improve screening and differential diagnosis of learning disabilities (Algozzine & Ysseldyke, 1986). Furthermore, teacher education programs and efficacious classroom interventions should have greater potential to increase the academic performance of students with learning disabilities if indeed theory and research inform such practice.

The imprecision and fluctuation of the definition of learning disabilities has engendered changing diagnostic criteria, inconsistent and conflicting research data, and the lack of a unified direction for research. The resulting confusion has seriously impeded the progress of the field. Consensus among professionals in the field of learning disabilities (from classroom teachers to theoreticians and researchers) as to what constitutes a learning disability may well be so elusive as a result of the multidimensional and frequently overlooked developmental and context-dependent nature of learning problems manifested by students who have neither mental retardation nor primarily emotional disabilities. The field of learning disabilities may best serve its constituency by focusing efforts on developing an alternative paradigm for learning disabilities, one that may provide a framework for replicable research and efficacious interventions.

THE INTERACTIVE DEVELOPMENTAL PARADIGM

As has been stated, the interactive developmental paradigm does include elements of earlier conceptualizations of learning disabilities. However, its interactive developmental emphasis is in marked contrast to the earlier models (and practices), which espoused single-deficit explanations for learning disabilities. The interactive developmental paradigm reflects a trend present since the late 1970s to investigate multidimensional mechanisms underlying manifest learning disabilities. This paradigm represents an attempt to formulate a more holistic conceptual framework, one that takes the field beyond global diagnostic labels. The emphasis is placed instead on rich clinical description and the rigorous study of the interactions among *elemental functions* and *task production components* that contribute to *school-related outcomes*.

The *interactive dimension* of the paradigm operates at three levels. First, the paradigm emphasizes the importance of analyzing school-related tasks into their requisite subskills (production components) and mapping psychological processes (elemental functions) onto those subskills (see Torgesen, 1979; chap. 8, this volume). Recognizing the interactions between subskills associated with school-related tasks and constituent cognitive processes overcomes the limitations of deficit models of learning disabilities that target training of a deficient process in isolation from specific academic tasks. This paradigm emphasizes skill-based, task-related analyses of performance patterns in research and diagnosis and the tailoring of interventions based on a student's individual profile of strengths, weaknesses, and affinities (Palinscar & Brown, 1988). Second, the paradigm stresses the transactions occurring among and between elemental functions that underlie task production components. Such a framework allows for investigations that focus on how the elemental functions develop in relation to each other and the implications of these interactive processes for performance. Third, the model takes account of relationships between elemental functions and a range of environmental and historical factors in generating critical production components and, ultimately, school-related outcomes.

The *developmental dimension* of the paradigm accounts for the observed fact that students may be "learning disabled" at a particular age or grade level, but may not manifest learning disabilities at a subsequent age or grade level. In addition, students' learning disabilities at one age or grade level may differ qualitatively and in degree of severity from those manifested at a later period. The developmental dimension also acknowledges change in individual elemental functions in relation to intensifying and evolving task demands and performance expectations.

The interactive developmental paradigm has four characteristics that may prove to be advantageous for the field of learning disabilities. First, the paradigm attempts to account for the heterogeneity of learning disabilities by using a comprehensive approach to differential diagnosis within the category of learning disabilities. Second, the paradigm emphasizes a developmental approach to the assessment of intra- and interindividual differences. By using grade/age-appropriate school-related outcomes, diagnosticians and investigators are able to produce ecologically valid assessments of students' learning problems. Third, the paradigm is focused on the interactions between the inherent characteristics of tasks or expectations and the cognitive profiles of students. Fourth, the paradigm has practical implications for both research and practice. By using the first three characteristics of the paradigm, research may be conducted that advances theories of learning disabilities and produces generalizable research.

Elemental Functions and Production Components

Elemental functions are defined as fundamental neurocognitive operations that contribute ultimately to one or more school-related outcomes. Individual elemental functions interact to achieve developmentally specific task production components, which, in turn, operate in synchrony to yield developmentally appropriate school-related outcomes. The latter, in turn, interact with a multitude of exogenous factors to yield life adjustment outcomes, outcomes that extend beyond the school day and the school years. Central to this paradigm is the notion that age- or grade-specific academic competencies emerge from intact synergies between their requisite elemental functions (Figure 1). A deficient school-related outcome at a specific point in time (e.g., a reading problem in second grade) entails one or more deficient elemental functions (e.g., a weakness of phonological awareness and/or active working memory) precipitating the breakdown of a necessary production component (e.g., decoding).

Task-analytic techniques, as promoted by Torgeson (1979, 1988) and others, can be used to develop hypotheses regarding the transactions between specific elemental functions and the generation of production components to which they are presumed to contribute (Figure 2). Validation of the existence and task-related roles of individual elemental functions derives from rigorous research using multiple sources of information, including empirical data based on direct sampling of academic performance, reports from teachers, perceptions of parents and of students themselves, direct cognitive testing, and published studies of learning disorders, academic skill acquisition, learning processes, and normal development. Elemental functions can be thought of as subconstructs grouped within well-established interdependent neurodevelopmental constructs, which

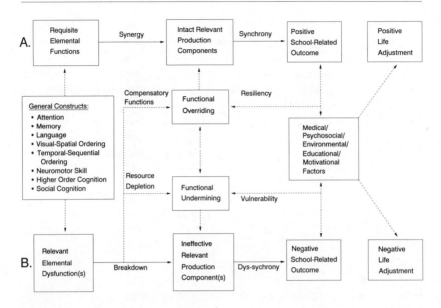

Figure 1. Pathways of positive and negative school-related outcomes. In this overview of the model presented in this chapter, the eight general constructs are depicted on the left side of the diagram. Within each there exist some elemental functions that either operate effectively or are dysfunctional. Together the elemental functions interact to create important production components needed for specific school-related outcomes. It can be seen in this diagram that there are multiple factors that interact to create such outcomes.

include language, memory, attention, neuromotor skill, visual-spatial ordering, temporal-sequential ordering, social cognition, and higher order cognition (thinking skills). Some elemental functions may be subsumed under more than one construct. For example, word retrieval may be thought of as an elemental function within language and/or an elemental function within memory.

No production components, and thus no academic outcomes, entail single elemental functions operating in isolation. Successful completion of a task demands the selective recruitment and integration of multiple elemental functions. This means that one *or more* of the contributing elemental functions is likely to be deficient when a student is unable to meet the challenge of a particular task. Researchers in several domains have alluded to this process. In fact, several investigators of reading have supported and elaborated the concept of interactive processes operating within a system of limited resources (LaBerge & Samuels, 1974; Perfetti & Lesgold; 1977; Rummelhart, 1977; Stanovich, 1980; see also Stanovich, chap. 13, this volume). Implicit in such models is the notion that the delineation of the elemental functions and production components required for the attainment of a school-related outcome facilitates the formu-

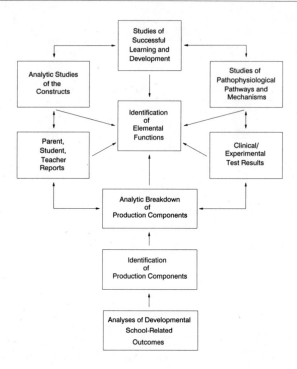

Figure 2. The derivation and validation of elemental functions. Many different techniques are used to identify the significant elemental functions that must be accounted for in evaluating a performance of schoolchildren.

lation of a developmental differential diagnosis of failure with respect to that outcome.

As noted by many researchers in the field of learning disabilities, we must acknowledge the developmental nature of these phenomena (Kavanagh & Truss, 1988). Specific elemental functions assume greater or lesser importance over the course of the school years. Moreover, because of the effects of altered academic expectations from grade level to grade level, some specific school-related outcomes at one grade level become production components for academic outcomes at a higher grade level. For example, single word decoding skill, an academic outcome in early elementary school, eventually evolves into a production component essential for sophisticated reading comprehension in late elementary and secondary school.

School-related outcomes are developmental as well. Thus, successful reading in ninth grade is substantially different in its production components from reading mastery in second grade. Also, new school-related outcomes (e.g., foreign language proficiency) emerge over time. Consequently, the manifest "learning disabilities" of one age group or of a particular grade level may differ significantly from those of another (see Fletcher, Francis, Rourke, Shaywitz, & Shaywitz, chap. 3, this volume). Moreover, as other researchers have suggested (Shepherd, 1988), chronically deficient academic performance can ultimately exert a negative impact on the elemental functions and/or other cognitively based functions of a specific academic domain. For example, poor reading skills may eventually take their toll on word retrieval. These negative recursive phenomena have been called "Matthew effects" (the rich get richer, the poor get poorer), a frequent complicating factor involved in the assessment of older students (Stanovich, 1986; see also chap. 13, this volume).

Interactive Developmental Effects

In the presence of one or more deficient elemental functions, the adequacy of relevant production components is dependent in part on the availability or absence of strengths in other elemental functions. It has been suggested that an individual with advanced capacities in certain elemental functions may utilize such capacities to override the effects of one or more deficient elemental functions (Spiro & Myers, 1984). An example of such *functional overriding* is seen when a student with excellent language skills and deficient nonverbal reasoning conceptualizes conventionally nonverbal mathematics concepts through a linguistic route. Such alternative or unorthodox tactics may or may not engender success. However, their frequent existence complicates research and clinical evaluation.

It is also the case that certain unsuccessful students may exhibit signs of *functional undermining,* circumstances in which one elemental function is so inadequately developed or insufficiently automatized that it drains excessive mental effort (i.e., cognitive/ mnemonic/attentional resources) from one or more other (ordinarily intact) elemental functions needed to generate a production component. For example, a child with a motor dyspraxia may have to exert so much effort to form letters that little if any resource remains for adequate spelling. Such a child may be able to spell certain words with accuracy in a spelling bee or when writing single words on a spelling test, but may misspell the identical words in a written paragraph. In such a case, an apparent but task-specific spelling deficit results from inadequacies in the neuromotor system. This phenomenon of functional undermining has been shown to exist at the level of production components, particularly in the reading domain, and has led to what has been called the "bottleneck" hypothesis by Perfetti and Lesgold (1977), whereby text comprehension can be severely undermined in children with major decoding problems.

The overt manifestations of deficient elemental functions may also be *content specific*. Individual orientations toward or away from discrete subject domains or topical materials are likely to influence clinical patterns. Thus, a student with a strong content affinity toward animals may exhibit superior reading skills and more effective memory functions in a biology course than he or she demonstrates during history and English classes. So it is that the specific content area in which production components are to be deployed may exert a potent influence over their effectiveness. There is also reason to believe that elemental functions as well as production components may be strengthened through their direct utilization in domains for which a student displays a strong content affinity. It is likely that reading skill, for example, can be enhanced by reading material about which one knows a great deal.

Elemental functions and production components develop over time. Nonspecific factors such as speed, "chunk size," automaticity, and versatility commonly characterize the progressive enhancement of individual elemental functions. The extent and rate of such progressions are highly dependent on multiple factors, many of which have been studied extensively in longitudinal investigations of childhood development. Among the critical variables are genetic endowment, socioeconomic status, environmental nurturance, experience (practice), physical health, critical life events, the quality of education, interactions with teachers (and other mentors), and the effects of a student's cumulative "track record" on motivation, level of aspiration, overall mental health, and self-esteem. Such forces may exert their effects primarily on the intrinsic *resiliency* and *malleability* of children. Resiliency is the capacity to withstand stress and disadvantage, and malleability refers to the degree to which children are responsive to interventions. Both of these critical dimensions have been found to be highly dependent on the multiple environmental and endogenous forces enumerated above (Gallagher & Ramey, 1987). In addition, however, it is likely that the extent of resiliency and malleability is in part dependent on a child's broad profile of strengths and weaknesses among the critical elemental functions. Different patterns of strength, intactness, and deficiency among elemental functions are likely to harbor the potential for greater or lesser resiliency and malleability.

THE EXAMPLE OF WRITING

To illustrate the interactive developmental paradigm, it will be helpful to examine one specific school-related outcome, successful written output in middle childhood (ages 9–15). Although the bulk of research in learning disabilities is focused on reading decoding, writing is an equally germane school-related outcome. Many students underachieve and lose all motivation to an agonizing extent because they cannot keep pace with the progressively heightening demand for written output. Writing is inherently developmental, and represents a final common pathway composed of multiple production components and their subsumed elemental functions.

We have identified six major production components that contribute meaningfully to the ability to keep pace with writing demands. These are observable and readily identified by teachers (Cicci, 1980). These six written output production components (see Figure 3) are handwriting/legibility, writing rate, written linguistics, ideational written exposition, mechanics, and spelling. Any as-

| | The Primary Production Components and Elemental Functions Potentiating Written Output in Middle Childhood | | | | | | | | | | | | | | | | | | | | | | | | |
| Relevant Neurodevelopmental Constructs → | Attention | | | | Neuromotor Skill | | | | | | Memory | | | | Language | | | | | Higher Cognition | | | | | |
Relevant Elemental Functions → / Production Components ↑	Sustained Mental Effort	Reflection/Planning	Tempo Control	Self-monitoring	Praxis-Previsual	Praxis-Procedural	Praxis-Direct Visual *	Praxis-Direct Verbal **	Motor Production	Motor Feedback/Regulation	Convergent Retrieval	Simultaneous Retrieval	Active Working Memory	Automatization	Phonological Processing	Lexical Knowledge	Word Finding/Lexical Retrieval	Semantic/Syntactic Expression	Narrative/Expository Expression	Brainstorming	Concept Formation/Utilization	Problem Solving	Critical Thinking	Sequential Ideation	Task Staging
Handwriting/Legibility	X	X			X	X			X	X	X	X													
Writing Rate	X	X			X	X			X	X	X	X	X				X	X	X						X
Written Linguistics	X	X													X	X	X	X	X						
Ideational Written Exposition	X	X	X									X	X	X		X	X	X	X	X	X	X	X	X	X
Mechanics	X			X							X	X	X	X											
Spelling	X			X							X	X	X	X	X	X									
Reading Ability	X												X	X	X	X						X			

* Related to Copying ** Related to Notetaking Abilities

Figure 3. Primary production components and elemental functions potentiating written output in middle childhood. It can be seen that a multitude of elemental functions are needed for effective writing. These elemental functions can contribute in varying combinations to the seven production components of written output.

sessment of the developmental adequacy of a child's writing, therefore, should include the measurement and accurate description of these six production components. Research studies that focus on writing must take account of these production components in compiling sampling criteria or, at the very least, in composing replicable sample descriptions and in being vigilant for critical interactions between production components.

The production components of writing subsume interactions between specific elemental functions. Myklebust (1973) discussed a hierarchy of developmental language abilities essential for the acquisition of writing skills. Litowitz (1981) pointed out a number of additional cognitive and psychological abilities that contribute to the writing process. There are five relevant neurodevelopmental constructs that encompass the elemental functions contributing to the production components for written output: attention, neuromotor skill, memory, language, and higher cognition. It is implicit in this developmental paradigm that these constructs and their various constituent elemental functions may play greater or lesser roles at different grade levels. For example, spatial abilities are more germane to the writing process early in elementary school than during secondary education.

Given the linguistic contributions to writing, many of the same receptive and expressive language processes related to oral expression are likely to contribute to writing, despite there being well-defined disparities between the oral and written domains (Rubin, 1987). The most relevant language elements for a "first-pass" written product are those directly related to spoken language, including sublexical (i.e., *phonological processing*), *lexical* (i.e., word knowledge and retrieval), and *sentential* (i.e., semantic-syntactic sentence formulation and expression) processes. Another relevant element may include a *suprasentential process* (e.g., narrative or expository macrostructure).

Consistent in many respects with the overall structure and organization of current models of discourse and sentence production (e.g., Levelt, 1989), the writing process too may be profitably viewed as top-down and interactive. The writing process may begin with a writer selecting an idea or concept (top-down initiation) that he or she wants to express. Next, a writer presumably must map his or her idea onto some organizational structure (i.e., narrative or expository macrostructure). This macrostructure, reflected in *narrative or expository expression,* serves as the organizational framework in which the idea inherits an overall coherent structure (e.g., Mandler & Johnson, 1977; Rummelhart, 1975). The organized idea or concept then must be translated and expressed in written form via various language-specific processes. These language-specific processes entail at least the following elemental functions: 1) *semantic-syntactic expression,* which is reflected as the output from the sentence formulation/generation process; 2) *lexical retrieval* and *selection* (i.e., lexical selection being motivated in part by *lexical knowledge*—semantic and relational word knowledge), whereby lexical items appropriate to the content and semantic-syntactic sentential context are retrieved from the lexicon; and 3) *phonological processing,* whereby the phonological forms (i.e., individual phonetic units) of the selected words are accessed and subsequently converted into their appropriate graphemic representations.

Much as in spoken language, the linguistic functions in writing in all likelihood also occur in an interactive fashion such that information activated and accessed at one level (e.g., semantic-syntactic level) spreads to and activates information at other levels, thus allowing for a functional system wherein there are both bottom-up and top-down interactions (Bock, 1982; Levelt, 1989). In the context of this model, writing failure may result from any one or more deficient language-specific elemental functions. A developmental model of writing as proposed in this chapter has the potential to uncover the dynamic nature of the relative contributions of these proposed language-specific elemental functions over time, as well as their intimate interactions with nonlinguistic elemental functions.

Higher order cognitive activities are also essential to the writing process. The challenge of generating ideas for written discourse, or *brainstorming,* represents a salient elemental function from elementary school through college. Writing also requires *sequential ideation,* a process in which ideas are presented in a logical expression. As students progress through school, metacognitive executive functions such as *task staging* become increasingly relevant to writing. Similarly, higher order functions such as viewpoint and sense of audience are most salient in the written discourse of college students (Gregg & Hoy, 1989).

Under the construct of attention, four elemental functions appear to be primarily involved (Hill & Caramazza, 1989). The first is *sustained mental effort,* or cognitive stamina, to complete writing tasks. The second entails *reflection and planning* needed to impose appropriate structures over content. Writing also necessitates ongoing *tempo control,* so as to allow for the synchronization of relevant elemental functions. If a child is generating ideas too frenetically, the recall of letter formation, spelling, or mechanics may not keep pace. Finally, *self-monitoring,* the ability to detect and correct errors during and after a writing activity, constitutes another of the attentional elemental functions contributing to writing. It has been shown that a significant proportion of children with attention deficits have learning disabilities, often affecting written output (Barkley, 1989). Conversely, many children with writing disabilities have attention deficits (Speece, McKinney, & Appelbaum, 1985). A number of studies of the efficacy of stimulant medication have demonstrated substantial improvement in the writing of children with attention deficits who are treated with stimulant medication (Lerer, Lerer, & Artner, 1977). In many cases, it is likely that stimulants enable such students to sustain mental effort, plan, control tempo, and self-monitor effectively enough to be productive on paper.

The motor components of writing, or graphomotor functions, have been extensively studied (Denckla, 1984; O'Hare & Brown, 1989). In general, the neuromotor loops required for written output entail motor planning (praxis), motor production, and ongoing feedback and regulation. There exist multiple forms of motor praxis (Sugden & Keogh, 1990). The instantaneous and precise recall of letter and word configurations constitutes *previsual praxis,* and the retrieval of motor engrams or "kinetic melodies" (Luria, 1980) comprises *procedural praxis.* Effective written output requires the nearly simultaneous recall of such configurations and motor sequences. Graphomotor dysfunction, therefore, may ensue when a child has difficulties with previsual praxis or with procedural praxis. It can be seen in Figure 3 that more specialized writing activities, such as copying or notetaking, may additionally call for the integration of direct visual or direct verbal inputs into motor plans.

Motor production entails the assignment and activation of discrete muscle groups (most commonly in the fingers, wrist, and forearm) to accomplish letter/word formation. The ability to coordinate smoothly in-hand movements of the writing utensil while stabilizing specific muscle groups and joints is especially important (Exner, 1989). Poor eye–hand coordination, poor visual-motor integration, and poor isolation of finger movements may impair graphomotor fluency as well.

Finally, during writing there needs to be ongoing *propriokines- thetic (reafferent) feedback,* so that the position of the writing utensil can be monitored from instant to instant and, thereby, its continuing movements guided appropriately (Sovik, Arntzen, & Thygesen, 1986). Students who harbor finger agnosia have deficient feedback systems and may experience considerable difficulty with writing. They also tend to have problems in a number of other academic areas (Satz, Taylor, Friel, & Fletcher, 1978).

Discrete breakdowns in short-term memory (Jorm, 1979) and retrieval strategies (Brainerd, Kingma, & Howe, 1986) have been implicated as major contributors to learning disabilities. *Convergent retrieval* (e.g., the ability to recall precise spelling configurations) is a critical elemental function for writing. *Simultaneous retrieval* (e.g., the capacity to recall multiple task components virtually in parallel) also is essential because a student must access spelling, punctuation, grammar, capitalization, prior knowledge, vocabulary, and letter formations all at once. *Active working memory,* the ability to maintain (rather than retrieve) multiple task components while working with them also contributes to the writing process. Thus, a student must remember what she or he intends to write about while deciding how to punctuate or whether to capitalize a particular word. Finally, *automatization* (of memory demands) enables students to engage in more sophisticated cognitive processes during the act of writing. Breakdowns in any or all of these memory systems are likely to obstruct written output. Students whose retrieval is slow (or poorly automatized) or overly divergent may have devastating trouble with the simultaneous manipulation of multiple task components during writing. Such students may be able to copy neatly, but legibility deteriorates in a written expository paragraph (functional undermining). Even language abilities may decay while a child is writing. A student may be eloquent during a class discussion, but his or her ideas on paper appear primitive and underdeveloped. In such a case, the multiple memory and/or motor demands of writing undermine language and ideation.

Visual–spatial processing and *spatial organization* abilities are likely to be important elemental functions in the writing process of young children. Perceptual disorders have been implicated in some children with "dysgraphia" (Critchley, 1968). O'Hare and Brown (1989) described a group of children with "visual-perceptual dysgraphia" whose writing was characterized by illegible handwriting, inconsistent spacing, and sloping lines.

IMPLICATIONS OF THE PARADIGM

An important thrust of research efforts in learning disabilities entails the identification, ongoing addition, and understanding of the elemental functions contributing to production components necessary for successful school-related outcomes. Future research should explore the interactions of identified elemental functions and their impacts on the efficacy of production components and school-related outcomes. Longitudinal research that investigates developmental changes in elemental functions and production components and their impacts on performance will aid in our understanding of evolving intraindividual differences over time. Although neat classifications of learning disabilities are empirically desirable, it is important that efforts at subtyping not result in artificial clusters that are too global or that have little resemblance to clinical reality and fail to probe for deficiencies in critical elemental functions (see Morris, chap. 5, this volume). There is also a need to acknowledge the existence within the population with learning disabilities of multiple, relatively low prevalence patterns of deficient elemental functions that may be highly germane clinically, but may become obscured by a blind faith in multivariate techniques such as cluster or exploratory factor analysis.

Clinical Assessment

Many of the relevant elemental functions and production components, such as those required for successful written output, are not routinely assessed on IQ tests or on group achievement tests. To assess learning disabilities comprehensively, our observations and/ or "diagnoses" must be guided by a priori knowledge and hypotheses regarding interactions between production components and elemental functions at specific chronological ages and/or grade levels. Clinical assessment should occur on four levels, examining systematically: 1) the school-related outcomes, 2) the intactness of relevant production components, 3) the adequacy of subsumed elemental functions relevant to production components for a given age and grade level, and 4) the interactions among elemental functions, learning contexts, and exogenous factors (e.g., home and school environment). Instead of defining phenomena exclusively on the basis of test results, we must keep reshaping our testing procedures and our diagnostic algorithms based on our expanding knowledge of relevant elemental functions and how they relate to each other and to the production components to which they contribute. We cannot rely on existing tests simply because they are well established and rigorously validated. Their relevance to essential production components must be demonstrable. As new contributing elemental functions are identified, refined assessment procedures will have to be designed for their proper developmental evaluation. We cannot abide by the notion that "there are already enough tests." Our diagnostic techniques should always be undergoing refinement!

Toward a Definition

The continuing study of elemental functions will advance our efforts to develop more appropriate definitions for learning disabilities. Rather than relying on relatively arbitrary discrepancy formulas, the presence of a learning disability can be established by documenting the existence of one or more weak elemental functions thwarting the development of a critical production component.

Within this model, intraindividual discrepancies should be demonstrable because children with learning disabilities presumably would exhibit intact elemental functions and production components along with their deficient elemental functions and production components. Developmentally calibrated criteria for deficient elemental functions and impaired production components should be established. The demonstration of a student's jagged profile of relevant elemental functional variation would constitute evidence for a learning disability. Among other advantages, we would become less susceptible to the inherent biases of global IQ and achievement scores as the exclusive standards for discrepancy.

It is essential that we resist simplistic, reductionist labeling. Such nomenclature has been helpful in identifying a global area of compelling need (i.e., "learning disabilities"). However, in the future, we should not be restrained by this convenience. Too many children have been excluded from services as a result of arbitrary and mutually exclusivistic categorical systems. They have fallen between the cracks because their particular dysfunctional profiles have eluded detection on the subtests of an intelligence test or within the parameters quantified on an achievement test. Moreover, conceptual models of "learning disability" often have failed to factor in the social contexts and developmental progressions of school-related outcomes and the expectation for progressive enhancement and automatization of relevant elemental functions. Consequently, the evolving needs of children with learning disabilities have often gone unmet. A child may be deemed eligible for services at one age and then ineligible at another.

Even when educational intervention is unavailable, ineffective, or inappropriate, there remains justification for enlightenment, for the prevention of the malignant effects of false attributions on the part of teachers, parents, the community, and the childhood victims themselves, none of whom may be aware of a student's deficient elemental functions and their manifestations.

Implications for Training

The education of professionals to deal with academic failure and underachievement represents a most critical need. Future research using an interactive developmental paradigm should yield a vocabulary and an approach that can transcend traditional disciplinary boundaries and barriers. Concurrently, there must be a recognition that the study of "learning disabilities" is inseparable from the study of normal and gifted learning and from the investigation of child development in general. Our ideas about developmental dysfunction or disability should not diverge widely from what is known of the pathways of "normal" development, "normal" education, and the physiology of cognitive processes. There is a need for a common vocabulary as well as shared systems of observation and descriptive assessment.

It might well be argued that no one component of this interactive developmental paradigm for learning disabilities is, in itself, innovative or unique. The ideas espoused in this chapter represent more of a revision than an entirely new pathway for research, clinical activity, and education. What is important in this paradigm is that there is a reaffirmation of the need to view learning disabilities in a developmental context, a framework that evolves over time and one in which a multiplicity of exogenous and endogenous factors interact reciprocally and often recursively. At present, research into learning disabilities, criteria for service delivery, and clinical diagnostic algorithms assume an unrealistically narrow view. By combining well-established principles of child development within a comprehensive paradigm, we are in a far better position to develop a more generalizable and scientifically rigorous construct of intraindividual differences and the ways in which such differences engender failure in school, as well as maladaptation and underachievement in the years beyond formal education.

REFERENCES

Adelman, H.S., & Taylor, L. (1986a). Moving the LD field ahead: New paths, new paradigms. *Journal of Learning Disabilities, 19*(10), 602–608.

Adelman, H.S., & Taylor, L. (1986b). Summary of the survey of fundamental concerns controlling the LD field. *Journal of Learning Disabilities, 19,* 391–393.

Algozzine, B.J., & Ysseldyke, J.E. (1986). The future of the LD field: Screening and diagnosis. *Journal of Learning Disabilities, 19,* 394–398.

Association for Children with Learning Disabilities. (1985). ACLD offers new definition. *Special Education Today, 2,* 19.

Ayres, A. (1978). Learning disabilities and the vestibular system. *Journal of Learning Disabilities, 11,* 18–29.

Ayres, A. (1981). *Sensory integration and the child.* Los Angeles: Western Psychological Services.

Baddeley, A. (1989). *Working memory.* Oxford, England: Clarendon Press.

Barkley, R.A. (1989). Attention deficit-hyperactivity disorder. In E.J. Mash & R.A. Barkley (Eds.), *Treatment of childhood disorders* (pp. 39–72). New York: Guilford Press.

Bartoli, J.S. (1990). On defining learning and disability: Exploring the ecology. *Journal of Learning Disabilities, 23*(10), 628–631.

Bender, L.A. (1956). *Psychology of children with organic brain disorders.* Springfield, IL: Charles C Thomas.

Bender, L.A. (1957). Specific reading disabilities as a maturational lag. *Bulletin of the Orton Society, 7,* 9–18.

Birch, H.G., & Belmont, S. (1964). Auditory-visual integration in normal and retarded readers. *American Journal of Orthopsychiatry, 34,* 852–861.

Birch, H.G., & Belmont, S. (1965). Auditory-visual integration, intelligence, and reading ability in school children. *Perceptual and Motor Skills, 20,* 295–305.

Blachman, B.A. (1988). The futile search for a theory of learning disabilities. *Journal of Learning Disabilities, 21*(5), 286–289.

Bock, K. (1982). Toward a cognitive psychology of syntax: Information processing contributions to sentence processing. *Psychological Review, 62,* 1–47.

Brainerd, C.J., Kingma, J., & Howe, M.L. (1986). Long-term memory developmental learning disability: Storage and retrieval loci of disabled/nondisabled differences. In S.J. Ceci (Ed.), *Handbook of cognitive, social and neuropsychological aspects of learning disabilities* (pp. 161–184). Hillsdale, NJ: Lawrence Erlbaum Associates.

Bryan, T., Bay, M., & Donahue, M. (1988). Implications for the learning disabilities definition for the regular education. *Journal of Learning Disabilities, 21*(1), 23–28.

Cannon, L. (1991). Construct of learning disabilities: Classification and definition. *LDA Newsbriefs, 26*(1), 1, 16.

Cicci, R. (1980). Written language disorders. *Bulletin of the Orton Society, 30,* 240–251.

Critchley, M. (1968). Dysgraphia and other anomalies of written speech. *Pediatric Clinics of North America, 15,* 639–650.

Delacato, C. (1966). *Neurological organization and reading.* Springfield, IL: Charles C Thomas.

Denckla, M.B. (1984). Developmental dyspraxia: The clumsy child. In M.D. Levine & P. Satz (Eds.), *Middle childhood: Development and dysfunction.* Baltimore: University Park Press.

Exner, C. (1989). Development of hand function. In P. Pratt & A. Allen (Eds.), *Occupational therapy for children* (pp. 87–96). St. Louis: C.V. Mosby.

Frostig, M. (1964). *Frostig Developmental Test of Visual Perception.* Palo Alto, CA: Consulting Psychologist Press.

Gallagher, J.J., & Ramey, C.T. (Eds.). (1987). *The malleability of children.* Baltimore: Paul H. Brookes Publishing Co.

Gavelek, J.R., & Palincsar, A.S. (1988). Contextualism as an alternative world view of learning disabilities: A response to Swanson's "Toward a metatheory of learning disabilities." *Journal of Learning Disabilities, 21* (5), 267–270.

Getman, G. (1965). The visuomotor complex of the acquisition of motor skills. In J. Hellmuth (Ed.), *Learning disorders* (Vol. 1, pp. 112–126). Seattle: Special Child Publications.

Gregg, N., & Hoy, C. (1989). Coherence: The comprehension and production abilities of normally achieving, learning disabled and underprepared college writers. *Journal of Learning Disabilities, 22,* 370–373.

Hammill, D.D., Leigh, J.E., McNutt, G., & Larsen, S.C. (1981). A new definition of learning disabilities. *Learning Disabilities Quarterly, 4,* 336–342.

Harris, K.R. (1988). Learning disabilities research: The need, the integrity, and the challenge. *Journal of Learning Disabilities, 21*(5), 267–270.

Hill, A.E., & Caramazza, A. (1989). The graphemic buffer and attentional mechanisms. *Brain and Language, 36,* 208–235.

Hinshelwood, J. (1895). Word-blindness and visual memory. *Lancet, i,* 1506–1508.

Hooper, S.R., & Willis, W.G. (1989). *Learning disability subtyping: Neuropsychological foundations, conceptual models, and issues in clinical differentiation.* New York: Springer-Verlag.

Interagency Committee on Learning Disabilities. (1987). *Learning disabilities: A report to the U.S. Congress.* Washington, DC: U.S. Government Printing Office.

Jorm, A.F. (1979). The cognitive and neurological basis of developmental dyslexia: A theoretical framework and review. *Cognition, 7,* 19–33.

Kahneman, D. (1973). *Attention and effort.* Englewood Cliffs, NJ: Prentice Hall.

Kavale, K.A. (1990). Variances and verities in learning disability interventions. In T.E. Scruggs & B.Y.L. Wong (Eds.), *Intervention research in learning disabilities* (pp. 3–33). New York: Springer-Verlag.

Kavanagh, J.F., & Truss, T.J., Jr. (Eds.). (1988). *Learning disabilities: Proceedings of the national conference.* Parkton, MD: York Press.

Keogh, B.K. (1986). Future of the LD field: Research and practice. *Journal of Learning Disabilities, 19,* 455–460.

Kephart, N.C. (1971). *The slow learner in the classroom* (2nd ed.). Columbus, OH: Charles E. Merrill.

Kussmaul, A. (1877). Disturbance of speech. *Cyclopedia of Practical Medicine, 14,* 581.

LaBerge, D., & Samuels, S. (1974). Toward a theory of automatic information processing. *Cognitive Psychology, 6,* 293–323.

Lerer, R.J., Lerer, M.P., & Artner, J. (1977). The effects of methylphenidate on the handwriting of children with minimal brain dysfunction. *Journal of Pediatrics, 91,* 127–132.

Levelt, L.J.M. (1989). *Speaking: From intention to articulation.* Cambridge, MA: MIT Press.

Litowitz, B. (1981). Developmental issues in written language. *Topics in Language Disorders, 1,* 73–89.

Luria, A.R. (1980). *Higher cortical functions in man.* New York: Basic Books.

Mandler, J., & Johnson, N. (1977). Rememberance of things past: Story structure and recall. *Cognitive Psychology, 9,* 111–151.

Myklebust, H.R. (1973). *Development and disorders of written language: Studies of normal and exceptional children.* New York: Grune & Stratton.

O'Hare, A.E., & Brown, J.K. (1989). Childhood dysgraphia. Part 2: A study of hand function. *Child: Care, Health and Development, 15,* 151–166.

Orton, S.T. (1928). Specific reading disability—strephosymbolia. *Journal of the American Medical Association, 90,* 1005–1009.

Palincsar, A.S., & Brown, A. (1988). Advances in improving the cognitive performance of handicapped students. In M.C. Wang, M. Reynolds, & H.J. Walberg (Eds.), *Handbook of special education: Research and practice* (Vol. 1, pp. 93–112). New York: Pergamon Press, Inc.

Perfetti, C., & Lesgold, A. (1977). Discourse comprehension and sources of individual differences. In M. Just & P. Carpenter (Eds.), *Cognitive processes in comprehension* (pp. 215–237). Hillsdale, NJ: Lawrence Erlbaum Associates.

Public Law 91-230, Education of the Handicapped Act, Title VI, of 1970.
Public Law 94-142, Education for All Handicapped Children Act of 1975. (23 August 1977). 20 U.S.C. 1401 et seq: *Federal Register, 42,* 42474-42518.
Public Law 99-457, Education of the Handicapped Act Amendments of 1986. (22 September 1986). *Congressional Record, 132* (125), H 7893-7912.
Public Law 102-119, Individuals with Disabilities Education Act Amendments of 1991. (7 October 1991). Title 20, U.S.C. 1400 et seq: *U.S. Statutes at Large, 105,* 587–608.
Rourke, B.P. (1983). Outstanding issues in research on learning disabilities. In M. Rutter (Ed.), *Developmental neuropsychiatry* (pp. 564–574). New York: Guilford Press.
Rubin, D.L. (1987). Divergence and convergence between oral and written communication. *Topics in Language Disorders, 7*(4), 1–18.
Rummelhart, D.E. (1975). Notes on a schema for stories. In D.G. Brown & A. Collins (Eds.), *Representation and understanding: Studies in cognitive science* (pp. 211–236). New York: Academic Press.
Rummelhart, D.E. (1977). Toward an interactive model of reading. In S. Domio (Ed.), *Attention and performance* (Vol. 6, pp. 37–67). Hillsdale, NJ: Lawrence Erlbaum Associates.
Satz, P., Taylor, H.G., Friel, J., & Fletcher, J.M. (1978). Some developmental and predictive precursors of reading disabilities. In A.L. Benton & D. Pearl (Eds.), *Dyslexia: An appraisal of current knowledge* (pp. 313–348). New York: Oxford University Press.
Schwartz, R.G., Leonard, L.B., Folger, M.K., & Wilcox, M.J. (1980). Early phonological behavior in normal-speaking and language disordered children: Evidence for a synergistic view of linguistic disorders. *Journal of Speech and Hearing Disorders, 45,* 357–377.
Scruggs, T.E., & Wong, B.Y.L. (1990). *Intervention research in learning disabilities.* New York: Springer-Verlag.
Shepherd, M.J. (1988). Discussion. In J.F. Kavanagh & T.J. Truss (Eds.), *Learning disabilities: Proceedings of the national conference* (pp. 164–167). Parkton, MD: York press.
Siegel, L.S. (1988). Definitional and theoretical issues and research on learning disabilities. *Journal of Learning Disabilities, 21*(5), 264–270.
Silver, L.B. (1988). A review of the federal government's Interagency Committee on Learning Disabilities Report to the U.S. Congress. *Learning Disabilities Focus, 2*(2), 73–80.
Sovik, N., Arntzen, O., & Thygesen, R. (1986). Effects of feedback training on 'normal' and dysgraphic students. In H.R.S. Kao (Ed.), *Graphonomics: Contemporary research in handwriting* (pp. 140–149). Amsterdam: North-Holland.
Speece, D.L., McKinney, J.D., & Appelbaum, M.I. (1985). Classification and validation of behavioral subtypes of learning disabled children. *Journal of Educational Psychology, 77,* 67–77.
Spiro, R., & Myers, A. (1984). Individual differences and underlying cognitive processes. In P.D. Pearson (Ed.), *Handbook of reading research* (pp. 471–504). New York: Longman.
Stanovich, K.E. (1980). Toward an interactive-compensatory model of individual differences in the development of reading fluency. *Reading Research Quarterly, 16,* 32–71.

Stanovich, K.E. (1986). Matthew effects in reading: Some consequences of individual differences in the acquisition of literacy. *Reading Research Quarterly, 21,* 360.

Sugden, D.A., & Keogh, J.F. (1990). *Problems in movement skill development.* Columbia: University of South Carolina Press.

Swanson, H.L. (1988). Toward a metatheory of learning disabilities. *Journal of Learning Disabilities, 21,* 196–209.

Torgesen, J.K. (1979). What shall we do with psychological processes? *Journal of Learning Disabilities, 12* (8), 514–521.

Torgesen, J.K. (1986). The future of the LD field: Its current state and future prospects. *Journal of Learning Disabilities, 19* (7), 399–407.

Torgesen, J.K. (1988). Applied research and metatheory in the context of contemporary cognitive theory. *Journal of Learning Disabilities, 21* (5), 271–274.

Wepman, J.M. (1960). Auditory discrimination. *Elementary School Journal, 9,* 325–333.

12

LEARNING DISABILITIES FROM AN EDUCATIONAL PERSPECTIVE

Naomi Zigmond

Learning disability as an educational phenomenon has a rather short history. Whereas schools have recognized and provided services for students with physical, sensory, and intellectual disabilities since the turn of the century, students with learning disabilities came to the attention of the schools as late as the 1960s, and large-scale provision of special education services for this population of students dates only to 1975 and the passage of P.L. 94-142 (see Zigmond & Semmel, in press). Since then, the numbers of students with learning disabilities identified and served in public school programs have soared from 1.8% of school-age students in 1976–1977 (the first year for which national figures on the numbers of students with disabilities were kept) to nearly 5% in 1988–1989. In 1976–1977, students with learning disabilities comprised 22% of school-age students with disabilities; by 1988–1989 it was closer to 50% (U.S. Department of Education, 1989).

The simplest explanation for the large, and growing, numbers is that "learning disabilities" is not a distinct disability, but an invented category. Some have argued that classification of students as having learning disabilities is a sociological phenomenon, unrelated to issues of differential diagnosis or definitional criteria (Coles,

This chapter was written while the author was a Visiting Scholar in the Post-Doctoral Training Program in Special Education, Special Education Research Laboratories, University of California, Santa Barbara.

1987). In fact, Coles and others (Gartner & Lipsky, 1989; Reynolds, Wang, & Walberg, 1987) contend that most students labeled as "learning disabled" do not have disabilities at all; instead, they are victims of poor pedagogy, of inadequate instructional programs, or of limited educational opportunity. It is the failure of schools to tolerate and accommodate individual differences that *creates* in students what appear to be disabilities (Gerber & Semmel, 1984).

It is true that, during the same 15-year period in which there has been this dramatic rise in the number of students identified as having learning disabilities who are served in public schools, American schooling has come under fierce public scrutiny and attack. Educational reform is high on the national agenda: There have been calls to increase the academic press of the schools, to increase achievement in core skills, to increase student competence in higher order thinking skills, and to produce high school graduates who are better prepared to enter the workforce so that America can compete successfully with Europe and the Pacific Rim countries. Reform at the high school level has meant tougher, more uniform standards; increased graduation requirements in mathematics, science, foreign languages, and technology; harsher grading; and less leniency. Reform at the elementary level has meant challenging students and teachers to work harder, strive for more, and achieve more.

With reform have come pressures for teacher accountability and for conformity to established curricula, standardized teaching practices, and rigid pacing. Many students are finding this new school environment unwelcoming. Dropout rates, failure rates, and referral rates to special services all have increased. Students who are not being taught well, are being turned off by school, and are falling farther and farther behind as they progress through the grades may seem to have learning disabilities, although they may not. Any discussion of learning disabilities from an educational perspective must be viewed against this larger backdrop.

However, the purpose of this chapter is not to debate whether the condition of learning disability exists; I begin with the premise that it does. Instead, my aim is to explore the ways in which the schools have dealt with learning disabilities. I will try to explain that, from an educational perspective, the question of interest is not "Who has a learning disability?", but "Who is eligible for special education services as a student with learning disabilities?" This is a very different question, but one whose answer will have a profound impact on the outcomes of research conducted with populations of students identified by the schools as having learning disabilities.

"DISCOVERY" OF LEARNING
DISABILITIES BY THE EDUCATIONAL ESTABLISHMENT

Definition of Learning Disabilities

The authors of special education textbooks written before 1962 make no reference to the term *learning disabilities*. This is hardly surprising. Although histories of learning disabilities in the field date to concerns in the mid-19th century regarding disorders of spoken language (see Wiederholt, 1974), it has been only within the last 30 years that *learning disabilities* has been accepted as the generic educational term under which a variety of syndromes affecting language, learning, and communication could be grouped.

In 1962, Kirk used the term *learning disability* for the first time in the first edition of his now-classical textbook, *Educating Exceptional Children*. Kirk defined learning disabilities as: "a retardation, disorder, or delayed development in one or more of the processes of speech, language, reading, spelling, writing, or arithmetic resulting from a possible cerebral dysfunction and not from mental retardation, sensory deprivation or cultural or instructional factors" (p. 263). To Kirk, learning disabilities represented a discrepancy between a child's achievement and his or her apparent capacity to learn (Kirk, 1963). They reflected unexpected learning problems in a seemingly capable child. It is important to note that, even in this earliest definition of learning disabilities, Kirk recognized that they were a heterogeneous collection of disabilities, all subsumed under a single label. Learning disability was not synonymous with reading disability then, and is not now.

The term *learning disability* caught on. It was not stigmatizing. It was preferred by parents and educators over such etiological labels as brain injured, minimal brain dysfunction, or perceptually handicapped (Mercer, Forgnone, & Wolking, 1976). It was an optimistic term: Children with learning disabilities had adequate intelligence, hearing, vision, motor capacity, and emotional adjustment, and learned some things well; yet, despite these integrities, specific verbal or nonverbal skills were acquired only with great difficulty (Johnson & Myklebust, 1967). Learning disabilities were not the inevitable consequence of reaching the ceiling of ability, nor the consequence of a disturbed home environment or deep-seated emotional disorders. The problem and the apparent solution were simpler than that: Students with learning disabilities failed to achieve under existing rigid and prescribed school or classroom conditions, but could be successful under changed learning conditions (Johnson & Myklebust, 1967). To parents and educators alike, learning disabilities made intuitive sense.

By 1963, when the Association for Children with Learning Disabilities (ACLD) was formed, the term *learning disability,* despite its vagueness or perhaps because of it, had been accepted into medical, psychological, and educational lexicons. In 1969, the following definition was presented to Congress by the National Advisory Committee on Handicapped Children. This definition served as the basis for the 1969 Learning Disabilities Act (Title VI-G, the Education of the Handicapped Act of 1970, of P.L. 91-230), later appeared in the Education for All Handicapped Children Act of 1975 (P.L. 94-142), and most recently appeared in the Individuals with Disabilities Education Act Amendments of 1991 (P.L. 102-119):

> The term "children with specific learning disabilities" means those children who have a disorder in one or more basic psychological process involved in understanding or in using language, spoken or written, in which the disorder may manifest itself in imperfect ability to listen, think, speak, read, write, spell, or do mathematical calculations. Such disorders include such conditions as perceptual handicaps, brain injury, minimal brain dysfunction, dyslexia and developmental aphasia. Such term does not include children who have learning problems which are primarily the result of visual, hearing or motor handicaps, of mental retardation, of emotional disturbance, or environmental, cultural, or economic disadvantage. (Education of the Handicapped Law Report, 1992; U.S. Department of Health, Education and Welfare, 1977)

The final sentence of the definition has come to be known as the "exclusion clause" and has been interpreted in at least three ways. First, the exclusion clause referred to the possibility of co-morbidity; learning disability was a separate condition and was not *primarily* the result of visual, hearing, or motor handicaps; mental retardation; emotional disturbance; or environmental, cultural, or economic disadvantage, but it could coexist with these other disabilities in the same child. Second, the exclusion clause was meant to identify as eligible for special education services students who were not eligible based on any already existing category. A diagnosis of visual handicap, hearing impairment, mental retardation, emotional disturbance, or cultural disadvantage automatically made a student eligible for a special program paid for, at least in part, by federal education funds. Learning disabilities was an additional category; it defined students who had serious school learning problems but could not access special federally funded education programs or services because they did not meet the criteria for diagnosis within already existing categories. Finally, the exclusion clause was a way of describing the concept of "discrepancy," which has come to be a defining feature of learning disabilities. A learning disability could be diagnosed if learning problems existed despite the adequacy of internal and external facilitators of learning. In other words, in a student with a learning disability, a discrepancy existed between the expectations for learning that grew from the presence of adequate vision, hearing, or intellectual capabilities; emotional stability; and environmental or cultural advantages and the student's actual performance on certain specific learning tasks.

Problems in Applying the Federal Definition

The early federal definition created the parameters to be used by schools to diagnose pupils as having learning disabilities—at least in terms of making them eligible to be served in state-mandated special education programs or in a national network of federally funded public education Child Service Demonstration Centers (CSDCs) (Sontag, 1976). However, three studies of the students served in the CSDCs (Kirk & Elkins, 1975; Mann, Davis, Boyer, Metz, & Wolford, 1983; Norman & Zigmond, 1980) demonstrated the inadequacy of the federal language as an operational definition. Mann et al. (1983) reviewed all CSDC reports and federal documentation to understand what the CSDCs did with their funding from the federal treasury. Kirk and Elkins (1975) queried directors of CSDCs regarding their placement practices. Norman (Norman & Zigmond, 1980) visited CSDCs across the nation and reviewed placement records of all students served.

The data in all three studies showed little commonality among the pupils served, either within or across sites. Furthermore, in assigning students to learning disabilities programs, little attention had been paid to what seemed implicit in the federal definition and what the field at that time considered to be the three "critical elements" of a diagnosis of learning disabilities: 1) IQ not more than 1 standard deviation below normal (i.e., the student was neither mentally retarded nor "slow learning" [Kephart, 1960]); 2) evidence of some sort of psychological process disorder (i.e., low scores on some measures of auditory or visual perceptual processing or on memory tests); and 3) lack of other disability or clear evidence of cultural deprivation (i.e., the student was not already eligible for special services through some other diagnostic label). Only 3 of the 30 CSDC sites on which data were available adhered to all three of these "critical elements." Overall, a significant proportion of the pupils served in the CSDCs scored well below IQ 85 (Norman & Zigmond 1980). In most sites, underachievement, without mention of process deficits, was synonymous with learning disabilities; evidence of the technical inadequacy of tests of perceptual and memory skills as well as questions about their relevance (Mann, 1979) had led to their disuse in the diagnosis of learning disabilities in the schools. In addition, many CSDCs, responding explicitly to the call from the Office of Special Education Programs to focus attention on inner city and rural pupils (Mann et al., 1983), were providing services to students who were primarily culturally and economically disadvantaged. Mann et al. (1983) concluded that, for the CSDC programs, learning disabilities was "an opinion not a diagnosis" (p. 16). Local needs, not federal guidelines, determined eligibility, and school systems considered it more important to keep constituencies happy than to adhere to an abstract definition.

In the dozen or so years since the CSDCs (funding was terminated in 1975 with the passage of P.L. 94-142), considerable attention has been paid to developing a clearer, more precise definition of learning disabilities and a better understanding of the nature of the condition. Research on the psychological, cognitive, neurological, and neuropsychological characteristics of students with learning disabilities has flourished (Kavale & Nye, 1986), and new definitions have been proposed. For example, after several years of discussion, the National Joint Committee on Learning Disabilities (a conference of officials from eight professional groups representing scholars and practitioners engaged in the study of and in the provision of services to students with learning disabilities) published an alternative definition (McLoughlin & Netick, 1983):

> Learning disabilities is a generic term that refers to a heterogeneous group of disorders manifested by significant difficulties in the acquisition and use of listening, speaking, reading, writing, reasoning, or mathematical abilities. These disorders are intrinsic to the individual and presumed to be due to central nervous system dysfunction. Even though a learning disability may occur concomitantly with other handicapping conditions (e.g. sensory impairment, mental retardation, social and emotional disturbance) or environmental influences (e.g. cultural differences, insufficient/inappropriate instruction, psychogenic factors), it is not the direct result of those conditions or influences. (p. 22)

This definition reflected a growing consensus regarding the intrinsic nature of the disorder, the heterogeneity of the group of students who exhibit the disorder, and the possibility that learning disabilities could exist between both students who do not fit other classifications of disability and those for whom the learning disability is a secondary disability (Hammill, Leigh, McNutt, & Larsen, 1981).

THE SEARCH FOR AN OPERATIONAL DEFINITION

Any definition is a theoretical statement that specifies the delimiting or boundary characteristics of the condition and is not a set of specific operational criteria for identifying individual cases (Hammill et al., 1981; see also Fletcher, Francis, Rourke, Shaywitz, & Shaywitz, chap. 3, this volume; Kavale, chap. 9, this volume; Keogh, chap. 14, this volume; Morris, chap. 5, this volume). As long as learning disabilities was a clinical phenomenon, predominantly the domain of physicians (pediatric neurologists and pediatricians), clinicians (psychologists, language pathologists), and researchers, as was the case from 1962 to 1975, a theoretical definition was adequate. However, with the passage of P.L. 94-142, the Education for All Handicapped Children Act, in 1975, the need for an *operational* definition of learning disabilities became acute. The services mandated by P.L. 94-142 represented a limited, targeted resource, available only to eligible students. School districts needed fair and equitable ways to make the dichotomous decision of who would and would not have access to these resources (Burbules, Lord, & Sherman, 1982). Imprecision in their application of a definition could leave school districts open to legal action for overidentification or underidentification of specific groups.

The problem of defining eligibility is not unique to the field of learning disabilities. For example, there is no universally accepted definition of emotional disturbance/behavior disorder (see Fletcher, Francis, Rourke, Shaywitz, & Shaywitz, chap. 3, this volume), nor are there generally accepted tests that can be used to identify emotionally disturbed students for special education programs (Hallahan & Kauffman, 1991). Experts (and school districts) have felt free to construct individual working definitions that fit their own purposes, although research has failed to show that disorders having primarily an emotional base can be discriminated reliably from other types of disorders (Center, 1989; Kauffman, 1989). Also, a heated debate currently continues over whether socially maladjusted students should be included within the definition of students eligible for special education services as having serious emotional disturbance (Benson, Edwards, Rosell, & White, 1986; Clarizio, 1987; Nelson, Rutherford, Center, & Walker, 1991).

Similarly, the definition of mental retardation has changed considerably over the years (see Kavale & Forness, 1985; MacMillan, Meyers, & Morrison, 1980; Robinson & Robinson, 1976; see also MacMillan, chap. 7, this volume). Whereas at one time it was common practice to diagnose mental retardation solely on the basis of an IQ score below 85, today a student must demonstrate deficits in adaptive behavior *and* an IQ score below 75 or 70 to be classified as having mental retardation. Operationally, criteria related to adaptive behavior are interpreted differently in different settings. There is even considerable variance across states on the cutoff IQ score that defines educable mental retardation.[1] For example, included in the American Association on Mental Retardation (AAMR) definition

---

[1]The AAMR is currently revising the definitional criteria for mental retardation and the role that IQ scores play in the definition.

of mental retardation is an IQ score of at least 2 standard deviations below the mean (IQ of 68–70 on an individually administered IQ test) (Grossman, 1983); yet, in the Commonwealth of Pennsylvania, students with IQ scores below 80 (only *1.3* standard deviations below the mean) are eligible to be served in programs for children with mental retardation (Department of Education of Pennsylvania 1990, p. 4).

Discrepancy Formulas

The search for a more operational definition of learning disabilities resulted in the adoption of severe discrepancy formulas (Danielson & Bauer, 1978; Reynolds, 1984). These formulas were attempts to quantify what was assumed to be the fundamental concept underlying learning disabilities—an imbalance between achievement and potential. With formulas, school districts sought to distinguish objectively between those whose academic achievement was consistent with intellectual capacity and those whose academic achievement was not, with only the latter eligible to be classified as having disabilities. Four major classes of achievement discrepancy models have been proposed (see Cone & Wilson, 1981):

1. Difference between expected and actual grade-equivalent scores (Bateman, 1965; Johnson & Myklebust, 1967)
2. Ratio of actual to expected grade-equivalent scores (Bond & Tinker, 1957; Harris, 1970; Kaluger & Kolson, 1969; Myklebust, 1968)
3. Difference between IQ and achievement standard (Z) scores (Erickson, 1975)
4. Difference between expected and actual achievement level based on the regression of IQ on achievement (Cone & Wilson, 1981; Shepard, 1980)

The fourth model is generally preferred by mathematicians, statisticians, and experts in tests and measurement (Reynolds et al., 1984). Obtained scores are corrected for reliability and for intercorrelations among measures so that one is comparing the best estimates of a student's true aptitude and achievement.

Criticisms of Discrepancy Formulas

The use of formulas has given state education agencies and school districts new confidence that they are using sound, objective criteria to assign only the most appropriate students to learning disabilities special education services (although many admit that there is wide variability in the application of these formulas and their attendant cutoff scores in response to local pressures and individual student needs.) However, the use of formulas has also generated considerable criticism. Some claim that efforts to reduce complex learning problems to a single formula are simply inappropriate (McLoughlin & Netick, 1983). Learning disabilities is a complex, multivariate problem. We know more and more about the linguistic, social, cognitive, perceptual, memory, attention, and neuropsychological difficulties of students with learning disabilities (see Kavale & Nye, 1986). How could the discrepancy alone diagnose learning disabilities (see Kavale, 1987)?

Others believe that the concept of an aptitude–achievement discrepancy is flawed. It is not just that a discrepancy formula like the fourth model above is too complex for most practitioners to use "on the job," so that what are actually used in practice are inadequate, inappropriate calculations. It is also that discrepancy formulas are based on naive and erroneous assumptions about the accuracy and adequacy of IQ as a general measure of capacity to learn (see *Journal of Learning Disabilities,* October 1989, for a more complete discussion), and about the technical adequacy and equivalence of tests of language and academic achievement (see Hessler, 1987; Ysseldyke & Thurlow, 1984; see also Fletcher et al., chap. 3, this volume; Stanovich, chap. 13, this volume).

My contention is that the aptitude–achievement discrepancy is the wrong comparison (although I contributed in 1965 to the invention and use of an aptitude–achievement formula called a learning quotient; see Myklebust, 1968). The error is in characterizing the discrepancy as between "potential" (intelligence) and achievement. More consistent with the clinical and educational picture of learning disabilities would have been a quantification of the differences *between* achievements (i.e., between rate of learning X and rate of learning Y). When one has a learning disability, an extraordinary combination of individual differences makes it more difficult than it should be to learn "some things." To learn those things, either the student must work much harder than would be predicted from the presence of basic integrities and his or her ability to learn "other things," or the teacher must teach much better than is necessary for most students to achieve the same outcome, or both. The discrepancy is intraindividual across learning tasks, not norm-referenced to IQ; it is a discrepancy in the ease with which "some things" are acquired as compared with "other things." From this orientation, dynamic assessment research in cognitive science may contribute to both defining and evaluating potential learning disabilities.

Dynamic assessment refers to approaches of measuring an individual's receptiveness to instruction (Feuerstein, 1979). In contrast to static assessment, usually used to diagnose a learning disability, dynamic assessment requires an ongoing interaction between the examiner and the examinee so that specific problem-solving behaviors can be assessed (Rothman & Semmel, 1990; see also Swanson, chap. 10, this volume). The examiner provides an instructional intervention, often a systematic approach to modifying task components and providing prompts and other forms of mediation to aid the student in solving the presented problem. Generally, in dynamic assessment, the examiner compares the student's baseline ability with his or her performance following the instructional intervention (see Bransford, Delclos, Vye, Burns, & Hasselbring, 1987; Brown & French, 1979; Budoff, 1972, 1974; Burns, 1985; Campione, Brown, Ferrara, Jones, & Steinberg, 1985; Feuerstein, 1979). Dynamic assessment approaches could also compare a student's receptivity to instruction *across* various domains to evaluate differences in performance that may signal a learning disability.

However, even if the "correct" discrepancy formula were to be developed, the discrepancy would be inadequate in defining *who is served* in programs for students with learning disabilities in the schools (as differentiated from *who has learning disabilities*) because, in the educational context, "classification as having disabilities" is not synonymous with "eligible for special education services." There are two features to the eligibility decision, two questions that must be answered: 1) "Does the child have disabilities?" and 2) "Is the child in need of *special* educational services?" The answer to the first question requires a differential diagnosis. After completing all necessary examinations, a multidisciplinary team may conclude that a child is "normal" or has any one or more of the disabilities specified in federal or state special education regulations. The answer to the second question requires a judgment of whether the student is in need of "specially designed instruction" (Hallahan & Kauffman, 1991, p. 8). The issue is not whether the student needs a better education or a more personalized education, because *all* students need those things; the issue is whether the student needs a *special* education, a special curriculum, one not available to other students, taught in a special way, using different texts, different ways of presenting the information, different pacing of instruction, different amounts of guided practice, different examinations, and different grading standards.

An answer of "no" to either the first or the second eligibility question renders the child "not disabled" for educational purposes. Take the case of the child with spina bifida who is functioning well in his second grade classroom; the child with hearing impairment who is getting *B*s and *C*s in all of her middle school subjects, or the anorexic or severely depressed, perhaps even suicidal, teenager who, when not hospitalized, achieves passing grades in high school. All of these students probably qualify has having disabilities, but, if they are functioning *adequately* in a regular education classroom and are not in need of a *special* education (i.e., a special curriculum and specially designed instruction), they do not have physical disabilities, hearing impairment, or emotional disturbance *from the educational perspective.* Similarly, a student with attention problems, poor handwriting, atrocious spelling, or inadequate social or organizational skills may be diagnosed as having a severe discrepancy and a learning disability, but if he or she is performing adequately in the ordinary school program and is not in need of a special education, he or she does not have learning disabilities from an educational perspective.

LEARNING DISABILITIES AS A CONTEXTUAL PROBLEM

Not all students with disabilities have difficulty with school, but, even among those who do, not all of them are referred for special services. A recent analysis indicated that 23% of students with achievement scores in the lowest quartile were not receiving any special services whatsoever—not special education, not Chapter 1, not anything (Gerber, 1989). Obviously, teachers tolerate student failure; researchers have shown that, for every child labeled as "learning disabled," there are others *not referred* who match the labeled child on academic underachievement (Bryan, Bay, & Donahue, 1988). That may be the key to understanding learning disabilities from an educational perspective—not the significant discrepancy, but *the referral.*

Medical and psychological models of learning disabilities tend to be unidirectional. Teachers teach; students learn or fail to learn because of some unique (in)capacities. Failing students are recognized by their teachers, referred to special services, and, if a significant discrepancy is detected, these students are labeled as "learning disabled" and placed in special education programs.

In real schools, however, the problem of "failure to learn" is not unidirectional. It is transactional, a breakdown in the *interaction* between student and teacher, between learner and environment (Gerber & Semmel, 1984). In this alternative, educational model, failure to learn is a function of both within-child (in)capacities and teacher behaviors. Students with learning disabilities may or may not fail; failing students may or may not be recognized and referred. Students with similar innate capabilities may succeed in one environment and fail in another.

Referral Is the Key

Teachers work to maintain the forward flow of activities in their classrooms (Gerber & Semmel, 1984). Most teachers orient instruction toward students whose abilities and performance are perceived to be modal for that particular classroom (Semmel & Englert, 1978; Shavelson & Stern, 1981). However, students with learning disabilities are not modal; they are "hard to teach" (Zigmond, 1983). They have developmental imbalances, intraindividual gaps, uneven patterns of skills, and wide variations in performance across cognitive or academic tasks (Gallagher, 1966). Because these students can learn *some* things easily, the teacher has an expectation that *all* educational tasks will be mastered with ease. When, instead, the students run into difficulty, it is an unexpected difficulty (Bryan et al., 1988) to which the teacher responds in one of two ways: he or she feels challenged or gives up.

Teachers who feel challenged accommodate these children and their unexpected difficulties well. Just as emotional temperament interacts with caregiver characteristics to influence the course of development of emotional adjustment and stability in children (see Thomas & Chess, 1984), so learning temperament interacts with the educational environment to influence the course of achievement in school (Thomas, 1968). Children with learning disabilities require more time and effort (both their own and the teacher's) to learn, and more explicit and intensive instruction from the teacher, than do peers who are achieving normally to achieve the same outcomes. Some teachers recognize the potential in students with learning disabilities, remain optimistic about their capacity to adjust to the students' needs, make explicit the use of strategies and tactics for learning effectively, and do not refer these students for special services.

These same students, in other classrooms with other teachers, might fare quite differently. If the teacher gives up and does not adjust instruction beyond the modal student, the result, over time, will likely be fragmented acquisition of ideas, inaccuracies in the understanding of concepts, inability to transfer concepts to the next lesson, development of "islands of knowledge," and a cumulative instructional loss that can be devastating (Bryan et al., 1988). As time passes, these students become even harder to teach. Classrooms are, of course, more manageable when such "hard-to-teach" students are removed, so the teacher makes referrals to special education. The referral is a signal that the teacher has reached the limits of his or her tolerance of individual differences, is no longer optimistic about his or her capacity to deal effectively with a particular student in the context of the larger group, and no longer perceives that the student is teachable *by him- or herself* (Gerber & Semmel, 1985).

Ysseldyke and Algozzine (1983) have concluded, after a series of studies on the placement process, that the most important decision that gets made in the assignment of students to learning disabilities programs is the decision by the regular classroom teacher to refer. The recent work of Zigmond, McCall, and George (1990) at the University of Pittsburgh confirms this. They have been trying to understand what school-related factors account for extreme differences in special education service rates among school districts in Pennsylvania. In a study of 24 school districts scattered across the Commonwealth, we collected data on fiscal and demographic characteristics and on the availability and extent of use of more than a score of intervention alternatives to special education, including Chapter 1 and non–Chapter 1 remedial services, counseling for troublesome or troubling students, educational and psychological consultation for their teachers, school-based child study teams, and classroom-based instructional accommodations. Zigmond et al. (1990) also interviewed teachers in elementary, middle, and high schools in these districts about their current practices regarding students with learning problems in their classes, and they used case study simulations to explore how frequently and for what reasons these teachers referred students to special education.

The only variable that differentiated school districts that serve very large proportions (11%–15%) of their student population in programs for children with mild disabilities (which include students diagnosed as having learning disabilities, mild mental retardation, and emotional disturbance, the latter two in relatively small proportions) from school districts that serve very small proportions (2%–4%) of their student population in such programs came from the interviews of classroom teachers. Neither fiscal nor demographic variables helped to explain differences in service rates, nor did the availability or extent of use of prereferral options at the school building level. However, teachers in low-classification–rate districts were significantly more optimistic about the likelihood of success of the non–special education strategies and interventions as alternatives to special education for problem children in their classes. These teachers were more likely than their counterparts in high-classification–rate districts to work harder, persist longer, and maintain their optimism about students who were having difficulty (or with whom they were having difficulty), and were less likely to make a referral.

Therefore, not all students with significant intraindividual discrepancies in learning capacity, who find it unexpectedly difficult to learn "some things," who have serious attention disorders, spelling problems, handwriting difficulties, or problems in mastering a foreign language, are in learning disabilities programs in the schools. Many of these students with learning disabilities are performing adequately in school because they have a caring teacher who adapts to some of their individual differences, who encourages, prods, sets high expectations, rewards effort, and makes allowances—the kind of teacher all parents want for all children.

Who Gets Assigned to Special Education?

Assignment to special education is reserved by school districts for the few (3%–8% of the school population [U.S. Department of Education, 1989]) who need even more: a curriculum not taught in the mainstream, and instruction delivered and paced quite differently from instruction in the mainstream. Studies of special education environments for students with learning disabilities show that they are, indeed, special places, places where there is lower cognitive demand, and slower paced, more deliberate instruction. At the elementary level, it has been observed that students with learning disabilities in self-contained special education classes spend small amounts of each day engaged in reading orally or silently, in composing written texts, or in instructional interactions with their teachers (see Leinhardt, Zigmond, & Cooley, 1981; Silverman, Zigmond, Zimmerman, & Vallecorsa, 1981; Zigmond & Baker, 1990). At the secondary level it has been found that students with learning disabilities spend 85% of their resource room time (36 minutes of each 42-minute period) assigned to independent seatwork, practicing very basic academic skills (Zigmond, 1990). In two ethnographic studies of high school students with learning disabilities, it was shown that, in their special education classes, students receive "watered down" content instruction (see Miller, Leinhardt, & Zigmond, 1988; Zigmond & Miller, 1991) that is accommodating and helps students achieve passing grades, but is seriously limited in substance. Clearly, placement in special education classes for students with learning disabilities is not for everyone who needs a personalized education.

Moreover, not all students in learning disabilities programs truly have learning disabilities (even if all of them have significant discrepancy scores). School district selections of students for special services tell as much about a particular system and its tolerance for individual differences as about the condition itself. In a school district (or individual teacher's class) where there is pressure to in-

crease the achievement levels of modal students, and where tolerance of student variance is low, there is an advantage to identifying
a student as having learning disabilities *if* it permits that student to
access special services reserved only for students with that label
and removes the student from the responsibility (and accountability
mechanisms) of mainstream education. Under these circumstances,
many underachievers with *and without* disabilities may be assigned
to special education programs for students with learning disabilities. Conversely, one could speculate that, if there is no advantage
to the school district (or the individual teacher) to identifying a
student as having learning disabilities—if diagnosis produces no
change in resource allocation, no access to a restricted service, and
no exclusion from accountability mechanisms—then referral and
placement rates would decline. Here again, the work at the University of Pittsburgh is instructive.

Project MELD (Mainstream Experiences for the Learning Disabled) (Zigmond & Baker, 1990) was designed as one response to the
movement to serve students with disabilities in regular education
classes; it is an experimental program currently being implemented
in five elementary schools across the Commonwealth of Pennsylvania. Phase I of MELD consists of a year of planning that includes
workshops to allay teacher anxieties, teach mainstream teachers
new techniques for literacy instruction to students who are hard to
teach, and prepare learning disabilities special education teachers
for a new role; students with learning disabilities assigned to special
education programs continue to be served in pull-out programs during this planning year. In Phase II, all students with learning disabilities in the school building are returned full time to mainstream
class placements, and special education teachers assume the role
of co-teacher and consultant, providing services to the students
with learning disabilities in the regular classroom by assisting with
and/or advising the mainstream teachers on accommodations for all
children in that regular education class. Phase II implementation is
underway in all five sites, and it appears that, with training, encouragement, and support, mainstream teachers *can* accommodate well
a range of individual differences, and students who find it hard to
learn and who are hard to teach will not need to be served in pull-out
special education programs.

One outcome of the MELD implementations, however, has been
that, once Phase II began, there were virtually no new referrals to
special education. This did not mean that there were no students
with learning disabilities in those five elementary schools. It meant,
instead, that there were no children teachers felt they could give
upon. My contention is that, because in the MELD model any stu-

dent diagnosed as having learning disabilities remains the primary responsibility of the referring classroom teacher, there is no longer any advantage to referring a student for a diagnostic workup. So, if programs such as MELD continue to proliferate—and there is every reason to believe that they will (see Kauffman, 1989; Reynolds et al., 1987)—each school's capacity to accommodate individual differences as a function of local talent, resources, and resolve will determine the nature of the learning disabilities population in that school. Therefore, school-identified populations of students with learning disabilities may look quite different from school to school.

Problems with School-Identified Populations

There are two broad foci of research in the field of learning disabilities. One group of researchers studies the internal processes of the child and/or the responsiveness of the child to various instructional strategies. Basic biological research, cognitive research, and experimental instructional research all fit into this first focus. For research of this kind, the problems of definition are critical. The subject of study is certain to influence the findings. Researchers in this group would do well to maintain a healthy skepticism about "school-identified" populations of students with learning disabilities. These populations will always include some students who would not meet a definition of learning disabilities that required *more* than a severe discrepancy (e.g., neurological dysfunction; integrities of sensory, cognitive, and emotional capacities; adequate exposure to cultural and instructional opportunities). Researchers will also miss students who *do* have learning disabilities, but who have not been referred by their teacher for special education services. Defining a subject population for this kind of research will require additional diagnostic testing to cast *both* a narrower and a wider net.

The second focus of research in learning disabilities is on how schooling can be organized to serve better the needs of all children. This is research on school organization, school reform, and public policy. It includes research on the economics, sociology, or politics of education. In my own case, it is research on how schools deal with difficult children and how these children deal with school. Since 1980, I have been studying why students with learning disabilities drop out of school at a rate nearly twice that of classmates without disabilities (see deBettencourt, Zigmond, & Thornton, 1989; Thornton & Zigmond, 1988; Zigmond, 1990; Zigmond & Thornton, 1986). My colleagues and I have completed detailed studies of what school is like for high school students in learning disabilities programs and in the normal school program; what students say about their schooling experience as they are going through it and later, after they have graduated or dropped out; and what school and personal events lead a student who is in a learning disabilities program to make the decision to leave school before graduation. In this research, we talk about our subject population as "students placed in a learning disabilities program." That designation stands for students who were set aside, pulled out, sheltered from the cognitive demands of the mainstream, and, often inadvertently, made to feel less capable than they might actually be. All of the students we study qualified for placement in the learning disabilities program according to state guidelines and local practice. Most of them had significant discrepancies between achievement and IQ at the time of placement into special education; all of them had severe discrepancies after several years in the learning disabilities program because they fell farther behind their age cohorts in academic skill development, in large part because students in special education programs are taught less, more slowly. Studying these "learning disabled" students and their schooling reveals much about what is wrong with public education and in particular what is wrong with how schools cope with students who are not easy to teach. However, studying all of these students, and only these students, will not help researchers who are interested in understanding the fundamental nature of learning disabilities.

As Keogh (1983; see also chap. 14, this volume) has pointed out, there are several reasons for a definition: to serve as a focal point for advocacy, to channel the flow of dollars for school programs, and to establish a valid basis for replicable research. Problems occur when the purposes are confused, as, for example, when children identified as having learning disabilities by school districts so that they can access special education services become the subjects for psychological or neuropsychological research. Students assigned to learning disabilities programs in the schools were never intended to serve that purpose.

REFERENCES

Bateman, B. (1965). An educator's view of a diagnostic approach to learning disorders. In J. Hellmuth (Ed.), *Learning disorders* (Vol. 1, pp. 219–239). Seattle: Special Child Publications.

Benson, D., Edwards, L., Rosell, J., & White, M. (1986). Inclusion of socially maladjusted children and youth in the legal definition of the behaviorally disordered population: A debate. *Behavior Disorders, 11,* 213–222.

Bond, G.L., & Tinker, M.A. (1957). *Reading difficulties, their diagnosis and corrections.* New York: Appleton-Century-Crofts.

Bransford, J.D., Delclos, V.R., Vye, N.J., Burns, M.S., & Hasselbring, T.S. (1987). State of the art and future directions. In C.S. Lidz (Ed.), *Dynamic assessment: Foundations and fundamentals* (pp. 479–496). New York: Guilford Press.

Brown, A.L., & French, L.A. (1979). The zone of proximal development. In J. Wertsch (Ed.), *Culture, communication and cognition: Vygotskian perspectives* (pp. 273–305). Cambridge, England: Cambridge University Press.

Bryan, T., Bay, M., & Donahue, M. (1988). Implications of the learning disabilities definition for the regular education initiative. *Journal of Learning Disabilities, 21,* 23–28.

Budoff, M. (1972). Measuring learning potential: An alternative to the traditional intelligence test. *Studies in Learning Potential, 3*(39).

Budoff, M. (1974). *Learning potential and educability among the educable mentally retarded* (Final Report, Project No. 312312). Cambridge, MA: Research for Educational Problems, Cambridge Mental Health Association.

Burbules, N.C., Lord, B.T., & Sherman, A.L. (1982). Equity, equal opportunity, and education. *Educational Evaluation and Policy Analysis, 4,* 169–187.

Burns, M.S. (1985). *Comparison of "graduated prompt" and "mediational" dynamic assessment and static assessment with young children.* Nashville: John F. Kennedy Center for Research on Human Development, Vanderbilt University.

Campione, J.C., Brown, A.L., Ferrara, R.A., Jones, R.S., & Steinberg, E. (1985). Differences between retarded and non-retarded children in transfer following equivalent learning performance: Breakdowns in flexible use of information. *Intelligence, 9,* 297–315.

Center, D.B. (1989). Social maladjustment: Definition, identification, and programming. *Focus on Exceptional Children, 22*(1), 1–12.

Clarizio, H. (1987). Differentiating emotionally impaired from socially maladjusted students. *Psychology in the Schools, 24,* 237–243.

Coles, G. (1987). *The learning mystique.* New York: Pantheon.

Cone, T.E., & Wilson, L.R. (1981). Quantifying a severe discrepancy: A critical analysis. *Learning Disabilities Quarterly, 4,* 359–371.

Danielson, L.C., & Bauer, J.N. (1978). A formula-based classification of learning disabled children: An examination of the issues. *Journal of Learning Disabilities, 11,* 50–63.

deBettencourt, L., Zigmond, N., & Thornton, H. (1989). Follow-up of post secondary age rural learning disabled graduates and dropouts. *Exceptional Children, 56*(1), 40–49.

Department of Education of Pennsylvania. (1990). *Title 22: Education, Part XVI: Standards, Chapter 342: Special education services and programs.* Harrisburg: Author.

Education of the Handicapped Law Report: Statutes, regulations, indices & highlights. (1992). Horsham, PA: LRP Publications.

Erickson, M.T. (1975). The Z-score discrepancy method for identifying reading disabled children. *Journal of Learning Disabilities, 8,* 308–312.

Feuerstein, R. (1979). *The dynamic assessment of retarded performers: The learning potential assessment device, theory, instruments, and techniques.* Baltimore: University Park Press.

Gallagher, J.J. (1966). Children with developmental imbalances: A psychoeducational definition. In W.M. Cruickshank (Ed.), *The teacher of brain-*

injured children (pp. 23–33). Syracuse, NY: Syracuse University Press.

Gartner, A., & Lipsky, D.K. (1989). *The yoke of special education: How to break it.* Rochester, NY: National Center on Education and the Economy.

Gerber, M. (1989). The new "diversity" and special education: Are we going forward or starting again? *California Public Schools Forum, 3,* 1–13.

Gerber, M., & Semmel, M.I. (1984). Teacher as imperfect test: Reconceptualizing the referral process. *Educational Psychologist, 19,* 1–12.

Gerber, M., & Semmel, M.I. (1985). The microeconomics of referral and reintegration: A paradigm for evaluation of special education. *Studies in Educational Evaluation, 11,* 13–29.

Grossman, H.J. (Ed.). (1983). *Classification in mental retardation.* Washington, DC: American Association on Mental Retardation.

Hallahan, D.P., & Kauffman, J.M. (1991). *Exceptional children: Introduction to special education* (5th ed.). Englewood Cliffs, NJ: Prentice Hall.

Hammill, D.D., Leigh, J.E., McNutt, G., & Larsen, S.C. (1981). A new definition of learning disabilities. *Learning Disabilities Quarterly, 4,* 336–342.

Harris, A. (1970). *How to increase reading abilities* (5th ed.). New York: David McKay.

Hessler, G.L. (1987). Educational issues surrounding learning disabilities. *Learning Disabilities Research, 3*(1), 43–49.

Johnson, D., & Myklebust, H. (1967). *Learning disabilities: Educational principles and practices.* New York: Grune & Stratton.

Journal of Learning Disabilities, 22(8), 1989, October.

Kaluger, G., & Kolson, C. (1969). *Reading and learning disabilities.* Columbus, OH: Charles E. Merrill.

Kauffman, J.M. (1989). *The regular education initiative as Reagan-Bush education policy: A trickle-down theory of education of the hard-to-teach.* Charlottesville: Commonwealth Center for Education of Teachers & Virginia Educational Policy Analysis Center, University of Virginia.

Kavale, K.A. (1987). Theoretical issues surrounding severe discrepancy. *Learning Disabilities Research, 3*(1), 12–20.

Kavale, K.A., & Forness, S.R. (1985). *The science of learning disabilities.* San Diego: College-Hill Press.

Kavale, K.A., & Nye, C. (1986). Parameters of learning disabilities in achievement, linguistics, neuropsychological and social-behavioral domains. *Journal of Special Education, 19,* 443–458.

Keogh, B.K. (1983). Classification, compliance and confusion. *Journal of Learning Disabilities, 16,* 25.

Kephart, N.C. (1960). *The slow learner in the classroom.* Columbus, OH: Charles E. Merrill.

Kirk, S.A. (1962). *Educating exceptional children.* Boston: Houghton Mifflin.

Kirk, S.A. (1963). Behavioral diagnosis and remediation of learning disabilities. In *Proceedings of the conference on exploration into the problems of the perceptually handicapped child* (Vol. 1, pp. 1–7). Evanston, IL: Fund for Perceptually Handicapped Children, Inc.

Kirk, S.A., & Elkins, J. (1975). Characteristics of children enrolled in Child Service Demonstration Centers. *Journal of Learning Disabilities, 8,* 630–637.

Leinhardt, G., Zigmond, N., & Cooley, W.W. (1981). Reading instruction and its effects. *American Educational Research Journal, 18,* 343–361.

MacMillan, D.L., Meyers, C.E., & Morrison, G.M. (1980). System-identification of mildly retarded children: Implications for integrating and conducting research. *American Journal of Mental Deficiency, 85,* 108–115.

Mann, L. (1979). *On the trail of process.* New York: Grune & Stratton.

Mann, L., Davis, C.H., Boyer, C.W., Metz, C.M., & Wolford, B. (1983). LD or not LD, that was the question: A retrospective analysis of Child Service Demonstration Centers' compliance with the federal definition of learning disabilities. *Journal of Learning Disabilities, 16,* 14–17.

McLoughlin, J.A., & Netick, A. (1983). Defining learning disabilities: A new and cooperative direction. *Journal of Learning Disabilities, 16,* 21–23.

Mercer, C.D., Forgnone, C., & Wolking, W.D. (1976). Definitions of learning disabilities used in the United States. *Journal of Learning Disabilities, 9,* 47–57.

Miller, S.E., Leinhardt, G., & Zigmond, N. (1988). Influencing engagement through accommodation: An ethnographic study of at-risk students. *American Educational Research Journal, 25*(4), 465–488.

Myklebust, H.R. (1968). Learning disabilities: Definition and overview. In H.R. Myklebust (Ed.), *Progress in learning disabilities* (pp. 1–15). New York: Grune & Stratton.

Nelson, C.M., Rutherford, R.B., Center, D.B., & Walker, H.M. (1991). Do public schools have an obligation to serve troubled children and youth? *Exceptional Children, 57*(5), 406–415.

Norman, C.A., Jr., & Zigmond, N. (1980). Characteristics of students labelled and served in school systems affiliated with child service demonstration centers. *Journal of Learning Disabilities, 13*(10), 546–547.

Public Law 91-230, Education of the Handicapped Act, Title VI, of 1970.

Public Law 94-142, Education for All Handicapped Children Act of 1975. (23 August 1977). 20 U.S.C. 1401 et seq: *Federal Register, 42,*(163), 42474-42518.

Public Law 102-119, Individuals with Disabilities Education Act Amendments of 1991. (7 October 1991). 20 U.S.C. 1400 et seq: *U.S. Statutes at Large, 105,* 587–608.

Reynolds, C.R. (1984). Critical measurement issues in learning disabilities. *Journal of Special Education, 18,* 451–475.

Reynolds, C.R., Berk, R.A., Boodoo, G.M., Cox, J., Gutkin, T.B., Mann, L., Page, E.B., & Willson, V.C. (1984–85). *Critical measurement issues in learning disabilities.* Report of the Work Group on Measurement Issues in the Assessment of Learning Disabilities. Washington, DC: U.S. Office of Education.

Reynolds, M.C., Wang, M.C., & Walberg, H.J. (1987). The necessary restructuring of special and regular education. *Exceptional Children, 53,* 391–398.

Robinson, N.M., & Robinson, H.B. (1976). *The mentally retarded child: A psychological approach.* New York: McGraw-Hill.

Rothman, H.R., & Semmel, M.I. (1990). Dynamic assessment: A comprehensive review of the literature. In R. Gaylord-Ross (Ed.), *Issues and research in special education* (Vol. 1, pp. 355–386). New York: Teachers College Press.

Semmel, M.I., & Englert, C.S. (1978). A decision-making orientation applied to student teaching supervision. *Teacher Education and Special Education, 1*(2), 28–36.

Shavelson, R., & Stern, P. (1981). Research on teachers' pedagogical thoughts, judgements, decisions and behavior. *Review of Educational Research, 51,* 455–498.

Shepard, L. (1980). An evaluation of the regression method for identifying children with learning disabilities. *The Journal of Special Education, 14*(1), 79–91.

Silverman, R., Zigmond, N., Zimmerman, J., & Vallecorsa, A. (1981). Improving written expression in learning disabled students. *Topics in Language Disorders, 1*(2), 91–99.

Sontag, E. (1976). Specific learning disabilities program. *Exceptional Children, 43*(3), 157–159.

Thomas, A. (1968). Significance of temperamental individuality for school functioning. In J. Hellmuth (Ed.), *Learning disorders* (Vol. 3, pp. 345–358). Seattle: Special Child Publications.

Thomas, A., & Chess, S. (1984). Genesis and evolution of behavioral disorders: From infancy to early adult life. *American Journal of Psychiatry, 141,* 1–9.

Thornton, H., & Zigmond, N. (1988). Secondary vocational training outcomes and their relationship to school completion status and post school outcomes. *Illinois School Journal, 67*(2), 37–54.

U.S. Department of Education. (1989). *To assure the free appropriate public education of all handicapped children: Eleventh annual report to Congress on the implementation of the Education of the Handicapped Act.* Washington, DC: Author.

U.S. Department of Health, Education and Welfare, Office of Education. (1977, December). Part III. Additional procedures for evaluating specific learning disabilities. *Federal Register, 42*(250), 65083.

Wiederholt, J.L. (1974). Historical perspectives on the education of the learning disabled. In L. Mann & D.A. Sabatino (Eds.), *The second review of special education* (pp. 103–152). Austin, TX: PRO-ED.

Ysseldyke, J.E., & Algozzine, B. (1983). LD or not LD: That's not the question! *Journal of Learning Disabilities, 16*(1), 29–31.

Ysseldyke, J.E., & Thurlow, M.L. (1984). Assessment practices in special education: Adequacy and appropriateness. *Educational Psychologist, 9*(3), 123–126.

Zigmond, N. (1983). *Towards a new definition of learning disabilities.* Paper presented at the annual meeting of the American Educational Research Association, Montreal, Quebec, Canada.

Zigmond, N. (1990). Rethinking secondary school programs for students with learning disabilities. *Focus on Exceptional Children, 23*(1), 1–12.

Zigmond, N., & Baker, J. (1990). Mainstreaming experiences for learning disabled students: A preliminary report. *Exceptional Children, 57*(2), 176–185.

Zigmond, N., McCall, R., & George, J. (1990). *The effects of availability, extent of use and teachers' perceived effectiveness of prereferral interventions on classification rates of mildly handicapped students in school districts in the Commonwealth of Pennsylvania.* Paper presented at the annual meeting of the American Educational Research Association, Boston.

Zigmond, N., & Miller, S.E. (1991). Improving high school programs for students with learning disabilities: A matter of substance as well as form. In F.R. Rusch, L. DeStefano, J. Chadsey-Rusch, L.A. Phelps, & E.

Szymanski (Eds.), *Transition from school to adult life*. Champaign, IL: Sycamore Publishing Company.

Zigmond, N., & Semmel, M.I. (in press). Educating the nation's handicapped children: The federal role in special education. In K. Lloyd (Ed.), *Risking American educational competitiveness in a global economy: Federal education and training policies 1980–1990*. Arlington, VA: Center for Educational Competitiveness.

Zigmond, N., & Thornton, H. (1986). Follow-up of post-secondary age LD graduate and dropouts. *LD Research, 1*(1), 50–55.

13

THE CONSTRUCT VALIDITY OF DISCREPANCY DEFINITIONS OF READING DISABILITY

Keith E. Stanovich

In this chapter I hope to clarify some of the confusion that many different investigators agree (see Vaughn & Bos, 1987) surrounds our current attempts to develop a conceptually coherent definition of learning disability in the domain of reading. The way I have phrased the issue in fact reveals my first recommendation. It is not a new or innovative recommendation, having been suggested by several commentators at the 1987 National Conference on Learning Disabilities. The recommendation is that we stop using the term *learning disabilities* in scientific contexts (however useful it may be in school or public policy contexts) and only talk about disabilities defined in terms of reasonably coherent and operational domains. Scientific investigations of some generically defined entity called "learning disability" simply make little sense given what we already know about heterogeneity across various learning domains. Research investigations must define groups specifically in terms of the domain of deficit (e.g., reading disability, arithmetic disability). The extent of co-occurrence of these dysfunctions then becomes an empirical question, not something decided a priori by definition practices. For

Portions of this chapter have been adapted from material appearing in Stanovich, K.E. (1991). Discrepancy definitions of reading disability: Has intelligence led us astray? *Reading Research Quarterly, 26,* 7–29. Preparation of this chapter was supported by a grant from the Social Sciences and Humanities Research Council of Canada.

this reason, this chapter focuses on reading disability as a more specific form of learning disability.

My call for domain specificity in our scientific definitions of learning disabilities echoes previous arguments for this definitional practice. For example, Shepherd (1988) has argued "I believe the time has come to assign the term learning disabilities to historical accounts of research on these developmental disorders . . . and to replace it with a taxonomy of those disorders which it subsumes" (p. 164). Similarly, Torgesen (1988) argued that

> We should stop using the unqualified term learning disabilities in the title of our research reports. Our subject selection procedures should be openly guided by our particular assumptions about the nature of the abilities we are studying. Thus, we might have some studies of language impaired [LD] children, or perhaps others of [LD] children with above average intelligence. (p. 175)

As obvious as this point may seem, it is still not adhered to with regularity in our professional literature—one regularly sees in our literature studies the subject selection characteristics that Torgesen and Shepherd recommended against: undifferentiated groups of children with disabilities in heterogeneous domains lumped together and tested on a battery of cognitive tasks. This, then, is the first reform that must be undertaken to extricate ourselves from the current conceptual muddle in which the term *learning disabilities* resides. Consistent with the recommendation, I should reiterate that the rest of this chapter deals with reading disability exclusively.

The second step in escaping our definitional muddle is to be more aware of a point repeatedly emphasized by Keogh (1987; see also Galaburda, 1990; Keogh, chap. 14, this volume): there are different types of learning disabilities definitions for different purposes. For example, she has printed out that definitions of learning disabilities for purposes of advocacy efforts, for purposes of delivery of services, and for purposes of scientific research may well diverge from each other. Thus, it is extremely important in discussions of learning disabilities for all parties to be absolutely clear about what type of definition is taken as a background assumption for their argument. We routinely violate this injunction in our discussion of learning disabilities, and this accounts for a lot of the "talking past each other" that goes on in the field. It is not uncommon to hear debates in which one disputant is assuming that the definitional issue being discussed concerns school-based service delivery and the other disputant assumes the discussion concerns a scientifically justifiable definition. It is no wonder, given that we often cannot even achieve agreement on the premises for the debate, that there is so much contention in our field.

With these preliminaries out of the way, I now turn to the main concern of this chapter: to consider why, after decades of intense research effort, we have yet to demonstrate construct validity for the concept of reading disability. I believe that this shocking state of affairs has been in part brought about by our failure to think seriously about the role of intelligence in definitions of reading disability.

THE CRUX OF THE PROBLEM

The initial formulations of professional and legal definitions of reading disability all emphasized the existence of discrepancies between actual school achievement and assumed intellectual capacity (see Doris, chap. 6, this volume). During the 1960s and 1970s, several proposed definitions of reading disability had considerable influence on both research and service delivery debates. The definition of the World Federation of Neurology had many features that became canonical for many researchers and practitioners. Specific developmental dyslexia was characterized as "A disorder manifested by difficulty in learning to read despite conventional instruction, adequate intelligence, and socio-cultural opportunity. It is dependent upon fundamental cognitive abilities which are frequently of constitutional origin" (Critchley, 1970, p. 11).

This particular definition highlighted the well-known "exclusionary criteria" that subsequently caused much dispute in discussions of dyslexia (e.g., Applebee, 1971; Ceci, 1986; Doehring, 1978; Eisenberg, 1978; Rutter, 1978)—in particular, "adequate" intelligence is required to qualify for the dyslexia label. The exclusionary criteria became the indirect way of operationalizing the assumption of neurological etiology in the absence of direct evidence of neurological dysfunction.

The use of exclusionary criteria was carried over into the definition of learning disability employed in the landmark Education for All Handicapped Children Act (P.L. 94-142) passed in 1975. The National Joint Committee for Learning Disabilities responded to criticisms of the exclusionary criteria by proposing that

> These disorders are intrinsic to the individual and presumed to be due to central nervous dysfunction. Even though a learning disability may occur concomitantly with other handicapping conditions (e.g., sensory impairment, mental retardation, social and emotional disturbance) or environmental influences (e.g., cultural differences, or inappropriate

instruction, psycholinguistic factors), it is not the direct result of those conditions or influences. (Hammill, Leigh, McNutt, & Larsen, 1981, p. 336)

Thus, this definition emphasized that the mere presence of other impairments or of environmental deprivation should not exclude children from the learning disabilities categorization (see also Kavanagh & Truss, 1988).

All of these professional and legal definitions highlight the same salient feature: the fact that a child with dyslexia has an "unexpected" disability in the domain of reading, one not predicted by his or her general intellectual competence and socioeducational opportunities. Practically, this has meant a statistical assessment of the difference between objectively measured reading ability and general intelligence (Frankenberger & Fronzaglio, 1991; Frankenberger & Harper, 1987; Kavale, 1987; Kavale & Nye, 1981; Reynolds, 1985; Shepard, 1980). Typically, very little effort is expended in ascertaining whether adequate instruction has been provided or whether the child suffers from sociocultural disadvantage—in short, in ascertaining whether the disability is "intrinsic to the individual." So much conceptual confusion has surrounded the more operational discrepancy criterion that researchers and theoreticians have been reluctant to take on the potential additional complications of the other criteria. In short, despite repeated admonitions that the diagnosis of reading disability should be multidimensional (Johnson, 1988; McKinney, 1987; Tindal & Marston, 1986), in actual educational practice it is the assessment of a discrepancy between aptitude as measured by an individually administered intelligence test and reading achievement that is the key defining feature (Frankenberger & Fronzaglio, 1991). In identifying their samples, researchers have typically followed the lead of practitioners in this respect.

The choice of IQ test performance as the baseline from which to measure achievement discrepancies was accepted by teachers, schools, professional organizations, and government agencies in the absence of much critical discussion or research evidence. Until quite recently, the field seems never to have grappled very seriously with the question of why the benchmark should have been IQ. It is thus not surprising that the concept of intelligence is the genesis of so many of the conceptual paradoxes that plague the concept of dyslexia (Stanovich, 1986a, 1986b, 1988b) and that the use of IQ in the differential diagnosis of reading disability has been called into question (Aaron, 1991; Rispens, van Yeren, & van Duijn, 1991; Seidenberg, Bruck, Fornarolo, & Backman, 1986; Share, McGee, & Silva, 1989; Siegel, 1988, 1989).

Why was professional assent to the use of IQ test scores in the discrepancy definition given so readily? Undoubtedly there were many reasons, but probably one factor was the belief that IQ scores were valid measures of intellectual potential. One major problem, however, was that most psychometricians, developmental psychologists, and educational psychologists long ago gave up the belief that IQ test scores measured potential in any valid sense. Indeed, standard texts in educational measurement and assessment routinely warn against interpreting IQ scores as measures of intellectual potential (Anastasi, 1988; Cronbach, 1984; Thorndike, 1963). At their best, IQ test scores are gross measures of current cognitive functioning (Detterman, 1982; Humphreys, 1979). Indeed, some work in developmental psychology might even force a weakening of this characterization (Ceci, 1990; Siegel, 1989).

However, advocates of current practices might counter some of these criticisms by arguing that, despite conceptual difficulties, a strictly empirical orientation would support current procedures. That is, an advocate of the status quo might argue that all of the philosophical and conceptual criticisms are beside the point because measuring discrepancy from IQ in the current manner distinguishes a group of children who, cognitively and behaviorally, are sufficiently distinct that the use of current procedures is justified on empirical grounds. Here we are getting to the heart of the empirical question that in part determines the validity of the reading disability concept.

RESEARCH DESIGNS AND CONSTRUCT VALIDITY

The critical assumption that has fueled theoretical interest in the dyslexia concept from the beginning—and that has justified differential educational classification and treatment—has been that the degree of discrepancy from IQ is meaningful. Thus, the reading difficulties of the child with dyslexia (I am referring to a discrepancy-defined child) stem from problems different from those characterizing the poor reader without IQ discrepancy, the so-called garden-variety poor reader (to use Gough & Tunmer's [1986] term); or, alternatively, if they stem from the same factors, the degree of severity is so extreme for the child with dyslexia that it constitutes, in effect, a qualitative difference.

The operationalization of this assumption for purposes of empirical tests has been dominated by two different research designs. One is the reading-level match design, where an older group of children with dyslexia is matched on reading level with a younger group of children without dyslexia, and the cognitive profiles of the two groups are compared. The logic here is fairly straightforward. If the reading-related cognitive profiles of the two groups do not match, it would seem that they are arriving at their similar reading levels via different routes. In contrast, if the reading subskill profiles of the two groups are identical, this would seem to undermine the rationale for the theoretical differentiation of children with dyslexia. If such children are reading just like other children who happen to be at their reading level, and are using the same cognitive skills to do so, they become much less interesting from a theoretical point of view.

The second major design—one not only pertinent to theoretical issues, but also quite relevant to the educational politics of reading disability—compares children with dyslexia with children of the same age who are reading at the same level, but who are not labeled "dyslexic," and who, of course, have lower IQs. Adapting the terminology of Gough and Tunmer (1986), I have termed this design the *garden-variety control* design. Again, the inferences drawn are relatively straightforward. If the reading subskill profiles of the two groups do not match, this is at least consistent with the assumption that they are arriving at their similar reading levels via different routes. In contrast, if the reading subskill profiles of the two groups are identical, this would certainly undermine the rationale for the differential educational treatment of children with dyslexia and would again make these children considerably less interesting theoretically.

WHAT MIGHT WE EXPECT TO FIND?

Before summarizing the current state of the evidence on the cognitive differentiation of dyslexic poor readers using these two designs I outline what patterns, given current conceptions of dyslexia, data should show in the best of all possible worlds. I have summarized the idealized situation in a model that I have termed the *phonological-core variable-difference framework* (Stanovich, 1988a).

The model rests on a clear understanding of the assumption of specificity in definitions of dyslexia (Stanovich, 1986a). This assumption underlies all discussions of the concept of dyslexia, even if it is not explicitly stated. It is the idea that a child with this type of learning disability has a brain/cognitive deficit that is reasonably specific to the reading task. That is, the concept of dyslexia requires that the deficits displayed by such children not extend too far into other domains of cognitive functioning. If they did, this would depress the constellation of abilities we call intelligence and thus reduce the reading–intelligence discrepancy that is central to all current definitions.

In short, the key deficit in dyslexia must be a vertical faculty rather than a horizontal faculty—a domain-specific process rather than a process that operates across a variety of domains. For this and other reasons, many investigators have located the proximal locus of dyslexia at the word recognition level (e.g., Bruck, 1988, 1990; Gough & Tunmer, 1986; Morrison, 1984, 1987; Perfetti, 1985; Siegel, 1985, 1988; Siegel & Faux, 1989; Stanovich, 1986b, 1988b) and have been searching for the locus of the flaw in the word recognition module.

Research in the last 10 years has focused intensively on phonological processing abilities. It is now well established that dyslexic children display deficits in various aspects of phonological processing. They have difficulty making explicit reports about sound segments at the phoneme level, they display naming difficulties, their utilization of phonological codes in short-term memory is inefficient, their categorical perception of certain phonemes may be other than normal, and they may have speech production difficulties (Ackerman, Dykman, & Gardner, 1990; Bruck & Treiman, 1990; Cossu, Shankweiler, Liberman, Katz, & Tola, 1988; Hurford & Sanders, 1990; Kamhi & Catts, 1989; Liberman & Shankweiler, 1985; Lieberman, Meskill, Chatillon, & Schupack, 1985; Mann, 1986; Pennington, 1986; Pratt & Brady, 1988; M.A. Reed, 1989; Snowling, 1987; Taylor, Lean, & Schwartz, 1989; Wagner & Torgesen, 1987; Werker & Tees, 1987; Williams, 1984, 1986; Wolf, 1991). Importantly, there is increasing evidence that the linkage from phonological processing ability to reading skill is a casual one (Adams, 1990; Ball & Blachman, 1991; Blachman, 1989; Bradley & Bryant, 1985; Bryant, Bradley, Maclean, & Crossland, 1989; Cunningham, 1990; Lie, 1991; Lundberg, Frost, & Peterson, 1988; Lundberg & Hoien, 1989; Maclean, Bryant, & Bradley, 1987; Perfetti, Beck, Bell, & Hughes, 1987; Stanovich, 1986b, 1988b; Treiman & Baron, 1983; Wagner & Torgesen, 1987). Whether all of these phonologically related deficits are reflective of a single underlying processing problem and whether all of them can be considered causal or are instead incidental correlates are matters for future research, but some important progress is being made on this issue (e.g., Pennington, Van Orden, Smith, Green, & Haith, 1990).

Thus, there is now voluminous evidence indicating that phonological deficits are the basis of the dyslexic performance pattern. This is an oversimplification because it ignores the possibility of core deficits in the realm of orthographic processing. In fact, there is growing evidence for the utility of distinguishing a group of children with dyslexia who have severe problems in accessing the lexicon on a visual/orthographic basis (see Stanovich, 1992; Stanovich & West, 1989). Suggestive evidence comes from the work on acquired reading disability that has revealed the existence of surface dyslexia (Patterson, Marshall, & Coltheart, 1985), a condition in which the individual appears to have difficulty forming and/or accessing orthographic representations of words in memory. However, the interpretation of these cases has recently been somewhat clouded by claims that the performance patterns can be simulated by connectionist models without the dual-route architectures that in some sense define a separable concept of orthographic processing (Seidenberg & McClelland, 1989).

Nevertheless, further indirect evidence for an additional processing deficit—perhaps one in the visual/orthographic domain—comes from multivariate investigations indicating that efficient phonological processing is a necessary but not sufficient condition for attaining advanced levels of word recognition skill (Juel, Griffith, & Gough, 1986; Tunmer & Nesdale, 1985). If efficient phonological processing ability is a necessary but not sufficient condition for rapid reading acquisition, this suggests that there must be at least one other sticking point for some children.

Finally, some research has indicated the presence of visually based deficits (Lovegrove, Martin, & Slaghuis, 1986; Martin & Lovegrove, 1988; Solman & May, 1990; Willows, 1991; Willows, Kruk, & Corcos, in press), but these remain controversial (Hulme, 1988). Irrespective of how this research dispute is eventually resolved, it is the case that any smaller group of children with dyslexia with visual/orthographic core deficits would mirror the phonological-core group in all of the other processing characteristics of the model. What are those characteristics?

In the phonological-core variable-difference model (Stanovich, 1988a), the term *variable difference* refers to the key performance contrasts between the garden-variety poor reader and the reader with dyslexia *outside* of the phonological domain. Research has indicated that the cognitive status of the garden-variety poor reader appears to be well described by a developmental lag model. Cognitively, this reader is remarkably similar to younger children reading at the same level (Stanovich, Nathan, & Vala-Rossi, 1986; Stanovich, Nathan, & Zolman, 1988). A logical corollary of this pattern is that the garden-variety poor reader will have a variety of cognitive deficits when compared to chronological-age controls who are reading at normal levels. However, it is important to understand that the garden-variety poor reader does share the phonological problems of the reader with dyslexia, and these deficits also appear to be a causal factor in his or her poor reading (Juel, 1988; Juel et al., 1986; Perfetti, 1985; Stanovich, 1986b). For the garden-variety poor reader, however, the deficits—relative to chronological-age controls—extend into a variety of domains (see Ellis & Large, 1987) and some of these (e.g., vocabulary, language comprehension) may also be causally linked to reading comprehension. Such a pattern should not characterize the child with dyslexia who should have a deficit localized in the phonological core.

The phonological-core variable-difference model assumes multidimensional continuity for reading ability in general and for all its related cognitive subskills. There is considerable evidence from a variety of different sources supporting such a continuity assumption (Ellis, 1985; Jorm, 1983; Olson, Kliegl, Davidson, & Foltz, 1985; Scarborough, 1984; Seidenberg, Bruck, Fornarolo, & Backman, 1985; Share, McGee, McKenzie, Williams, & Silva, 1987; Shaywitz, Escobar, Shaywitz, Fletcher, & Makugh, 1992; Silva, McGee, & Williams, 1985; Vogler, Baker, Decker, DeFries, & Huizinga, 1989). However, the fact that the distribution is a graded continuum does not necessarily render the concept of dyslexia scientifically useless, as some critics charge. Ellis (1985) has argued that the proper analogy for dyslexia is obesity. Everyone agrees that the latter condition is a very real health problem, despite the fact that it is operationally defined in a somewhat arbitrary way by choosing a criterion in a continuous distribution.

The framework of the phonological-core variable-difference model meshes nicely with the multidimensional continuum notion. Consider the following characterization: As we move in the multidimensional space of individual differences in cognitive subskills—from the reader with dyslexia to the garden-variety poor reader—we will move from a processing deficit localized in the phonological core to the global deficits of the developmentally lagging garden-variety poor reader. Thus, the actual cognitive differences that are displayed will be variable depending on the type of poor reader who is the focus of the investigation. The differences on one end of the continuum will consist of deficits located only in the phonological core (the reader with dyslexia) and will increase in number as we run through the intermediate cases that are less and less likely to pass strict psychometric criteria for dyslexia. Eventually we will reach the part of the multidimensional space containing relatively "pure" garden-variety poor readers who will not qualify for the label "dyslexic" (by either regression or exclusionary criteria), will have a host of cognitive deficits, and will have the cognitively immature profile of a developmentally lagging individual.

This framework provides an explanation for why almost all processing investigations of dyslexia have uncovered phonological deficits, but also why some investigations have found deficits in many other areas as well (see Stanovich, 1986b)—a finding that is paradoxical if one takes the definition of dyslexia seriously. However, this outcome can, with some additional assumptions, be explained by the phonological-core variable-difference model, which posits that virtually all poor readers have a phonological deficit, but that other processing deficits emerge as one drifts in the multidimensional space from readers with "pure" dyslexia toward garden-variety poor readers. Thus, the model's straightforward prediction is that those studies that revealed a more isolated deficit will be those that had more psychometrically select readers with dyslexia. To state the model's prediction in another way, the reading–IQ discrepancy of the subject populations should be significantly greater in those studies displaying more specific deficits. Presumably, studies finding deficits extending beyond the phonological domain are in the "fuzzy" area of the multidimensional space and are picking up the increasing number of processing differences that extend beyond the phonological domain as one moves toward the garden-variety area of the space.

The phonological-core variable-difference model provides a parsimonious but realistic way of conceptualizing the idea of dyslexia. The model would, if true, preserve at least some of the clinical insights of practitioners within the learning disabilities field who prefer traditional assumptions; yet, its emphasis on continuity removes some of the more objectionable features of the term *dyslexia*— features that actually have stigmatized the term within some reading research subcommunities. Of course, the true test is the state of the empirical evidence on the model, and it is to this that we now turn.

DO WE FIND THE EXPECTED DATA PATTERNS?

Unfortunately, well-controlled studies employing the garden-variety control and reading-level match designs have begun to appear in sufficient numbers only recently. For a considerable period, the dyslexia literature was dominated by studies employing only chronological-age controls, a design of low diagnosticity (Bryant & Goswami, 1986). It was not until the mid-1970s that we had the data from the ground-breaking epidemiological comparison of readers with dyslexia and garden-variety poor readers conducted by Rutter and Yule (1975), and only in the last 5 years or so has their data been supplemented by other garden-variety control investigations. Additionally, only recently have enough studies employing reading-level matches been accumulated so that patterns were discernible.

The data from investigations employing reading-level match designs were once a confusing mass of contradictions (see Stanovich et al., 1986). However, Rack, Snowling, and Olson (1992) have recently completed a meta-analysis of these studies that explains some of the discrepancies in the literature. It appears that children with dyslexia, when matched with younger children on word recognition ability, will display inferior phonological coding skills, particularly in the case of pseudoword naming. This conclusion is based on data from dozens of subjects collected by numerous investigators from several different continents (Aaron, 1989b; Baddeley, Ellis, Miles, & Lewis, 1982; Bradley & Bryant, 1978; Bruck, 1990; Holligan & Johnston, 1988; Kochnower, Richardson, & DiBenedetto, 1983; Lundberg & Hoien, 1989; Olson et al., 1985; Olson, Wise, Conners, Rack, & Fulker, 1989; Siegel & Faux, 1989; Siegel & Ryan, 1988; Snowling, 1980, 1981; Snowling, Stackhouse, & Rack, 1986). It is true that there are some exceptions to the pattern (Baddeley, Logie, & Ellis, 1988; Beech & Harding, 1984; Bruck, 1988; Treiman & Hirsh-Pasek, 1985; Vellutino & Scanlon, 1987), but most of these can be explained by a variety of factors that Rack et al. (1992) discussed in their meta-analysis. For example, the nature of the words on the word recognition test must be carefully considered, as must the pseudowords used in the nonword naming test.

Additionally, some studies have demonstrated that children with dyslexia perform relatively better on orthographic processing tasks than they do on phonological processing tasks when compared with younger readers without dyslexia matched on word recognition skill (Olson et al., 1985; Pennington et al., 1986; Siegel, in press). Readers with dyslexia, despite inferior phonological skills, appear to maintain word recognition levels equal to younger controls because they have better orthographic representations in their lexicon— perhaps because they have had more print exposure (see Cunningham & Stanovich, 1990, 1991; Stanovich, in press; Stanovich & Cunningham, 1992; West & Stanovich, 1991). In short, readers with dyslexia may require more exposure to words to reach a given level of word recognition skill. Thus, when tested on an orthographic task that relies heavily on the quality of the orthographic representation, they do better because they have had more exposure to words (and hence letter patterns) than younger children who reached that level of word recognition in less time.

It would be interesting to see how easily a connectionist model of word recognition (e.g., Seidenberg & McClelland, 1989) could simulate this type of compensation by deleting hidden units or lesioning the model, but compensating by providing more exposure to words. Such an investigation might help to differentiate whether it is mere differential experience that accounts for this pattern or whether it is some experience-independent superiority in accessing orthographic representations that characterizes readers with dyslexia. Alternatively, a connectionist model with too many hidden units might be the appropriate neural model. Galaburda (1991) has suggested that the atypical symmetry in the planum temporale found in children with dyslexia may be due to too many neurons rather than too few. Interestingly, Seidenberg and McClelland (1989) noted that "It is known that in some cases, networks with too many hidden units 'memorize' the training examples, but fail to extract important regularities, and thus lack the ability to respond to novel inputs" (p. 561), and Besner, Twilley, McCann, and Seergobin (1990, p. 435) suggested that too many hidden units may be the reason that the data simulations of certain connectionist models show lower nonword naming performance (as do children with dyslexia) than they should. If the phenotypic performance pattern of poor readers is indeed inferior phonological processing and superior orthographic processing compared to reading level–matched younger readers without disabilities, then neurophysiological and connectionist models may be converging on a coherent theory of why this is the case.

However these theoretical issues are resolved, there is evidence for a different organization of cognitive subskills within the word recognition module when readers with dyslexia are compared to younger readers without disabilities. However, when we turn our attention to studies employing garden-variety matches, where we would expect a similar pattern—if, that is, the concept of discrepancy-defined dyslexia has construct validity—we find something very puzzling indeed. The literature provides no strong support for a differential organization of cognitive subskills within the word recognition module among readers of different IQ levels. Several studies have failed to find differences in tasks tapping word recognition subprocesses, such as pseudoword naming, regular word naming, exception word naming, phonological choice tasks, and orthographic choice tasks (Fredman & Stevenson, 1988; Share, Jorm, et al., 1987; Siegel, 1988). Additionally, Olson, Wise, Conners, and Rack (1990) have failed to find a correlation between the degree of discrepancy within their sample of twins with dyslexia and the degree of phonological deficit, a statistical test not quite equivalent to a garden-variety control design, but troublesome nonetheless.

It is interesting to note that both Olson (Olson et al., 1985, 1990) and Siegel (1988, in press) have found a mismatch in processing abilities between readers with dyslexia and younger word-level controls, but no such mismatch between readers with dyslexia and poor readers across the IQ range. Age thus appears to be a better predictor of the reorganization cognitive skills in reading than does IQ. Or, rather than age, one might say that it is reading failure that is a better predictor because, of course, reading failure is something that the readers with dyslexia and the garden-variety poor readers also have in common. Here might be the key to the apparent puzzle (see Snowling, 1987). Whether low phonological sensitivity is due to developmental lag, neurological insult, or whatever, the key fact is that the necessity of confronting the demands of the reading task on entering school triggers the reorganization of skills we see in readers with dyslexia and garden-variety poor readers when either are compared to younger matched controls.

This interpretation—and the finding it seeks to explain: the nondifferentiability of readers with dyslexia and garden-variety poor readers—is, however, a bit of a threat to the construct validity of IQ-based discrepancy measurement. This is because when it comes to the critical locus of dyslexia—word recognition—the structure of processing looks remarkably similar across the IQ range (see Siegel, 1988, 1989). One must at least conclude that it has often been surprisingly difficult to differentiate discrepancy-defined readers with dyslexia from garden-variety poor readers on tasks that tap critical processing components of reading. This is surprising because it is *intelligence* that is supposed to be the more encompassing construct. Consider, for example, the data published by Siegel (1988). It is *reading skill* and *not* IQ that separates subject groups more strongly on such variables as visual processing, phonological processing, Illinois Test of Psycholinguistic Abilities performance, cloze performance, sentence correction tasks, short-term memory tasks, working memory tasks, and, of course spelling, but also arithmetic performance, which tracks reading more closely than IQ. As a general cognitive probe, reading ability seems to be a more sensitive indicator than IQ test performance.

FURTHER MISSING EVIDENCE OF CONSTRUCT VALIDITY

The lack of differentiation based on IQ is a cause for some soul-searching. Indeed, the empirical picture is, if anything, even more incomplete than I have portrayed it here, for there are still inadequate data on several other foundational assumptions. For example, outside of the pioneering work of Lyon (1985), there are very few data on differential response to treatment. There are, for example, very few data indicating that discrepancy-defined readers with dyslexia respond differently to various educational treatments than do garden-variety poor readers of the same age or younger children without dyslexia reading at the same level (Pressley & Levin, 1987; van der Wissel, 1987; however, also see Torgesen, Dahlem, & Greenstein, 1987). This is not a trivial gap in our knowledge. Differential treatment effects are, in large part, the raison d'être of special education.

We are equally unenlightened on several other crucial issues. The data on differential prognosis for reading are contradictory. Rutter and Yule (1975) found differential growth curves for readers with specific disabilities and garden-variety poor readers. The garden-variety poor readers displayed greater growth in reading, but less growth in arithmetic ability than the children with specific disabilities. However, this finding of differential reading growth rates has failed to replicate in some other studies (Bruck, 1988; Labuda & DeFries, 1989; McKinney, 1987; Share, McGee, et al., 1987; van der Wissel & Zegers, 1985).

Until convincing data on such issues as differential response to treatment are provided, the utility of the concept of dyslexia will continue to be challenged because the reading disabilities field will have no rebuttal to assertions that it is more educationally and clinically relevant to define reading disability without reference to IQ discrepancy (Seidenberg et al., 1986; Share et al., 1989; Siegel, 1988, 1989).

BACK TO SQUARE ONE: THE ISSUE OF INTELLIGENCE

How could the field of learning disabilities venture so far down the road of resting its conceptual foundations on discrepancy measurement from IQ when it is so difficult to distinguish poor readers on the basis of discrepancy? I leave the answer to this question to sociologists who specialize in behavioral contagion. I would only motivate their study of this social phenomenon by noting that it is surprising that for so long the concept of intelligence received so little discussion in the learning disabilities literature. Researchers and practitioners in the field seem not to have realized that it is a foundational concept for the very idea of reading disability. As currently defined, IQ is a superordinate construct for the classification of a child as having reading disability. Without a clear conception of the construct of intelligence, the notion of a reading disability, as currently defined, dissolves into incoherence.

However, problems with the IQ concept are numerous. Consider the fact that researchers, let alone practitioners, cannot agree on the type of IQ score that should be used in the measurement of discrepancy. For example, it has often been pointed out that changes in the characteristics of the IQ test being used will result in somewhat different subgroups of children being identified as discrepant and also alter the types of processing deficits that they will display in comparison studies (Bowers, Steffy, & Tate, 1988; Fletcher et al., 1989; Lindgren, DeRenzi, & Richman, 1985; Reed, 1970; Shankweiler, Crain, Brady, & Macaruso, 1992; Siegel & Heaven, 1986; Stanley, Smith, & Powys, 1982; Torgesen, 1985; Vellutino, 1978). Yet, it is not hard to look in the research literature and find recommendations that are all over the map.

For example, a very common recommendation that one finds in the literature is that performance and/or nonverbal IQ tests be used to assess discrepancy (e.g., Beech & Harding, 1984; Perfetti, 1985 [p. 18], 1986; Siegel & Heaven, 1986; Stanovich, 1986a; Thomson, 1982) because verbally loaded measures are allegedly unfair to children with dyslexia. In complete contrast, in an issue of *Learning Disabilities Research* devoted to the issue of measuring severe discrepancy, Hessler (1987) argued for the use of *verbally loaded* tests because

> Using a nonverbal test of intelligence because an individual has better nonverbal cognitive abilities than verbal cognitive abilities does not, of course, remove the importance of verbal processing and knowledge structures in academic achievement; it only obscures their importance and perhaps provides unrealistic expectations for an individual's academic achievement. (p. 46)

Of course, the use of full-scale IQ scores results in some unprincipled amalgamation of the above two diametrically opposed philosophies, but is still sometimes recommended precisely *because* the field is so confused and so far from consensus on this issue (Harris & Sipay, 1985, p. 145). Finally, there is a sort of "either" strategy that is invoked by investigators who require only that performance *or* verbal IQ exceed 90 in samples of readers with dyslexia (e.g., Olson et al., 1985). As Torgesen (1986) pointed out, the naturally occurring multidimensional continuum of abilities guarantees that such a criterion ends up creating more discrepancies with performance IQ.

The choice of different aptitude measures relates strongly to the possibility of isolating a modular cognitive dysfunction (see Stanovich, 1988b), perhaps in the phonological domain (Brady & Shankweiler, 1991; Liberman & Shankweiler, 1985; Shankweiler & Liberman, 1989; Stanovich, 1988a), that differentiates readers with dyslexia. The point is this: Do we really want to look for a group of poor readers who are qualitatively differentiable in terms of etiology and neurophysiology? Officials at the National Institutes of Health (NIH) in the United States who are funding several program projects on the neurological, genetic, and behavioral underpinnings of dyslexia certainly want to look for such a group (Gray & Kavanagh, 1985). Many in the learning disabilities field share their enthusiasm for the quest to isolate—behaviorally, genetically, and physiologically— a select group of "different" poor readers.

Let us, for purposes of argument, accept this as a goal whether we believe in it or not. I want to argue that, if we do, a somewhat startling conclusion results. The conclusion is that we must move away from measures of abstract intelligence as benchmarks for discrepancy analysis and toward more educationally relevant indices. In short, to get NIH's neurologically differentiable groups, we need an aptitude benchmark of more educational relevance than IQ— nonverbal IQ in particular, contrary to some common recommendations.

However, it must be emphasized that the context for any such discussion must be the voluminous body of prior research on the cognitive correlates of individual differences in reading achievement. Our knowledge of the structure of human abilities in this domain puts severe constraints on the ability patterns that can be observed in studies of dyslexia. For example, an extremely large body of research has demonstrated that reading skill is linked to an incredibly wide range of verbal abilities. Vocabulary, syntactic knowledge, metalinguistic awareness, verbal short-term memory, phonological awareness, speech production, inferential comprehension, semantic memory, and verbal fluency form only a partial list (Baddeley, Logie, Nimmo-Smith, & Brereton, 1985; Byrne, 1981; Carr, 1981; Chall, 1983; Cunningham, Stanovich, & Wilson, 1990; Curtis, 1980; Evans & Carr, 1985; Frederiksen, 1980; Harris & Sipay, 1985; Jackson & McClelland, 1979; Just & Carpenter, 1987; Kamhi & Catts, 1989; Palmer, MacLeod, Hunt, & Davidson, 1985; Perfetti, 1985; Rapala & Brady, 1990; Rayner & Pollatsek, 1989; Siegel & Ryan, 1988, 1989; Stanovich, 1985, 1986a; Stanovich, Cunningham, & Feeman, 1984; Stanovich et al., 1988; Vellutino, 1979; Vellutino & Scanlon, 1987).

In contrast, the nonverbal abilities linked to reading are much more circumscribed (Aman & Singh, 1983; Carr, 1981; Daneman & Tardif, 1987; Hulme, 1988; Lovegrove & Slaghuis, 1989; Siegel & Ryan, 1989; Stanovich, 1986a; Vellutino, 1979; however, also see Carver, 1990, for an opposing view). Here, the abilities associated with reading are more likely to be distinct and domain specific (e.g., orthographic storage, processing of certain spatial frequencies). In the verbal domain, however, there are many more abilities that are related to reading and that are more likely to have more global influences (e.g., inferential comprehension, verbal short-term memory, vocabulary), thereby affecting general verbal IQ. Therefore, matching readers with and without dyslexia on performance IQ will necessarily lead to broad-based deficits on the verbal side. However, even if there *are* visual/orthographic deficits linked to reading disability, the converse is not true. Because there are not as many reading-related nonverbal processes and because those that do exist will certainly be more circumscribed than something like vocabulary or verbal memory, verbal IQ matching will not necessarily result in subjects with dyslexia with severely depressed performance IQs.

We now travel across the continuum of potential aptitude candidates for discrepancy measurement with this research context and the goal of differentiating children with dyslexia in mind. It immediately becomes apparent that the use of reading achievement discrepancies from performance IQ will make it extremely difficult to cognitively differentiate children with dyslexia from other poor readers. Such performance-discrepancy children with dyslexia—because they are allowed to have depressed verbal components—will have a host of verbal deficits, some at levels higher than phonology, and they will not display the cognitive specificity required of the dyslexia concept. Torgesen (1986) has discussed how definitional practices that require only that verbal *or* performance scales be above some criterion value will have the same effect. The verbal scale IQ for readers with dyslexia is allowed to be considerably under that of the control group, and it is not surprising that, subsequently, a range of verbal deficits are observed (see Vellutino, 1979). A behaviorally and neurologically differentiable core deficit will be virtually impossible to find, given such classification.

In contrast, discrepancies based on verbal aptitude measures would be likely to isolate a more circumscribed disability that may be more readily identifiable by neurophysiological and/or genetic methods. Such a procedure would preclude the possibility of deficits in broad-based verbal processes. It could potentially confine deficits exclusively to the phonological module. For example, Bowers et al. (1988) demonstrated that, if only performance IQ was controlled, subjects with dyslexia were differentiated from subjects without dyslexia on the basis of rapid naming performance and on digit span and sentence memory. However, controlling for verbal IQ removed the association between reading disability and memory abilities. Importantly, an association with rapid naming remained. In short, verbal IQ control resulted in the isolation of a more circumscribed processing deficit.

Similarly, verbal IQ–based discrepancy measurement would be much more likely to demarcate a visual/orthographic deficit, if one exists (see Lovegrove & Slaghuis, 1989; Solman & May, 1990; Willows et al., in press). Verbal IQ matching in a comparison study would, of course, allow the performance IQ of the dyslexic group to fall below that of the control group, but because the number of abilities linked to reading is much more circumscribed in the nonverbal than in the verbal domain, the groups would not become unmatched on a commensurately large number of abilities. Additionally, subtle, visually based deficits would not be "adjusted away" by a procedure of performance IQ matching. Thus, verbal IQ control provides a greater opportunity for these visual/orthographic deficits—which are much harder to track than those in the phonological domain—to emerge in comparison studies.

In summary, by adopting verbal IQ as an aptitude measure, we would be closer to a principled definition of potential in the reading domain, that is, the academic level that would result from instruction if the person's dysfunction were totally remediated. We would also be more likely to isolate a circumscribed deficit that would at least be more amenable to cognitive and neurological differentiation than are the deficits in samples of children defined by other methods. Nevertheless, there is empirical evidence that should make us skeptical that discrepancy measurement from any type of IQ test will establish the cognitive differentiability that is inherent in the dyslexia concept (Fletcher et al., 1989; Siegel, 1988, 1989; Taylor, Satz, & Friel, 1979).

AN ALTERNATIVE TO IQ

In fact, there is a baseline for discrepancy measurement that leads to many fewer conceptual problems than does IQ. This proposal for an alternative baseline has been around for quite some time, but has never received a proper hearing because studies and definitions of dyslexia have been so unthinkingly fixated on the measurement of intelligence. Many educationally oriented reading researchers have long suggested that measuring the discrepancy between reading ability and *listening comprehension* would be more educationally relevant and would seem to have been a more logical choice in the first place (see Aaron, 1989a, 1991; Carroll, 1977; Carver, 1981; Durrell, 1969; Gillet & Temple, 1986; Gough & Tunmer, 1986; Hood & Dubert, 1983; Royer, Kulhavy, Lee, & Peterson, 1986; Spring & French, 1990; Sticht & James, 1984). Certainly, a discrepancy calculated in this way seems to have more face validity and educational relevance than one calculated by the traditional procedure (Aaron, 1989a, 1991; Durrell & Hayes, 1969; Hoover & Gough, 1990; Spache, 1981). Children who do not understand written material as well as they would understand the same material if it were read to them appear to be in need of educational intervention. Presumably, their listening comprehension exceeds their reading comprehension because word recognition processes are inefficient and are a "bottleneck" that impedes comprehension (Gough & Tunmer, 1986; Perfetti, 1985; Perfetti & Lesgold, 1977). Listening comprehension correlates with reading comprehension much more highly than full-scale or even verbal IQ. Children simultaneously low in reading and listening do not have an "unexplained" reading problem (Carroll, 1977; Hoover & Gough, 1990), and we must always remember that the idea of "unexplained" reading failure is the puzzle that enticed us into the idea of dyslexia in the first place.

As with verbal IQ but more so, listening comprehension isolates a modular deficit because, in a comparison study, subjects with dyslexia would not become unmatched from subjects without dyslexia on a host of reading-related verbal abilities. Additionally, even though the idea of visual deficits as an explanation of dyslexia is out of favor at the moment, this "layman's conception of dyslexia" (not totally without support in the literature; see Lovegrove et al., 1986; Solman & May, 1990; Willows, 1991) would receive a fairer test if discrepancies from listening comprehension were the criteria for subject selection in research. Any potential visual deficits would not be "adjusted away" by performance IQ matching. Thus, not only would we get a better chance of demarcating the modular phonological deficits that are of great interest in current work on dyslexia (Liberman & Shankweiler, 1985; Stanovich, 1988b), but more tenuous hypotheses in the visual domain would get a fairer hearing. In short, a large discrepancy between reading comprehension and listening comprehension has probably isolated—as well as we are ever going to get it—a modular decoding problem that then may or may not be amenable to genetic and neurological analysis in the manner of the ongoing NIH program projects.

There are, of course, several obstacles to implementing procedures of measuring reading disability with reference to discrepancies from listening comprehension. For example, although several individual measures of listening comprehension ability have been published (Carroll, 1972, 1977; CTB/McGraw-Hill, 1981; Durrell & Hayes, 1969; Spache, 1981), it may be the case that none has been standardized across the range of ages, nor attained the psychometric properties, needed to serve as an adequate measure from which to assess discrepancy (Johnson, 1988). Other complications may also arise, such as hearing problems or unfamiliarity with standard English. However, many of these problems are no more severe for listening comprehension measures than they are for certain IQ tests. It is encouraging that work on listening comprehension as a diagnostic benchmark has recently been increasing in quantity;

some important progress is being made (see Aaron, 1989a, 1991; Carlisle, 1989; Hoover & Gough, 1990; Horowitz & Samuels, 1985; Royer, Sinatra, & Schumer, 1990; Spring & French, 1990).

Using listening comprehension as an aptitude benchmark also solves the perennially knotty problem of deciding what type of test to use as the *reading* rest in a discrepancy analysis. When investigators use a word recognition test—because they believe that the key to reading disability lies somewhere in the word recognition module—they are often accused of ignoring the real educational context and real educational goal of reading, which is comprehension. The proposal to use listening comprehension as the aptitude benchmark dissolves this problem because it would *allow* the use of a reading *comprehension* test as the achievement benchmark in educational settings (word recognition tests would still be preferable in strictly research contexts). Such a procedure simultaneously renders these criticisms ineffectual, but ends up isolating word recognition problems fairly exclusively.

Investigators advocating the use of a word recognition test exclusively are often accused of prejudging the issue of the causes of reading difficulties and, on the surface, it seems as if they are (the critics ignore the fact that this practice is motivated by the outcome of voluminous research). By using a reading comprehension test, the bulk of the identified discrepancies would represent phonologically based word recognition problems for the reasons I outlined above. Yet, investigators could not be accused of prejudging the issue by employing a word recognition test. It would be subsequent testing that would reveal the word recognition problem, which would *result* from classification using other procedures, not an a priori restriction to identification based on word recognition tests. This procedure might be more convincing to those in the reading education community who still doubt that reading disability has, as its main source, problems in word recognition.

MATTHEW EFFECTS
COMPLICATE DISCREPANCY MEASUREMENT

There remains, however, a further obstacle to measuring reading disability by reference to aptitude–achievement discrepancy— irrespective of the indicator used for the aptitude benchmark. Let us again consider the recommendation against the use of verbally loaded tests for discrepancy measurement. This admonition stems from the either tacit or explicit assumption that the reading difficulties themselves may lead to depressed performance on such measures. One reason that this may occur is because of so-called Matthew effects associated with reading: situations wherein reading itself develops other related cognitive abilities (see Stanovich, 1986b; Walberg & Tsai, 1983). However, the recognition of such phenomena perniciously undermines the whole notion of discrepancy measurement by weakening the distinction between aptitude and achievement. It serves to remind us that the logic of the learning disabilities field implicitly has given all of the causal power to IQ. That is, it is reading that is considered discrepant from IQ rather than IQ that is discrepant from reading. However, this is a vast oversimplification because there are potent effects running in both directions.

Much evidence has now accumulated to indicate that reading itself is a moderately powerful determinant of vocabulary growth, verbal intelligence, and general comprehension ability (Hayes, 1988; Hayes & Ahrens, 1988; Juel, 1988; Nichols, Inglis, Lawson, & McKay, 1988; Share & Silva, 1987; Share et al., 1989; Stanovich, 1986b; Stanovich & West, 1989; van den Bos, 1989). These Matthew effects (reciprocal causation effects involving reading and other cognitive skills) highlight a further problematic aspect of discrepancy-based classification. The possibility of Matthew effects prevents us from ignoring the possibility that poor listening comprehension or verbal intelligence could be the *result* of poor reading.

Thus, Matthew effects are interrelated in some very complicated ways with the conceptual logic of discrepancy-based disability definitions. It appears, then, that any discrepancy-based conceptualization is going to require considerable refinement based on how Matthew effects alter the course of development, bringing education-related cognitive skills more into congruence with age. Thus, conceptually justified discrepancy-based classification—even of reading comprehension from listening comprehension—will be maddeningly tricky to carry out in a principled fashion. A serious consideration of the potential complications that Matthew effects cause for discrepancy-based classification should force a serious consideration of whether reading disability should cease to be conceptualized based on aptitude–achievement discrepancies. Alternative proposals to classify poor readers simply on the basis of the proximal processing problem in virtually all cases of poor reading—phonological deficits that impair word recognition processes—are currently being given more serious consideration by researchers (Fletcher et al., 1989; Leong, 1989; Siegel, 1988, 1989; Stanovich, 1989).

It is interesting to note that the question of whether a discrepancy-defined disability is different from a disability defined purely in terms of chronological age occurs in analogous form—

complete with accompanying practical implications—in another area: that of language delay. Cole, Dale, and Mills (1990) described how, prior to more recent concerns about the relation between cognition and language, "Any child who demonstrated a discrepancy between chronological age and language age would generally have been considered a candidate for language intervention by speech-language pathologists" (p. 291). However, an assumed tight link between language and cognition has recently led to what is called the cognitive referencing model, which has the implication that "Children who have developed language skills at a level equal to their cognitive skills are not considered to be language delayed, even if their language skills are significantly below chronological age" (Cole et al., 1990, p. 292). However, just as in the area of reading disability, Cole et al. pointed out that "Given the importance of this decision [for whom to provide speech-language services], it is surprising that there is *little or no empirical evidence for evaluating the Cognitive Referencing model*" [italics added] (1990, p. 292). Cole et al. argued that "The profound clinical implications of excluding from service a substantial subgroup of children who exhibit a marked language delay relative to their chronological age demands that the practice be supported by empirical evidence" (p. 293).

Thus, Cole et al. (1990) provided a description of another field so confident in the construct validity of IQ that it recommends changes in practice without thoroughly testing the empirical adequacy of its assumptions about intelligence. Given the previous review, it is not surprising that this idea of "cognitive referencing" leads to exactly the same conundrums as are present in the field of reading disability. For example, Cole et al. (1990) pointed out that "Because specific intelligence tests include various domains with varying weights (particularly the balance of verbal and nonverbal skills), the identification of children as language delayed will vary considerably as a function of the general cognitive test utilized" (p. 293).

Cole et al. (1990) conducted a study that compared the effect of a 1-year language intervention on discrepancy-defined and chronologically defined children with language delay (the language analogue to the garden-variety control design) and found that the effects of the intervention were largely similar across a variety of language measures. In short, there was no differential response to treatment. Thus Cole et al. were led to conclude that "The current practice of selecting students for language service only when they have a discrepancy between language and cognitive skills is questionable" (1990, p. 300). While admitting that the cognitive referencing hypothesis is "an elegant and intriguing theoretical construct," they end with a warning that is an equally fitting caution for the field of reading disabilities: "Elegant and intriguing theoretical models should be subjected to empirical examination before their wide acceptance and application by the field, or we risk saying more than we know" (p. 301).

SUMMARY

The history of the concept of dyslexia has followed a confused "cart before the horse" path in part because too many practitioners and researchers accepted at face value claims that IQ tests were measures of special "unlocked potential" in particular groups of children with low reading achievement. Research has failed to show that discrepancy-defined poor readers are cognitively differentiable from other poor readers on processes that are causally linked to the reading disability. An alternative proposal for measuring aptitude–achievement discrepancies with reference to listening comprehension ability was explored and found to be superior to that of IQ assessment. Nevertheless, it was argued that complications stemming from the increasing difficulty of differentiating aptitude from achievement as a child gets older will plague all definitional efforts based on the discrepancy notion. Problems such as these have led to Siegel's (1988, 1989) suggestion that reading disability be defined solely on the basis of decoding deficits, without reference to discrepancies from aptitude measures. Some in the reading research community may find this a disappointing outcome, but others may find it a useful way to redirect research energy from a fixation on psychometric instruments of dubious relevance to the reading process to the reading processes that characterize virtually all poor readers.

It is also important to reiterate that the focus on reading disability in this chapter was a planned attempt to depart from the use of the term *learning disability* because learning disability represents such a vague construct, complicated by substantial heterogeneity. This chapter instead sought to help clarify our current definitional woes by dealing exclusively with the domain-specific area of reading.

REFERENCES

Aaron, P.G. (1989a). *Dyslexia and hyperlexia*. Dordrecht, The Netherlands: Kluwer Academic.

Aaron, P.G. (1989b). Qualitative and quantitative differences among dyslexic, normal, and nondyslexic poor readers. *Reading and Writing: An Interdisciplinary Journal, 1,* 291–308.

Aaron, P.G. (1991). Can reading disabilities be diagnosed without using intelligence tests? *Journal of Learning Disabilities, 24,* 178–186.

Ackerman, P.T., Dykman, R.A., & Gardner, M.Y. (1990). ADD students with and without dyslexia differ in sensitivity to rhyme and alliteration. *Journal of Learning Disabilities, 23,* 279–283.

Adams, M.J. (1990). *Beginning to read: Thinking and learning about print.* Cambridge, MA: MIT Press.

Aman, M., & Singh, N. (1983). Specific reading disorders: Concepts of etiology reconsidered. In K. Gadow & I. Bialer (Eds.), *Advances in learning and behavioral disabilities* (Vol. 2, pp. 1–47). Greenwich, CT: JAI Press.

Anastasi, A. (1988). *Psychological testing* (6th ed.). New York: Macmillan.

Applebee, A.N. (1971). Research in reading retardation: Two critical problems. *Journal of Child Psychology & Psychiatry, 12,* 91–113.

Baddeley, A., Logie, R., Nimmo-Smith, I., & Brereton, N. (1985). Components of fluent reading. *Journal of Memory and Language, 24,* 119–131.

Baddeley, A.D., Ellis, N.C., Miles, T.R., & Lewis, V.J. (1982). Developmental and acquired dyslexia: A comparison. *Cognition, 11,* 185–199.

Baddeley, A.D., Logie, R.H., & Ellis, N.C. (1988). Characteristics of developmental dyslexia. *Cognition, 30,* 198–227.

Ball, E.W., & Blachman, B.A. (1991). Does phoneme segmentation training in kindergarten make a difference in early word recognition and developmental spelling. *Reading Research Quarterly, 26,* 49–66.

Beech, J., & Harding, L. (1984). Phonemic processing and the poor reader from a developmental lag viewpoint. *Reading Research Quarterly, 19,* 357–366.

Besner, D., Twilley, L., McCann, R., & Seergobin, K. (1990). On the association between connectionism and data: Are a few words necessary? *Psychological Review, 97,* 432–446.

Blachman. (1989). Phonological awareness and work recognition: Assessment and intervention. In A.G. Kamhi & H.W. Catts (Eds.), *Reading disabilities* (pp. 133-158). Boston: College-Hill.

Bowers, P., Steffy, R., & Tate, E. (1988). Comparison of the effects of IQ control methods on memory and naming speed predictors of reading disability. *Reading Research Quarterly, 23,* 304–319.

Bradley, L., & Bryant, P.E. (1978). Difficulties in auditory organization as a possible cause of reading backwardness. *Nature, 271,* 746–747.

Bradley, L., & Bryant, P.E. (1985). *Rhyme and reason in reading and spelling.* Ann Arbor: University of Michigan Press.

Brady, S., & Shankweiler, D. (Eds.). (1991). *Phonological processes in literacy.* Hillsdale, NJ: Lawrence Erlbaum Associates.

Bruck, M. (1988). The word recognition and spelling of dyslexic children. *Reading Research Quarterly, 23,* 51–69.

Bruck, M. (1990). Word-recognition skills of adults with childhood diagnoses of dyslexia. *Developmental Psychology, 26,* 439–454.

Bruck, M., & Treiman, R. (1990). Phonological awareness and spelling in normal children and dyslexics: The case of initial consonant clusters. *Journal of Experimental Child Psychology, 50,* 156–178.

Bryant, P.E., Bradley, L., Maclean, M., & Crossland, D. (1989). Nursery rhymes, phonological skills and reading. *Journal of Child Language, 16,* 407–428.

Bryant, P.E., & Goswami, U. (1986). Strengths and weaknesses of the reading level design: A comment on Backman, Mamen, and Ferguson. *Psychological Bulletin, 100,* 101–103.

Byrne, B. (1981). Deficient syntactic control in poor readers: Is a weak phonetic memory code responsible? *Applied Psycholinguistics, 2,* 201–212.

Carlisle, J.F. (1989). The use of the sentence verification technique in diagnostic assessment of listening and reading comprehension. *Learning Disabilities Research, 5,* 33–44.

Carr, T.H. (1981). Building theories of reading ability: On the relation between individual differences in cognitive skills and reading comprehension. *Cognition, 9,* 73–114.

Carroll, J.B. (1972). Defining language comprehension: Some speculations. In J.B.T. Carroll & R. Freedle (Eds.), *Language, comprehension, and the acquisition of knowledge* (pp. 1–29). Washington, DC: W.H. Winston & Sons.

Carroll, J.B. (1977). Developmental parameters of reading comprehension. In J.T. Guthrie (Ed.), *Cognition, curriculum, and comprehension* (pp. 1–15). Newark, DE: IRA.

Carver, R.P. (1981). *Reading comprehension and reading theory.* Springfield, IL: Charles C Thomas.

Carver, R.P. (1990). Intelligence and reading ability in grades 2–12. *Intelligence, 14,* 449–455.

Ceci, S.J. (1986). *Handbook of cognitive, social, and neuropsychological aspects of learning disabilities* (Vol. 1). Hillsdale, NJ: Lawrence Erlbaum Associates.

Ceci, S.J. (1990). *On intelligence . . . more or less: A bio-ecological treatise on intellectual development.* Englewood Cliffs, NJ: Prentice-Hall.

Chall, J.S. (1983). *Stages of reading development.* New York: McGraw-Hill.

Cole, K.N., Dale, P.S., & Mills, P.E. (1990). Defining language delay in young children by cognitive referencing: Are we saying more than we know? *Applied Psycholinguistics, 11,* 291–302.

Cossu, G., Shankweiler, D., Liberman, I.Y., Katz, L., & Tola, G. (1988). Awareness of phonological segments and reading ability in Italian children. *Applied Psycholinguistics, 9,* 1–16.

Critchley, M. (1970). *The dyslexic child.* London: William Heinemann Medical Books.

Cronbach, L.J. (1984). *Essentials of psychological testing* (4th ed.). New York: Harper & Row.

CTB/McGraw-Hill. (1981). *Listening test.* Monterey, CA: McGraw-Hill.

Cunningham, A.E. (1990). Explicit versus implicit instruction in phonemic awareness. *Journal of Experimental Child Psychology, 50,* 429–444.

Cunningham, A.E., & Stanovich, K.E. (1990). Assessing print exposure and orthographic processing skill in children: A quick measure of reading experience. *Journal of Educational Psychology, 82,* 733–740.

Cunningham, A.E., & Stanovich, K.E. (1991). Tracking the unique effects of print exposure in children: Associations with vocabulary, general knowledge, and spelling. *Journal of Educational Psychology, 83,* 264–274.

Cunningham, A.E., Stanovich, K.E., & Wilson, M.R. (1990). Cognitive variation in adult students differing in reading ability. In T. Carr & B.A. Levy (Eds.), *Reading and development: Component skills approaches* (pp. 129–159). New York: Academic Press.

Curtis, M. (1980). Development of components of reading skill. *Journal of Educational Psychology, 72,* 656–669.

Daneman, M., & Tardif, T. (1987). Working memory and reading skill re-examined. In M. Coltheart (Ed.), *Attention and performance* (Vol. 12, pp. 491–508). London: Lawrence Erlbaum Associates.

Detterman, D. (1982). Does "g" exist? *Intelligence, 6,* 99–108.

Doehring, D.G. (1978). The tangled web of behavioral research on developmental dyslexia. In A.L. Benton & D. Pearl (Eds.), *Dyslexia* (pp. 123–135). New York: Oxford University Press.

Durrell, D.D. (1969). Listening comprehension versus reading comprehension. *Journal of Reading, 12,* 455–460.

Durrell, D.D., & Hayes, M. (1969). *Durrell listening-reading series.* New York: Psychological Corporation.

Eisenberg, L. (1978). Definitions of dyslexia: Their consequences for research and policy. In A.L. Benton & D. Pearl (Eds.), *Dyslexia* (pp. 29–42). New York: Oxford University Press.

Ellis, A.W. (1985). The cognitive neuropsychology of developmental (and acquired) dyslexia: A critical survey. *Cognitive Neuropsychology, 2,* 169–205.

Ellis, N., & Large, B. (1987). The development of reading: As you seek so shall you find. *British Journal of Psychology, 78,* 1–28.

Evans, M.A., & Carr, T.H. (1985). Cognitive abilities, conditions of learning, and the early development of reading skill. *Reading Research Quarterly, 20,* 327–350.

Fletcher, J.M., Espy, K., Francis, D., Davidson, K., Rourke, B., & Shaywitz, S. (1989). Comparisons of cutoff and regression-based definitions of reading disabilities. *Journal of Learning Disabilities, 22,* 334–338.

Frankenberger, W., & Fronzaglio, K. (1991). A review of states' criteria and procedures for identifying children with learning disabilities. *Journal of Learning Disabilities, 24,* 495–500.

Frankenberger, W., & Harper, J. (1987). States' criteria and procedures for identifying learning disabled children: A comparison of 1981/82 and 1985/86 guidelines. *Journal of Learning Disabilities, 20,* 118–121.

Frederiksen, J.R. (1980). Component skills in reading: Measurement of individual differences through chronometric analysis. In R. Snow, P. Federico, & W. Montague (Eds.), *Aptitude, learning, and instruction* (Vol. 1, pp. 105–138). Hillsdale, NJ: Lawrence Erlbaum Associates.

Fredman, G., & Stevenson, J. (1988). Reading processes in specific reading retarded and reading backward 13-year-olds. *British Journal of Developmental Psychology, 6,* 97–108.

Galaburda, A. (1991). Anatomy of dyslexia: Argument against phrenology.

In D. Duane & D. Gray (Eds.), *The reading brain: The biological basis of dyslexia* (pp. 119–131). Parkton, MD: York Press.

Galaburda, A.M. (1990). Response to Hammill. *Journal of Learning Disabilities, 23*, 525.

Gillet, J.W., & Temple, C. (1986). *Understanding reading problems: Assessment and instruction* (2nd ed.). Boston: Little, Brown.

Gough, P.B., & Tunmer, W.E. (1986). Decoding, reading, and reading disability. *Remedial and Special Education, 7*, 6–10.

Gray, D.B., & Kavanagh, J.K. (1985). *Biobehavioral measures of dyslexia.* Parkton, MD: York Press.

Hammill, D., Leigh, J., McNutt, G., & Larsen, S. (1981). A new definition of learning disabilities. *Learning Disabilities Quarterly, 4*, 336–342.

Harris, A.J., & Sipay, E.R. (1985). *How to increase reading ability* (8th ed.). White Plains, NY: Longman.

Hayes, D.P. (1988). Speaking and writing: Distinct patterns of word choice. *Journal of Memory and Language, 27*, 572–585.

Hayes, D.P., & Ahrens, M. (1988). Vocabulary simplification for children: A special case of 'motherese'? *Journal of Child Language, 15*, 395–410.

Hessler, G.L. (1987). Educational issues surrounding severe discrepancy. *Learning Disabilities Research, 3*, 43–49.

Holligan, C., & Johnston, R.S. (1988). The use of phonological information by good and poor readers in memory and reading tasks. *Memory & Cognition, 16*, 522–532.

Hood, J., & Dubert, L.A. (1983). Decoding as a component of reading comprehension among secondary students. *Journal of Reading Behavior, 15*, 51–61.

Hoover, W.A., & Gough, P.B. (1990). The simple view of reading. *Reading and Writing: An Interdisciplinary Journal, 2*, 127–160.

Horowitz, R., & Samuels, S.J. (1985). Reading and listening to expository text. *Journal of Reading Behavior, 17*, 185–198.

Hulme, C. (1988). The implausibility of low-level visual deficits as a cause of children's reading difficulties. *Cognitive Neuropsychology, 5*, 369–374.

Humphreys, L.G. (1979). The construct of general intelligence. *Intelligence, 3*, 105–120.

Hurford, D.P., & Sanders, R.E. (1990). Assessment and remediation of a phonemic discrimination deficit in reading disabled second and fourth graders. *Journal of Experimental Child Psychology, 50*, 396–415.

Jackson M.D., & McClelland, J.L. (1979). Processing determinants of reading speed. *Journal of Experimental Psychology: General, 108*, 151–181.

Johnson, D.J. (1988). Review of research on specific reading, writing, and mathematics disorders. In J.F. Kavanagh, & T.J. Truss (Eds.), *Learning disabilities: Proceedings of the national conference* (pp. 79–163). Parkton, MD: York Press.

Jorm, A. (1983). Specific reading retardation and working memory: A review. *British Journal of Psychology, 74*, 311–342.

Juel, C. (1988). Learning to read and write: A longitudinal study of 54 children from first through fourth grades. *Journal of Educational Psychology, 80*, 437–447.

Juel, C., Griffith, P.L., & Gough, P.B. (1986). Acquisition of literacy: A longitudinal study of children in first and second grade. *Journal of Educational Psychology, 78;* 243–255.

Just, M., & Carpenter, P.A. (1987). *The psychology of reading and language comprehension.* Needham Heights: Allyn & Bacon.

Kamhi, A., & Catts, H. (1989). *Reading disabilities: A developmental language perspective.* Boston: College-Hill Press.

Kavale, K.A. (1987). Theoretical issues surrounding severe discrepancy. *Learning Disabilities Research, 3,* 12–20.

Kavale, K.A., & Nye, C. (1981). Identification criteria for learning disabilities: A survey of the research literature. *Learning Disabilities Quarterly, 4,* 363–388.

Kavanagh, J.F., & Truss, T.J. (Eds.). (1988). *Learning disabilities: Proceedings of the national conference.* Parkton, MD: York Press.

Keogh, B.K. (1987). Learning disabilities: In defense of a construct. *Learning Disabilities Research, 3,* 4–9.

Kochnower, J., Richardson, E., & DiBenedetto, B. (1983). A comparison of the phonic decoding ability of normal and learning disabled children. *Journal of Learning Disabilities, 16,* 348–351.

Labuda, M., & DeFries, J.C. (1989). Differential prognosis of reading-disabled children as a function of gender, socioeconomic status, IQ, and severity: A longitudinal study. *Reading and Writing: An Interdisciplinary Journal, 1,* 25–36.

Leong, C.K. (1989). The locus of so-called IQ test results in reading disabilities. *Journal of Learning Disabilities, 22,* 507–512.

Liberman, I.Y., & Shankweiler, D. (1985). Phonology and the problems of learning to read and write. *Remedial and Special Education, 6,* 8–17.

Lie, A. (1991). Effects of a training program for stimulating skills in word analysis in first-grade children. *Reading Research Quarterly, 26,* 234–250.

Lieberman, P., Meskill, R.H., Chatillon, M., & Schupack, H. (1985). Phonetic speech perception deficits in dyslexia. *Journal of Speech and Hearing Research, 28,* 480–486.

Lindgren, S.D., De Renzi, E., & Richman, L.C. (1985). Cross-national comparisons of developmental dyslexia in Italy and the United States. *Child Development, 56,* 1404–1417.

Lovegrove, W., Martin, F., & Slaghuis, W. (1986). A theoretical and experimental case for a visual deficit in specific reading disability. *Cognitive Neuropsychology, 3,* 225–267.

Lovegrove, W., & Slaghuis, W. (1989). How reliable are visual differences found in dyslexics? *Irish Journal of Psychology, 10,* 542–550.

Lundberg, I., Frost, J., & Peterson, O. (1988). Effects of an extensive program for stimulating phonological awareness in preschool children. *Reading Research Quarterly, 23,* 263–284.

Lundberg, I., & Hoien, T. (1989). Phonemic deficits: A core symptom of developmental dyslexia? *Irish Journal of Psychology, 10,* 579–592.

Lyon, G.R. (1985). Educational validation studies of learning disability sub-types. In B.P. Rourke (Ed.), *Neuropsychology of learning disabilities* (pp. 228–253). New York: Guilford Press.

Maclean, M., Bryant, P., & Bradley, L. (1987). Rhymes, nursery rhymes, and reading in early childhood. *Merrill-Palmer Quarterly, 33,* 255–281.

Mann, V. (1986). Why some children encounter reading problems. In J. Torgesen & B. Wong (Eds.), *Psychological and educational perspectives on learning disabilities* (pp. 133–159). New York: Academic Press.

Martin, F., & Lovegrove, W. (1988). Uniform & field flicker in control and specifically-disabled readers. *Perception, 17,* 203–214.

McKinney, J.D. (1987). Research on the identification of learning-disabled children: Perspectives on changes in educational policy. In S. Vaughn & C. Bos (Eds.), *Research in learning disabilities* (pp. 215–233). Boston: College-Hill Press.

Morrison, F. (1984). Word decoding and rule-learning in normal and disabled readers. *Remedial and Special Education, 5,* 20–27.

Morrison, F., Giordani, B., & Nagy, J. (1977). Reading disability: An information processing analysis. *Science, 196,* 77–79.

Morrison, F.J. (1987). The nature of reading disability: Toward an integrative framework. In S. Ceci (Ed.), *Handbook of cognitive, social and neuropsychological aspects of learning disabilities* (pp. 33–62). Hillsdale, NJ: Lawrence Erlbaum Associates.

Nichols, E.G., Inglis, J., Lawson, J.S., & McKay, I. (1988). A cross-validation study of patterns of cognitive ability in children with learning difficulties, as described by factorially defined WISC-R verbal and performance IQs. *Journal of Learning Disabilities, 21,* 504–508.

Olson, R., Kliegl, R., Davidson, B., & Foltz, G. (1985). Individual and developmental differences in reading disability. In T. Waller (Ed.), *Reading research: Advances in theory and practice* (Vol. 4, pp. 1–64). London: Academic Press.

Olson, R., Wise, B., Conners, F., & Rack, J. (1990). Organization, heritability, and remediation of component word recognition and language skills in disabled readers. In T. Carr & B.A. Levy (Eds.), *Reading and its development: Component skills approaches* (pp. 261–322). New York: Academic Press.

Olson, R., Wise, B., Conners, F., Rack, J., & Fulker, D. (1989). Specific deficits in component reading and language skills: Genetic and environmental influences. *Journal of Learning Disabilities, 22,* 339–348.

Palmer, J., MacLeod, C.M., Hunt, E., & Davidson, J.E. (1985). Information processing correlates of reading. *Journal of Memory and Language, 24,* 59–88.

Patterson, K., Marshall, J., & Coltheart, M. (1985). *Surface dyslexia.* London: Lawrence Erlbaum Associates.

Pennington, B.F. (1986). Issues in the diagnosis and phenotype analysis of dyslexia: Implications for family studies. In S.D. Smith (Ed.), *Genetics and learning disabilities* (pp. 69–96). San Diego: College-Hill Press.

Pennington, B.F., McCabe, L.L., Smith, S., Lefly, D., Bookman, M., Kimberling, W., & Lubs, H. (1986). Spelling errors in adults with a form of familial dyslexia. *Child Development, 57,* 1001–1013.

Pennington, B.F., Van Orden, G.C., Smith, S.D., Green, P.A., & Haith, M.M.

(1990). Phonological processing skills and deficits in adult dyslexics. *Child Development, 61,* 1753–1778.

Perfetti, C.A. (1985). *Reading ability.* New York: Oxford University Press.

Perfetti, C.A. (1986). Continuities in reading acquisition, reading skill, and reading disability. *Remedial and Special Education, 7,* 11–21.

Perfetti, C.A., Beck, I., Bell, L., & Hughes, C. (1987). Phonemic knowledge and learning to read are reciprocal: A longitudinal study of first grade children. *Merrill-Palmer Quarterly, 33,* 283–319.

Perfetti, C.A., & Lesgold, A.M. (1977). Discourse comprehension and sources of individual differences. In M. Just & P. Carpenter (Eds.), *Cognitive processes in comprehension* (pp. 141–183). Hillsdale, NJ: Lawrence Erlbaum Associates.

Pratt, A.C., & Brady, S. (1988). Relation of phonological awareness to reading disability in children and adults. *Journal of Educational Psychology, 80,* 319–323.

Pressley, M., & Levin, J.R. (1987). Elaborative learning strategies for the inefficient learner. In S.J. Ceci (Ed.), *Handbook of cognitive, social, and neuropsychological aspects of learning disabilities* (Vol. 2, pp. 175–212). Hillsdale, NJ: Lawrence Erlbaum Associates.

Public Law 94-142, Education for All Handicapped Children Act of 1975. (23 August 1977). 20 U.S.C. 1401 et seq: *Federal Register, 42,* (163), 42474-42518.

Rack, J.P., Snowling, M.J., & Olson, R.K. (1992). The nonword reading deficit in developmental dyslexia: A review. *Reading Research Quarterly, 27,* 28–53.

Rapala, M.M., & Brady, S. (1990). Reading ability and short-term memory: The role of phonological processing. *Reading and Writing: An Interdisciplinary Journal, 2,* 1–25.

Rayner, K., & Pollatsek, A. (1989). *The psychology of reading.* Englewood Cliffs, NJ: Prentice Hall.

Reed, J.C. (1970). The deficits of retarded readers—Fact or artifact? *The Reading Teacher, 23,* 347–357.

Reed, M.A. (1989). Speech perception and the discrimination of brief auditory cues in reading disabled children. *Journal of Experimental Child Psychology, 48,* 270–292.

Reynolds, C.R. (1985). Measuring the aptitude-achievement discrepancy in learning disability diagnosis. *Remedial and Special Education, 6,* 37–55.

Rispens, J., van Yeren, T., & van Duijn, G. (1991). The irrelevance of IQ to the definition of learning disabilities: Some empirical evidence. *Journal of Learning Disabilities, 24,* 434–438.

Royer, J.M., Kulhavy, R., Lee, S., & Peterson, S. (1986). The relationship between reading and listening comprehension. *Educational and Psychological Research, 6,* 299–314.

Royer, J.M., Sinatra G.M., & Schumer, H. (1990). Patterns of individual differences in the development of listening and reading comprehension. *Contemporary Educational Psychology, 15,* 183–196.

Rutter, M. (1978). Prevalence and types of dyslexia. In A. Benton & D. Pearl (Eds.), *Dyslexia: An appraisal of current knowledge* (pp. 5–28). New York: Oxford University Press.

Rutter, M., & Yule, W. (1975). The concept of specific reading retardation. *Journal of Child Psychology and Psychiatry, 16,* 181–197.

Scarborough, H.S. (1984). Continuity between childhood dyslexia and adult reading. *British Journal of Psychology, 75,* 329–348.

Seidenberg, M.S., Bruck, M., Fornarolo, G., & Backman, J. (1985). Word recognition processes of poor and disabled readers? Do they necessarily differ? *Applied Psycholinguists, 6,* 161–180.

Seidenberg, M.S., Bruck, M., Fornarolo, G., & Backman, J. (1986). Who is dyslexic? Reply to Wolf. *Applied Psycholinguistics, 7,* 77–84.

Seidenberg, M.S., & McClelland, J.L. (1989). A distributed, developmental model of word recognition and naming. *Psychological Review, 96,* 523–568.

Shankweiler, D., Crain, S., Brady, S., & Macaruso, P. (1992). Identifying the causes of reading disability. In P. Gough, L. Ehri, & R. Treiman (Eds.), *Reading acquisition* (pp. 275–305). Hillsdale, NJ: Lawrence Erlbaum Associates.

Shankweiler, D., & Liberman, I.Y. (1989). (Eds.). Phonology and reading disability: Solving the reading puzzle. Ann Arbor: The University of Michigan Press.

Share, D.L., Jorm, A., McGee, R., Silva, P.A., Maclean, R., Matthews, R., & Williams, S. (1987). *Dyslexia and other myths.* Unpublished manuscript, University of Otago Medical School, Dunedin, New Zealand.

Share, D.L., McGee, R., McKenzie, D., Williams, S., & Silva, P.A. (1987). Further evidence relating to the distinction between specific reading retardation and general reading backwardness. *British Journal of Developmental Psychology, 5,* 35–44.

Share, D.L., McGee, R., & Silva, P. (1989). IQ and reading progress: A test of the capacity notion of IQ. *Journal of the American Academy of Child and Adolescent Psychiatry, 28,* 97–100.

Share, D.L., & Silva, P.A. (1987). Language deficits and specific reading retardation: Cause or effect? *British Journal of Disorders of Communication, 22,* 219–226.

Shaywitz, S.E., Escobar, M.D., Shaywitz, B.A., Fletcher, J.M., & Makugh, R. (1992). Evidence that dyslexia may represent the lower tail of a normal distribution of reading ability. *The New England Journal of Medicine, 326,* 145–150.

Shepard, L. (1980). An evaluation of the regression discrepancy method for identifying children with learning disabilities. *Journal of Special Education, 14,* 79–91.

Shepherd, M.J. (1988). Discussion. In J.F. Kavanagh & T.J. Truss (Eds.), *Learning disabilities: Proceedings of the national conference* (pp. 164–167). Parkton, MD: York Press.

Siegel, L.S. (1985). Psycholinguistic aspects of reading disabilities. In L. Siegel & F. Morrison (Eds.), *Cognitive development in atypical children* (pp. 45–65). New York: Springer-Verlag.

Siegel, L.S. (1988). Evidence that IQ scores are irrelevant to the definition and analysis of reading disability. *Canadian Journal of Psychology, 42,* 201–215.

Siegel, L.S. (1989). IQ is irrelevant to the definition of learning disabilities. *Journal of Learning Disabilities, 22,* 469–478.

Siegel, L.S. (in press). Phonological processing deficits as the basis of developmental dyslexia: Implications for remediation. In J. Riddoch & G. Humphreys (Eds.), *Cognitive neuropsychology and cognitive rehabilitation*. Hillsdale, NJ: Lawrence Erlbaum Associates.

Siegel, L.S., & Faux, D. (1989). Acquisition of certain grapheme-phoneme correspondences in normally achieving and disabled readers. *Reading and Writing: An Interdisciplinary Journal, 1*, 37–52.

Siegel, L.S., & Heaven, R.K. (1986). Categorization of learning disabilities. In S.J. Ceci (Ed.), *Handbook of cognitive, social, and neuropsychological aspects of learning disabilities* (Vol. 1, pp. 95–121). Hillsdale, NJ: Lawrence Erlbaum Associates.

Siegel, L.S., & Ryan, E.B. (1988). Development of grammatical-sensitivity, phonological and short-term memory skills in normally achieving and learning disabled children. *Developmental Psychology, 24*, 28–37.

Siegel, L.S., & Ryan, E.B. (1989). Subtypes of developmental dyslexia: The influence of definitional variables. *Reading and Writing: An Interdisciplinary Journal, 1*, 257–287.

Silva, P.A., McGee, R., & Williams, S. (1985). Some characteristics of 9-year-old boys with general reading backwardness or specific reading retardation. *Journal of Child Psychology and Psychiatry, 26*, 407–421.

Snowling, M. (1980). The development of grapheme-phoneme correspondence in normal and dyslexic readers. *Journal of Experimental Child Psychology, 29*, 294–305.

Snowling, M. (1987). *Dyslexia*. Oxford: Basil Blackwell.

Snowling, M., Stackhouse, J., & Rack, J. (1986). Phonological dyslexia and dysgraphia—a developmental analysis. *Cognitive Neuropsychology, 3*, 309–339.

Solman, R.T., & May, J.G. (1990). Spatial localization discrepancies: A visual deficiency in poor readers. *American Journal of Psychology, 103*, 243–263.

Spache, G.D. (1981). *Diagnostic reading scales*. Monterey, CA: CTB/McGraw-Hill.

Spring, C., & French, L. (1990). Identifying children with specific reading disabilities from listening and reading discrepancy scores. *Journal of Learning Disabilities, 23*, 53–58.

Stanley, G., Smith, G., & Powys, A. (1982). Selecting intelligence tests for studies of dyslexic children. *Psychological Reports, 50*, 787–792.

Stanovich, K.E. (1985). Explaining the variance in reading ability in terms of psychological processes: What have we learned? *Annals of Dyslexia, 35*, 67–96.

Stanovich, K.E. (1986a). Cognitive processes and the reading problems of learning disabled children: Evaluating the assumption of specificity. In J. Torgesen & B. Wong (Eds.), *Psychological and educational perspectives on learning disabilities* (pp. 87–131). New York: Academic Press.

Stanovich, K.E. (1986b). Matthew effects in reading: Some consequences of individual differences in the acquisition of literacy. *Reading Research Quarterly 21*, 360–407.

Stanovich, K.E. (1988a). Explaining the differences between the dyslexic and the garden-variety poor reader: The phonological-core variable-difference model. *Journal of Learning Disabilities, 21*, 590–612.

Stanovich, K.E. (1988b). The right and wrong places to look for the cognitive locus of reading disability. *Annals of Dyslexia, 38,* 154–177.

Stanovich, K.E. (1989). Has the learning disabilities field lost its intelligence? *Journal of Learning Disabilities, 22,* 487–492.

Stanovich, K.E. (1992). Speculations on the causes and consequences of individual differences in early reading acquisition. In P. Gough, L. Ehri, & R. Treiman (Eds.), *Reading acquisition* (pp. 307–342). Hillsdale, NJ: Lawrence Erlbaum Associates.

Stanovich, K.E. (in press). Does reading make you smarter? Literacy and the development of verbal intelligence. *Advances in Child Development and Behavior, 24.*

Stanovich, K.E., & Cunningham, A.E. (1992). Studying the consequences of literacy within a literate society: The cognitive correlates of print exposure. *Memory & Cognition, 20,* 51–68.

Stanovich, K.E., Cunningham, A.E., & Feeman, D.J. (1984). Intelligence, cognitive skills, and early reading progress. *Reading Research Quarterly, 19,* 278–303.

Stanovich, K.E., Nathan, R., & Vala-Rossi, M. (1986). Developmental changes in the cognitive correlates of reading ability and the developmental lag hypothesis. *Reading Research Quarterly, 21,* 267–283.

Stanovich, K.E., Nathan, R.G., & Zolman, J.E. (1988). The developmental lag hypothesis in reading: Longitudinal and matched reading-level comparisons. *Child Development, 59,* 71–86.

Stanovich, K.E., & West, R.F. (1989). Exposure to print and orthographic processing. *Reading Research Quarterly, 24,* 402–433.

Sternberg, R. (1985). *Beyond IQ: A triarchic theory of human intelligence.* Cambridge, England: Cambridge University Press.

Sticht, T.G., & James, J.H. (1984). Listening and reading. In P.D. Pearson (Ed.), *Handbook of reading research* (pp. 293–317). New York: Longman.

Taylor, H.G., Lean, D., & Schwartz, S. (1989). Pseudoword repetition ability in learning-disabled children. *Applied Psycholinguistics, 10,* 203–219.

Taylor, H.G., Satz, P., & Friel, J. (1979). Developmental dyslexia in relation to other childhood reading disorders: Significance and clinical utility. *Reading Research Quarterly, 15,* 84–101.

Thomson, M. (1982). Assessing the intelligence of dyslexic children. *Bulletin of the British Psychological Society, 35,* 94–96.

Thorndike, R.L. (1963). *The concepts of over- and under-achievement.* New York: Teachers College Press.

Tindal, G., & Marston, D. (1986). Approaches to assessment. In J.K. Torgeson & B.Y.L. Wong (Eds.), *Psychological and educational perspectives on learning disabilities* (pp. 55–84). Orlando, FL: Academic Press.

Torgesen, J. (1985). Memory processes in reading disabled children. *Journal of Learning Disabilities, 18,* 350–357.

Torgesen, J.K. (1986). Controlling for IQ. *Journal of Learning Disabilities, 19,* 452.

Torgesen, J.K. (1988). Discussion. In J.F. Kavanagh, & T.J. Truss (Eds.), *Learning disabilities: Proceedings of the national conference* (pp. 174–177). Parkston, MD: York Press.

Torgesen, J. K., Dahlem, W. E., & Greenstein, J. (1987). Using verbatim text recordings to enhance reading comprehension in learning disabled adolescents. *Learning Disabilities Focus, 3,* 30–38.

Trieman, R., & Baron, J. (1983). Phonemic-analysis training helps children benefit from spelling-sound rules. *Memory & Cognition, 11,* 382–389.

Treiman, R., & Hirsh-Pasek, K. (1985). Are there qualitative differences in reading behavior between dyslexics and normal readers? *Memory & Cognition, 13,* 357–364.

Tunmer, W.E., & Nesdale, A.R. (1985). Phonemic segmentation skill and beginning reading. *Journal of Educational Psychology, 77,* 417–427.

van den Bos, K.P. (1989). Relationship between cognitive development, decoding skill, and reading comprehension in learning disabled Dutch children. In P. Aaron & M. Joshi (Eds.), *Reading and writing disorders in different orthographic systems* (pp. 75–86). Dordrecht, The Netherlands: Kluwer Academic.

van der Wissel, A. (1987). IQ profiles of learning disabled and mildly mentally retarded children: A psychometric selection effect. *British Journal of Developmental Psychology, 5,* 45–51.

van der Wissel, A., & Zegers, F.E. (1985). Reading retardation revisited. *British Journal of Developmental Psychology, 3,* 3–9.

Vaughn, S., & Bos, C.S. (1987). *Research in learning disabilities: Issues and future directions.* Boston: College-Hill Press.

Vellutino, F.R. (1978). Toward an understanding of dyslexia: Psychological factors in specific reading disability. In A.L. Benton & D. Pearl (Eds.), *Dyslexia* (pp. 59–111). New York: Oxford University Press.

Vellutino, F.R. (1979). *Dyslexia: Theory and research.* Cambridge, MA: MIT Press.

Vellutino, F.R., & Scanlon, D.M. (1987). Phonological coding, phonological awareness, and reading ability: Evidence from a longitudinal and experimental study. *Merrill-Palmer Quarterly, 33,* 321–363.

Vogler, G., Baker, L.A., Decker, S.N., DeFries, J.C., & Huizinga, D. (1989). Cluster analytic classification of reading disability subtypes. *Reading and Writing: An Interdisciplinary Journal, 1,* 163–177.

Wagner, R.K., & Torgesen, J.K. (1987). The nature of phonological processing and its causal role in the acquisition of reading skills. *Psychological Bulletin, 101,* 192–212.

Walberg, H.J., & Tsai, S. (1983). Matthew effects in education. *American Educational Research Journal, 20,* 359–373.

Werker, J.F., & Tees, R.C. (1987). Speech perception in severely disabled and average reading children. *Canadian Journal of Psychology, 41,* 48–61.

West, R.F., & Stanovich, K.E. (1991). The incidental acquisition of information from reading. *Psychological Science, 2,* 325–330.

Williams, J. (1984). Phonemic analysis and how it relates to reading. *Journal of Learning Disabilities, 17,* 240–245.

Williams, J.P. (1986). The role of phonemic analysis in reading. In J. Torgesen & B. Wong (Eds.), *Psychological and educational perspectives on learning disabilities* (pp. 399–416). New York: Academic Press.

Willows, D.M. (1991). Visual processes in learning disabilities. In B. Wong (Ed.), *Learning about learning disabilities* (pp. 163–193). New York: Academic Press.

Willows, D.M., Kruk, R., & Corcos, E. (Eds.). (in press). *Visual processes in reading and reading disabilities.* Hillsdale, NJ: Lawrence Erlbaum Associates.

Wolf, M. (1991). Naming speed and reading: The contribution of the cognitive neurosciences. *Reading Research Quarterly, 26,* 123–141.

IV

IMPACT OF SOCIAL AND POLICY ISSUES ON LEARNING DISABILITIES

As Keogh points out in the first chapter in this section, the classification of learning disabilities has been more of a social-political process than a scientific one. This should not be surprising because learning disabilities as a field emerged not from any particular initial interest to study how children of average or above-average intelligence who were failing in school could be understood, diagnosed, and taught. The field was initiated because, 25 years ago, children who displayed unusual learning characteristics were disenfranchised from any formal special education services because their cognitive and educational features did not correspond to any other categories of disability recognized at that time. This disenfranchisement has successfully driven a social, political, and educational movement designed to protect children from being underserved by our educational system. Thus, the development of the field has not been guided by well-thought-out scientific initiatives and programmatic research, but by the strength of advocacy and political forces. As a result, capricious changes in public and educational policies are clearly reflected in inconsistencies in definitions of learning disabilities and in eligibility criteria. In essence, each state has been left to operationalize its definition of learning disabilities, and each has done so with widely varying standards and procedures. It is not uncommon that a student may be identified as having learning disabilities in one state, but not in its neighbor. Although science has taken a back seat to the forces of advocacy and public and social policy, there is an increasing recognition that more equal contributions from scientific and social policy arenas must be made if the field is to be expected to flourish.

In the first chapter in this section, Keogh brings to bear her wisdom and experience in describing and discussing this very complex relationship among social, political, and scientific forces in the classification and definition of learning disabilities. Keogh illuminates the influences that history, special interests, economics, litigation, and different disciplinary perspectives have had on the current learning disabilities mosaic. In the following chapter, Martin provides a detailed analysis of the development of federal education policy for children with learning disabilities. From this analysis, Martin points out that two myths about learning disabilities have emerged that lead to false impressions about the relative severity of the disorder and the degree of instructional intensity and expertise that is required to enable competent remediation to take place.

14

LINKING PURPOSE AND PRACTICE
Social–Political and Developmental Perspectives on Classification

Barbara K. Keogh

In a 1985 article in *American Psychologist,* Sandra Scarr argued for a constructionist position in psychology, suggesting that "We do not discover scientific facts; we invent them. Their usefulness to us depends both on shared perceptions of the 'facts' (consensual validation) and on whether they work for various purposes, some practical and some theoretical" (p. 499). Her paper might well have been written with learning disabilities in mind because few problem conditions so clearly exemplify the constructive process. The constructions in learning disabilities represent a variety of disciplines and perspectives, and include a range of constructs and variables. Given this variation, it is not surprising that there have been continuing definition and classification problems and an inconsistent research literature. It is also not surprising that differences in "constructions" have led to diverse treatment and intervention approaches, and to strongly held advocacy positions.

With this as backdrop, I argue that classification in special education in general, and learning disabilities in specific, has been more a social–political process than a scientific one. The social–political basis of classification is particularly salient in learning disabilities where the most powerful reasons for classification have been advocacy and services, not scientific enquiry. For the most part, science has followed, not preceded, social–political decisions. Thus, over time, we have changing and inconsistent definitions, diverse findings from many different disciplinary perspectives, and markedly discrepant incidence and prevalence figures.

311

These differences do not necessarily negate the reality of this problem condition, but underscore the need for a more powerful conceptual system of classification and more precise operational definitions and measures. In the development of such a system, there are at least three aspects of classification that are important: purpose, developmental appropriateness, and applicability and clinical utility. These requirements are in addition to the technical criteria of reliability, coverage, descriptive validity, and predictive validity, as delineated by Blashfield and Draguns (1976), or the internal and external validation of typologies as proposed by Skinner (1981). In addition, from a constructionist position, it is necessary to weigh the impact of the social–political or secular context in which classification schemes are developed, that is, to take into account the context of classification.

CONTEXT OF CLASSIFICATION

In a sense, the nature and definition of categories reflect a society's views of difference, of deviance, even of threat. From this perspective, anthropologist Robert Edgerton's argument that deviance is "negotiable"—that is, that normative and nonnormative concepts vary with the values and beliefs of a given social group—deserves our attention. As example, in a discussion of at-risk conditions from an anthropological perspective, T. Weisner (1990, personal communication) stressed that risk or problems are defined and shaped by ecocultural context so that specifics of problems differ in time and in place. Horticultural societies, dependent on subsistence crops and livestock, value compliance to family subsistence needs and expect competence in domestic chores, child care, and the like. In societies dependent on literacy, competencies related to learning spoken and written text are emphasized. From this perspective we would expect learning disabilities to be expressed differently in specific societies and in different times; particular symptoms or signs vary in diagnostic significance as a function of context. Learning disabilities indeed represent a negotiated category of problem. Importantly, the primary negotiators have been parents and special interest groups. Their purpose was to secure services, not to further scientific enquiry, and the construct is embedded in a secular, political context as well as a scientific one.

INFLUENCES ON CLASSIFICATION

A number of secular and scientific influences have affected the definition of learning disabilities and the ways in which definitions have been operationalized and implemented. On a practical level, in contemporary society, politics and economics have had profound effects on classification and identification. A striking example may be found in California, where a volatile and litigative educational-political environment led to legislative mandates for changes in assessment, identification, and classification procedures. A consequence was a shift in prevalence figures in categories of mental retardation and learning disabilities. In 1 year, approximately 12,000–14,000 pupils identified as having mental retardation were "rediagnosed" (i.e., reclassified); during the same year, the number of pupils with educational disabilities (i.e., learning disabilities) increased by almost 9,000. The bulk of pupils whose classification changed were of minority ethnic backgrounds. Clearly, the impetus for change was social-political rather than scientific.

Similar findings are reported by Tucker (1980) based on an analysis of data from 50 school districts in the southwestern United States. The school population in Tucker's analysis was made up of primarily three groups: Anglo, African-American, and Mexican-American pupils, the total number equalling more than 40,000. In the early 1970s, slightly more than 4% of the pupils were in special education; this percentage increased to almost 12% in 1977, following passage of P. L. 94-142, the Education for All Handicapped Children Act of 1975. This legislation, of course, provided states with financial incentives and resources to serve children with disabilities up to a 12% "cap." When the figures were examined according to category of services, Tucker found that the percentage of pupils in programs for students with learning disabilities increased from 1971 to 1977, while the percentage of pupils in programs for "educable mentally retarded" students decreased. The changes were particularly apparent for African-American pupils, who had been overrepresented in programs for students with mild mental retardation, but who were increasingly categorized as having learning disabilities. This led Tucker to raise the possibility that the new learning disabilities category was being used as a convenient and socially acceptable special education placement for pupils from minority backgrounds.

Current funding limitations and the philosophical underpinnings of the regular education initiative (Will, 1986) will undoubtedly affect the number of pupils identified or not identified as having learning disabilities because more inclusive services in regular education programs will presumably reduce the need for categorical programs. The point to be emphasized is that findings of incidence, prevalence, and even expression of problem conditions are influenced by social and political conditions and pressures, not just by the nature of the condition itself.

Context is not just political; the history of learning disabilities suggests the importance of disciplinary perspectives on classification and definitions. Kavale and Forness (1985) noted that professional perspectives and professional "politics" affect resources for research. Priorities change with changes in social–political conditions and as knowledge accrues. According to Kavale and Forness, there were five major stages in the definition of learning disabilities: brain injury, minimal brain injury, educational discrepancy, legislative, and operational. The definitions proposed in each stage served as working guides for practices of identification and for treatment or intervention. In the early years, many popular diagnostic techniques were directed at specifying neurological dysfunctions characteristic of the "Strauss syndrome." Interventions designed specifically for children with brain injury were widely implemented (e.g., Cruickshank, Bentzen, Ratzeberg, & Tannhauser, 1961; Strauss & Lehtinen, 1947). Currently, there are paralleling interests in cognitive processing models of learning failure and in neuropsychological underpinnings of learning disabilities. The contemporary literature contains many examples of techniques designed to identify individuals with learning disabilities with specific information-processing problems (e.g., Swanson, 1987a, 1987b). These approaches represent somewhat different views of the problem, including definitional boundaries and the methods and techniques appropriate for study of the condition. The approaches also lead to different decisions about treatment. The politics of science, therefore, affect both research and practice in learning disabilities.

Another source of influence, and a very practical one, also deserves brief note. I refer specifically to "institutional" politics, to the workings of schools and clinics that serve pupils with learning disabilities. Whereas in an ideal setting, all pupils who need special help would get it, the reality of schools is that only selected children are served. The availability and quality of services vary across school districts, across schools, and even within schools. These discrepancies do not stem from purposeful selection policies or from neglect, but reflect financial and personnel resources and functional characteristics of service agencies. These influences are well illustrated by Mehan and his associates (Mehan, Meihls, Hertweck, & Crowdes, 1981), who conducted an ethnographic case study of referral and service procedures in a southern California school district. The numbers of pupils referred for assessment and possible identification and placement varied relative to a number of very practical, functional considerations: the availability and case loads of school psychologists, the volume of paperwork to be completed by teachers, building principals' attitudes and beliefs about special education services, and the nature of alternative programs such as compensatory education classes. These practical constraints, along with the social–political and scientific influences already noted, make it difficult, if not impossible, to determine how many "real" students with learning disabilities are represented in a given population and what are the most effective intervention programs.

In sum, social–political, economic, professional, and institutional conditions affect how a condition such as learning disabilities is conceptualized and operationalized. These influences almost preclude a meaningful empirical mapping of the condition because the operational boundaries change over time and place. Rather than a description of the expression and prevalence of the reality of a condition, it may be more productive to acknowledge classification systems and definitions as constructions that reflect the social and political context in which problems are defined. This does not lessen their importance or their value, but does imply caution in inference and generalization about the intrinsic nature of problem conditions, especially of a somewhat ambiguous condition such as learning disabilities. The very ambiguity of the condition argues for the importance of a meaningful classification system that could order the diversity within the broad construct. I suggest that such a classification system must take into account purpose, developmental appropriateness, and utility.

PURPOSES OF CLASSIFICATION

I have argued elsewhere (Keogh, 1983) that there are three primary purposes for classification of problem conditions: advocacy, services, and scientific study. Because the purpose of classification leads to different operational practices in identification, the number of individuals identified in any given category, and their characteristics or attributes, may, and often will, differ according to purpose. In contrast to many classification systems developed in the physical and natural sciences, the purpose of classification in special education has been advocacy and the perceived need for services. Early categories of disability and services were physical and sensory impairments, profound mental retardation, and severe emotional disturbance. Although we might question the adequacy of the services provided, the classification system at least acknowledged the existence of a problem condition and carried implications for services, including schooling. Powerful parent and professional groups have led the advocacy effort and have successfully lobbied for services, making learning disabilities the fastest growing category of special education services. From an advocacy point of view, arguments that a problem is widespread, affects many individuals, and has long-term consequences increase its salience and importance and contribute to its political power. Thus, advocates are not concerned about the heterogeneity of identified groups. Rather, they are concerned with demonstrating the importance of a problem and the need for services.

These are worthwhile and necessary purposes, yet they have resulted in major confusion for the efforts in scientific enquiry. Because the purposes of classification determine the size and shape of the operational net used to identify individuals, individuals or groups identified for one purpose may be different from individuals identified for another. This is, in part at least, a function of the negotiation process. As a consequence, however, the bulk of research in learning disabilities has been confounded by the use of subjects (usually elementary school-age children) identified as failing in the regular educational program and in need of specialized services. This net captures a broad array of problems, and, as noted above, the attributes of the catch reflect the socioeconomic conditions, philosophy, and organizational and procedural characteristics of the identifying agencies or individuals. It should come as no surprise, then, that the range of subject variance in any identified groups of individuals with learning disabilities is broad, and that some individuals not identified exhibit characteristics of learning disabilities. "System-identified subjects" (Keogh & MacMillan, 1983; MacMillan, Meyers, & Morrison, 1980)—that is, subjects identified under selection criteria and practices defined for purposes of advocacy or for the provision of services—do not necessarily meet the classification criteria requisite for scientific study.

These differences in purposes, along with vagaries of measurement, lack of precision in identification procedures, and the resulting inconsistencies in characteristics of individuals categorized as having learning disabilities, present serious challenges to the viability, even reality, of the condition. A number of investigators (Shepard, 1983; Ysseldyke & Algozzine, 1983) have documented these differences, and have shown also that many individuals with characteristics of learning disabilities are not identified. They have also questioned the adequacy of measures and techniques used in identification procedures. These are valid challenges to the adequacy of the operational procedures used in identification. They also are classic examples of the confusion between classification and identification. As Bailey (1973) has argued, classification is conceptual and measurement is free; identification is operational and measurement-bound, and, thus, subject to the limitations and inconsistencies of the technical adequacy of instruments and the expertise of those responsible for the identification. Identification is also affected by purpose and by context. It comes as no surprise that empirically determined groups are heterogeneous. However, this does not necessarily challenge the construct and the class of problems. It is obvious, however, that increased understanding of the substantive nature of learning disabilities requires clearer and more precise conceptualization and identification practices linked to the purposes of identification. I argue, in addition, that understanding learning disabilities requires a developmental perspective or framework.

DEVELOPMENTAL APPROPRIATENESS

Questions posed from a developmental perspective have to do with the appropriateness and applicability of classification systems over the life span, the changing expression of learning disabilities over time, and the impact of experience on problem status. We might ask if definitional criteria, including the widely discussed aptitude–achievement discrepancy, are useful when applied to toddlers, preschool children, and adults. To date, the bulk of empirical research has focused on school-age children, and a good deal of the work has been directed at learning disabilities defined within specific subject matter areas (e.g., reading, spelling, and/or arithmetic). This focus, although useful for a restricted age group, has serious limitations. Indeed, a rapidly growing literature documents that learning disabilities are not restricted to a particular age group, but are apparent in adults and in secondary as well as elementary schoolchildren (Vogel, 1986; White, 1985).

According to U. S. Department of Education figures, in 1987–1988 more than 1 million secondary-school pupils were identified as having learning disabilities, and more than half of special education pupils age 12 and above were so classified. In a study of learning disabilities in secondary schools, Wagner (1990) found that the majority of secondary-school pupils with learning disabilities were in regular education classrooms, but that many did not fare well, as evidenced by failing grades and higher than average dropout rates. These findings are consistent with those of a 10-year follow-up study of 114 children identified as having learning disabilities in elementary school (Hartzell & Compton, 1984). When compared with their siblings without disabilities, the subjects with learning disabilities in Hartzell and Compton's study had lower academic success, as indicated by poorer grades, higher dropout rates, lower rates of continuation to higher education, and less success socially. Such findings argue that learning disabilities are not limited to younger children, but may require continuing services throughout the school years.

At the other end of the spectrum, current legislation (P.L.102-119) directs the early identification and treatment of problem conditions in preschool children and encourages identification and interventions during infancy. Although this legislation targets children with serious and major disabilities, in many states learning disabilities are included. Clearly, the expression or evidence of learning disabilities will differ relative to the age of the individual. In the early years, biological markers are the primary indicators of problem development. However, unless severe, these markers tend to be nonspecific (i.e., they could infer mental retardation, learning disabilities, or other developmental disabilities). There are, in addition, questions of stability or continuity of problem conditions and the impact of social–environmental influences on development.

In their follow-up of the large National Collaborative Study Sample, Nichols and Chen (1981) found that few pre-, peri-, or neonatal signs predicted later learning problems. In contrast, social–environmental conditions were strongly correlated, a conclusion similar to that reached by Horn and Packard (1985) in their meta-analysis of 58 studies of reading problems. Indeed, considerable evidence documents the increasingly powerful contribution of social–environmental conditions as children grow older (Badian, 1988; Hartzell & Compton, 1984; Werner & Smith, 1982). Especially interesting is the recognition of protective or compensating attributes and conditions in problem development and expression (see Garmezy, 1983; Rutter, 1979; Werner, 1986). In summary, consideration of learning disabilities from a developmental perspective involves inclusion of both intrinsic, within-child characteristics, and social–contextual, extra-child influences. It also involves the recognition that problem expression may change as a function of age. This, of course, raises questions about the continuity of defining variables over time, and about the appropriateness of identification techniques with particular age groups.

Not only may learning disabilities be expressed differently in various developmental periods, but problems also may be expressed in a variety of domains. The definition proposed by the Interagency Committee on Learning Disabilities (1987), for example, includes disorders of social skills. This addition to the definition is clear recognition that learning disabilities are not limited to academic achievement, but may affect many aspects of living. The broadened view of learning disabilities has implications for identification techniques and decisions. It may also muddy the definitional boundaries between learning disabilities and other problem conditions, particularly behavior disorders and mild emotional conditions. However, the inclusion of social skill problems as an indicator of learning disabilities may be particularly important for identification of individuals outside the school-age range (e.g., preschoolers and adults).

A major point, then, is that classification and identification must be developmentally appropriate and must take into account both individual and social–environmental conditions. A clear research need is the documentation of the nature of these person–environment interactions and transactions. A further scientific question of importance is whether there are underlying and unifying consistencies that are unique to the learning disabilities condition(s) and/or that identify valid subgroups within and across developmental periods. A related question has to do with the nature of the organization or structure of such a multivariate taxonomy: Are typologies categorical or hierarchical, and are they based on etiology or psychological–behavioral characteristics (see Skinner, 1981, for discussion)?

APPLICABILITY AND CLINICAL UTILITY

A third major consideration in the definition and classification of learning disabilities relates to utility or applicability. As noted by Doris (1986), "The diagnosis of an entity in either medicine or education is an academic exercise unless it is related to prognosis, therapeutic intervention, and/or prevention" (p. 39). To have clinical utility, a classification system and the operational definitions that follow must link to treatment. Unfortunately, the research or scientific basis for treatment or intervention decisions is limited, and the array of treatment options is broad (see Doris, 1986; Lloyd, 1988, for comprehensive reviews). The state of the art reflects the many disciplinary perspectives on learning disabilities, but it is also a function of a lack of rigor in the analysis and evaluation of treatments. Examination of the research literature on interventions identifies a diverse set of techniques based on or derived from different views of, or beliefs about, the nature and etiology of learning disabilities. Unfortunately, the efficacy studies yield mixed findings. Even when positive outcomes are reported, it is often difficult to determine if effects are due to specifics of the treatment program, to the "individualization" of treatments, to particular characteristics of the subjects participating in the program, or to other unspecified sources of variance.

CONCLUSIONS AND IMPLICATIONS

In describing the organization of this volume, editors David Gray and Reid Lyon indicated that a major goal was to consider how the construct of learning disabilities could be operationalized at the definitional and diagnostic levels. Consideration of both social–political and developmental aspects underscores several points. These are not new or original, but gain relevance when viewed from these perspectives.

First, it can be argued that the inconsistencies among empirically defined groups are in part a function of identification for different purposes and in part related to confusions between classification and identification. Despite the difficulties in operationalizing the concept, learning disabilities describes a class or category of problems that are different from those identified in other diagnostic categories. There is, however, obvious need for a defensible taxonomy and for the development and refinement of operational measures and techniques that allow accurate and reliable identification of individual exemplars.

Second, it is clear that learning disabilities may be expressed in a number of ways. An individual child may have learning disabilities in one domain, but not in another; problems in one domain do not necessarily imply problems in another. Thus, for both research and intervention purposes, global identification or categorization of that child as having learning disabilities is inadequate. On an operational/applied level, classification and diagnosis must specify domains of learning disabilities.

Third, it is also clear that learning disabilities are not independent of a developmental period. Problem expression is embedded in development. As a consequence, on a conceptual level, classification and definitional systems must accommodate a potentially changing pattern of learning disabilities over time. Similarly, operational procedures for identification of individuals must be developmentally appropriate.

Fourth, and closely related, from a clinical, developmental perspective, it is important to recognize that individuals may change diagnostic status over time. This does not necessarily infer errors in diagnosis, but acknowledges situational influences and the transactional nature of development, particularly the importance of mediating or protective factors in the individual and in the social environment. Learning disabilities evident early on may be amenable to change, may be compensated by other strengths, or may be ameliorated with powerful treatments. In contrast, seemingly intact and problem-free children may evidence specific learning disabilities as they move into different developmental periods and face more complex intellectual and social demands. Recognizing that diagnostic status changes, Gordon and Jens (1988) proposed a "moving risk model" that may appropriately be applied to the study of learning disabilities. Developmentalists are increasingly concerned with understanding discontinuities, not just continuities, in development, and we might profit by taking a page from their book. The systematic mapping of the expression of learning disabilities and of the influences on continuity and discontinuity are major research needs.

Fifth, the continuing confusion, even controversy, over treatment/intervention procedures poses serious problems for parents and professionals. Intervention decisions are based partly on evidence of efficacy, beliefs, and availability. There have been few large-scale, comprehensive tests of most approaches, and only limited tests on competing treatments. The study of treatment effects is obviously not simple. However, from both clinical and theoretical perspectives, there is clear need for comprehensive and objective study of a range of therapeutic approaches to learning disabilities.

I began this discussion with the propositions that learning disabilities is a constructed, negotiated category of problem, and that perceived need precedes science. It is likely that this situation will continue for some time because the course of science is slow and there are many controversies and unanswered questions. However, there is both conceptual and empirical support for the notion of learning disabilities as a class of problems. Importantly, large numbers of individuals and their families are affected. It would be neither humane nor responsible to deny or withdraw services while waiting for the scientific validation of the condition.

REFERENCES

Badian, N. (1988). The prediction of good and poor reading before kindergarten entry: A nine-year follow-up. *Journal of Learning Disabilities, 21,* 98–103.

Bailey, K.D. (1973). Monothetic and polythetic typologies and their relation to conceptualization, measurement, and scaling. *American Sociological Review, 38,* 18–33.

Blashfield, R.K., & Draguns, J.G. (1976). Evaluative criteria for psychiatric classification. *Journal of Abnormal Psychology, 85,* 140–150.

Cruickshank, W.M., Bentzen, F., Ratzeberg, F., & Tannhauser, M.A. (1961). *Teaching method for brain-injured and hyperactive children.* Syracuse, NY: Syracuse University Press.

Doris, J. (1986). Learning disabilities. In S.J. Ceci (Ed.), *Handbook of cognitive, social, and neuropsychological aspects of learning disabilities* (Vol. 1, pp. 3–54). Hillsdale, NJ: Lawrence Erlbaum Associates.

Garmezy, N. (1983). Stressors of childhood. In N. Garmezy & M. Rutter (Eds.), *Stress, coping and development in children* (pp. 43–84). New York: McGraw-Hill.

Gordon, B.N., & Jens, K.G. (1988). A conceptual model for tracking high-risk infants and making service decisions. *Developmental and Behavioral Pediatrics, 2,* 279–286.

Hartzell, H.E., & Compton, C. (1984). Learning disability: A ten-year follow-up. *Pediatrics, 74,* 1058–1064.

Horn, W.I., & Packard, T. (1985). Early identification of learning problems: A meta analysis. *Journal of Educational Psychology, 5,* 597–607.

Interagency Committee on Learning Disabilities. (1987). *Learning disabilities: A report to the U.S. Congress.* Washington, DC: National Institutes of Health.

Kavale, K., & Forness, S. (1985). *The science of learning disabilities.* Boston: Little, Brown.

Keogh, B.K. (1983). Classification, compliance, and confusion. *Journal of Learning Disabilities, 16,* 25.

Keogh, B.K., & MacMillan, D.L. (1983). The logic of sample selection: Who represents what? *Exceptional Educational Quarterly, 4,* 84–96.

Lloyd, J.W. (1988). Direct academic interventions in learning disabilities. In M.C. Wang, M.C. Reynolds, & H.J. Walberg (Eds.), *Handbook of special education research and practice* (pp. 345–366). Oxford, England: Pergamon Press.

MacMillan, D.L., Meyers, C.E., & Morrison, G.M. (1980). System identification of mildly mentally retarded children: Implications for conducting and interpreting research. *American Journal of Mental Deficiency, 85,* 108–115.

Mehan, H., Meihls, J.L., Hertweck, A., & Crowdes, M.J. (1981). Identifying handicapped students. In S.T. Bacharach (Ed.), *Organizational behavior in school and school districts* (pp. 381–427). New York: Praeger.

Nichols, P.L., & Chen, T.C. (1981). *Minimal brain dysfunction.* Hillsdale, NJ: Lawrence Erlbaum Associates.

Public Law 94-142, Education for All Handicapped Children Act of 1975. (23 August 1977). 20 U.S.C. 1401 et seq: *Federal Register, 42,* (163), 42474–42518.

Public Law 102-119, Individuals with Disabilities Education Act Amendments of 1991. (7 October 1991). 20 U.S.C. 1400 et seq: *U.S. Statutes at Large, 105,* 587–608.

Rutter, M. (1979). Protective factors in children's responses to stress and disadvantage. In M.W. Kent & J.E. Rolf (Eds.), *Primary prevention of psychopathology. Vol. III: Social competence in children* (pp. 49–74). Hanover, VT: University Press of New England.

Scarr, S. (1985). Constructing psychology: Making facts and fables for our times. *American Psychologist, 40,* 499–512.

Shepard, L. (1983). The role of measurement in educational policy: Lessons from the identification of learning disabilities. *Educational Measurement: Issues in Policy and Practice, 2*(3), 4–8.

Skinner, H.A. (1981). Toward the integration of classification theory and methods. *Journal of Abnormal Psychology, 90,* 68–86.

Strauss, A., & Lehtinen, L.E. (1947). *Psychopathology and education of the brain-injured child.* New York: Grune & Stratton.

Swanson, H.L. (1987a). Information processing theory and learning disabilities. *Journal of Learning Disabilities, 20,* 3–7.

Swanson, H.L. (1987b). Information processing theory and learning disabilities: A commentary and future perspective. *Journal of Learning Disabilities, 20,* 155–166.

Tucker, J.A. (1980). Ethnic proportions in classes for the learning disabled: Issues in nondisabled assessment. *Journal of Special Education, 14,* 92–107.

Vogel, S. (1986). Levels and patterns of intellectual functioning among learning disabled adults: Clinical and educational implications. *Journal of Learning Disabilities, 19,* 71–79.

Wagner, M. (1990). *The school programs and school performance of secondary students classified as learning disabled: Findings from the National Longitudinal Transition Study of Special Education Students.* Menlo Park, CA: SRI International.

Werner, E.E. (1986). The concept of risk from a developmental perspective. In B.K. Keogh (Ed.), *Advances in special education, Vol. 5: Developmental problems in infancy and the preschool years* (pp. 1–24). Greenwich, CT: JAI Press.

Werner, E.E., & Smith, R. (1982). *Vulnerable but invincible: A longitudinal study of resilient children and youth.* New York: McGraw-Hill.

White, W.J. (1985). Perspectives in the education and training of learning disabled adults. *Learning Disabilities Quarterly, 8,* 231–236.

Will, M.C. (1986). Educating children with learning problems: A shared responsibility. *Exceptional Children, 52,* 411–415.

Ysseldyke, J.E., & Algozzine, B. (1983). LD or not LD: That's not the question! *Journal of Learning Disabilities, 16,* 29–31.

15

LEARNING DISABILITIES AND PUBLIC POLICY
Myths and Outcomes

Edwin W. Martin

The field of learning disabilities has not had an outcome orientation toward special education, particularly one that looked at postsecondary activities. Without a determination of the long-term effects of disability and the effectiveness of different interventions on disabilities, we are left with a system of assumptions that are frequently based on little empirical information. The first of these assumptions is that learning disabilities are "mild" disorders, similar in nature to mild mental retardation and mild emotional disorders. This assumption has led to further assumptions that heterogeneous grouping of such children for educational purposes might be in order. A second assumption is that children with learning disabilities are being effectively educated by being offered brief special education supplements to their regular education. A third assumption, perhaps not as widespread as the first two, is that learning disabilities do not really exist, but are simply signs of slow learning or poor instruction. The combination of these assumptions has provided impetus for what has been termed the *regular education initiative.*

To counter these assumptions, outcome studies indicate that students with learning disabilities have a very poor record in finishing school, with a majority dropping out or leaving for unknown reasons. Furthermore, few students with learning disabilities pursue postsecondary education, and, until recently, none were considered to have problems severe enough to warrant their inclusion in federally funded vocational rehabilitation programs. These bleak outcomes indicate that the prevailing assumptions about learning disabilities may be no more than myths. In addition, programs at the high school and college level designed to assist students with learning and physical disabilities reported high success rates and participant satisfaction. Obviously, there exists a clear need to understand why these more positive outcomes were obtained versus the limited outcomes observed following traditional programs for students with learning disabilities.

These reports illustrate the fact that little substantive information about long-term effectiveness is available to parents and educators and that many education programs are considered effective only because they are structured along philosophically attractive dimensions. To provide effective service and to grow as a responsible profession, educators, related specialists, and research workers must examine the outcomes of treatment programs over time in such "commonsense" dimensions as higher education, employment, self-satisfaction, and independent living.

DEVELOPMENT OF FEDERAL EDUCATION
POLICY FOR STUDENTS WITH LEARNING DISABILITIES

The development of federal policy in the United States in relation to the education of children with learning disabilities has been controversial from its inception (Martin, 1984, 1987b). A definition of "handicapping conditions" eligible for special education appeared in 1963 in P.L. 88-164, which authorized a program of federal support for training special educators and for research in special education. The definition did not refer directly to learning disabilities.

In 1967, the first Education of the Handicapped Act (Title VI, Elementary and Secondary Education Act, P.L. 89-750) began a program of grants to the state to "initiate, expand and improve" special education programs for children with disabilities. Although Congress heard testimony from the parents of children with learning disabilities prior to its enactment, Title VI did not include learning disabilities in the federal definition of "handicapping conditions" (U. S. House of Representatives, 1966). Although no official reason was expressed for this choice, personal conversations with a key professional staff member of Congress indicated a number of concerns. There were doubts as to the nature of the disorder and the possible inclusion of children with learning problems as a result of poverty and related factors rather than traditional disabilities. Fear was also expressed that the large numbers of children cited by advocates would take scarce resources from smaller groups, such as children who were deaf (Martin, 1984, 1987b). In many ways these arguments have persisted for the more than 20 years since then (U. S. Senate, 1975).

Federal education law finally recognized children with learning disabilities as requiring special education, in two stages and in separate acts. Programs supporting model service programs and teacher education and research were approved in 1970 and, in 1975, when Congress passed the Education for All Handicapped Children Act (P.L. 94-142), children with learning disabilities (specific learning disabilities in the statute) were assisted for the first time in local programs receiving federal funds. In practice, some children had been assisted in federally supported programs when the local school districts categorized them as neurologically impaired, under a provision of earlier statutes that recognized "other health impairments."

Congress showed continuing uncertainty about learning disabilities even while including the category in P.L. 94-142. A provision in the legislation provided that a maximum of one sixth of children enrolled in special education (i.e., a maximum of 2% of all school-age children) could be identified as having learning disabilities and be counted for federal entitlement purposes (P.L. 94-142, 1975). This "capping" provision was to be removed when the Bureau of Education for the Handicapped promulgated new regulations making more specific the identification procedures that would be acceptable under federal law. The regulations that were published were acceptable to Congress and to most state agencies and advocates at the time, but have been recognized as at least somewhat troublesome ever since (Code of Federal Regulations, 1990). No consensus has developed around alternative approaches, however.

In the years since the implementation of P.L. 94-142, there has been rapid growth in the numbers of children identified as having learning disabilities who are enrolled in special education programs, although this growth has leveled off in recent years (U. S. Department of Education, 1990). Earlier estimates by federal officials that the population would encompass about 1%–3% of all school-age children have been surpassed in some communities and states, with enrollment of children with learning disabilities comprising approximately 4% of the school-age population. This growth has resulted in various financial and educational concerns and continues to have an impact on both formal and informal public policy at state, local, and federal levels. The term *informal public policy* refers to actions taken by local school administrators to reduce the identification and classification of children who might be diagnosed as having learning disabilities. This policy generally is not stated publicly, but is made clear to teachers and diagnosticians. At the federal level, efforts to encourage education of more children with disabilities in regular classrooms, rather than refer them to special education, has some similar roots.

In support of public policy, both formal and informal, are two central assumptions regarding learning disabilities that I believe may be better labeled as myths. The first is that learning disabilities are similar in nature to mild mental retardation and mild emotional disorders and, therefore, may be seen as one of a cluster of "mild" disabilities. This assumption leads to further assumptions about placement, treatment, and such procedures as "heterogeneous grouping" of these children for educational purposes. Within this context, a number of state departments of education offer what are sometimes called "noncategorical" certifications for those teachers who will be called on to teach such groups. The second myth is that children with learning disabilities are being effectively educated by receiving brief special education supplements to their regular education. These are services that are typically offered by resource room teachers.

Both of these myths, and perhaps others, have had, and will continue to have effects on public policy, and it is now appropriate to issue various scientific disclaimers. It is not possible at present to demonstrate conclusively through research citations that the above assumptions are myths, but it is possible to present arguments about them within the context of an informed discussion of public policy, with support from empirical research data. It is expected that researchers will find there is not sufficient evidence to support these myths, however philosophically attractive they might be to some people.

LEARNING DISABILITIES MYTHS: RAISING POLICY QUESTIONS BASED ON OUTCOMES

Myth 1—Learning Disabilities Is a Mild Disorder

The belief that learning disabilities represent a disorder with "mild" impact is countered by pointing to the universal recognition that children and adults with learning disabilities are a very hetero-geneous population (see Fletcher, Francis, Rourke, Shaywitz, & Shaywitz, chap. 3, this volume; Morris, chap. 5, this volume; Mac-Millan, chap. 7, this volume; Keogh, chap. 14, this volume). This heterogeneity implies that such disabilities are distributed along various continuua, often in the shape of a normal curve. Severity of disability is one such continuum (for a similar comment on children with behavior disorders, see Kauffman, Braaten, Nelson, Polsgrove, & Braaten, 1990).

The perception that learning disabilities represent only mild disorders is beginning to change in response to new evidence to the contrary. Government statistics indicate that a considerable percentage of high school students identified as having learning disabilities (26.7%) drop out of school prior to graduation. Another 16% of students with learning disabilities exit school for "unknown" reasons without a diploma and without reaching maximum age. These percentages not only defy the myth of mildness, but also exceed expectations based on a normal curve of severity. In fact, almost 50% of all children with disabilities who drop out are children with learning disabilities (U. S. Department of Education, 1990).

Equally impressive and troubling is a report by Fairweather and Shaver (1990) of a national sample of students leaving school prior to graduation. The authors found only 17.1% of students identified as having learning disabilities enrolled in any postsecondary course, including vocational courses, 1 year after leaving school (see Table 1). Only 6.8% of the students participated in 2-year higher education programs, and a startlingly low 1.8% participated in 4-year programs. These figures do not report successful completions, just participation. In this context, the successful demonstrations of transition to higher education are especially significant.

Despite the failures in long-term outcomes of education suggested by these reports, one may infer that the major support for the assumption that children with learning disabilities can be educated

Table 1.   Postsecondary education participation of youth with disabilities

Primary disability[a]	Any postsecondary course		Vocational course (%)	2-year course (%)	4-year course (%)
	%	No.			
Learning disabled	17.1	243	8.5	6.8	1.8
Emotionally disturbed	12.4	128	7.3	3.8	1.3
Mentally retarded	5.9	161	4.2	1.1	0.6
Speech impaired	32.0	82	6.6	16.4	9.0
Visually impaired	42.6	108	2.2	12.6	27.8
Deaf	38.7	152	5.3	18.2	15.2
Hard of hearing	30.1	101	10.8	12.6	6.7
Orthopedically disabled	29.1	104	9.0	10.4	9.7
Health impaired	32.6	63	10.3	13.4	8.9
Multiply handicapped	4.8	73	0.6	3.9	0.3
Deaf–blind	8.3	27	8.3	0	0
Total	15.1	1,242	7.2	5.7	2.2

From Fairweather, J. S., & Shaver, D. M. (1990). Making the transition to postsecondary education and training. *Exceptional Children, 57,* 264–270; reprinted by permission.

[a] Categories of disability were as identified by student's school.

successfully with children with other disabilities considered to be mild grows out of the research on differential diagnosis. Within this context, a number of studies have demonstrated difficulties in identifying important differences on diagnostic measures between groups of children identified as having learning disabilities and other low achievers (Ysseldyke, Algozzine, Shinn, & McGue, 1982). In addition, there have been reports of educational efforts in which children identified by several different labels have been taught successfully, using similar methods (Chalfant, Pysh, & Moultine, 1979; Idol-Maestas et al., 1981).

In general, however, comprehensive studies of outcome seem to be minimal. The problems in differential diagnosis, even though seen as valid, do not necessarily mean that heterogeneous grouping for instructional purposes is valid. There is no absolute linkage between issues of identification and procedures for remediation. Numerous successful treatments in medicine as well as behavioral sciences may occur while differential diagnosis continues, or perhaps is never resolved. For example, speech-language therapy may proceed for nonverbal preschool children while attempts to identify etiology continue. Differentiation of emotional, neurological, and other components of the etiology of the disability may be very difficult. Also familiar are situations in which treatment of gastrointestinal disorders such as those sometimes called preulcerous may proceed after appropriate diagnostic tests, even if the existence of an ulcer is not confirmed. If the treatment alleviates the symptoms to the physicians' and patient's satisfaction, the ultimate question of "ulcer" may be moot.

My inferences come primarily from my experience as a clinician and college teacher. In many conversations with graduate students who are practicing teachers, they report being troubled by the heterogeneity they face. They believe their efforts have value, but they often report being frustrated by having to respond to very different learning needs and behaviors among students who have emotional problems, developmental disabilities, and learning disabilities. Gerber and Semmel (1985) discussed similar observations in what they called the "microeconomics of teachers' behavior."

Unfortunately, the myth of mildness also has had an effect on public policy in the area of vocational rehabilitation. In recent years, I have been concerned about employment issues, and have frequently observed the difficulty many young adults with learning disabilities have in securing and maintaining employment. These individuals present employment problems that are by no means "mild" in their negative impact on the person (see also Edgar, Levine, Levine, & Dubey, 1988; Hasazi, Gordon, & Roe, 1985; Mithaug, Horiuchi, & Fanning, 1985).

While serving as an assistant secretary for special education and rehabilitation in the U. S. Department of Education during 1980–1981, I urged one of the component agencies, the Rehabilitation Services Administration (RSA), to include persons with learning disabilities within the larger group of persons eligible for their services. After considerable debate, the RSA complied, but only with grave reservations about being inundated with persons with "mild" disabilities (Martin, Smith, & Zwerlein, 1985).

Ten years later, persons with learning disabilities were categorized as "mildly disabled" by this agency. In the Projects With Industry program, which fosters cooperative relationships between business and rehabilitation and gives extra credit to recipients of federal grants that help place persons with severe disabilities in competitive employment, *no* person with learning disabilities could be counted as a person with severe disabilities. Until recently, the power of this myth made it difficult for rehabilitation centers to convince policymakers that learning disabilities can be severe.

The key premise put forward here, and throughout this chapter, is that, as practitioners and researchers, we have failed to place sufficient emphasis on the *outcomes* of special education. We have tended to ignore the macro-issues, such as school leaving, enrollment and success in higher education or vocational training, successful employment in the competitive sector, independent living, social adequacy, and positive feelings about oneself that become the basis for community adjustment. When one begins to consider these types of output data, they put a new perspective on issues such as "mildness" and "homogeneity."

Myth 2—Current Supplemental Education Is Sufficient

In recent years professionals have had considerable interest in encouraging greater and more successful relationships between persons with disabilities and those viewed as not having disabilities. This value system has led to a number of related social policies, including deinstitutionalization of persons with mental illness and mental retardation, mainstreaming of children with disabilities within regular classrooms, and greater efforts to employ persons with disabilities in the competitive work force. Changes in federal education and rehabilitation policies, as well as in health-related areas, have been matched recently, on an even broader societal basis, by P.L. 101-336, the Americans with Disabilities Act (1990), which prohibits discrimination against persons with disabilities and provides for certain reasonable accommodations that must be made to avoid such discrimination.

There are few persons in the United States who would argue against this general policy, and, in fact, there is considerable interest around the world in pursuing similar ends (Organization for Economic Cooperation and Development, 1985, 1988).[1] Within this context, most special educators have applauded efforts to educate children with disabilities with their peers without disabilities, and one of the areas within special education in which the highest levels of inclusion have occurred is in developing programs for children with learning disabilities (U. S. Department of Education, 1990).

The strength of our commitment to inclusion of persons with disabilities into our society has been so strong that many professional specialists seem to have assumed that inclusive placements automatically mean successful educational programs. As a government official, I, and others, have presented enrollment figures indicating that more children were being educated in inclusive settings as a demonstration of the success of special education under the federal law. There is little doubt that there are successes in such programs, but increasingly one may wonder what careful outcome studies of these programs would show. Do we really know what is occurring in the tens of thousands of classrooms across the nation, and in the lives of the children during and after they leave schooling?

The issue here is not the value of inclusion as a socially desirable end, but the question of whether children are, in fact, benefiting in the various programs. We still have a variety of programs being offered by schools, ranging from those in which children with learning disabilities are engaged full time in regular classrooms, through those in which children are "pulled out" part time for extra assistance, to those in which children spend most of their time in a special class, resource room, or special school placement. Within any one of these placements on what has been called the continuum of services, there may be very different educational procedures from school to school or even class to class. Furthermore, it is well known by teachers and other specialists that budget and policy considerations frequently result in programs offering fewer services than instructional staff recommend. What is quite clear is that we do not know enough about how children benefit from these educational placements, and favoring one over another may be based primarily on an emotional rather than on an instructional or scientific basis. The time has come to stop assuming that the effectiveness of a

---

[1] A number of unpublished "expert papers," written through 1990 and dealing with integration in various nations, are also available from the Organization.

program may be judged primarily on whether it is located in setting A or setting B. Education policy should be based on increasing knowledge concerning effectiveness rather than solely on achieving philosophically desirable ends. This does not imply that the two are mutually exclusive, but that we should seek to know the results of the implementation philosophies.

Results of Program Implementation With regard to the importance of program effectiveness, the results of two programs have influenced my thinking. Both of these programs are based on the work of my colleagues at the National Center for Disability Services.

Postsecondary Schooling Assistance for Students with Learning Disabilities Michaels (1987) and Martin, Michaels, and Gottlieb (1990) reported a demonstration project that assisted a number of young adults with learning disabilities to successfully attend several community colleges. The 108 young people selected were then in their senior year in 25 different high schools in local school districts. Despite the rapidly approaching end of their secondary schooling, these young people had no specific postsecondary plans and were not expected to attend college. Although their average IQ scores on the Wechsler Adult Intelligence Scale–Revised were 97.66 on the performance scale and 97.54 on the verbal scale, they had not taken the Scholastic Aptitude Test. Neither they nor their regular or special education teachers had specific plans for their postsecondary experiences. The project was designed to see if these students could participate successfully in community college programs, with a limited degree of assistance from our center. One specialist in education for people with learning disabilities was assigned to each of these colleges. The specialist had weekly meetings with students, arranged some peer tutoring, and met with occasional faculty members to explain the problems associated with learning disabilities. In sum, it was a commonsense approach, not a labor-intensive intervention. The project also involved the state vocational rehabilitation agency as indicated.

There were a variety of interesting results from this project, including positive outcomes in the community colleges for the majority of the students who enrolled. The project was also designed to have an impact on the referring school faculties, the community college faculties, and the vocational rehabilitation agency counselors. Secondary school faculty members, for example, reconsidered such issues as the kind of English instruction the students had been receiving. Faculty members stated that they would have provided more emphasis on composition skills if they had thought the young people might attend college.

Most of the students with learning disabilities (85%) failed all four modules of one college's mathematics placement examination, in contrast to a 25% failure rate among students overall. The project helped the college faculty modify the procedures, but not the content, of the remedial program, resulting in a pass rate of 75% for the students with learning disabilities. The general success rate after remediation for all students had been 15%. These surprising results led to a revision of the program for all students.

These results not only demonstrate the program's effectiveness, but also point out the more general failure of the education system to be concerned with outcomes. Note the contrast with the Fairweather and Shaver (1990) report of only 8.6% of a national sample of students with learning disabilities participating in 2- or 4-year college programs (see Table 1). In the present demonstration project, students who proved to be able to complete community college work had been moving through well-meaning secondary special education programs focused on day-to-day activities with no real thought about postschool outcomes. When these outcomes became relevant, not only were the lives of students dramatically changed, but the subject of curriculum reform also became relevant. Somewhat similar effects were found for the participating colleges and rehabilitation professionals.

High School Program for Students with Physical Disabilities   In a followup survey of persons who had graduated during a 20-year period from a secondary school program for children with severe physical disabilities (Liebert, Lutsky, & Gottlieb, 1990), of 106 respondents, 72% said they were generally satisfied with their high school education program. Various program offerings rated most useful included driver's education, training in independent living, and various therapies (e.g., speech-language, physical, and occupational). Suggestions for program improvement included more exposure to peers without disabilities (23%), although most students said it had been easy to make friends at college. Fourteen percent recommended more guidance counseling.

Most significantly, more than 75% of these students attended or were attending college (see Table 2). (Average full-scale IQ of the group was 98, with an average verbal IQ of 105.) This exceeds postsecondary enrollment figures for students without disabilities. Edgar et al. (1988) reported that only 50% of students without disabilities were enrolled in postsecondary programs 6 months after high school graduation. Another impressive finding of the Liebert et al. study was that 62% of these graduates were employed, 45% full time (see Table 3). Another 15% were not seeking work because they were still in education programs. Using U. S. Department of Labor

Table 2. Postsecondary educational achievements of participants in high school program for students with severe physical disabilities

Achievement	Percentage
Current school status[a]	
In college or training program	32.4
In other type of program	2.9
Not in school or training program	64.8
Attended college or training program[a]	
Full-time college	66.7
Part-time college	11.4
Full-time training	6.7
Part-time training	1.0
Degree earned[b]	
A.A.	14.6
B.A.	19.5
M.A.	8.5
Ph.D., LL.B.	2.4
Degree expected	
A.A.	7.3
B.A.	18.3
M.A.	3.7
Ph.D.	1.2

From Liebert, D., Lutsky, L., & Gottlieb, A. (1990). Post-secondary experiences of young adults with severe physical disabilities. *Exceptional Children, 57*, 58; reprinted by permission.
[a] $n = 105$.
[b] $n = 82$.

methodology for determining those persons in the work force and those out of it, only 25% of these graduates were not in the work force. In contrast, a recent national sampling survey reported that 62% of adults with disabilities were out of the work force (Louis Harris & Associates, 1986).

These data may be enough to demonstrate the point that an education program for students with disabilities and average intelligence can produce rather impressive outcomes for its graduates. How many other such programs can be cited? Data from these programs would be helpful to parents, and, perhaps equally importantly, the long-term results could enable teachers and administrators to modify program content to promote more positive outcomes for students with disabilities.

The results of this report contrast sharply with figures cited by Fairweather and Shaver (1990) in their national sample of students with physical disabilities gathered from local school district programs. They reported that only 20.1% of their sample participated

Table 3. Employment outcomes of participants in high school program for students with severe physical disabilities

Outcome	Percent (N)
Employed full-time	45.3 (48)
Employed part-time	17.0 (18)
Unemployed (and seeking work)	12.2 (13)
Not seeking work (student)	15.1 (16)
Not seeking work (health reasons)	2.0 (2)
Not seeking work (other reasons)	8.4 (9)

From Liebert, D., Lutsky, L., & Gottlieb, A. (1990). Post-secondary experiences of young adults with severe physical disabilities. *Exceptional Children, 57,* 60; reprinted by permission.

in 2- or 4-year college programs by taking at least one postsecondary course. Another 9.0% in their sample participated in a vocational course (for other examples of follow-up reports, see Edgar et al., 1988; Hasazi et al., 1985; Mithaug et al., 1985; Rogan & Hartman, 1990).

The Liebert et al. (1990) longitudinal study also provides information of value to rehabilitation specialists and to persons interested in community service planning. Their impressive results were gathered from a special day-school program offered by a tuition-free, state-supported, special school. This point is made to emphasize that evaluation of programs' outcomes must go beyond making value judgments on integration. In essence, to develop and/or recommend any program for students with learning disabilities, we must know more about the program's effectiveness in producing favorable long-term outcomes. However, it is important to note that we should not assume programs are inadequate given less than optimal outcome data until we have an idea of what objectively constitutes a favorable outcome.

ADDITIONAL PUBLIC POLICY ISSUES

There are several other current public policy issues that may be of significance to research workers and other professional specialists. First, there is a hidden assumption that learning disabilities do not really exist. The policy issues associated with this view result in efforts to end special programs for children with learning disabilities and to provide them with more generic education programs. This concept seems to be associated with concerns about the possibility that children with general problems in school that are of unknown origin are frequently labeled as having learning disabilities, thereby resulting in increased enrollments. Others see the literature on differential diagnosis, cited earlier, as meaning that no discrete, identifiable learning disability condition can be demonstrated. For others, the heterogeneity of the population with learning disabilities decreases the clinical usefulness of the concept of "learning disability" (Shepherd, 1988). These assumptions may be reflected in skepticism by some legislators and general educators about the entity we call learning disabilities, and have added considerable fuel to the fire that has been called the regular education initiative (Wang, Reynolds, & Walberg, 1986).

There is a danger that the public at large, as well as persons with learning disabilities and their families, will be affected negatively by this erroneous belief. Certainly, lowered public support for educational programs for students with learning disabilities might be anticipated, and this might produce psychological harm in persons struggling with problems that others think are illusory. Perhaps it is appropriate to publish a research synthesis for policymakers and the general public that would sample neurological, neurophysiological, neuropsychological, linguistic, educational, and other areas of study to demonstrate the concrete nature of observations of the phenomena we call learning disabilities.

Discrepancy Criteria

Parents have reported at meetings of the Learning Disability Association of America and other gatherings that various policies and practices are limiting and result in an arbitrary rendering of services to children with learning disabilities. One such practice is the misuse of the "discrepancy" approach to identification as a single criterion for the diagnosis of learning disabilities. The federal regulations suggested that, after a multifaceted evaluation of a child, discrepancies might be noted between achievement and various ability (IQ) scores, most specifically in reading, writing, listening, speaking, and mathematics. However, final judgments about eligibility of that child for classification as having learning disabilities were to be made by professional specialists weighing all variables, and were not to be the result of one or more arbitrary test procedures (Code of Federal Regulations, 1990; Dangel & Ensminger, 1988). Unfortunately, it has been reported to me by parents that certain school districts, and perhaps entire states, have established a rigid discrepancy criterion—for example, a 50% gap between achievement and ability as measured by IQ tests. This approach appears to be illegal under P.L. 94-142 and inconsistent with federal court rulings in cases dealing with intelligence testing as a sole criterion for determining placement of children with mental retardation.

From an educational perspective, one may be repulsed by the thought that a given child, showing clear signs of difficulty in reading and other related subject matter, might be refused special education because his or her scores failed by several points, or by some months of academic achievement, to be severe enough to reach an arbitrary cutoff. This child would have to fail until he or she reached the critical point before intervention could begin. There are clinical reports, equally frustrating, of children who raise their performances as the result of much hard work and effective educational interventions, and then find themselves ineligible for additional special educational services or even untimed tests. The time has come to hold this approach up to scientific scrutiny as well as to legal challenge, and to determine more appropriate eligibility procedures.

Regular versus Special Education

Much has been written for and against merging regular and special education, and the policy implications thereof (Bryan & Bryan, 1988; Hallahan, Keller, McKinney, Lloyd, & Bryan, 1988; Kauffman et al., 1990; Martin, 1987a; McKinney & Hocutt, 1988; Stainback & Stainback, 1984; Wang et al., 1986); a review of those arguments here in any detail is unnecessary. However, it is important to remind ourselves that there exist no compelling data to warrant such a merger at this time. The lives of many children will be affected; and yet, there is very little research support for the belief that proposed changes in educational placement into "regular" settings will be beneficial. A much more rational and appropriate public policy would parallel that which emerged during planning for early childhood education for children with disabilities in the 1970s and 1980s.

In that instance, the federal government, primarily the Bureau of Education for the Handicapped and the Head Start program, created priorities for the funding of early childhood research and demonstration programs. These projects, funded over a number of years, created a literature and data base on program characteristics and program effectiveness. Research workers in child development and early childhood education for children without disabilities and researchers studying disability began to interact, and the result was the creation of a substantial academic and clinical discipline. Based on that process, state, and ultimately federal, policies that provided for broad-scale services evolved. Although research continues and arguments persist, there is, for all practical purposes, a consensus that early childhood educational experiences, when properly provided, can be beneficial to children. On that basis, planning for comprehensive implementation strategies is responsible and appropriate.

What is of concern today is that some advocates for the regular education initiative want to bypass this research and demonstration process and put their value judgments into practice immediately. Given the lack of outcome observations mentioned, one can only assume that thousands, perhaps hundreds of thousands, of children will be involved in programs and there will be no careful monitoring of the impact on their lives either in the short term or, particularly, in the long term. The research and clinical communities cannot be silent in the face of that possibility. It is, of course, possible to support multiple, controlled research and demonstration studies. As mentioned previously, the counterargument that research does not support current programs is not sufficient to justify a radical change from long-established practice and from hard-won legal protections.

Declining Support for Special Education

Finally, and perhaps somewhat pessimistically, there seems to be a decline in the commitment of the community at large to education programs for children with disabilities, including learning disabilities. This perception is apparent from discussions with parents and professionals across the nation, as well as from articles in the press citing special education costs as contributions to high local taxes. In addition, the New York State Regents, for example, recently increased class sizes for students with learning disabilities and other "mild" disorders. The past decade has seen a decline in federal willingness to share in special education costs. In 1981, when I left the government, our last federal budget provided for about 12% of excess costs of special education. In 1992, the federal share is 10%, which actually represents an increase after the sharp declines of the Reagan era. State and local expenditures have peaked as well. There are consistent reports from parents and teachers of failure to offer services and failure to identify children who may have disabilities. In this climate it is even more essential that we begin to determine the practical outcomes of special educational interventions.

We should be concerned that the recent calls for reform of education activities have ignored children with learning disabilities, and that some of the reforms designed to emphasize academic achievement may make inclusion and proper educational programs for children with learning disabilities even more difficult. The widely publicized America 2000 program lacks demonstrable concern for education of children with learning and other disabilities.

In 1965, Congress demonstrated a great interest in improving education, particularly for low-income and minority children. Children with disabilities, however, were not included in these new federal initiatives. During the 1970s, the situation gradually changed and public consciousness about disability increased. A broad commitment to persons with disabilities continues to this time, as can be seen in the Americans with Disabilities Act of 1990. At the same time, the failure by current education leaders and reformers to find an appropriate place in their deliberations for the 10%–12% of schoolchildren with disabilities does not bode well for such children in the present structure.

Despite this somewhat negative observation, there is a lesson to be learned from the development of public policy on disability in the past 20 years: advocates for the population with disabilities have been successful when their jointly developed goals have been clearly conceived and articulated. Despite relatively few dollars, virtually every public policy goal forged through a consensus of parents and professionals has succeeded in gaining congressional support for children with learning disabilities. This should stimulate hope that, as we focus on the results of special education and rehabilitation programs in terms of outcome measures such as higher education, employment, social adequacy, self-satisfaction, and independent living, we will be able to obtain the public policy support necessary to achieve our educational goals. Our task now is to refine our questions and to begin to provide answers to the basic outcome questions that, for the most part, have been ignored.

REFERENCES

Bryan, J.H., & Bryan, T.H. (1988). Where's the beef? A review of published research on the adaptive learning environment model. *Learning Disabilities Focus, 4*(1), 9–14.

Chalfant, J.C., Pysh, M.V., & Moultine, R. (1979). Teacher assistance teams: A model for within building problem solving. *Learning Disabilities Quarterly, 2,* 85–96.

Code of Federal Regulations. (1990). C.F.R. Sect. 300. 540–543. (original citation [1977] C.F.R. 100. 540–543.)

Dangel, H.L., & Ensminger, E.E. (1988). The use of a discrepancy formula with LD students. *Learning Disability Focus, 4*(1), 24–31.

Edgar, E., Levine, P., Levine, R., & Dubey, M. (1988). *Washington State follow-along studies 1983–87: Final report.* Seattle, WA: Experimental Education Unit, Child Development and Mental Retardation Center.

Fairweather, J.S., & Shaver, D.M. (1990). Making the transition to postsecondary education and training. *Exceptional Children, 57,* 264–270.

Gerber, M.M., & Semmel, M.I. (1985). The microeconomics of referral and reintegration: A paradigm for evaluation of special education. *Studies in Educational Evaluation, 11,* 13–29.

Hallahan, D.P., Keller, C.E., McKinney, J.D., Lloyd, J.W., & Bryan, T. (1988). Examining the research base of the regular education initiative: Efficacy studies and the adaptive learning environments model. *Journal of Learning Disabilities, 21,* 29–35, 55.

Hasazi, S.B., Gordon, L.R., & Roe, C.A. (1985). Factors associated with the employment status of handicapped youth in high school from 1979 to 1983. *Exceptional Children, 51,* 455–469.

Idol-Maestas, L., Lloyd, S., & Lilly, M.S. (1981). A non-categorical approach to direct service and teacher education. *Exceptional Children, 48,* 213–220.

Kauffman, J.M., Braaten, S., Nelson, C.M., Polsgrove, L., & Braaten, B. (1990). The regular education initiative and patent medicine: A rejoinder to Alzozzine, Maheady, Sacca, O'Shea, & O'Shea. *Exceptional Children, 56,* 558–560.

Liebert, D., Lutsky, L., & Gottlieb, A. (1990). Post-secondary experiences of young adults with severe physical disabilities. *Exceptional Children, 57,* 56–63.

Louis Harris & Associates. (1986). *The ICD survey of disabled Americans: Bringing disabled people into the mainstream.* New York: author.

Martin, E.W. (1984). Developmental variation and dysfunction: Observations on labeling, public policy and individualization of instruction. In M.D. Levine & P. Satz (Eds.), *Middle childhood: Development and dysfunction* (pp. 435–445). Baltimore: University Park Press.

Martin, E.W. (1987a). Developing public policy concerning "regular" or "special" education for children with learning disabilities. *Learning Disability Focus, 3*(1), 11–16.

Martin, E.W. (1987b). Learning disabilities and public policy: A role for research workers. In S. Vaughn & C.S. Bos (Eds.), *Research in learning disabilities: Issues and future directions* (pp. 203–214). College-Hill Press.

Martin, E.W., Michaels, C., & Gottlieb, A. (1990). Enhancing success in community colleges for high school students with learning disabilities. In G.T. Pavlidis (Ed.), *Perspectives on dyslexia: Vol. 2. Cognition, language and treatment* (pp. 229–244). New York: John Wiley & Sons.

Martin, E.W., Smith, M.A., & Zwerlein, R.A. (1985). Vocational rehabilitation and learning disabilities: The camel's nose is getting under the edge of the tent. In D.D. Duane & C.K. Leong (Eds.), *Understanding learning disabilities: International and multidisciplinary views* (pp. 167–178). New York: Plenum.

McKinney, J.D., & Hocutt, A.M. (1988). Policy issues in the evaluation of the regular education initiative. *Learning Disability Focus, 4*(1), 15–23.

Michaels, C.A. (1987). Assisting students with learning disabilities in transition from high school to college. In *Proceedings of the 1987 Annual Conference of the Association on Handicapped Student Service Programs in Postsecondary Education* (pp. 140–150). City: Publisher.

Mithaug, D., Horiuchi, C.N., & Fanning, P.N. (1985). A report on the Colorado statewide follow-up survey of special education students. *Exceptional Children, 51,* 397–404.

Organization for Economic Cooperation and Development. (1985). *Integration of the handicapped in secondary schools: Five case studies.* Paris: Centre for Educational Research and Innovation, Organization for Economic Cooperation and Development.

Organization for Economic Cooperation and Development. (1988). *Disabled youth: The right to adult status.* Paris: Centre for Educational Research and Innovation, Organization for Economic Cooperation and Development.

Public Law 88-164, Mental Retardation Facilities and Community Mental Health Centers Construction Act of 1963. (1963). #77 Stat 282.

Public Law 89-750, The Elementary and Secondary Education Amendment of 1966. (1966). #80 Stat 1191.

Public Law 91-230, Education of the Handicapped Act, Title VI, of 1970.

Public Law 94-142. (1975). Sec. 611.(5)(A)(ii). Entitlements and Allocations.

Public Law 101-336, Americans with Disabilities Act of 1990 (ADA). (July 26, 1990). Title 42, U.S.C. 12101 et seq: *U.S. Statutes at Large, 104*, 327–378.

Rogan, L.L., & Hartman, L.D. (1990). Adult outcome of learning disabled students 10 years after initial follow-up. *Learning Disability Focus, 5*(2), 91–102.

Shepherd, M.J. (1988). Discussion. In J.F. Kavanaugh & T.J. Truss (Eds.), *Learning disabilities: Proceedings of the national conference* (pp. 164–167). Parkton, MD: York Press.

Stainback, W., & Stainback, S. (1984). A rationale for the merger of special and regular education. *Exceptional Children, 51*, 102–111.

U. S. Department of Education. (1990). *12th Annual Report on the Implementation of P.L. 94-142*. Washington, DC: U. S. Government Printing Offices.

U. S. House of Representatives. (1966). Hearings, Ad Hoc Subcommittee on the Handicapped, 89th Congress.

U. S. Senate. (1975). Report No. 94–168: Education for All Handicapped Children Act, June 2 (pp. 9–10). Washington, DC: U. S. Government Printing Office.

Wang, M.C., Reynolds, M.C., & Walberg, H.J. (1986). Rethinking special education. *Educational Leadership, 44*(1), 26–31.

Ysseldyke, J.E., Algozzine, B., Shinn, M.R., & McGue, M. (1982). Similarities and differences between low achievers and students classified learning disabled. *The Journal of Special Education, 16*, 73–85.

16

CONCLUSIONS
AND FUTURE DIRECTIONS

Duane Alexander, David B. Gray,
and G. Reid Lyon

The "Wingspread" conference, which served as the foundation
and a forum for the development of the chapters in this book,
constituted a major activity for the National Institute of Child
Health and Human Development (NICHD). The conference itself
was more than 2 years in the planning, and we believe that the
products that have been generated from the discussions and proceedings have been well worth the effort. In essence, the "Wingspread" conference and this book punctuate a critical time in the
development of the field of learning disabilities and the NICHD's
commitment to research programs in this area. As is explained below, the NICHD has had a long-standing interest in the study of
learning disabilities. By 1990, a number of our NICHD-funded scientists had been studying reading disorders and other learning disabilities for more than 20 years, and we thought that it was time to
bring together these investigators, as well as other leaders in the
field, to discuss our findings to date and to identify new research
questions and initiatives for our learning disabilities research port-
folio. As with all scientific endeavors, our investigative work in
learning disabilities represents an incremental process and one that
has required a substantial amount of time and money, primarily
because of the extensive ambiguity and confusion that characterize
the field. However, we now believe that a solid foundation has been
forged such that we can begin to build our knowledge on a set of
replicable findings. We also believe that we are now in a position to
identify more precisely what the major scientific goals in the field

This chapter is in the public domain.

should be and how we should approach the achievement of these goals. In order to provide a context for a discussion of future NICHD goals and initiatives, we briefly review our past efforts in this area.

THE NICHD RESEARCH PROGRAM
IN DYSLEXIA AND OTHER LEARNING DISABILITIES

The NICHD, one of the 16 institutes within the National Institutes of Health, is committed to the study of learning disabilities and disorders that adversely affect the development of attentional, listening, speaking, reading, writing, and mathematics abilities of children and adults in the United States. Since its inception in 1963, the NICHD has funded research to delineate the basic biological and behavioral mechanisms that underlie deficits in attention, perception, language, cognition, and academic skills. Our early research in this area focused on basic learning mechanisms related to sensation, perception, and cognitive operations involving memory and language. In 1968, the NICHD formally marshalled an attack on reading disabilities and began this initiative with a conference titled "The Reading Process."

As the attention of educators, clinicians, and legislators turned toward providing individualized education programs for all children with disabilities, the research supported by the NICHD broadened its scope to include studies of children who were classified as manifesting dyslexia, learning disabilities, attention deficit disorder, and developmental language disorders. With the passage of P.L. 94-142, the Education for All Handicapped Children Act, in 1975, NICHD funding for research in learning disorders and disabilities increased dramatically. For example, support for research projects related to specific learning disabilities (to include reading disorders) grew from $1.75 million in 1975 to $11 million in 1990, with the greatest increase occurring between 1985 and 1992. However, along with this substantial increase in funding, particularly during the early 1980s, came the realization that much of the research being conducted in the late 1970s and early 1980s was uncoordinated and severely hampered by the lack of an operational definition and a reliable and valid classification system for learning disabilities. This resulted in great difficulty in comparing findings of studies on learners with disabilities and in establishing accurate prevalence rates. In addition, scientific analysis was further complicated by differences in the expression of a range of learning disabilities manifested at different ages, as well as the psychometric and technical vagaries of existing measurement tools, the overlap between general and specific cognitive deficits, and issues related to co-morbidity, gender differences, and cultural factors.

In an effort to address these issues, the Health Research Extension Act of 1985 (P.L. 99-158) mandated the establishment of an Interagency Committee on Learning Disabilities to review and assess federal research priorities, activities, and findings regarding learning disabilities. The NICHD was designated as the lead agency for this congressional initiative and immediately began to take steps to increase the effectiveness of research on learning disabilities; to improve the dissemination of findings; and to prioritize research on the causes, diagnosis, treatment, and prevention of learning and attention disorders. Within this context, the NICHD subsequently funded five program projects to develop a classification system and a valid definition for dyslexia and three specialized multidisciplinary learning disability research centers to define and classify learning disabilities, conduct disorders, and attention deficit disorders and their interrelationships. To date, the five program projects, located at the University of Miami, the University of Colorado, Yale University, the Bowman Gray School of Medicine, and Harvard University, and the three learning disability research centers (LDRCs) at Johns Hopkins University, Yale University, and the University of Colorado have made substantial gains and discoveries in their efforts to advance knowledge relevant to the etiology, definition, and diagnosis of learning disabilities.

Although space does not permit a comprehensive review of the products obtained to date by these program projects and LDRCs (see Duane & Gray, 1991, and Lyon, 1991, for complete reviews), a brief review may be informative for two reasons. First, the findings obtained by each of the scientific teams at the five program project sites and LDRC sites were presented to the "Wingspread" conference participants. Therefore, in many cases the chapters within this volume reflect the methodological concerns highlighted by program project and LDRC research. Second, the information derived to date from the program projects and LDRCs provides a foundation for a blueprint for future initiatives and challenges. In short, we have learned a great deal over the past several years about the science of classification, the nature of reading disabilities, and the effects of co-morbidity on learning in children. More importantly, we have learned a great deal about where to focus our investigative energies during the next decade. With this as background, we take a small amount of space to discuss what it is we now know about learning disabilities (to include dyslexia) and what we still need to know.

WHAT WE KNOW AND WHAT WE NEED TO KNOW

What We Know

Not surprisingly, a number of the findings obtained by our scientists at the program project and LDRC sites have indicated that some of our most basic assumptions about learning disabilities are in error and must be revised. For example, research teams at Yale University under the direction of Bennett Shaywitz and at the University of Colorado under the direction of John DeFries have reported that children with dyslexia differ from one another along a continuous distribution and do not "cluster" together in well-defined syndromes marked by distinctive diagnostic boundaries. Thus, dyslexia is not an all-or-none phenomenon, but, like hypertension, occurs in degrees. The Yale group also has devised methods using a normal-distribution model to quantify and predict the variability inherent in the diagnosis of dyslexia. These findings will no doubt alter the way we conceptualize dyslexia and thus the manner in which we set criteria for diagnosis and identification.

In addition, scientists at the Bowman Gray School of Medicine under the direction of Frank Wood and at the University of Miami under the direction of Herb Lubs have discovered, contrary to popular belief, that males and females are represented equally in the population with reading disability. These findings have been confirmed in epidemiological studies undertaken by the Yale group and in twin studies conducted by the Colorado group. These discoveries will undoubtedly have a positive impact on identification and diagnostic practices in the public schools. Moreover, Wood's group at Bowman Gray has been the first to report with replicable evidence that reading disability and attention deficits constitute separable disorders and have different cognitive effects and electrophysiological correlates. In view of this finding, it is now being recognized in the field that the separation of cognitive effects of attention disorders from those of dyslexia is necessary in constructing a reliable and valid definition of dyslexia. In addition, the Miami group has discovered that reading disability with co-morbid attention deficit disorder results in significantly greater severity of the reading deficit, which necessitates differential approaches to treatment.

Since the program projects and LDRC research sites have been developed to enhance multidisciplinary research, a number of exciting findings related to how the brain is organized for complex behaviors have emerged in the last 5 years. For example, the Bowman Gray group has reported replicable evidence from regional blood flow studies that persons with dyslexia demonstrate an altered cortical landscape of abnormal patterns of activation in the left cerebral hemisphere. Basic neurophysiological investigations being carried out by Al Galaburda and his colleagues at Harvard and the Beth Israel Hospital are beginning to shed light on the neuroanatomical features that accompany dyslexia and their origins during development. Equally informative are the behavioral genetic studies of twins with dyslexia carried out by DeFries and his colleagues at the University of Colorado. His group has pioneered a multiple-regression analytic procedure that allows for the analysis of the genetic etiology of deviant scores as well as individual differences in language and reading development. This is a highly unique and flexible methodology that can be extended to assess a range of possible main effects and interactions and to test for differential genetic and environmental influences on a number of complex cognitive behaviors.

From a phenotypic perspective, converging evidence from the Yale, Bowman Gray, Colorado, and Johns Hopkins groups has established that both childhood and adult reading disabilities are significantly associated with deficits in phonological awareness that are manifested in poor performance on segmentation, phonemic analysis, and confrontation naming tasks. In addition, the Bowman Gray group has discovered that deficits in the recognition of whole words are significantly related to word retrieval errors, whereas deficits in word attack skills are referable to separable deficiencies in phonological awareness. An important applied research finding obtained by the Bowman Gray group with their longitudinal sample clearly supports the hypothesis that specific forms of early intervention with youngsters at risk for reading failure are highly influential in increasing reading abilities in later grades, and that the interventions that are informed by linguistic theory and have a code emphasis are more powerful than approaches that rely solely on reading context.

In the main, the research advances briefly discussed here result from the NICHD's emphasis on developmental, longitudinal research. In contrast to cross-sectional and "single-shot" studies using school-identified samples of children diagnosed as having learning disabilities, our longitudinal efforts have a firm grounding in classification methodology and provide a research context wherein the same children can be repeatedly observed and studied without the need for any a priori assumptions about preconceived diagnoses. The findings reported here as well as those summarized by Duane and Gray (1991) and Lyon (1991) provide a stable context for additional epidemiological studies on various learning disorders (e.g., mathematics, written language, social competencies) and allow better data to be gathered about their prevalence, developmental course, and response to various interventions. However, there is no doubt that we have a tremendous distance to travel before we have a clear picture of who has a learning disability, why they have such a disability, and most importantly how we can combat the disability and ensure healthy cognitive and academic development in childhood. Within this context, we must recognize our shortcomings and identify critical areas for research. Some of our thoughts relevant to these critical areas are provided next.

What We Need To Know

By way of background, it is clear that those who study learning disabilities must be aware of past research practices that have confounded and confused efforts to understand and intervene with children who display unexpected and debilitating learning difficulties. More specifically, we must know what conditions have to be in place with respect to selecting samples of children with learning disabilities. Numerous reviews of the literature as well as the chapters in this book uniformly attest to the danger of studying samples that have been selected on the basis of ambiguous criteria set forth in school and/or clinic policies. It goes without saying that studies of the population with learning disabilities must have comparable inclusion and exclusion criteria if any progress is to be expected. Editors of scientific journals must also know that our understanding of learning disabilities can only be advanced when stringent criteria are applied to manuscripts undergoing review, particularly to those sections that detail the sampling methodology. Clearly, if a study cannot be replicated because of vague descriptions of intellectual, demographic, and academic achievement variables, the scientific merit of the study has been compromised.

We also need to know what measurement and assessment conditions must be in place in order to provide reliable and valid descriptions of the behaviors that we are studying over time. Recent initiatives on measurement of learning disabilities carried out by our NICHD extramural scientists are attempting to delineate what factors must be considered when attempting to assess developmental change and to disentangle this change from that which occurs in response to treatment (Lyon, 1994). Despite the fact that the learning disabilities field has been in existence for more than 2 decades, a review of the literature reveals that minimal attention has been paid to how we measure complex developmental events.

Our work in cognitive neuroscience clearly needs to be expanded so we can begin to know more about how the brain is organized for complex behaviors, and to know more specifically how the child with learning disabilities and the child without such disabilities differ with respect to central nervous system functioning. Within this context, it is important for us to know how such physiological and neuroanatomical differences are related to indices of heritability as well as environmental influences. Our ability to assess brain–behavior relationships in an accurate, yet noninvasive manner, is improving significantly as we better understand how to utilize magnetic resonance imaging in the study of anatomical structures and positron emission tomography and regional cerebral blood flow analysis in the study of brain function and information processing. However, before this technology can be used to its maximum potential in the study of learning and learning differences, we must know how best to register functional brain information to structural brain data in order to achieve a precise picture of the complex workings of the brain. We also must know the limits of individual variability in the brain structures in which we are interested. At the time of this writing, Drs. Norman Krasnegor and Reid Lyon in the Human Learning and Behavior Branch within NICHD are developing research initiatives and protocols that address these complex issues.

Very importantly, we need to aggressively expand our basic and applied research programs to understand how different treatment interventions affect well-defined learning deficits in children with learning disabilities. Importantly, we must know what teaching conditions must be in place in order to move a youngster along in a critical academic and social skill. We must know which interventions or combination of interventions are most efficacious for particular types of learners at different developmental epochs, in different content areas. It would seem that our ability to prepare professionals to teach children with learning disabilities would necessarily depend on a clear understanding of these conditions. Because of the tremendous importance of conducting highly controlled and replicable treatment/intervention research, G. Reid Lyon and his colleagues within the human learning and behavior branch have recently initiated a request for applications (RFA) to carry out investigations on treatment effectiveness for children with learning disabilities. The general research question to be addressed within this RFA is: Which single treatment/intervention or combination of interventions, provided in which setting or combination of settings, has (have) the most effective impact on well-defined domains of child functioning, for how long, and for what reasons? We are hopeful that studies carried out in response to this RFA will more clearly delineate the critical instructional factors that must be considered when one addresses the well-defined needs of a child with learning disabilities.

CONCLUSIONS

We have attempted in this chapter to provide a brief overview of some of the reasons that the NICHD developed the "Wingspread" conference and supported a significant amount of the research that is discussed within the chapters in this book. We clearly are at a critical juncture in our research on learning disabilities. We now have a good understanding of the basic methodological factors that must be addressed when conducting research on this tremendously heterogeneous population of learners with disabilities, and we are using this information to discover and develop robust measurement procedures for both behavioral and biological studies. We are also at a stage where we can begin highly controlled intervention studies with well-defined groups of youngsters. As importantly, the scholars writing in this book have provided us with a detailed look at those issues that continue to confuse and confound our research and, better still, have provided us with well-thought-out ideas for improving the clarity and effectiveness of future research and intervention practices.

REFERENCES

Duane, D.D., & Gray, D.B. (1991). *The reading brain: The biological basis of dyslexia.* Parkton, MD: York Press.

Lyon, G.R. (1991). *Research in learning disabilities* (technical report). Bethesda, MD: The National Institute of Child Health and Human Development.

Lyon, G.R. (1994). *Frames of reference for the assessment of learning disabilities: New views on measurement issues.* Baltimore: Paul H. Brookes Publishing Co.

Public Law 94-142, Education for all Handicapped Children Act of 1975. (23 August 1977). 20 U.S.C. 1401 et seq: *Federal Register, 42,* (163), 42474-42518.

INDEX

AAMR, *see* American Association on Mental Retardation
Academic outcomes
  developmental nature of, 236–237
    see also Interactive developmental paradigm
  policy questions based on, 328–336
  production components and, elemental functions and, 233, 234–237
  theory development and, 157
  see also Performance; Underachievement
Academic skills
  discrepancy relative to, classification and, 45–46
  psychometric research focus on, 210
Accessibility, knowledge representation and, in assessment, 212
Achievement discrepancy models, *see* Discrepancy
ACLD, *see* Association for Children with Learning Disabilities
Active working memory, writing and, 243
Adaptive behavior
  linkage between definition and identification practices and, 136–137
  mental retardation and, 120–121, 128
ADD, *see* Attention-deficit disorder
ADHD, *see* Attention-deficit hyperactivity disorder
Advocacy, classification and, 315–316
African-American children, overrepresentation of, mental retardation and, 122–127, 313
Alphabetic principle, in phonological reading disabilities, 161–162
American Association on Mental Retardation (AAMR)
  classification system of, 119
  comorbidity and, 135
  mental retardation definition of, 119–121, 257–258
  arbitrary criteria and, 140
  dimensions of behavior in, 128
  DSM–III–R definition versus, 121
  etiological patterns and, 130–132
  homogeneous subcategories and, 129–130

American Psychiatric Association (APA), mental retardation definition of, 121
  comorbidity and, 135
Americans with Disabilities Act (P.L. 101-336), 331–332, 340
APA, *see* American Psychiatric Association
Aptitude–achievement discrepancy, *see* Discrepancy
Arbitrary criteria, in identification, 140–142
Assessment
  cognitive psychology applications in, 212–215
  dynamic, 214–215
  discrepancy formulas and, 259–260
  interactive developmental paradigm and, 244
  see also Measurement practices
Assessment instruments
  extensive batteries of, advantages and disadvantages of, 87–89
  IQ tests, *see* IQ tests
  standardized, problems with, 85–87
Association for Children with Learning Disabilities (ACLD), 254
  learning disabilities definition of, 231
Attention, writing and, interactive developmental paradigm and, 241–242
Attention-deficit disorder (ADD), hyperactivity versus, 105–107
Attention-deficit hyperactivity disorder (ADHD), 106–107
Autocorrelation, of IQ tests and achievement tests, 138–140
Automatization, memory and, writing and, 243

Behavior
  adaptive, *see* Adaptive behavior
  dimensions of, selection for inclusion in definitions, 127–129
Behavior disorder, operational definitions of, 257
Behavioral impairment, neurological lesions and, 101–103

351

Secondary characteristics, development of, theories about, 155–157
Self-monitoring, writing and, 241
Semantic-syntactic expression, writing and, 240, 241
Sentence production, interactive developmental paradigm and, 240–241
Sentential process, writing and, 240
Sequential ideation, writing and, 241
Services, classification for, 316
Severely and profoundly mentally retarded (SPMR), 130
Short-term memory, writing and, 242–243
Simultaneous retrieval, writing and, 243
Single-deficit models, 230
Skinner model, 80–84
  see also Theoretical classification model
Social–political perspective on classification, 311–321
  see also Public policy
Social movement, learning disabilities as, 154–155
Social skills, in learning disabilities definition, 128
"Socio-culturally retarded," 132
Spatial organization, writing and, 243
Special education
  assignment to, 264–266
  programs of, detection rates and, 146, 147
  regular education versus, 338–339
  support for, decline in, 339–340
SPMR, see Severely and profoundly mentally retarded
Standardized assessment instruments
  extensive batteries of, advantages and disadvantages of, 87–89
  IQ tests, see IQ tests
  problems with, 85–87
State definitions, identification criteria and, 138, 139
State education codes, classification and, 122
Statistical classification, 29
  see also Empirical classification
Strategy instruction, 216–222
  principles of
    comparable performance versus comparable strategies, 218–219
    different purposes of strategies, 217
    expert strategies versus strategies taught, 221–222
    law of parsimony, 217–218
    processing differences and, 218
    relation to student's capacity, 219–221

residual performance differences and, 221
students with versus without learning disabilities and, 218
"Strauss syndrome," 314
Strephosymbolia, 100
Structure of Scientific Revolutions, The (Kuhn), 188
Students with learning disabilities, see Children with learning disabilities
Subject domains, elemental functions and, 238
Sublexical process, see Phonological processing
Subtypes
  defined, 58–62
  by environment, school placement and, 65–69
  homogeneity of, 59–61
  operational definitions and, 129–135
  usefulness of, in individual classification, 61–62
  see also specific subtypes
Subtyping, defined, 58
Supplemental education, current, myth of sufficiency of, 331–336
Suprasentential, writing and, 240
System identification
  classification and, purposes of, 316
  definitions and, 142–144
  see also Referral

Task production components, see Production components
Task staging, writing and, 241
Task-analytic techniques, elemental functions and, production components and, 234–235
Taxonomy of learning disabilities, classification models as related to, 17–25
Teachers, see Educators; Professionals
Tempo control, writing and, 241
Theoretical classification model, 80–84
  operationalization of, clinical versus empirical, 84–89
Theory of learning disabilities, 153–167, 171–190
  comparison of causal theories, 163–167
  definition and, 95–96
  see also Definition
  development of secondary characteristics and, 155–157
  dilemmas in, 179–182